MODERN ELOQUENCE
LIBRARY OF
POLITICAL ORATORY

W·A·C·

PATRICK HENRY

Photogravure after an engraving by W. G. Jackman

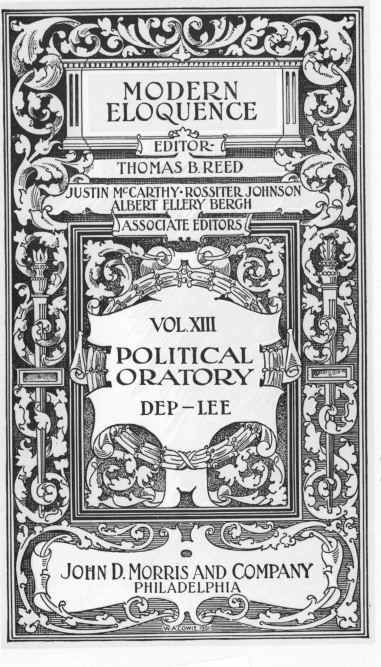

MODERN ELOQUENCE

EDITOR-
THOMAS B. REED

JUSTIN McCARTHY · ROSSITER JOHNSON
ALBERT ELLERY BERGH
ASSOCIATE EDITORS

VOL. XIII

POLITICAL ORATORY

DEP — LEE

JOHN D. MORRIS AND COMPANY
PHILADELPHIA

W.A.COWIE. 1901.

COMMITTEE OF SELECTION

EDWARD EVERETT HALE, Author of "The Man Without a Country."

JOHN B. GORDON, Former United States Senator.

NATHAN HASKELL DOLE, Associate Editor "International Library of Famous Literature."

JAMES B. POND, Manager Lecture Bureau; Author of "Eccentricities of Genius."

GEORGE MCLEAN HARPER, Professor of English Literature, Princeton University.

LORENZO SEARS, Professor of English Literature, Brown University.

EDWIN M. BACON, Former Editor "Boston Advertiser" and "Boston Post."

J. WALKER MCSPADDEN, Managing Editor "Édition Royale" of Balzac's Works.

F. CUNLIFFE OWEN, Member Editorial Staff "New York Tribune."

TRUMAN A. DEWEESE, Member Editorial Staff "Chicago Times-Herald."

CHAMP CLARK, Member of Congress from Missouri.

MARCUS BENJAMIN, Editor, National Museum, Washington, D. C.

CLARK HOWELL, Editor "Atlanta Constitution."

EPIPHANIUS WILSON, Managing Editor.

INTRODUCTIONS AND SPECIAL ARTICLES BY

THOMAS B. REED,	HAMILTON WRIGHT MABIE,
LORENZO SEARS,	JONATHAN P. DOLLIVER,
CHAMP CLARK,	EDWARD EVERETT HALE,
GEORGE F. HOAR,	CHARLES W. EMERSON,
ALBERT J. BEVERIDGE,	ALBERT ELLERY BERGH.

NOTE.—A large number of the most distinguished speakers of this country and Great Britain have selected their own best speeches for this Library. These speakers include Whitelaw Reid, William Jennings Bryan, Henry van Dyke, Henry M. Stanley, Newell Dwight Hillis, Joseph Jefferson, Sir Henry Irving, Arthur T. Hadley, John D. Long, David Starr Jordan, and many others of equal note.

THE POWER OF ORATORY

EVERY form of human expression, being a manifestation of power, possesses power. All great art is
powerful to move the will of the spectator or the hearer. In
most forms of art this influence is indirect: the art product,
through the lofty conceptions of life which it presents to the
mind, is a power in molding character. Every ideal, whether
in nature or in art, is to some extent formative; the mind,
like the body, grows in accordance with that upon which it
is fed. But there is one form of art which has ever been
preeminently powerful in impelling men to immediate and
definite action, even to the extent of the sacrifice of life and
of all that life holds dear. This smiting, compelling, irresistible power is the art of oratory.

It is true that we can sometimes, in tracing the origin of
an act or a course of conduct, find that an impulse was given
by a specific expression in some line of art other than oratory. In this respect, music is the most closely allied to
oratory. Martial strains and songs of patriotism have had
no slight influence in directing the fortunes of battle; hymns
of praise have touched and softened hardened hearts that
have persistently resisted the eloquent pleadings of the
preacher. Direct power upon the will of man is also sometimes exerted by the artist in literature. No one could
measure the potency of the impulse that one woman through
a single book gave to the cause of freeing the slaves in the
United States. A great English novelist, whose power is less
definable but no less real, promoted reforms in civic and
educational life in England through this expression of a
direct, specific purpose in his novels.

But although these instances might be multiplied, yet we
recognize that our minds recur to them at once because they

are exceptional; it is their very unusualness that makes them striking. Masses of men have not been moved to immediate, definite action so naturally and so directly, throughout all the ages, by any other art as by oratory. To describe the moving power of other arts, indeed, we have borrowed from oratory a term descriptive of its power. We say that a poem, a painting, a symphony is "eloquent"; i.e., that it "speaks out." This is a tacit recognition of the *direct appeal* of the art from which we borrow the figure. The figurative language employed by men is revelatory of many unconscious mental processes. We pay homage to the sight as the leading avenue of perception by "seeing" with the intellect— "I 'see' that truth." So we say of any work of art that has moving power, that it "speaks" to the heart or to the understanding.

The medium through which the orator moves out upon the hearts of men in power received the supreme recognition of its distinction when the inspired apostle said, as his primary utterance, "In the beginning was the Word." Jesus Christ, the one complete expression of God's thought, was the *Logos*, the Word! The choice of the term was no accident. Insight more profound is shown nowhere in the gospels. The apostle discerned that spirit and expression are inseparable; that spirit must of necessity express itself —"*in the beginning was the Word.*" Each thought of God, from the beginning, has found its expression in some form. But when John calls the supreme manifestation of the spirit the "Word," he sets the seal upon the sovereignty of word-language as the most natural if not the highest form of human expression.

What does history tell us of the rank of the orator as a power in molding nations? It tells us that the orators of the past were not only associated with the great movements, religious and political, but they were the immediate causes of those movements. The orators of Greece shaped her destiny. When Philip of Macedon essayed to conquer Greece, doubtless expecting through Greece to conquer Persia and the surrounding nations, he recognized that the one thing necessary to these great achievements was the cooperation of the best orators of Greece. If he could buy the orators of a state, he knew that he could conquer that state. He bought many eloquent men of Greece, but there was one orator whom all his rich possessions could not buy. Over in Macedon stood a man with the helmet, the shield, and the sword, leading men to battle and to conquest. Over against him in Athens stood a man with only such arms as equip the orator. Which was destined to be the ruler? The historians tell us that Philip conquered the states primarily by his orators, secondly by his gold, and thirdly by his armies. Philip and all his armies arrayed against one man, the consummate orator of the ages, met ignominious defeat.

Where shall we find the history of progress in England? In the lives and works of her orators. The elemental upheaval which, centering in France, revolutionized Europe and started the world along new thoroughfares of thought and motive, owed its main impulse to the orators of the time. The heart of the American colonies was fired by oratory—the *Word*, fraught with Liberty!

The orator must be the king, the ruler, the leader. He must be able to say to one " Go," and he goeth, and to another " Come," and he cometh. All men must wait upon his words and act as he wishes them to act. The orator rules those who sit upon thrones—he is king over kings.

What is the secret of this power of direct appeal which is preeminently that of the orator? It is largely the secret of personality—of presence. If you can analayze the power of personal presence, you can explain why the orator exerts an influence over men more direct than that exerted by the painter, the sculptor, or even the poet. Henry Ward Beecher said that " the greatest thing in oratory is the orator." Personality is the greatest power in the universe. Oratory is the most personal of all the arts, in the sense that the entire being of the artist is the medium through which his thought is flashed to the world. True education in oratory, more than any other training, involves the culture of the entire individual, because oratory as an art employs directly every personal power at the command of the individual. True, all art is the product of the entire being; no one can *express*— " press out "—through any medium, anything that is not within, neither can he by any act of will refrain from reflect-

ing something of his personality in his art. Figs do not
grow upon thistles; the law of cause and effect cannot be
circumvented. But certain it is that no other art can in the
nature of things be so revelatory of the artist, the outer and
the inner man, as this art whose direct medium is the person
of the artist. The "flash of the will that can" is existent
behind the laws governing every act, is revealed in every art
product; but when the medium is the printed page, the keys
of a piano, colors on a canvas, the personality through which
it is manifest is at most a little more remote.

What is this power of personal presence, which, more
than the words he utters, influences those whom the orator
addresses? It is not physical bulk—men of powerful presence have been short of stature and slight of build. Saint
Bernard, a man of such mighty presence that people were
impressed by him even when he did not utter a word, is said
to have weighed seventy-five pounds. Presence is not a
thing of weight or of bulk. It is something which eludes
analysis. It stands over the material man like the power
that stands behind a throne. This subtle power is the manifestation of the personal character of the individual. It cannot be assumed. It results as a growth, from surrendering
the soul daily to the high behests of truth and right.

Young men, observing that orators have each an individual manner, sometimes think that is the secret of their success. Yet it may be that the manner is a positive hindrance
to the orator; that he succeeds in spite of it rather than
because of it. The young man, imitating the manner of the
orator, wonders that he does not succeed. So subtly does
personality command forms of expression that it seems to
the observer to be identified with the peculiar mannerisms
of the speaker. No artist's mannerisms account for his
power. Mannerisms are accidental; they are not to be con-
founded with individuality. Any eccentricity of expression,
indeed, stands more or less in the way of the highest development of individuality. Were an artist developed to a
point of perfect freedom of expression, there would be an
absence of distinguishing mannerisms, eccentricities, in his
art, while, on the other hand, his individuality would find its
highest expression.

Another secret of the orator's power is the plasticity of his art. In this respect, again, music and oratory are akin. Here are no fixed forms, no crystalizations. If living forms only are powerful in art, surely no limit can be set to the power of the art whereby the soul, on fire with zeal for a lofty cause, continually molds glowing forms from flesh and blood and living speech. Here is infinite variety, infinite wealth of suggestion. Even music, with all its marvelous reach and sweep, is more formal than oratory, knows not such utter freedom from conscious art. The exquisite tribute which Browning makes Abt Vogler, in an ecstasy of appreciation, pay to music, applies to its kindred art:—

" All through my keys that gave their sounds to a wish of my soul,
All through my soul that praised as its wish flowed visibly forth,
All through music and me! For think, had I painted the whole,
Why, there it had stood, to see, nor the process so wonder-worth;
Had I written the same, made verse—still, effect proceeds from cause,
Ye know why the forms are fair, ye hear how the tale is told;
It is all triumphant art, but art in obedience to laws,
Painter and poet are proud in the artist-list enrolled:—

" But here is the finger of God, a flash of the will that can,
Existent behind all laws, that made them and, lo, they are!"

The instrument upon which the orator plays is, in its highest perfection, the most wonderful mechanism that ever gave its sounds at a wish of the soul.

Ralph Waldo Emerson has said "the soul knows only soul." In true, spontaneous oratory, guiltless of affectation or of tricks of manner, soul speaks through kindling eye, through vibrant voice, through every fiber of the physical frame, and thrills the soul of the listener as a direct current of thought, emotion, and purpose.

But there are certain fixed laws of power in oratory, obedience to which has always determined the success of the public speaker, the degree of his growth in oratory. Foremost among these laws is that which demands that the speaker lose *himself in the service of others.*

If the soul knows only soul, and oratory owes its power of direct appeal to the fact that it employs the most direct and immediate avenues of expression, then surely the ideal of the orator must be to eliminate everything that might interpose between his thought and the mind of the hearer. It is said that in converting coal into electricity, from ten to forty per cent. of the original power is lost. But as science applies new inventions, the percentage of loss grows less. An orator should be able to express his thought through such free channels that he will not waste from ten to forty per cent. of his power in transmitting it. If self is in the way of the thought, friction will result, and power will be misdirected and lost.

How may self be in the way of the speaker's thought ? In many ways. In the first place, the physical person may obtrude itself upon the attention of the audience from lack of freedom. The physical agents may be so restricted from wrong habits of action that they may oppose hindrances to the current of thought. In this lack of freedom of the physical agents there is double loss of power. Besides the loss resulting from friction, there is a loss from misdirection; the attention of the hearer, directed to the effort exerted by the speaker, loses much of his motive. Effort always calls attention to itself. Ease is force, a maximum of result with a minimum of effort is an important ideal for the orator.

But there is a form of self-consciousness in oratory which is not only more offensive than that resulting from an uncultured, unresponsive body and voice, but which is also destructive to the powers of the speaker. If a man endeavor humbly, persistently, and ardently to impart truth to men for their good, if he be single-minded in his desire and his purpose to efface self and hold up truth, his every endeavor will in itself be conducive to culture of the stubborn agents. *Truth will make channels for itself* if the desire of the soul to serve men through truth be single and strong. Uncouth, ungainly men have become great orators, and men, under the spell of their eloquence, have thought them kingly in presence. Such men have succeeded in spite of their physical limitations, because the soul, fired with zeal for noble ends, was great enough to command its instrument. But when a man says, " Go to, now ; I will edify this people with the charm of my manner, the beauty of my cadences, the grace of my movements; I will win their approval for my matchless eloquence"—he is signing the death-warrant of his powers of oratory.

Nothing is beautiful in art that does not serve; necessity is the criterion of beauty. A beautiful voice, graceful gestures, brilliant figures, and smooth-flowing periods, however much they may elevate art, do not in themselves constitute art in oratory. If they attract attention to themselves, they as certainly defeat the end of the discourse—the legitimate end—as would harsh tones, angular features, unpolished speech. The most beautiful voice is the one that is the best servant of the speaker's thought, feeling, and purpose; the most highly cultivated body is that which the truth can most freely possess; the highest discourse is that which most directly and adequately conveys the meaning of the speaker to his hearers. In a word, the straightest line beween the mind of the speaker and the mind of his auditor is the path through which his thought should travel. Anything that interposes, whether it be a beautiful voice or an unmusical one, is impertinent. The highest ideal of personal culture for the public speaker is that he become a transparent medium through which truth may shine unhindered.

We have spoken of oratory as the most personal of the arts, in the sense that it enlists all of the personal powers of being and brings the personality of the artist in the closest contact with men. We see here that in another sense the highest oratory, like all great art, is strictly impersonal. While the personality of the speaker is the power through which truth speaks to men, it is not the center of that truth. The orator never says to men, either in manner or in words, "This is truth because I give it to you." He has no desire to attract the attention of his audience to himself, because that, being a diversion from the main subject, would defeat his purpose. His dominant desire is to bring into the presence of their minds, as directly as possible, the truth which he wills shall influence them. He knows that no tricks of manner or of speech will serve him, that nothing is effective to influence men long but the power of truth in living forms. He knows, furthermore, that he can arouse men to interest and thence to action in proportion as he can make them think. The enthusiasm of an audience is in the ratio of the activity of their minds. The Truth has declared, "And I, if I be lifted up, will draw all men unto Me." It is the business of the orator to lift up the truth; if he be able to elevate it so high that men can see it, he need never fear that they will not be drawn to it.

How may I overcome my self-consciousness? By becoming conscious of the needs of others. You are before the audience neither for their approval nor their disapproval: you are before them to serve their highest needs, to influence them toward higher ideals *by the action of their own minds.* The potter does not pose before the clay, neither does he ask permission of the clay to mold it into shapes he chooses.

A speaker's words may not be imposed upon people as authority. There is no authority for man outside of the laws of his own being. That speaker is authoritative who has so perfectly obeyed the laws of his being that he is able to touch the constitution of other beings with a living touch, and so point out the truth to people as from an authority higher than himself. He has power to present truth so that it is clearly seen by the hearer and becomes authority for him. A man's opinion and his perception of truth are two different things. The orator recognizes that when man has been led to perceive truth, to realize it *as truth for him,* he bows to its authority. His spiritual horizon has been widened; he has attained heights which he has never reached before.

But there is another law which the orator must not disregard if he would lead men to heights commanding broader views. If he would lead men, he must first *meet them on common ground.* You cannot lead a child when you are remote from him. The orator cannot direct the thinking of men unless he first go where they are.

This matter of meeting men upon their own ground does not necessarily imply descent, as people are prone to think. The would-be orator who in conscious superiority says, "I did not succeed in moving these men because I would not descend to their level," knows not whereof he speaks. It is what the fool hath said in his heart. The common ground upon which men may meet is not the lowlands; men meet only on the heights. Sway a crowd by their lower instincts and you have a mob; move them by an appeal to their higher natures and you have a united force. There is at the center of being in every man a recognition of the divine authority of the universal principles of truth, justice, mercy, love, service. This general recognition of the sovereignty of truth and love in the world is the only bond of complete union among men.

A source of power in the orator is his knowledge of men. He must understand the instrument upon which he is to play; he must know the keys and the stops; he must be able to strike the common chords. And a knowledge of human nature implies sympathy with human nature. Sympathy, a feeling with men, follows an understanding of their environment and their motives. If you can command another man's point of view, you cannot fail to sympathize with him.

What constitutes power in the orator? A body educated for adequate service of its master, the soul; a breadth of vision that comprehends universal truth in its relation to men; a steadfast belief in the ultimate triumph of right; an unfaltering faith in the infinite possibilities and the infinite worth of every human soul; an unfailing love that desires the highest welfare of all conscious being; a strength of purpose that recognizes no defeat, no discouragement; habits of spontaneous service. The stream cannot rise higher than its source. Let him who would become a ruler of men look to it that he gain mastery over self and learn to wield the weapon of universal law.

Charles Wesley Emerson.

CONTENTS

VOLUME XIII

xviii   CONTENTS

ILLUSTRATIONS

VOLUME XIII

CHAUNCEY MITCHELL DEPEW

THE COLUMBIAN ORATION

[Chauncey Mitchell Depew possesses the gift of oratory in its widest sense. He is equally at home in the legislative hall, on the platform, or in the lighter graces and amenities of the after-dinner speech. He has in his veins a mingling of Huguenot, Dutch, and Irish blood, which perhaps suggests an explanation of his versatility. He was born in Peekskill, N. Y., April 23, 1834; was educated in his native town and at Yale College, finishing his college course in 1856. Law and politics next claimed his attention, and his popularity gained him the seat in the New York legislature of 1861-62, elected from a Democratic constituency. In the following year he rose to the secretaryship of New York State. In 1866 the duties of his profession, which had taken the form of consulting attorney for the New York and Harlem Railroad, caused him to withdraw from active politics, and after a time he became president of the New York Central Railroad. In the Republican National Convention of 1888 his name became prominent as a candidate for the Presidency. In January, 1899, he was elected to the United States Senate. During President McKinley's administration he was offered the post of United States minister to England. The following oration was delivered at the World's Fair, Chicago, in 1892.]

THIS day belongs not to America, but to the world. The results of the event it commemorates are the heritage of the peoples of every race and clime. We celebrate the emancipation of man. The preparation was the work of almost countless centuries; the realization was the revelation of one. The Cross on Calvary was hope; the cross raised on San Salvador was opportunity. But for the first, Columbus would never have sailed; but for the second, there would have been no place for the planting, the nurture, and the expansion of civil and religious liberty. Ancient history is a dreary record of unstable civilizations. Each reached its zenith of material splendor, and perished. The Assyrian, Persian, Egyptian, Grecian, and Roman empires were proofs of the possibilities and limitations of man for conquest and intellectual development. Their destruction involved a sum of misery and relapse which made their creation rather a curse than a blessing. Force was the factor in the government of the world when Christ was born, and force was the source and exercise of authority both by Church and State when Columbus sailed from Palos. The Wise Men traveled from the East towards the West under the guidance of the Star of Bethlehem. The spirit of the equality of all men before God and the law moved westward from Calvary with its revolutionary influence upon old institutions, to the Atlantic Ocean. Columbus carried it westward across the seas. The emigrants from England, Ireland, Scotland, and Wales, from Germany and Holland, from Sweden and Denmark, from France and Italy, from Spain and Portugal, under its guidance and inspiration, moved west, and again west, building states and founding cities until the Pacific limited their march. The exhibition of arts and sciences, of industries and inventions, of education and civilization, which the Republic of the United States will here present, and to which, through its Chief Magistrate, it invites all nations, condenses and displays the flower and fruitage of this transcendent miracle.

The anarchy and chaos which followed the breaking up of the Roman Empire necessarily produced the feudal system. The people, preferring slavery to annihilation by robber chiefs, became the vassals of territorial lords. The reign of physical force is one of perpetual struggle for the mastery. Power which rests upon the sword neither shares nor limits its authority. The king destroyed the lords, and the monarchy succeeded feudalism. Neither of these institutions considered or consulted the people. They had no part but to suffer or die in this mighty strife of masters for the mastery. But the throne, by its broader view and greater resources, made possible the construction of the highways of freedom. Under its banner, races could unite, and petty principalities be merged, law substituted for brute force, and right for might. It founded and endowed universities, and encouraged commerce. It conceded no political privileges, but unconsciously prepared its subjects to demand them.

Absolutism in the State and intolerance in the Church shackled popular unrest, and imprisoned thought and enterprise in the fifteenth century. The divine right of kings stamped out the faintest glimmer of revolt against tyranny, and the problems of science, whether of the skies or of the earth, whether of astronomy or geography, were solved or submerged by ecclesiastical decrees. The dungeon was ready for the philosopher who proclaimed the truths of the solar system, or the navigator who would prove the sphericity of the earth. An English Gladstone, or a French Gambetta, or a German Bismarck, or an Italian Garibaldi, or a Spanish Castelar, would have been thought a monster, and his death at the stake, or on the scaffold, and under the anathemas of the Church, would have received the praise and approval of kings and nobles, of priests and peoples. Reason had no seat in spiritual or temporal realms. Punishment was the incentive to patriotism, and piety was held possible by torture. Confessions of faith extorted from the writhing victim on the rack were believed efficacious in saving his soul from fires eternal beyond the grave. For all that humanity to-day cherishes as its best heritage and choicest gifts, there was neither thought nor hope.

Fifty years before Columbus sailed from Palos, Gutenberg and Faust had forged the hammer which was to break the bonds of superstition and open the prison doors of the mind. They had invented the printing-press and movable types. The prior adoption of a cheap process for the manufacture of paper at once utilized the press. Its first service, like all its succeeding efforts, was for the people. The universities and the schoolmen, the privileged and the learned few of that age, were longing for the revelation and preservation of the classic treasures of antiquity, hidden, and yet insecure in monastic cells and libraries. But the first-born of the marvelous creation of these primitive printers of Mayence was the printed Bible. The priceless contributions of Greece and Rome to the intellectual training and development of the modern world came afterwards, through the same wondrous machine. The force, however, which made possible America and its reflex influence upon Europe was the open Bible by the family fireside. And yet neither the enlightenment of the new learning, nor the dynamic power of the spiritual awakening, could break through the crust of caste which had been forming for centuries. Church and State had so firmly and dexterously interwoven the bars of privilege and authority that liberty was impossible from within. Its piercing light and fervent heat must penetrate from without.

Civil and religious freedom are founded upon the individual and his independence, his worth, his rights, and his equal status and opportunity. For his planting and development a new land must be found where, with limitless areas for expansion, the avenues of progress would have no bars of custom or heredity, of social orders or privileged classes. The time had come for the emancipation of the mind and soul of humanity. The factors wanting for its fulfilment were the new world and its discoverer.

God always has in training some commanding genius for the control of great crises in the affairs of nations and peoples. The number of these leaders is less than the centuries, but their lives are the history of human progress. Though Cæsar and Charlemagne and Hildebrand and Luther and William the Conqueror and Oliver Cromwell and all the epoch-makers prepared Europe for the event, and contributed to the result, the lights which illumine our firmament to-day are Columbus the discoverer, Washington the founder, and Lincoln the savior.

Neither realism nor romance furnishes a more striking and picturesque figure than that of Christopher Columbus. The mystery about his origin heightens the charm of his story. That he came from among the toilers of his time is in harmony with the struggles of our period. Forty-four authentic portraits of him have descended to us, and no two of them are the counterfeits of the same person. Each represents a character as distinct as its canvas. Strength and weakness, intellectuality and stupidity, high moral purpose and brutal ferocity, purity and licentiousness, the dreamer and the miser, the pirate and the Puritan, are the types from which we may select our hero. We dismiss the painter, and piercing with the clarified vision of the dawn of the twentieth century the veil of four hundred years, we construct our Columbus.

The perils of the sea in his youth upon the rich argosies of Genoa, or in the service of the licensed rovers who made them their prey, had developed a skillful navigator and intrepid mariner. They had given him a glimpse of the possibilities of the unknown beyond the highways of travel, which roused an unquenchable thirst for adventure and research. The study of the narratives of previous explorers, and diligent questionings of the daring spirits who had ventured far towards the fabled West, gradually evolved a theory which became in his mind so fixed a fact that he could inspire others with his own passionate beliefs. The words "That is a lie," written by him on the margin of nearly every page of a volume of the travels of Marco Polo, which is still to be found in a Genoese library, illustrate the skepticism of his beginning, and the first vision of the New World the fulfillment of his faith.

To secure the means to test the truth of his speculations, this poor and unknown dreamer must win the support of kings and overcome the hostility of the Church. He never doubted his ability to do both, though he knew of no man living who was so great in power, or lineage, or learning, that he could accomplish either. Unaided and alone he succeeded in arousing the jealousies of sovereigns, and dividing the councils of the ecclesiastics. " I will command your fleet and discover for you new realms, but only on condition that you confer on me hereditary nobility, the admiralty of the ocean and the vice-royalty and one-tenth the revenues of the New World," were his haughty terms to King John of Portugal. After ten years of disappointment and poverty, subsisting most of the time upon the charity of the enlightened monk of the Convent of Rabida, who was his unfaltering friend, he stood before the throne of Ferdinand and Isabella, and, rising to imperial dignity in his rags, embodied the same royal conditions in his petition. The capture of Granada, the expulsion of Islam from Europe, and the triumph of the cross, aroused the admiration and devotion of Christendom. But this proud beggar, holding in his grasp the potential promise and dominion of El Dorado and Cathay, divided with the Moslem surrender the attention of sovereigns and of bishops. France and England indicated a desire to hear his theories and see his maps while he was still a suppliant at the gates of the camp of Castile and Aragon, the sport of its courtiers and the scoff of its confessors. His unshakable faith that Christopher Columbus was commissioned from heaven, both by his name and by Divine command, to carry "Christ across the sea" to new continents and pagan peoples lifted him so far above the discouragements of an empty purse and a contemptuous court that he was proof against the rebuffs of fortune or of friends. To conquer the prejudices of the clergy, to win the approval and financial support of the state, to venture upon that unknown ocean, which, according to the beliefs of the age, was peopled with demons and savage beasts of frightful shape, and from which there was no possibility of return, required the zeal of Peter the Hermit, the chivalric courage of the Cid, and the imagination of Dante. Columbus belonged to that high order of "cranks" who confidently walk where "angels fear to tread," and often become the benefactors of their country or their kind.

It was a happy omen of the position which woman was to hold in America that the only person who comprehended the majestic scope of his plans and the invincible quality of his genius was the able and gracious Queen of Castile. Isabella alone of all the dignitaries of that age shares with Columbus the honors of his great achievement. She arrayed her kingdom and her private fortune behind the enthusiasm of this mystic mariner, and posterity pays homage to her wisdom and faith.

The overthrow of the Mohammedan power in Spain would have been a forgotten scene in one of the innumerable acts in the grand drama of history had not Isabella conferred immortality upon herself, her husband, and their dual crown, by her recognition of Columbus. The devout spirit of the queen and the high purpose of the explorer inspired the voyage, subdued the mutinous crew, and prevailed over the raging storms. They covered with the divine radiance of religion and humanity the degrading search for gold and the horrors of its quest, which filled the first century of conquest with every form of lust and greed.

The mighty soul of the great admiral was undaunted by

the ingratitude of princes and the hostility of the people by imprisonment and neglect.   He died as he was securing the means and preparing a campaign for the rescue of the Holy Sepulchre at Jersusalem from the infidel.   He did not know what time has revealed, that while the mission of the crusades of Godfrey of Bouillon and Richard of the Lion Heart was a bloody and fruitless romance, the discovery of America was the salvation of the world.   The one was the symbol, the other the spirit; the one death, the other life.   The tomb of the Saviour was a narrow and empty vault, precious only for its memories of the supreme tragedy of the centuries, but the new continent was to be the home and temple of the living God.

The rulers of the Old World began with partitioning the New.   To them the discovery was expansion of empire and grandeur to the throne.   Vast territories, whose properties and possibilities were little understood, and whose extent was greater than the kingdoms of the sovereigns, were the gifts to court favorites and the prizes of royal approval.   But individual intelligence and independent conscience found here haven and refuge.   They were the passengers upon the caravels of Columbus, and he was unconsciously making for the port of civil and religious liberty.   Thinkers who believed men capable of higher destinies and larger responsibilities, and pious people who preferred the Bible to that union of Church and State where each serves the other for the temporal benefit of both, fled to these distant and hospitable lands from intolerable and hopeless oppression at home.   It required three hundred years for the people thus happily situated to understand their own powers and resources and to break bonds which were still reverenced or loved, no matter how deeply they wounded or how hard they galled.

The nations of Europe were so completely absorbed in dynastic difficulties and devastating wars, with diplomacy and ambitions, that, if they heard of, they did not heed the growing democratic spirit and intelligence in their American colonies.   To them these provinces were sources of revenue, and they never dreamed that they were also schools of liberty.   That it exhausted three centuries under the most favorable conditions for the evolution of freedom on this continent demonstrates the tremendous strength of custom and heredity when sanctioned and sanctified by religion. The very chains which fettered became inextricably interwoven with the habits of life, the associations of childhood, the tenderest ties of the family, and the sacred offices of the Church from the cradle to the grave. It clearly proves that if the people of the Old World and their descendants had not possessed the opportunities afforded by the New for their emancipation, and mankind had never experienced and learned the American example, instead of living in the light and glory of nineteenth-century conditions they would still be struggling with mediæval problems.

The northern continent was divided among England, France, and Spain, and the southern between Spain and Portugal. France, wanting the capacity for colonization, which still characterizes her, gave up her western possessions and left the English, who have the genius of universal empire, masters of North America. The development of the experiment in the English domain makes this day memorable. It is due to the wisdom and courage, the faith and virtue of the inhabitants of this territory, that government of the people, for the people, and by the people was inaugurated and has become a triumphant success. The Puritan settled in New England and the Cavalier in the South. They represented the opposites of spiritual and temporal life and opinions. The processes of liberty liberalized the one and elevated the other. Washington and Adams were the new types. Their union in a common cause gave the world a Republic both stable and free. It possessed conservatism without bigotry, and liberty without license. It founded institutions strong enough to resist revolution, and elastic enough for indefinite expansion to meet the requirements in government of ever-enlarging areas of population and the needs of progress and growth. It was nurtured by the toleration and patriotism which bound together in a common cause the Puritans of New England and the Catholics of Maryland, the Dutch Reformers of New York and the Huguenots of South Carolina, the Quakers and Lutherans of Pennsylvania and the Episcopalians, Methodists, Presbyterians, Baptists, and religionists of all and of opposite opinions in the other colonies.

The "Mayflower," with the Pilgrims, and a Dutch ship
laden with African slaves, were on the ocean at the same
time, the one sailing for Massachusetts and the other for
Virginia. This company of saints and first cargo of slaves
represented the forces which were to peril and rescue free
government. The slaver was the product of the commercial
spirit of Great Britain, and the greed of the times to stimulate production in the colonies. The men who wrote in the
cabin of the "Mayflower" the first charter of freedom, a government of just and equal laws, were a little band of Protes-
tants against every form of injustice and tyranny. The leaven
of their principles made possible the Declaration of Independence, liberated the slaves, and founded the free commonwealths which form the Republic of the United States.

Platforms of principles, by petition or protest or statement,
have been as frequent as revolts against established authority.
They are a part of the political literature of all nations. The
Declaration of Independence proclaimed at Philadelphia, July
4, 1776, is the only one of them which arrested the attention
of the world when it was published, and has held its undivided interest ever since. The vocabulary of the equality of
man had been in familiar use by philosophers and statesmen
for ages. It expressed noble sentiments, but their application was limited to classes or conditions. The masses cared
little for them, nor remembered them long. Jefferson's superb crystalization of the popular opinion that "all men are
created equal, that they are endowed by their Creator with
certain inalienable rights, that among these are life, liberty,
and the pursuit of happiness," had its force and effect in
being the deliberate utterance of the people. It swept away
in a single sentence kings and nobles, peers and prelates. It
was Magna Charta and the Petition of Rights planted in the
virgin soil of the American wilderness and bearing richer and
riper fruit. Under its vitalizing influence upon the individual, the farmer left his plow in the furrow, the lawyer his
books and briefs, the merchant his shop, and the workman
his bench, to enlist in the patriot army. They were fighting
for themselves and their children. They embodied the idea
in their Constitution in the immortal words with which that
great instrument of liberty and order began:—

" We, the people of the United States, do ordain."

The scope and limitations of this idea of freedom have neither been misinterpreted nor misunderstood. The laws of nature in their application to the rise and recognition of men according to their mental, moral, spiritual, and physical endowments are left undisturbed. But the accident of birth gives no rank and confers no privilege. Equal rights and common opportunity for all have been the spurs of ambition and the motors of progress. They have established the common schools and built the public libraries. A sovereign people have learned and enforced the lesson of free education. The practice of government is itself a liberal education. People who make their own laws need no lawgivers. After a century of successful trial, the system has passed the period of experiment, and its demonstrated permanency and power are revolutionizing the governments of the world. It has raised the largest armies of modern times for self-preservation, and at the successful termination of the war returned the soldiers to the pursuits of peace. It has so adjusted itself to the pride and patriotism of the defeated, that they vie with the victors in their support of and enthusiasm for the old flag and our common country. Imported anarchists have preached their baleful doctrines, but have made no converts. They have tried to inaugurate a reign of terror under the banner of the violent seizure and distribution of property, only to be defeated, imprisoned, and executed by the law made by the people and enforced by juries selected from the people, and judges and prosecuting officers elected by the people. Socialism finds disciples only among those who were its votaries before they were forced to fly from their native land, but it does not take root upon American soil. The State neither supports nor permits taxation to maintain the Church. The citizen can worship God according to his belief and conscience, or he may neither reverence nor recognize the Almighty. And yet religion has flourished, churches abound, the ministry is sustained, and millions of dollars are contributed annually for the evangelization of the world. The United States is a Christian country, and a living and practical Christianity is the characteristic of its people.

Benjamin Franklin, philosopher and patriot, amused the jaded courtiers of Louis XVI. by his talks about liberty, and entertained the scientists of France by bringing lightning from the clouds. In the reckoning of time, the period from Franklin to Morse, and from Morse to Edison, is but a span, and yet it marks a material development as marvelous as it has been beneficent. The world has been brought into contact and sympathy. The electric current thrills and unifies the people of the globe. Power and production, highways and transports have been so multiplied and improved by inventive genius, that within the century of our independence sixty-four millions of people have happy homes and improved conditions within our borders. We have accumulated wealth far beyond the visions of the Cathay of Columbus or the El Dorado of De Soto. But the farmers and freeholders, the savings banks and shops illustrate its universal distribution. The majority are its possessors and administrators. In housing and living, in the elements which make the toiler a self-respecting and respected citizen, in avenues of hope and ambition for children, in all that gives broader scope and keener pleasure to existence, the people of this Republic enjoy advantages far beyond those of other lands. The unequalled and phenomenal progress of the country has opened wonderful opportunities for making fortunes, and stimulated to madness the desire and rush for the accumulation of money. Material prosperity has not debased literature nor debauched the press; it has neither paralyzed nor repressed intellectual activity. American science and letters have received rank and recognition in the older centers of learning. The demand for higher education has so taxed the resources of the ancient universities as to compel the foundation and liberal endowment of colleges all over the Union. Journals, remarkable for their ability, independence, and power, find their strength, not in the patronage of government, or the subsidies of wealth, but in the support of a nation of newspaper readers. The humblest and poorest person has, in periodicals whose price is counted in pennies, a library larger, fuller, and more varied than was within the reach of the rich in the time of Columbus.

The sum of human happiness has been infinitely increased

by the millions from the Old World who have improved
their conditions in the New, and the returning tide of lesson
and experience has incalculably enriched the fatherlands.
The divine right of kings has taken its place with the instruments of mediæval torture among the curiosities of the
antiquary.   Only the shadow of kingly authority stands
between the government of themselves, by themselves, and
the people of Norway and Sweden.   The union in one
empire of the states of Germany is the symbol of Teutonic
power and the hope of German liberalism.   The petty
despotisms of Italy have been merged into a nationality
which has centralized its authority in its ancient capitol on
the hills of Rome.   France was rudely roused from the sullen
submission of centuries to intolerable tyranny by her soldiers
returning from service in the American revolution.   The wild
orgies of the Reign of Terror were the revenges and excesses
of a people who had discovered their power, but were not
prepared for its beneficent use.   She fled from herself into
the arms of Napoleon.   He, too, was a product of the
American experiment.   He played with kings as with toys
and educated France for liberty.   In the processes of her
evolution from darkness to light, she tried Bourbon and
Orleanist and the third Napoleon, and cast them aside.   Now
in the fullness of time, and through the training in the school
of hardest experience, the French people have reared and
enjoy a permanent republic.   England of the "Mayflower"
and of James II., England of George III. and of Lord North,
has enlarged suffrage and is to-day animated and governed by
the democratic spirit.   She has her throne admirably occupied by one of the wisest of sovereigns and best of women,
but it would not survive one dissolute and unworthy successor.   She has her hereditary peers, but the House of
Lords will be brushed aside the moment it resists the will of
the people.

The time has arrived for both a closer union and greater
distance between the Old World and the New.   The former
indiscriminate welcome to our prairies and the present
invitation to these palaces of art and industry mark the passing period.   Unwatched and unhealthy immigration can no
longer be permitted to our shores.   We must have a national

quarantine against disease, pauperism, and crime. We do not want candidates for our hospitals, our poorhouses, or our jails. We cannot admit those who come to undermine our institutions and subvert our laws. But we will gladly throw wide our gates for, and receive with open arms, those who by intelligence and virtue, by thrift and loyalty, are worthy of receiving the equal advantages of the priceless gift of American citizenship. The spirit and object of this exhibition are peace and kinship.

Three millions of Germans, who are among the best citizens of the Republic, send greeting to the Fatherland their pride in its glorious history, its ripe literature, its traditions and associations. Irish, equal in number to those who still remain upon the Emerald Isle, who have illustrated their devotion to their adopted country on many a battle-field, fighting for the Union and its perpetuity, have rather intensified than diminished their love for the land of the shamrock and their sympathy with the aspirations of their brethren at home. The Italian, the Spaniard, and the Frenchman, the Norwegian, the Swede, and the Dane, the English, the Scotch, and the Welsh, are none the less loyal and devoted Americans because in this congress of their kin the tendrils of affection draw them closer to the hills and valleys, the legends and the loves associated with their youth.

Edmund Burke, speaking in the British Parliament with prophetic voice, said: "A great revolution has happened— a revolution made, not by chopping and changing of power in any of the existing states, but by the appearance of a new state, of a new species, in a new part of the globe. It has made as great a change in all the relations and balances and gravitations of power as the appearance of a new planet would in the system of the solar world." Thus was the humiliation of our successful revolt tempered to the motherland by pride in the state created by her children. If we claim heritage in Bacon, Shakespeare, and Milton, we also acknowledge that it was for liberties guaranteed Englishmen by sacred charters our fathers triumphantly fought. While wisely rejecting throne and caste and privilege and an Established Church in their new-born state, they adopted the substance of English liberty and the body of English law. Closer relations with England than with other lands, and a common language rendering easy interchanges of criticisms and epithet, sometimes irritate and offend, but the heart of republican America beats with responsive pulsations to the hopes and aspirations of the people of Great Britain.

The grandeur and beauty of this spectacle are the eloquent witnesses of peace and progress. The Parthenon and the cathedral exhausted the genius of the ancient and the skill of the mediæval architects, in housing the statue or spirit of Deity. In their ruins or their antiquity they are mute protests against the merciless enmity of nations, which forced art to flee to the altar for protection. The United States welcome the sister republics of the Southern and Northern continents, and the nations and peoples of Europe and Asia, of Africa and Australia, with the products of their lands, of their skill, and of their industry, to this city of yesterday, yet clothed with royal splendor as the Queen of the Great Lakes. The artists and architects of the country have been bidden to design and erect the buildings which shall fitly illustrate the height of our civilization and the breadth of our hospitality. The peace of the world permits and protects their efforts in utilizing their powers for man's temporal welfare. The result is this park of palaces. The originality and the boldness of their conceptions, and the magnitude and harmony of their creations, are the contributions of America to the oldest of the arts and the cordial bidding of America to the peoples of the earth to come and bring the fruitage of their age to the boundless opportunities of this unparalleled exhibition.

If interest in the affairs of this world is vouchsafed to those who have gone before, the spirit of Columbus hovers over us to-day. Only by celestial intelligence can it grasp the full significance of this spectacle and ceremonial.

From the first century to the fifteenth counts for little in the history of progress, but in the period between the fifteenth and the twentieth is crowded the romance and reality of human development. Life has been prolonged, and its enjoyment intensified. The powers of the air and the water, the resistless forces of the elements, which in the time of the discoverer were the visible terrors of the wrath of God, have been subdued to the service of man. Art and luxuries which could be possessed and enjoyed only by the rich and noble, the works of genius which were read and understood only by the learned few, domestic comforts and surroundings beyond the reach of lord or bishop, now adorn and illumine the homes of our citizens. Serfs are sovereigns and the people are kings. The trophies and splendors of their reign are commonwealths, rich in every attribute of great states, and united in a Republic whose power and prosperity and liberty and enlightenment are the wonder and admiration of the world.

All hail, Columbus, discoverer, dreamer, hero, and apostle! We, here, of every race and country, recognize the horizon which bounded his vision and the infinite scope of his genius. The voice of gratitude and praise for all the blessings which have been showered upon mankind by his adventure is limited to no language, but is uttered in every tongue. Neither marble nor brass can fitly form his statue. Continents are his monument, and unnumbered millions present and to come, who enjoy in their liberties and their happiness the fruits of his faith, will reverently guard and preserve, from century to century, his name and fame.

THE EARL OF DERBY

THE EMANCIPATION OF BRITISH NEGROES

[Edward Geoffrey Smith Stanley, Earl of Derby, an English statesman, three times Prime Minister of England and celebrated for a style
of oratory that won him the title of "the Rupert of Debate," was born
in Lancashire in 1799. He completed his education at Oxford and
entered Parliament at the age of twenty-one. His rise was rapid, and at
the age of thirty he was chief secretary for Ireland, in the Grey administration. In a few years more he was made secretary for the Colonies, and
by 1846 was leader in the House of Commons of the Opposition to the
Russell administration. Having succeeded his father as Earl of Derby,
he continued his brilliant public career until in 1852 he was made prime
minister, but his cabinet did not endure very long. He "went into
Opposition" and when the Palmerston ministry resigned he found himself Premier a second time, from 1858 to 1859. In 1866 he formed his
third ministry. He died in 1869. The following address to the House
of Commons was made in 1833, urging the emancipation of negroes in
the British West Indies.]

A SLAVE proprietor who was examined before the committee last year (I forget his name), told us that if a
slave only looked his master in the face he might order him
to receive thirty-nine lashes. Is this the way to teach him
to respect law and prepare him for the immunities of a free
man? Is it thus he is to be raised to a level with other men?
In 1826, Mr. Canning, talking of the dignity of man,
quoted the lines:—

"cælumque tueri
Jussit, et erectos ad sidera tollere vultus."

But how can you tell the negro that he shall look up as a free
man—how can you talk of hopes, encouragement, preparation for individual freedom, and general emancipation, when
even at this moment the slave dares not to raise his eyes to

his master's face without the risk of receiving thirty-nine lashes? I do not speak of the actual exercise of any such power—I do not believe it could be exercised—but that such a power exists there can be no doubt. In case of unjust infliction the slave must go before two magistrates, themselves slave masters; and if he can persuade them to believe him the master is to be prosecuted, and if found guilty by a jury subjected to fine and imprisonment; but if the magistrates think the evidence insufficient, without any malicious motive on the part of the slave, he is to be subjected to a second flogging for having made the complaint. This is the practical working in Jamaica of the law in favor of the slave. But there is a further punishment: in case aggravated, overwhelming cruelty be proved against a master, if a jury find that it has been atrocious, then an addition is to be made to the fine and imprisonment; and what is it? That the slave may be sold and the money handed over to the criminal master. This is the punishment inflicted on masters in Jamaica for conduct which is called atrocious. . . .

I am afraid I may disgust the House by details of the punishments inflicted; but they are a part of the system, and I must refer to them. I find that in 1829, when the slave population was 61,627, the number of punishments returned to the protectors was no less than 17,359; in the next year, when the population was 59,547, the punishments were increased to 18,324—the number of lashes in that time amounting to 194,744. In the year 1831, the population being then only 58,000, the number of punishments were 21,656, the lashes being 199,500.

This was the official record of the punishments supplied to the protectors of slaves by the owners themselves; it did not include any punishments inflicted under judicial authority; not one of those inflicted by direction of a magistrate; but those domestic punishments alone, which, in the present state of the law, are sanctioned; and this return also, let it be recollected, is confined to the Crown colonies, and represents the domestic, irresponsible punishments which the owners of slaves have inflicted by their own authority. I will not impute any guilt to the owners of the slaves—I will not impute to them anything more than that perversion of moral feeling which it is one of the greatest curses of slavery that it entails and impresses upon the mind of the enslaver— I will not impute any want of the ordinary feelings of humanity, further than that they are perverted by prejudice and rendered callous by custom and habit—but I call upon the House to consider where punishments are unrecorded, where no check is interposed by the legal authority, where no remedy or no efficient remedy is given to the slave by authority of the law—to consider if, in this comparatively free state of Demerara, this be the amount of punishment inflicted in one year, what must be the nature of the system which is carried on in other colonies where there are no checks. What must be the degradation of the system under which the other colonies of the British Empire at this moment labor! What is the amount of unredressed injustice—what is the amount of fatal oppression and cruel tyranny which calls upon this House to regulate, by interposing its solemn authority between this dreadful system of oppression and that which Mr. Canning called "the abstract love of the cart-whip"!   .   .   .

There is also another object on which I am sure his Majesty's government will not appeal in vain to the House or to the country. I feel perfect confidence in calling upon this House to pledge itself, whether in aid of the local legislatures of the colonies, or without any aid from those legislatures, to establish a religious and moral system of education for the negroes. We are about to emancipate the slaves; the old, after a trial of their industrious and other good qualities— the young immediately. With the young, therefore, our responsibility will immediately commence. If we place them in a state of freedom, we are bound to see that they are fitted for the enjoyment of that state; we are bound to give them the means of proving to themselves that the world is not for merely animal existence, that it is not the lot of man merely to labor incessantly from the cradle to the grave, and that to die is not merely to get to the end of a wearisome pilgrimage. We must endeavor to give them habits and to imbue them with feelings calculated to qualify them for the adequate discharge of their duties here; and we must endeavor to instil into them the conviction that when those duties shall be discharged they are not " as the brutes that perish."

Sir, I have now gone through the various points to which I think it necessary to call the attention of the House. I know the difficulties, the almost insurmountable obstacles, which attend almost any plan with reference to this subject; and I know the peculiar disadvantages under which I bring forward the present plan. But I entertain a confident hope that the resolutions which I shall have the honor to submit to the House contain a germ, which, in the process of time, will be matured, by better judgment and knowledge, into a perfect fruit; and that from the day on which the act passes there will be secured to the country, to the colonies, and to all classes of his Majesty's subjects, the benefit of a virtual extinction of all the horrors attendant on a state of slavery; and that, at no very distant period, by no uncertain operation, but by the effect of that machinery which the proposed plan will put in motion, the dark stain which disfigures the fair freedom of this country will be wholly wiped out. Sir, in looking to this most desirable object, it is impossible not to advert to those who first broached the mighty question of the extinction of slavery, the earliest laborers in that cause, the final triumph of which they were not destined to see. They struggled for the establishment of first principles—they were satisfied with laying the foundation of that edifice which they left it to their successors to rear; they saw the future, as the prophets of old saw "the days that were to come," but they saw it afar off, and with the eye of faith. It is not without the deepest emotion, I recollect that there is yet living one of the earliest, one of the most religious, one of the most conscientious, one of the most eloquent, one of the most zealous friends of this great cause, who watched it in its dawn. Wilberforce still remains to see, I trust, the final consummation of the great and glorious work which he was one of the first to commence, and to exclaim, like the last of the prophets to whom I have already alluded: " Lord, now lettest thou thy servant depart in peace."

Sir, it is with great regret that I have felt it necessary to detain the House so long; but on a subject of so much difficulty it was imperative upon me to do so. I will now, however, after thanking the House for the patience and attention with which they have been so good as to listen to me, conclude with offering up an ardent prayer that by the course which they may adopt they will for a second time set the world a glorious example of a commercial nation, weighing commercial advantages light in the balance against justice and religion; that they will achieve the great object of extinguishing slavery, gradually, safely, but at the same time completely—a result the more to be desired, if accomplished by a yielding on one side and the other, which may make both sides forget extreme opinion, and which will exhibit a great and proud example of a deliberative assembly, reconciling conflicting interests, liberating the slave without inflicting hardship on his master, gratifying the liberal and humane spirit of the age, without harming even those who stand in its way, and vindicating their high functions moderately, but with determination, and in a manner honorable to the people of whom they are the representatives, and acting in a manner on this important question which will afford a sure pledge of a successful termination of the glorious career on which they are about to enter.

CAMILLE DESMOULINS

ADVOCATING THE CONDEMNATION OF LOUIS XVI.

[Camille Desmoulins was a clever young journalist, and leader in the great French Revolution. He was born in 1760, educated for the law, and adopting the revolutionary principles of the day, by his great ability as a writer won the recognition of numerous radical groups in Paris. Next he became a leading figure in the Cordeliers Club of revolutionary agitators, was elected to the convention then administering the affairs of France, and voted to behead King Louis XVI. He had established a revolutionary paper in which he displayed his wit and supported Danton. He had also met and married beautiful Lucile Duplessis, who gave up everything for him. He fell at last under Robespierre's ban and was guillotined in 1794. The speech that follows was made in 1793, and was addressed to the National Convention, urging the speedy execution of the king.]

IT is no use for Necker to pretend that there is a contract between Louis XVI. and the nation, and to defend it by the principles of civil law. What does he gain by this, and according to these principles in how many ways will this contract not be nullified? Nullified, because it was not ratified by the contracting party; nullified, because Louis XVI. could not release himself without releasing the nation; nullified by the violence, the massacre of the Champ de Mars, and by that death-flag under which the revision was closed; nullified by default of cause and default of bond, in that the obligation rested on the nation, which gave all and received nothing in the way of " consideration," Louis XVI. entering into no obligation on his side, but being left free to commit all crimes with impunity.

But I am ashamed to follow the advocates of Louis XVI. in this discussion of civil law. It is by the law of nations that this trial ought to be regulated. The slavery of nations during ten thousand years has not been able to rescind their indefensible rights.   It was these rights that were a standing protest against the reigning of the Charleses, the Henrys, the Frederics, the Edwards, as they were against the despotism of Julius Cæsar.   It is a crime to be a king.   It was even a crime to be a constitutional king, for the nation had never accepted the constitution.   There is only one condition on which it could be legitimate to reign; it is when the whole people formally strips itself of its rights and cedes them to a single man, not only as Denmark did in 1660, but as happens when the entire people has passed or ratified this warrant of its sovereignty.   And yet it could not bind the next generation, because death extinguishes all rights.   It is the prerogative of those who exist, and who are in possession of this earth, to make the laws for it in their turn.   Otherwise, let the dead leave their graves and come to uphold their laws against the living who have repealed them.   All other kinds of royalty are imposed upon the people at the risk of their insurrection, just as robbers reign in the forests at the risk of the provost's punishment befalling them.   And now after we have risen and recovered our rights, to plead these feudal laws, or even the constitution, in opposition to republican Frenchmen, is to plead the black code to negro conquerors of white men.   Our constituents have not sent us here to follow those feudal laws and that pretended constitution, but to abolish it, or rather, to declare that it never existed, and to reinvest the nation with that sovereignty which another had usurped.   Either we are truly republicans, giants who rise to the heights of these republican ideas, or we are not giants, but mere pigmies.   By the law of nations Louis XVI. as king, even a constitutional king, was a tyrant in a state of revolt against the nation, and a criminal worthy of death. And Frenchmen have no more need to try him than had Hercules to try the boar of Erymanthus, or the Romans to try Tarquin, or Cæsar, who also thought himself a constitutional dictator.

But it is not only a king, it is a criminal accused of crimes that in his person we have to punish.

You must not expect me to indulge in undue exaggeration, and to call him a Nero, as I heard those do who have

CAMILLE DESMOULINS

Photogravure after an engraving by W. H. Mote

spoken the most favorably for him.   I know that Louis XVI.
had the inclinations of a tiger, and if we established courts
such as Montesquieu calls the courts of manners and
behavior, like that of the Areopagus at Athens, which
condemned a child to death for putting out his bird's eyes;
if we had an Areopagus, it would have a hundred times condemned this man as dishonoring the human race by the ca-
prices of his wanton cruelties.   But as it is not the deeds of
his private life, but the crimes of his reign that we are judging, it must be confessed that this long list of accusations
against Louis which our committee and our orators have
presented to us, while rendering him a thousand times worthy
of death, will nevertheless not suggest to posterity the horrors of the reign of Nero, but the crimes of constituents,
the crimes of Louis the King, rather than the crimes of Louis
Capet.

That which makes the former king justly odious to the
people is the four years of perjuries and oaths, incessantly
repeated into the nation's ear before the face of heaven,
while all the time he was conspiring against the nation.
Treason was always with every nation the most abominable
of crimes.   It has always inspired that horror which is
inspired by poison and vipers, because it is impossible to
guard against it.   So the laws of the Twelve Tables devoted
to the Furies the mandatary who betrayed the trust of his
constituent, and permitted the latter to kill the former where-
ever he should find him.   So, too, fidelity in fulfilling one's
engagements is the only virtue on which those pride themselves who have lost all others.   It is the only virtue found
among thieves.   It is the last bond which holds society—even
that of the robbers themselves—together.   This comparison, it
is, which best paints royalty, by showing how much less villain-
ous is even a robbers' cave than the Louvre, since the maxim of
all kings is that of Cæsar: "It is permissible to break one's faith
in order to reign."   So in his religious idiom, spoke Antoine
de Levre to Charles V.: "If you are not willing to be a rascal,
if you have a soul to save, renounce the empire."   So said
Machiaveli in terms very applicable to our situation.   For
this reason it was, that many years ago in a petition to the
National Assembly I quoted this passage: "If sovereignty

must be renounced in order to make a people free, he who is clothed with this sovereignty has some excuse in betraying the nation, because it is difficult and against nature to be willing to fall from so high a position." All this proves that the crimes of Louis XVI. are the crimes of the constituents who supported him in his position of king rather than his crimes, that is to say, of those who gave him the right by letters patent to be the " enemy of the nation" and a traitor. But all these considerations, calculated as they may be to soften the horror of his crimes in the eyes of posterity, are useless before the law, in mitigating their punishment. What! Shall the judges forbear to punish a brigand because in his cave he has been brought up to believe that all the possessions of those who pass his cave belong to him? Because his education has so depraved his natural disposition that he could not be anything but a robber? Shall it be alleged as a reason for letting the treason of a king go unpunished, that he could not be anything but a traitor, and as a reason for not giving the nations the example of cutting down this tree, that it can only bear poisons?

In two words, by the declaration of rights, by that code eternal, unchangeable (that provisional code which in all states precedes their complete organization, when special laws shall have modified general laws), the articles of which, effaced by the rust of centuries, the French people adopted with joy, and by the enactment (consecrated as the basis of its constitution) that the law is the same toward all, either for punishment or for protection, reestablished in all their purity, Louis XVI. was divested of his chimerical inviolability.

He can henceforth be regarded only as a conspirator. Followed by the people, he came on the tenth of August, — that famous " Commune"—came to seek an asylum among us, at the foot of the throne of national sovereignty, in the house which was found full of evidences of his plottings and of his crimes. We placed him under arrest and imprisoned him in the Temple, and now it only remains for us to pass sentence upon him.

"But who shall judge this conspirator?" It is astonishing and inconceivable what trouble this question has given to the best heads of the Convention.   Removed as we are from Nature and the primitive laws of all society, most of us have not thought that we could judge a conspirator without a jury of accusation, a jury of judgment, and judges who would apply the law, and all have imagined necessary a court more or less extraordinary.   So we leave the ancient ruts only to fall into new ones, instead of following the plain road of common sense.   Who shall judge Louis XVI.?   The whole people, if it can, as the people of Rome judged Manlius and Horatius, nor dreamt of the need of a jury of accusation, to be followed by a jury of judgment, and that in turn by a court which would apply the law to judge a culprit taken in the act.   But as we cannot hear the pleas of twenty-five millions of men we must recur to the maxim of Montesquieu: " Let a free people do all that it can by itself and the rest by representatives and commissioners!"   And what is the National Convention but the commission selected by the French people to try the last king and to form the constitution of the new republic?

Some claim that such a course would be to unite all the powers—legislative functions and judicial functions.   Those who have most wearied our ears by reciting the dangers of this cumulation of powers must either deride our simplicity in believing that they respect those limits, or else they do not well understand themselves.   For have not constitutional and legislative assemblies assumed a hundred times the functions of judges, whether in annulling the procedure of the Chatelet, and many other tribunals, or in issuing decrees against so many prisoners on suspicion whether there was an accusation or not?   To acquit Mirabeau and " P. Equality," or to send Lessart to Orleans, was not that to assume the functions of judges?   I conclude from this that those "Balancers," as Mirabeau called them, who continually talk of "equilibrium," and the balance of power, do not themselves believe in what they say.   Can it be contested, for example, that the nation which exercises the power of sovereignty does not "cumulate" all the powers?   Can it be claimed that the nation cannot delegate, at its will, this or that portion of its powers to whom it pleases?   Can any one deny that the nation has cumulatively clothed us here with its pow-

ers, both to try Louis XVI. and to construct the constitution?
One may well speak of the balance of power and the necessity of maintaining it when the people, as in England, exercises its sovereignty only at the time of elections.   But when
the nation, the sovereign, is in permanent activity, as formerly
at Athens and Rome, and as now in France, when the right
of sanctioning the laws is recognized as belonging to it, and
when it can assemble every day in its municipalities and sections, and expel the faithless mandataries, the great necessity
cannot be seen of maintaining the equilibrium of powers,
since it is the people who, with its arm of iron, itself holds
the scales ready to drive out the ambitious and the traitorous
who wish to make it incline to the side opposite the general
interest.   It is evident that the people sent us here to judge
the king and to give them a constitution.   Is the first of these
two functions so difficult to fulfill?   And have we anything
else to do than what Brutus did when the people caused him
to judge his two sons himself, and tested him by this, just as
the Convention is tested now?   He made them come to his
tribunal, as you must bring Louis XVI. before you.   It produced for him the proofs of their conspiracy as you must
present to Louis XVI. that multitude of overwhelming proofs
of his plots.   They could make no answer to the testimony
of a slave, as Louis XVI. will not be able to answer anything
to the correspondence of Laporte, and to that mass of written proofs that he paid his body-guard at Coblentz and
betrayed the nation.   And it only remains for you to prove,
as Brutus proved to the Roman people, that you are worthy
to begin the Republic and its constitution, and to appease
the shades of a hundred thousand citizens whom he caused
to perish in pronouncing the same sentence: [1] "I, lictor,
deliga ad palum."

---

[1] " Go, lictor, bind him to the stake."

GIRONDISTS ON THE WAY TO EXECUTION

Photogravure after a painting by C. von Piloty

JONATHAN PRENTISS DOLLIVER

THE AMERICAN OCCUPATION OF THE PHILIPPINES

[Jonathan Prentiss Dolliver, an American political leader, was born in 1858, in that part of Virginia from which West Virginia was formed. He received a good education, and graduated at the West Virginia University, subsequently becoming a lawyer. He practiced his profession with success and rose steadily to prominence, but never held public office until his election to Congress in 1901 as a Republican. In 1900 he was mentioned in connection with the vice-presidential nomination in the Republican National Convention at Philadelphia, but the honor fell to Theodore Roosevelt. In the year following he was appointed to the United States Senate to fill a vacancy, and in 1902 he was elected senator from Iowa for the full term, by the Legislature of the State. Senator Dolliver is a typical product of the higher culture of the Middle West. The son of a clergyman, and brought up amid refined surroundings, he has shown that the Western type of character is not only straightforward and strenuous, but educated in the best sense of the word. The speech that follows was delivered in the Senate in 1902, and expresses clearly the views of those who favor the expansion of territory for the United States.]

MUCH has been said intended to leave the impression that we entered the Philippine Islands with a lie on our tongues and treachery in our hearts, for the purpose of despoiling the land of its resources and the inhabitants of their liberties. It is discreditable to fill the air with such a clamor, unless somebody comes forward to identify and drag to light of day the authors of so gross an offense against mankind. The historian of these times, the student who deals with the unalterable facts of this case, will have no difficulty to find the monster who conceived and put into execution this atrocious conspiracy against the helpless people of these islands.

The policy which has been pursued has been assailed here with a rancor almost hysterical in its impotent rage. Senators have spoken by the day with words of incredible vehemence; epithet has followed epithet; accusation has been piled on accusation, as if the history of nations could be turned aside by a preconcerted series of gasoline explosions.

Gentlemen seem to forget that governments cannot move amid surroundings of such difficulty in paths of their own choosing. There may be no such thing as Divine Providence, though our fathers reverently believed that there is; there may be no such thing as destiny, though I am told the word is to be found in the files of Colorado newspapers, but nobody can doubt that forces are at work in this world altogether too large to be managed from a political headquarters; that there is a course of human events not to be combated, except at the most embarrassing disadvantages.

It is no depreciation of President McKinley to say that he looked upon the approaching conflict with Spain with fear and anxiety. He had devoted his whole life to the industrial and commercial questions which concern the investments of American capital and the wages of American labor. He had given no attention to our foreign affairs apart from the movements of commerce, and was the last man among his countrymen to give up the hope of peace.

He knew something, through the recollections of his boyhood, of the horrors of war, and better than any of his contemporaries he was able to look through the smoke of battle and beyond the noise of victory and to see distinctly, long before they came in sight of others, the perils involved in our disturbance of the peace of the world. He perceived at the time the fatal word was spoken by the joint resolution of Congress, that our victory over Spain carried with it not only the enlargement of our boundaries, but such an addition to our responsibilities as to dishearten even the most adventurous mind. Some said he was weak, others that he was timid, others that he was a creature of the commercial spirit, which is always conservative and does not like to risk any interference with business conditions.

Senators are sitting before me who saw much of him

during those days and nights of sleepless solicitude.   He
did not fear the military power of Spain.   He never doubted
that our operations on land and sea would make short work
of her armies and her fleets.

It was not the fear of defeat that appalled him.   It was
the moral certainty that the triumph over Spain in her colonial strongholds had in it a portentous national liability,
possibly beyond our strength, and at the very moment when
his partisan opponents, in the words of the most eloquent
Democratic leader in the House of Representatives, were
" dragging the Republican party into the war with Spain" the
overburdened Chief Magistrate of the people, with a troubled
heart, was pondering the very questions which to-day engage
the attention of both Houses of Congress.

I have listened with such patience as I could to the tirade
of stale and calumnious insinuations which for weeks has
filled this Chamber, intended to discredit the purposes and to
impeach the motives of the Government of the United States
in its dealings with the territory brought under our jurisdiction by the treaty of Paris.   Most of the men under whose
guidance these things were done, in the Senate, in the House
of Representatives, in the Cabinet, in the memorable sessions
of the Peace Commissioners at Paris, still live.   They can
answer for themselves, and I doubt not make their way
through this eruption of malice and prejudice without either
inconvenience or harm.

But one among them, more masterful than any other in
the influence of his persuasive leadership, can no longer
speak for himself.   He fell in the midst of his labors at the
post of his duty, in the maturity of his fame, after he had
seen the work which he had wrought lifted into the light of
universal history and his name enrolled among the founders
of states and the lawgivers of the world's progress.

In every step of the proceedings where the opportunity
to choose our course was given he exercised the part of a
practical wisdom which has never been successfully disparaged.   He could either have ordered Admiral Dewey, after
the victory at Manila, to assemble his ships and depart from
those waters, or to stay there and administer the situation
his guns had created—to take care of the wreck which had

been cast up by the sea. The first order would have been easy, and if it had been issued we would to-day have no Philippine problem and no paramount issue to become the football of our politics.

The President did not issue the order to retreat. Possibly he did not think of it, and there was no American, big or little, not even the micro-organisms of our politics, who did think of it till far after it was too late. Yet if we ever were to run away from the Philippine Islands that was the chance, that was the accepted time, that was the day of our cheap little salvation from the annoyances which have pestered us from that day to this.

William McKinley ordered him to stay at his post, and at once prepared the transports which carried the first detachment of our army of occupation to cooperate with his fleet. The alternative was presented to us either to go or to stay, and if there is a living American who denies that in remaining there we chose the part of courage and patriotism, such a man has not comprehended even the rudiments of our national character. If we had run away, within four weeks the nations of Europe, all of them having important commercial interests there, would have been compelled to restore order out of the chaos which we had brought about.

In fact, we had a hard time to keep them from helping us preserve order even while Dewey was there, and when the record of that faithful servant of the Republic is made up, the discriminating biographer will award to him as much credit for the prudence and sagacity of his administration during his long wait for the army transports as for the scientific skill with which his gunners wound up the affairs of the Spanish navy in the Pacific.

If he made any mistake at all it was in miscalculating the value of the help offered him by the leaders of native insurrectionary troops. I have heard his relations with these leaders discussed from every point of view. I have heard the letters of our consuls in those latitudes quoted, some claiming that things were said and done there which created an alliance between us and the native forces; but to my mind there is very little sense in such a controversy, for it did not need the prompt and sharp rebuke of the President to make it clear that neither the admiral nor the consuls were clothed with authority to lay upon the Government of the United States any obligations to sacrifice the whole Philippine people, not to speak of the foreign residents and Spanish subjects, to the ambitions or, if you please to call them, the aspirations of a few native adventurers.

It is clear that whatever civil institutions are at last established in the islands, if they include the whole archipelago or even the whole of the island of Luzon, they must be so ordered as to represent the aspirations of the entire community, and there has never been the slightest evidence of any general aspiration on the part of the Philippine people, outside of a single tribe, to subject themselves to the aspirations of an incompetent military dictatorship.

When the Peace Commission assembled at Paris, President McKinley had no immovable purpose in mind as to what ought to be done with the islands. He had been accustomed to speak in friendly consultation with his political associates of a commercial and naval headquarters at Manila somewhat on the lines of the British settlement at Hong-Kong, a sort of basis of supplies and operations in which our ships might find anchorage and from which the lines of our trade could be sent out through all the market places of the East.

Strangely enough, though he chose for the work of making the treaty men everywhere counted among the wisest and greatest of our statesmen—the honored president of the Senate [Mr. Frye]; the lamented Cushman K. Davis, of Minnesota; Whitelaw Reid, the veteran American journalist; George Gray, then a senator from the commonwealth of Delaware, and last, but not least, William R. Day, that modest country lawyer, whose extraordinary career as secretary of state, within less than a year's service, gave him a place among the famous diplomatists of his time—yet when it came to settling the momentous questions left undetermined by the protocol for peace the commissioners at Paris, unable to agree among themselves, turned for counsel to the President of the United States and left at last to his decision the whole question of the future of the Philippines.

He did not act in haste; he was slow to bring upon his countrymen the weight of such duties as were necessarily included in the act of assuming the sovereignty which the kingdom of Spain was no longer in a position to defend. What was done was so entirely free from the color of national greed and selfishness that his personal correspondence with the peace commissioners, conducted in the name of Secretary Hay, now a part of our public records, reveals the nobility of his character and the integrity of his motives more perfectly even than the more formal utterances of his official life.

He was not dazzled by the value of the prize we had captured; he did not seek to add to the humiliation of a prostrate enemy, and above all he understood the perplexities connected with administering or even overseeing the affairs of alien and backward races. What was it, then, that brought the President to the steadfast conviction that the summons of national duty called us to lay aside the ways of pleasantness, with which my friend from Tennessee [Mr. Carmack] adorned his eloquent peroration the other day, and take up the rugged task in which we have been ever since engaged?

For while the united judgment of our commissioners ultimately reached the same conclusion, after all the decision was his, and it needed only one line over his signature to have left the Philippine Islands exactly where we found them. Because that is so it has been hard for me, as I have heard the words lunatics, scoundrels, fools, thieves, murderers, land grabbers, carpetbaggers, plunderers, flying around this Chamber from the lips of all sorts and condition of Democratic statesmen, to keep my recollection from going back to those eventful days when alone in the executive chamber, pacing to and fro in restless meditation, weighing the circumstances in the fear of God, William McKinley set the seal of his approval upon the resolution of the American people to hold the Philippine Islands in trust for their inhabitants and to lift up that scattered population by the genius of our institutions to the privileges and the dignity of a free commonwealth.

Having thus located the authors of this wicked conspiracy against 10,000,000 of helpless and friendless people, I wish now to inquire in a general way into the progress and development of this plot against the liberties of the Philippine races. I wish to find out what has been undertaken and what measure of success has attended the enterprise.

The first problem with which the administration had to deal was the insurrectionary movement which arose while the treaty of peace was under debate in the Senate, and continued under normal military conditions until the collapse of the Mololos government and the flight of its military leaders to the mountain districts of Luzon. It is not easy and I do not think it is important to discuss the reasons of that rebellion against the United States, which took shape and gathered force during that long and unprofitable discussion which preceded the ratification of the treaty of peace.

I have never doubted that that period of controversy and delay brought on the disasters which have since fallen upon that people, and while I am not disposed to embitter this discussion with vain recriminations, yet it is due to truth to acquit the Government of the United States in any stage of this proceeding of any design to wrong or oppress the Philippine people.

Our navy went there to attack Spain, and our army went there to support the fleet. It lay in the trenches around Manila with explicit orders from the President that under no condition should it turn its guns on the native population, but on the other hand its commanding officers were charged with the duty of communicating our benignant purposes and doing whatever was in their power to win the regard and good will of the irregular militia encamped outside of their lines.

The United States was fortunate in the men selected to manage its affairs there—Merritt, Otis, MacArthur, Chaffee —all of them soldiers famous and honorable in the national service, and the American people, in my judgment, do not intend to spend very much of their time in trying to degrade their names in order to exalt the motives of the political and military cabal with which they were called upon to deal.

If the treaty had been promptly acted upon the provisional American government could have been forthwith inaugurated, and within thirty days might have reached an amicable adjustment, which would have disarmed the opposition even of the most ambitious and headstrong among the native popular leaders.

But whether that could have been done or not, it is too late now to review the mistakes and misunderstandings and follies which, in the opinion of some, were unhappily connected with the earlier stages of our military administration. If it ever was feasible to try to build up a permanent Philippine government, with the revolutionary congress and cabinet as its foundation, the prospect of that, nay, even the possibility of that, vanished when our volunteers in the trenches around Manila were compelled to fight for their lives against the aggressions of a formidable native armed force.

It is idle to say that the collision which resulted in the slaughter and flight and final destruction of that army could have been avoided.   It is certain, at any rate, that with such wisdom as we had the conflict was not avoided, and to spend our time on it now serves no good purpose of any sort.

For my own part, I am satisfied that an attempt to collect the elements of a permanent civil régime around the nucleus of the existing dictatorship would have fatally impeded every subsequent attempt to establish the social and political order of the islands.   And while we have succeeded in attaching nearly every important personal influence which survived the downfall of the government at Mololos to our present administration, their usefulness to their own people, according to their own frank admission, would have been limited indeed, without the direction of our strong hand.

It was the judgment of President McKinley, a judgment which, I think, will be affirmed by history, that underneath the civil institutions of the islands the firm foundation of our national authority must first of all be laid, and he therefore made the surrender of armed resistance the unalterable condition of peace.   Under his orders the rebellion was crushed and nothing left of it except scattered bands, ineffective for legitimate military purposes, hiding in the mountains wherever they could find a safe retreat.

Our army not only overthrew the rebellion in the field, but it did a thing which the Spanish government had never thought possible.   It pursued the guerilla operations of the enemy over impassable rivers, through impenetrable jungles, and across the summits of inaccessible mountains. And so completely was its work done that for more than a year, throughout the whole archipelago outside of three or four disturbed provinces, the Philippine insurrection as a military proposition has been a thing of the past.

But somebody says, " How can this be so when the newspapers even now are filled with reports of battles, captures, and other military outrages? " It has been apparently almost impossible for the American people to get into their minds a picture of these islands, and the government could well afford to put a map of the archipelago, with distances and provinces properly described, in every newspaper office and schoolhouse in the United States.

For incalculable mischief has arisen from our almost habitual failure to locate the field operations of our army. If the hearings before the Philippine Committee have had no other result than to define and identify the present scene of our warlike activities, they have served at least one useful purpose. Let me illustrate what I mean.

General Bell, trying to capture insignificant bands of roving guerillas in the provinces of Laguna and Batangas, issued orders requiring the friendly portion of the population, that portion that desired to cast in its lot with the Government of the United States, to reside within certain specified military limits, an order absolutely necessary for the success of his campaign, and executed without hardship and inhumanity of any kind—an order which has brought peace to the distracted provinces and prepared the way for the immediate establishment of civil government.

Yet half the newspapers in the United States took up the cry that we had adopted in the Philippine Islands the Weylerism of Spain, and a considerable portion, even of intelligent people, lost sight of the twenty-eight provinces enjoying the benefits of stable government and began again to speak the language of despair of the Philippine situation.

Not long ago, following the Balangigi massacre in the island of Samar, General Chaffee, in sending forward punitive expeditions, gave out a general order, which found its way into American newspapers, commending our troops to special vigilance and impressing the comrades of the men who had been killed by treachery to guard against similar misfortunes by treating the whole population with suspicion and distrust. He supposed that he was speaking about the island of Samar and the two remaining hostile provinces of Luzon, as the area of rebellion had dwindled to that small compass. He had himself officially reported the peaceful and prosperous situation that prevailed in practically all the other provinces.

Yet within a week after the newspapers had contained his expression about the war rebels, which included nearly everybody in the disturbed provinces, from his point of view, we find Dr. Schurman, who joined with Admiral Dewey and Professor Worcester in helping the President lay the foundation of his policy, with nothing to go on but a newspaper clipping, solemnly concluding that the terrorism inspired by guerillas and cattle thieves in the mountains of Batangas and Laguna, and the yells of blood-thirsty bolomen in the island of Samar, indicated that the whole Philippine archipelago had been welded together by the fires of war into a solid national mass which was ready and waiting for our tardy recognition as an independent state.

I will confess that there is enough yet to be done by the army to depress the feelings of the American people. At the same time the progress which has been made, the good and lasting work that has been done throughout the whole group of islands, outside of two or three provinces where the process of pacification has only just been finished, is such as to fill with hope and enthusiasm the heart of every man who has taken a sincere interest in the success of our arduous service in those remote and misunderstood regions of the earth.

We are not in the dark as to the present stage of our advancement toward the goal of self-government which we have set up for these islands. We have the testimony of the officers of the army as to the military conditions prevailing in the island of Luzon. Outside of the provinces of Batangas and Laguna they agree that the active work of the army is done, and General Chaffee's latest report indicates that General Bell has at last won a gratifying victory over the desperate obstacles with which his gallant brigade has so long contended in these two provinces. So that to-day the whole island of Luzon is living in peace, and civil government will soon be established in the two remaining unorganized provinces.

But we have not only the testimony of the officers of the army, but we have also the report of the Philippine Commission, and especially the testimony given by Governor Taft before the Senate committee during his recent visit to the capital. He says that, accompanied by his colleagues, and without military escort, he passed in perfect security from the capital of one province to another, kindly received everywhere by the inhabitants, and organized the local administration of municipalities and provinces on the basis of popular self-government, as authorized in the statutes which had been previously framed by the commission, finding the people everywhere ready to begin the work of building upon a safe foundation the political future of these scattered communities.

So that to-day courts of justice, schools crowded with eager pupils, highways, and progressive industrial conditions have everywhere followed the surrender of the vagrant armies which had been wandering over the island ever since the capitulation of the Spanish garrison at Manila; while throughout the whole civilized portion of the archipelago, except in two or three provinces, there is peace, order, and cheerful submission to the restraints of good laws. Even the bandits, who for centuries have infested the country, have in many regions recognized the efficiency of the new order of things, as they have stood before native judges, arrested by native policemen, and answered for crimes the like of which had gone almost unnoticed for generations.

I have in my hand what I regard as the most conclusive evidence of the state of affairs in the Philippine Archipelago —the reports made to the government at Manila by the provincial authorities all over the islands, including the period since the civil government has been organized and up to January 1, 1902. These reports cover the whole civilized portions of the islands outside of Samar, and the two provinces in Luzon, Bantangas and Laguna, where the disturbed conditions have only recently been pacified.

Notwithstanding my regard for the comfort and convenience of the Senate, I am disposed to read a few of them.

[The speaker here read extracts from the reports confirmatory of his
remarks.]

The record of this work reflects infinite honor upon the
commission which has executed it, upon the American army
which made it possible, and upon the people of the United
States who stood by President McKinley in the national election which saved the Philippine Islands to civilization.

To Governor William H. Taft, more than to any other
man, belongs the credit of this benign interpretation of the
national policy.

Unlike my friend the senator from Colorado [Mr. Patter-
son], who does me the honor to listen to me this moment,
he was not an original enthusiast on the acquisition of the
islands. The President sent for him, and he carelessly
boasted before he had had an opportunity to see him that he
had not the slightest intention of going into any such business. He was judge of a circuit court of the United States,
and before him there was a prospect clear as day to sit in the
Supreme Court of the United States. He said he was
opposed to the policy and knew nothing about it and cared
nothing about it. He thought it was a blunder and a course
of political stupidity.

President McKinley pressed his duty upon him. He was
five hours in the President's private apartments, and when
he came out he had been over " the road to Damascus," a
road which Victor Hugo says every man must travel who
looks to any great achievement in this world, for he himself
told me that in those five hours he received an altogether
new revelation of the significance of a man's relation to the
world in which we are living. And so, easily and happily,
he turned his back on the emoluments of a great profession,
laid aside the ambitions of a great career, gathered his wife
and children about him, and went out from among his kindred and his countrymen to become the servant of strange
peoples in their blind struggle toward a larger and a better
opportunity.

His perfect comprehension of the problems involved, his

brotherly heart leaning toward that people with a tender sympathy, his manly confidence in his country, his invincible optimism rising above all doubts and all fears—these have been the guaranties of his success, and these are the moral qualities that will place his name among the great figures in the history of our time.

He came here from a bed of sickness, and while he was here his body was racked with pain. Yet he could not keep to himself his anxiety to get back to his people, and when the other day he bade us good-by and anxious friends were heard to inquire about his health, he told them in words which thrilled me as few things have thrilled me in all my contact with men and with affairs, that if he knew he was going back to the Philippine Islands to die, nevertheless he would desire to be about the business which had been committed to his hands. My countrymen, it is impossible to overshadow the lofty heroism of a mission like that with the noise and dust and tempest of partisan controversy in the Senate.

This responsibility of ours is not a party responsibility. It is as completely national as the declaration of war against Spain. Men of all parties were with the late President when he began the work. Men of all parties will be with Theodore Roosevelt as, with a brave heart, keeping close to the counsel of the men who were nearest to McKinley when he died, he carries out in good faith the promise which he made to the American people in the hour of national sorrow, when he took upon him the oath of his high official duty.

Nor can this be a sectional question. The other day I heard a gallant knight step forth and offer his lance to defend the South if it should be attacked. The South is not likely to be attacked in this debate, and I warn those who are saving their ammunition to defend the South that they will have other need for their resources. A new generation is now on the stage of action in the United States, a generation which refuses to rekindle the fires of old animosities long since burned out, a generation that concedes to every section of the Union the right to work out the problems that have come upon them in the progress of society, not even offering them advice, but sympathy and good will rather, in the ordeal through which they are yet to pass.

For one I find comfort in the fact that to-day the affairs of the Philippines are in the hands of a broad-minded rebel general, Luke E. Wright, of Tennessee, honored as few men are honored throughout the South, and I never think of the trials of our little army in Luzon without seeing in my mind's eye a little old rebel cavalryman by the name of Joe Wheeler, yonder on the other side of the world, riding at the head of his division defending the sovereignty of the Republic, under our flag, the flag that never did stand and never can stand for anything except the liberties of the human race.

Nearly fifty years ago, Mr. Seward, speaking in the old Senate Chamber where the Supreme Court now sits, caught a prophetic glimpse of the future. He saw the conquest of the Rocky Mountains, and the Bay of San Francisco filled with ships; he saw the Isthmian Canal opened to the nations. He saw the unnumbered millions of the East, touched at last by the mighty forces of the modern world, making the Pacific Ocean the appointed highway of our traffic with far-off lands, then mysterious or unknown.

Within that fifty years the empire of Japan has risen up out of the ocean and to-day grasps the hand of Great Britain in a solemn covenant to guard the territorial unity of China and the equality of all commercial rights, while near at hand, on the very borders of Asia, are these islands, taking their first feeble steps toward constitutional government under our guidance; and I say to you, reflecting on the sacrifices we have made, counting the treasure we have poured out like water, considering the obligations we are under, and measuring the interests that are at stake, the Congress of the United States is just as likely to cede back the Mississippi Valley to the lawful heirs of Napoleon the Great as it is to leave the Philippine Archipelago to become a spoil of anarchy or a prize for European diplomacy. [Manifestations of applause in the galleries.]

STEPHEN ARNOLD DOUGLAS

REPLY TO LINCOLN

[Stephen Arnold Douglas was born in Brandon, Vt., in 1813. Ultimately he settled in Winchester, Ill., taught school, and studied law. In 1834 he was admitted to the bar of the Supreme Court, and his appointment to the office of attorney-general followed soon. In 1836 he entered the Illinois legislature; in 1840 he was appointed secretary of state, and the following year, though only twenty-seven, was elected a judge of the Supreme Court of Illinois. This office he resigned in 1843 to enter Congress. He remained in the lower house until 1847, when he was transferred to the Senate, and was twice reëlected. On three successive occasions, in 1852, 1856, and 1860, Mr. Douglas was nominated for the presidency by the Democrats or by a wing of that party. The campaign of 1860 was decided in favor of Abraham Lincoln. When the threatened secession of the Southern states became a certainty, Mr. Douglas proved his loyalty to the Constitution ; but he did not live to witness the struggle that followed, as he died in 1861. The following speech was delivered at Freeport, Ill., in 1858, and was a reply to a speech made by Lincoln advocating the abolition of slavery.]

I AM glad that at last I have brought Mr. Lincoln to the conclusion that he had better define his position on certain political questions to which I called his attention at Ottawa. He there showed no disposition, no inclination, to answer them. I did not present idle questions for him to answer merely for my gratification. I laid the foundation for those interrogatories by showing that they constituted the platform of the party whose nominee he is for the Senate. I did not presume that I had the right to catechise him as I saw proper, unless I showed that his party, or a majority of it, stood upon the platform and were in favor of the propositions upon which my questions were based. I desired simply to know, inasmuch as he had been nominated as the first, last, and only choice of his party, whether he concurred in the platform which that party had adopted for its government. In a few moments I will proceed to review the answers which he has given to these interrogatories; but in order to relieve his anxiety I will first respond to these which he has presented to me. Mark you, he has not presented interrogatories which have ever received the sanction of the party with which I am acting, and hence he has no other foundation for them than his own curiosity.

First, he desires to know if the people of Kansas shall form a constitution by means entirely proper and unobjectionable, and ask admission into the Union as a state, before they have the requisite population for a member of Congress, whether I will vote for that admission. Well, now, I regret exceedingly that he did not answer that interrogatory himself before he put it to me, in order that we might understand and not be left to infer on which side he is. Mr. Trumbull, during the last session of Congress, voted from the beginning to the end against the admission of Oregon, although a free state, because she had not the requisite population for a member of Congress. Mr. Trumbull would not consent, under any circumstances, to let a state, free or slave, come into the Union until it had the requisite population. As Mr. Trumbull is in the field fighting for Mr. Lincoln, I would like to have Mr. Lincoln answer his own question, and tell me whether he is fighting Trumbull on that issue or not. But I will answer his question. In reference to Kansas, it is my opinion that as she has population enough to constitute a slave state, she has people enough for a free state. I will not make Kansas an exceptionable case to the other states of the Union. I hold it to be a sound rule of universal application to require a territory to contain the requisite population for a member of Congress before it is admitted as a state into the Union. I made that proposition in the Senate in 1856, and I renewed it during the last session in a bill providing that no territory of the United States should form a constitution and apply for admission until it had the requisite population. On another occasion I proposed that neither Kansas nor any other territory should be admitted until it had the requisite population. Congress did not adopt any of my propositions containing this general rule, but did make an exception of Kansas. I will stand by that exception. Either Kansas must come in as a free state, with whatever population she may have, or the rule must be applied to all the other territories alike. I therefore answer at once, that it having been decided that Kansas has people enough for a slave state, I hold that she has enough for a free state. I hope Mr. Lincoln is satisfied with my answer; and now I would like to get his answer to his own interrogatory—whether or not he will vote to admit Kansas before she has the requisite population. I want to know whether he will vote to admit Oregon before that territory has the requisite population. Mr. Trumbull will not, and the same reason that commits Mr. Trumbull against the admission of Oregon commits him against Kansas, even if she should apply for admission as a free state. If there is any sincerity, any truth, in the argument of Mr. Trumbull in the Senate against the admission of Oregon, because she had not 93,420 people, although her population was larger than that of Kansas, he stands pledged against the admission of both Oregon and Kansas, until they have 93,420 inhabitants. I would like Mr. Lincoln to answer this question. I would like him to take his own medicine. If he differ with Mr. Trumbull, let him answer his argument against the admission of Oregon, instead of poking questions at me.

The next question propounded to me by Mr. Lincoln is: Can the people of the territory in any lawful way, against the wishes of any citizen of the United States, exclude slavery from their limits prior to the formation of a state constitution? I answer emphatically, as Mr. Lincoln has heard me answer a hundred times from every stump in Illinois, that in my opinion the people of a territory can, by lawful means, exclude slavery from their limits prior to the formation of a state constitution. Mr. Lincoln knew that I had answered that question over and over again. He heard me argue the Nebraska Bill on that principle all over the state in 1854, in 1855, and in 1856, and he has no excuse for pretending to be in doubt as to my position on that question. It matters not what way the Supreme Court may hereafter decide as to the abstract question whether slavery may or may not go into a territory under the constitution; the people have the lawful means to introduce it or exclude it as they please, for the reason that slavery cannot exist a day or an hour anywhere, unless it is supported by local police regulations. Those police regulations can only be established by the local legislature; and if the people are opposed to slavery, they will elect representatives to that body who will by unfriendly legislation effectually prevent the introduction of it into their midst. If, on the contrary, they are for it, their legislation will favor its extension. Hence, no matter what the decision of the Supreme Court may be on that abstract question, still the right of the people to make a slave territory or a free territory is perfect and complete under the Nebraska Bill. I hope Mr. Lincoln deems my answer satisfactory on that point.

In this connection I will notice the charge which he has introduced in relation to Mr. Chase's amendment. I thought that I had chased that amendment out of Mr. Lincoln's brain at Ottawa, but it seems that still haunts his imagination, and he is not yet satisfied. I had supposed that he would be ashamed to press that question further. He is a lawyer, and has been a member of Congress, and has occupied his time and amused you by telling you about parliamentary proceeding. He ought to have known better than to try to palm off his miserable impositions upon this intelligent audience. The Nebraska Bill provided that the legislative power and authority of the said territory should extend to all rightful subjects of legislation, consistent with the organic act and the Constitution of the United States. It did not make any exception as to slavery, but gave all the power that it was possible for Congress to give without violating the constitution to the territorial legislature, with no exception or limitation on the subject of slavery at all. The language of that bill which I have quoted gave the full power and the full authority over the subject of slavery, affirmatively and negatively, to introduce it or exclude it, so far as the Constitution of the United States would permit. What more could Mr. Chase give by his amendment? Nothing. He offered his amendment for the identical purpose for which Mr. Lincoln is using it, to enable demagogues in the country to try and deceive the people.

STEPHEN ARNOLD DOUGLAS

Photogravure after an engraving by John C. McRae

His amendment was to this effect.   It provided that the Legislature should have the power to exclude slavery; and General Cass suggested: "Why not give the power to introduce as well as exclude?" The answer was: "They have the power already in the bill to do both." Chase was afraid his amendment would be adopted if he put the alternative proposition, and so make it fair both ways, but would not yield. He offered it for the purpose of having it rejected. He offered it, as he has himself avowed over and over again, simply to make capital out of it for the stump. He expected that it would be capital for small politicians in the country, and that they would make an effort to deceive the people with it; and he was not mistaken, for Lincoln is carrying out the plan admirably. Lincoln knows that the Nebraska Bill, without Chase's amendment, gave all the power which the Constitution would permit. Could Congress confer any more? Could Congress go beyond the Constitution of the country? We gave all a full grant with no exception in regard to slavery one way or the other. We left that question, as we left all others, to be decided by the people for themselves, just as they pleased. I will not occupy my time on this question. I have argued it before all over Illinois. I have argued it in this beautiful city of Freeport. I have argued it in the North, the South, the East, and the West, avowing the same sentiments and the same principles. I have not been afraid to avow my sentiments up here for fear I would be trotted down into Egypt.

The third question which Mr. Lincoln presented is: "If the Supreme Court of the United States shall decide that a state of this Union cannot exclude slavery from its own limits, will I submit to it?" I am amazed that Lincoln should ask such a question. " A schoolboy knows better." Yes, a schoolboy does know better. Mr. Lincoln's object is to cast an imputation upon the Supreme Court. He knows that there never was but one man in America, claiming any degree of intelligence or decency, who ever for a moment pretended such a thing. It is true that the " Washington Union," in an article published on the seventeenth of last December, did put forth that doctrine, and I denounced the article on the floor of the Senate in a speech which Mr. Lincoln now pretends was against the President. "The Union" had claimed that slavery had a right to go into the free states, and that any provisions in the Constitution or laws of the free states to the contrary were null and void. I denounced it in the Senate, as I said before, and I was the first man who did. Lincoln's friends, Trumbull and Seward and Hale and Wilson and the whole Black Republican side of the Senate were silent. They left it to me to denounce it. And what was the reply made to me on that occasion? Mr. Toombs, of Georgia, got up and undertook to lecture me on the ground that I ought not to have deemed the article worthy of notice, and ought not to have replied to it; that there was not one man, woman, or child south of the Potomac, in any slave state, who did not repudiate any such pretension. Mr. Lincoln knows that that reply was made on the spot, and yet now he asks this question. He might as well ask me: "Suppose Mr. Lincoln should steal a horse, would you sanction it?" and it would be as genteel in me to ask him, in the event he stole a horse, what ought to be done with him. He casts an imputation upon the Supreme Court of the United States by supposing that they would violate the Constitution of the United States. I tell him that such a thing is not possible. It would be an act of moral treason that no man on the bench could ever descend to. Mr. Lincoln himself would never in his partisan feelings so far forget what was right as to be guilty of such an act.

The fourth question of Mr. Lincoln is: "Are you in favor of acquiring additional territory, in disregard as to how such acquisition may affect the Union on the slavery question?" This question is very ingeniously and cunningly put.

The Black Republican creed lays it down expressly, that under no circumstances shall we acquire any more territory unless slavery is first prohibited in the country. I ask Mr. Lincoln whether he is in favor of that proposition. Are you [addressing Mr. Lincoln] opposed to the acquisition of any more territory, under any circumstances, unless slavery is prohibited in it? That he does not like to answer. When I ask him whether he stands up to that article in the platform of his party he turns, Yankee fashion, and, without answering it, asks me whether I am in favor of acquiring territory without regard to how it may affect the Union on the slavery question. I answer that whenever it becomes necessary, in our growth and progress, to acquire more territory, that I am in favor of it, without reference to the question of slavery; and when we have acquired it, I will leave the people free to do as they please, either to make it slave or free territory, as they prefer. It is idle to tell me or you that we have territory enough. Our fathers supposed that we had enough when our territory extended to the Mississippi River, but a few years' growth and expansion satisfied them that we needed more, and the Louisiana territory, from the west branch of the Mississippi to the British possessions, was acquired. Then we acquired Oregon, then California and New Mexico. We have enough now for the present, but this is a young and a growing nation. It swarms as often as a hive of bees; and as new swarms are turned out each year, there must be hives in which they can gather and make their honey. In less than fifteen years, if the same progress that has distinguished this country for the last fifteen years continue, every foot of vacant land between this and the Pacific Ocean owned by the United States will be occupied. Will you not continue to increase at the end of fifteen years as well as now? I tell you, increase and multiply and expand is the law of this nation's existence. You cannot limit this great Republic by mere boundary lines, saying: "Thus far shalt thou go, and no further." Any one of you gentlemen might as well say to a son twelve years old that he is big enough, and must not grow any larger, and in order to prevent his growth put a hoop around him to keep him to his present size. What would be the result? Either the hoop must burst and be rent asunder, or the child must die. So it would be with this great nation. With our natural increase, growing with a rapidity unknown in any other part of the globe, with the tide of emigration that is fleeing from despotism in the Old World to seek refuge in our own, there is a constant torrent pouring into this country that requires more land, more territory upon which to settle; and just as fast as our interests and our destiny require additional territory in the North, in the South, or on the islands of the ocean, I am for it; and when we acquire it, will leave the people, according to the Nebraska Bill, free to do as they please on the subject of slavery and every other question.

I trust now that Mr. Lincoln will deem himself answered on his four points. He racked his brain so much in devising these four questions that he exhausted himself, and had not strength enough to invent the others. As soon as he is able to hold a council with his advisers, Lovejoy, Farnsworth, and Fred Douglass, he will frame and propound others. ["Good, good!"] You Black Republicans who say "Good," I have no doubt think that they are all good men. I have reason to recollect that some people in this country think that Fred Douglass is a very good man. The last time I came here to make a speech, while talking from the stand to you, people of Freeport, as I am doing to-day, I saw a carriage, and a magnificent one it was, drive up and take a position on the outside of the crowd; a beautiful young lady was sitting on the box-seat, whilst Fred Douglass and her mother reclined inside, and the owner of the carriage acted as driver. I saw this in your own town. ["What of it?"] All I have to say of it is this, that if you Black Republicans think that the negro ought to be on a social equality with your wives and daughters, and ride in a carriage with your wife, whilst you drive the team, you have a perfect right to do so. I am told that one of Fred Douglass's kinsmen, another rich black negro, is now traveling in this part of the state making speeches for his friend Lincoln as the champion of black men. ["What have you to say against it?"] All I have to say on that subject is, that those of you who believe that the negro is your equal and ought to be on an equality with you socially, politically, and legally, have a right to entertain these opinions, and, of course, will vote for Mr. Lincoln.

ROBERT EMMET

PROTEST AGAINST SENTENCE AS A TRAITOR

[Robert Emmet, an Irish patriot, was born in Dublin in 1778. He attended Trinity College in his native city, but did not take a degree. From his boyhood he attracted notice by his oratorical powers, and he was also deeply attached to the Irish revolutionary cause. He had grown up in an atmosphere of hatred to England, and even in his college days he had affiliated with secret societies of a character suspicious to the British government. For this reason, it appears, he had to leave Trinity before completing his studies. He went abroad and had interviews with French statesmen who were supposed to feel interest in an Irish uprising. He returned to Dublin and secretly raised a small force which he armed as well as he could. Then he issued proclamations and prepared to seize Dublin Castle. His movement spread panic for a time, but his followers were dispersed with no great difficulty and he himself fled. He lingered in Ireland, however, to bid farewell to Sarah Curran, to whom he was engaged to be married, and was captured and executed in 1803. The pathetic and eloquent speech that follows was made in Dublin, 1803, after he had been sentenced to death.]

I AM asked what have I to say why sentence of death should not be pronounced on me, according to law. I have nothing to say that can alter your predetermination, nor that it will become me to say, with any view to the mitigation of that sentence which you are to pronounce, and I must abide by. But I have that to say which interests me more than life, and which you have labored to destroy. I have much to say why my reputation should be rescued from the load of false accusation and calumny which has been cast upon it. I do not imagine that, seated where you are, your mind can be so free from prejudice as to receive the least impression from what I am going to utter. I have no hopes that I can anchor my character in the breast of a court constituted and trammeled as this is. I only wish—and that is the utmost that I expect—that your lordships may suffer it to float down your memories untainted by the foul breath of prejudice, until it finds some more hospitable harbor to shelter it from the storms by which it is buffeted. Were I only to suffer death, after being adjudged guilty by your tribunal, I should bow in silence, and meet the fate that awaits me without a murmur; but the sentence of the law which delivers my body to the executioner will, through the ministry of the law, labor in its own vindication to consign my character to obloquy; for there must be guilt somewhere; whether in the sentence of the court, or in the catastrophe, time must determine. A man in my situation has not only to encounter the difficulties of fortune, and the force of power over minds which it has corrupted or subjugated, but the difficulties of established prejudice. The man dies, but his memory lives. That mine may not perish, that it may live in the respect of my countrymen, I seize upon this opportunity to vindicate myself from some of the charges alleged against me. When my spirit shall be wafted to a more friendly port—when my shade shall have joined the bands of those martyred heroes who have shed their blood on the scaffold and in the field, in the defense of their country and of virtue, this is my hope: I wish that my memory and my name may animate those who survive me, while I look down with complacency on the destruction of that perfidious government which upholds its domination by blasphemy of the Most High; which displays its power over man as over the beasts of the forest; which sets man upon his brother, and lifts his hand, in the name of God, against the throat of his fellow who believes or doubts a little more or a little less than the government standard—a government which is steeled to barbarity by the cries of the orphans and the tears of the widows it has made. [Here Lord Norbury interrupted, saying that "the mean and wicked enthusiasts who felt as Emmet did were not equal to the accomplishment of their wild designs."]

I appeal to the immaculate God—I swear by the throne of Heaven, before which I must shortly appear—by the blood of the murdered patriots who have gone before me— that my conduct has been, through all this peril, and through all my purposes, governed only by the conviction which I

have uttered, and by no other view than that of the emancipation of my country from the superinhuman oppression
under which she has so long and too patiently travailed;
and I confidently hope that, wild and chimerical as it may
appear, there is still union and strength in Ireland to accomplish this noblest of enterprises. Of this I speak with the
confidence of intimate knowledge, and with the consolation
that appertains to that confidence. Think not, my lords, I
say this for the petty gratification of giving you a transitory
uneasiness. A man who never yet raised his voice to assert
a lie will not hazard his character with posterity by asserting
a falsehood on a subject so important to his country, and on
an occasion like this. Yes, my lords, a man who does not
wish to have his epitaph written until his country is liberated
will not leave a weapon in the power of envy, or a pretense
to impeach the probity which he means to preserve, even in
the grave to which tyranny consigns him. [Here he was
again interrupted by the court.]

Again I say, that what I have spoken was not intended
for your lordship, whose situation I commiserate rather than
envy—my expressions were for my countrymen. If there is
a true Irishman present, let my last words cheer him in the
hour of his affliction. [Here he was again interrupted.
Lord Norbury said he did not sit there to hear treason.]

I have always understood it to be the duty of a judge,
when a prisoner has been convicted, to pronounce the sentence of the law. I have also understood that judges sometimes think it their duty to hear with patience and to speak
with humanity; to exhort the victim of the laws, and to offer,
with tender benignity, their opinions of the motives by which
he was actuated in the crime of which he was adjudged
guilty. That a judge has thought it his duty so to have
done, I have no doubt; but where is the boasted freedom of
your institutions—where is the vaunted impartiality, clem-
ency, and mildness of your courts of justice, if an unfortunate prisoner, whom your policy, and not justice, is about
to deliver into the hands of the executioner, is not suffered
to explain his motives sincerely and truly, and to vindicate
the principles by which he was actuated? My lords, it may
be a part of the system of angry justice to bow a man's

mind by humiliation to the purposed ignominy of the scaffold; but worse to me than the purposed shame or the scaffold's terrors would be the shame of such foul and unfounded
imputations as have been laid against me in this court. You,
my lord, are a judge; I am the supposed culprit. I am a
man; you are a man also. By a revolution of power we
might change places, though we never could change characters. If I stand at the bar of this court and dare not vindicate my character, what a farce is your justice! If I stand
at this bar and dare not vindicate my character, how dare
you calumniate it? Does the sentence of death, which your
unhallowed policy inflicts on my body, condemn my tongue
to silence and my reputation to reproach? Your executioner
may abridge the period of my existence; but while I exist,
I shall not forbear to vindicate my character and motives
from your aspersions; and, as a man, to whom fame is dearer
than life, I will make the last use of that life in doing justice
to that reputation which is to live after me, and which is the
only legacy I can leave to those I honor and love, and for
whom I am proud to perish. As men, my lords, we must
appear on the great day at one common tribunal; and it will
then remain for the Searcher of All Hearts to show a col-
lective universe who was engaged in the most virtuous
actions, or swayed by the purest motive—my country's oppressors, or—[Here he was interrupted, and told to listen to
the sentence of the law.]

My lords, will a dying man be denied the legal privilege
of exculpating himself in the eyes of the community from an
undeserved reproach, thrown upon him during his trial, by
charging him with ambition, and attempting to cast away for
a paltry consideration the liberties of his country? Why did
your lordships insult me? Or rather, why insult justice, in
demanding of me why sentence of death should not be pronounced against me? I know, my lords, that form prescribes
that you should ask the question. The form also presents
the right of answering. This, no doubt, may be dispensed
with, and so might the whole ceremony of the trial, since
sentence was already pronounced at the castle before the jury
were empaneled. Your lordships are but the priests of the
oracle, and I insist on the whole of the forms.

I am charged with being an emissary of France.   An emissary of France! and for what end?   It is alleged that I wish to sell the independence of my country; and for what end? Was this the object of my ambition?   And is this the mode by which a tribunal of justice reconciles contradiction?   No; I am no emissary; and my ambition was to hold a place among the deliverers of my country, not in power nor in profit, but in the glory of the achievement.   Sell my country's independence to France! and for what?   Was it a change of masters?   No, but for ambition.   O my country! was it personal ambition that could influence me?   Had it been the soul of my actions, could I not by my education and fortune, by the rank and consideration of my family, have placed myself amongst the proudest of your oppressors? My country was my idol!   To it I sacrificed every selfish, every endearing sentiment; and for it I now offer up myself. O God!   No, my lords; I acted as an Irishman, determined on delivering my country from the yoke of a foreign and unrelenting tyranny, and the more galling yoke of a domestic faction, which is its joint partner and perpetrator in the patricide, from the ignominy existing with an exterior of splendor and a conscious depravity.   It was the wish of my heart to extricate my country from this doubly riveted despotism— I wished to place her independence beyond the reach of any power on earth.   I wished to exalt her to that proud station in the world.   Connection with France was, indeed, intended, but only as far as mutual interest would sanction or require. Were the French to assume any authority inconsistent with the purest independence, it would be the signal for their destruction.   We sought their aid—and we sought it as we had assurance we should obtain it—as auxiliaries in war, and allies in peace.   Were the French to come as invaders or enemies, uninvited by the wishes of the people, I should oppose them to the utmost of my strength.   Yes! my countrymen, I should advise you to meet them upon the beach with a sword in one hand and a torch in the other.   I would meet them with all the destructive fury of war.   I would animate my countrymen to immolate them in their boats, before they had contaminated the soil of my country. If they succeeded in landing, and if forced to retire before superior discipline, I would dispute every inch of ground, burn every blade of grass, and the last entrenchment of liberty should be my grave. What I could not do myself, if I should fall, I should leave as a last charge to my countrymen to accomplish; because I should feel conscious that life, any more than death, is unprofitable when a foreign nation holds my country in subjection. But it was not as an enemy that the succors of France were to land. I looked, indeed, for the assistance of France; but I wished to prove to France and to the world that Irishmen deserved to be assisted; that they were indignant at slavery, and ready to assert the independence and liberty of their country. I wished to procure for my country the guarantee which Washington procured for America; to procure an aid which, by its example, would be as important as its valor; disciplined, gallant, pregnant with science and experience; that of a people who would perceive the good, and polish the rough points of our character. They would come to us as strangers, and leave us as friends, after sharing in our perils and elevating our destiny. These were my objects: not to receive new taskmasters, but to expel old tyrants. It was for these ends I sought aid from France; because France, even as an enemy, could not be more implacable than the enemy already in the bosom of my country. [Here he was interrupted by the court.]

I have been charged with that importance in the emancipation of my country as to be considered the keystone of the combination of Irishmen; or as your lordship expressed it, "the life and blood of the conspiracy." You do me honor overmuch; you have given to the subaltern all the credit of a superior. There are men engaged in this conspiracy who are not only superior to me, but even to your own conceptions of yourself, my lord—men before the splendor of whose genius and virtues I should bow with respectful deference, and who would think themselves disgraced by shaking your blood-stained hand.

What, my lord, shall you tell me, on the passage to the scaffold, which that tyranny (of which you are only the intermediary executioner) has erected for my murder, that I am accountable for all the blood that has been and will be shed in this struggle of the oppressed against the oppressor

ROBERT EMMET

Photogravure after an engraving by John C. McRae

—shall you tell me this, and must I be so very a slave as not to repel it? I do not fear to approach the Omnipotent Judge to answer for the conduct of my whole life; and am I to be appalled and falsified by a mere remnant of mortality here? By you, too, although, if it were possible to collect all the innocent blood that you have shed in your unhallowed ministry in one great reservoir, your lordship might swim in it. [Here the judge interrupted.]

Let no man dare, when I am dead, to charge me with dishonor; let no man attaint my memory, by believing that I could have engaged in any cause but that of my country's liberty and independence; or that I could have become the pliant minion of power, in the oppression and misery of my country. The proclamation of the provisional government speaks for our views; no inference can be tortured from it to countenance barbarity or debasement at home, or subjection, humiliation, or treachery from abroad. I would not have submitted to a foreign oppressor, for the same reason that I would resist the foreign and domestic oppressor. In the dignity of freedom, I would have fought upon the threshold of my country, and its enemy should enter only by passing over my lifeless corpse. And am I, who lived but for my country, and who have subjected myself to the dangers of the jealous and watchful oppressor, and the bondage of the grave, only to give my countrymen their rights, and my country her independence—am I to be loaded with calumny, and not suffered to resent it? No; God forbid! [Here Lord Norbury told Mr. Emmet that his sentiments and language disgraced his family and his education, but more particularly his father, Doctor Emmet, who was a man, if alive, that would not countenance such opinions. To which Emmet replied:]

If the spirits of the illustrious dead participate in the concerns and cares of those who were dear to them in this transitory life, O, ever dear and venerated shade of my departed father! look down with scrutiny upon the conduct of your suffering son, and see if I have, even for a moment, deviated from those principles of morality and patriotism which it was your care to instill into my youthful mind, and for which I am now about to offer up my life. My lords, you are impatient for the sacrifice. The blood which you seek is not con-

gealed by the artificial terrors which surround your victim—
it circulates warmly and unruffled through the channels which
God created for noble purposes, but which you are now bent
to destroy for purposes so grievous that they cry to heaven.
Be yet patient! I have but a few more words to say—I am
going to my cold and silent grave—my lamp of life is nearly
extinguished—my race is run—the grave opens to receive
me, and I sink into its bosom. I have but one request to
ask at my departure from this world: it is—the charity of
its silence. Let no man write my epitaph; for, as no man
who knows my motives dares now vindicate them, let not
prejudice or ignorance asperse them. Let them and me
rest in obscurity and peace, and my tomb remain uninscribed,
and my memory in oblivion, until other times and other
men can do justice to my character. When my country
takes her place among the nations of the earth, then, and
not till then, let my epitaph be written. I have done.

LORD THOMAS ERSKINE

AGAINST THOMAS PAINE

[Lord Thomas Erskine, a British jurist, distinguished for the eloquence of his pleadings, was born in Edinburgh in 1750. He studied at St. Andrew's University, and entered the navy, which he abandoned for the army after some years, and finally devoted himself to the law. His success was decided. He revolutionized pleading at the English bar. He spoke with grace and eloquence to the court. He kept strictly to the subject matter, but he expressed his views of the law and the facts in fine English and with admirable wit. He defended Lord George Gordon, leader of the "No Popery" riots, and upon the trial of Stockdale, accused of libeling the House of Commons, delivered his finest plea, and the prisoner was acquitted. In 1806 he was made Lord Chancellor. His career as a member of the House of Commons was a failure from an oratorical point of view. His last public appearance was on the occasion of Queen Caroline's trial in 1820, in whose behalf he made some strong speeches. He died in 1823. The following speech, a denunciation of Thomas Paine's famous atheistic book, "The Age of Reason," was made in court, before Lord Kenyon, in the prosecution of his publisher for blasphemy, in 1797.]

GENTLEMEN OF THE JURY: The charge of blasphemy, which is put upon the record against the printer of this publication, is not an accusation of the servants of the crown, but comes before you sanctioned by the oaths of a grand jury of the country. It stood for trial upon a former day; but it happening, as it frequently does, without any imputation on the gentlemen named in the panel, that a sufficient number did not appear to constitute a full special jury, I thought it my duty to withdraw the cause from trial till I could have the opportunity, which is now open to me, of addressing myself to you, who were originally appointed to try it. I pursued this course, however, from no jealousy of the common juries appointed by the laws for the ordinary service of the court, since my whole life has been one continued experience of their virtues, but because I thought it of great importance that those who were to decide upon a cause so very momentous to the public should have the highest possible qualifications for the decision. That they should not only be men capable, from their education, of forming an enlightened judgment, but that their situations should be such as to bring them within the full view of their enlightened country, to which, in character and in estimation, they were in their own turns to be responsible.

Not having the honor, gentlemen, to be sworn for the king, as one of his counsel, it has fallen much oftener to my lot to defend indictments for libels than to assist in the prosecution of them. But I feel no embarrassment from that recollection, since I shall not be found to-day to express a sentiment or to utter an expression inconsistent with those invaluable principles for which I have uniformly contended in the defense of others. Nothing that I have ever said, either professionally or personally, for the liberty of the press, do I mean to deny, to contradict, or counteract. On the contrary, I desire to preface the discourse I have to make to you with reminding you that it is your most solemn duty to take care it suffers no injury in your hands. A free and unlicensed press, *in the just and legal sense of the expression*, has led to all the blessings, both of religion and government, which Great Britain, or any part of the world, at this moment enjoys, and is calculated still further to advance mankind to higher degrees of civilization and happiness. But this freedom, like every other, must be limited to be enjoyed, and, like every human advantage, may be defeated by its abuse.

Gentlemen, the defendant stands indicted for having published this book, which I have only read from the obligations of professional duty, and which I rose from the reading of with astonishment and disgust. Standing here with all the privileges belonging to the highest counsel for the Crown, I shall be entitled to reply to any defense that shall be made for the publication. I shall wait with patience till I hear it. Indeed, if I were to anticipate the defense which I hear and read of, it would be defaming, by anticipation, the learned counsel who is to make it. For if I am to collect it, even from a formal notice given to the prosecutors in the course of the proceedings, I have to expect that, instead of a defense conducted according to the rules and principles of English law and justice, the foundation of all our laws, and the sanctions of all our justice, are to be struck at and insulted. What is the force of that jurisdiction which enables the court to sit in judgment? What but the oath which his lordship as well as yourselves have sworn upon the Gospel to fulfil. Yet in the King's Court, where his majesty is himself also sworn to administer the justice of England in the King's Court, who receives his high authority under a solemn oath to maintain the Christian religion, as it is promulgated by God in the Holy Scriptures, I am nevertheless called upon, as counsel for the prosecution, to produce a certain book described in the indictment to be the Holy Bible. No man deserves to be upon the rolls of the court who dares, as an attorney, to put his name to such a notice. It is an insult to the authority and dignity of the court of which he is an officer; since it seems to call in question the very foundations of its jurisdiction. If this is to be the spirit and temper of the defense; if, as I collect from that array of books which are spread upon the benches behind me, this publication is to be vindicated by an attack on all the truths which the Christian religion promulgates to mankind, let it be remembered that such an argument was neither suggested nor justified by anything said by me on the part of the prosecution. In this stage of the proceedings I shall call for reverence to the sacred Scriptures, not from their merits, unbounded as they are, but from their authority in a Christian country; not from the obligations of conscience, but from the rules of law. For my own part, gentlemen, I have been ever deeply devoted to the truths of Christianity, and my firm belief in the Holy Gospel is by no means owing to the prejudices of education, though I was religiously educated by the best of parents, but arises from the fullest and most continued reflections of my riper years and understanding. It forms at this moment the great consolation of a life which, as a shadow, must pass away; and without it, indeed, I should consider my long course of health and prosperity, perhaps too long and uninterrupted to be good for any man, only as the dust which the wind scatters, and rather as a snare than as a blessing. Much, however, as I wish to support the authority of the Scriptures, from a reasoned consideration of them, I shall repress that subject for the present. But if the defense shall be as I have suspected, to bring them at all into argument or question, I shall then fulfil a duty which I owe not only to the court, as counsel for the prosecution, but to the public, to state what I feel and know concerning the evidences of that religion which is reviled without being examined, and denied without being understood.

I am well aware that by the communications of a free press, all the errors of mankind, from age to age, have been dissipated and dispelled; and I recollect that the world, under the banners of *reformed* Christianity, has struggled through persecution to the noble eminence on which it stands at this moment, shedding the blessings of humanity and science upon the nations of the earth. It may be asked by what means the Reformation would have been effected if the books of the reformers had been suppressed, and the errors of condemned and exploded superstitions had been supported as unquestionable by the state, founded upon those very superstitions formerly, as it is at present upon the doctrines of the Established Church? or how, upon such principles, any reformation, civil or religious, can in future be effected? The solution is easy. Let us examine what are the genuine principles of the liberty of the press, as they regard writings upon general subjects, unconnected with the personal reputations of private men, which are wholly foreign to the present inquiry. They are full of simplicity, and are brought as near perfection by the law of England as, perhaps, is consistent with any of the frail institutions of mankind.

Although every community must establish supreme authorities, founded upon fixed principles, and must give high powers to magistrates to administer laws for the preservation of the government itself, and for the security of those who are to be protected by it; yet, as infallibility and perfection belong neither to human establishments nor to human individuals, it ought to be the policy of all free establishments, as it is most peculiarly the principle of our own Constitution, to permit the most unbounded freedom of discussion, even by detecting errors in the Constitution or administration of the very government itself, so as that decorum is observed which every state must exact from its subjects, and which imposes no restraint upon any intellectual composition, fairly, honestly, and decently addressed to the consciences and understandings of men. Upon this principle I have an unquestionable right—a right which the best subjects have exercised—to examine the principles and structure of the Constitution, and by fair, manly reasoning, to question the practice of its administrators. I have a right to consider and to point out errors in the one or in the other; and not merely to reason upon their existence, but to consider the means of their reformation. By such free, well-intentioned, modest, and dignified communication of sentiments and opinions all nations have been gradually improved, and milder laws and purer religions have been established. The same principles which vindicate civil contentions, honestly directed, extend their protection to the sharpest controversies on religious faiths. This rational and legal course of improvement was recognized and ratified by Lord Kenyon as the law of England, in a late trial at Guildhall, when he looked back with gratitude to the labors of the reformers, as the fountains of our religious emancipation, and of the civil blessings that followed in their train. The English Constitution, indeed, does not stop short in the toleration of religious *opinions*, but liberally extends it to *practice*. It permits every man, even publicly, to worship God according to his own conscience, though in marked dissent from the national establishment, so as he professes the general faith, which is the sanction of all our moral duties, and the only pledge of our submission to the system which constitutes a state. Is not this system of freedom of controversy and freedom of worship sufficient for all the purposes of human happiness and improvement? and will it be necessary for either that the law should hold out indemnity to those who wholly abjure and revile the government of their country, or the religion on which it rests for its foundation?

I expect to hear, in answer to what I am now saying, much that will offend me. My learned friend, from the difficulties of his situation, which I know, from experience, how to feel for very sincerely, may be driven to advance propositions which it may be my duty, with much freedom to reply to; and the law will sanction that freedom. But will not the ends of justice be completely answered by the right to point out the errors of his discourse in terms that are decent and calculated to expose its defects? or will any argument suffer, or will public justice be impeded, because neither private honor and justice, nor public decorum, would endure my telling my very learned friend that he was a fool, a liar, and a scoundrel, in the face of the court, because I differed from him in argument or opinion? This is just the distinction between a book of free legal controversy and the book which I am arraigning before yon. Every man has a legal right to investigate, with modesty and decency, controversial points of the Christian religion; but no man, consistently with a law which only exists under its sanctions, has a right not only broadly to deny its very existence, but to pour forth a shocking and insulting invective, which the lowest establishments in the gradations of civil authority ought not to be permitted to suffer, and which soon would be borne down by insolence and disobedience, if they did.

The same principle pervades the whole system of the law, not merely in its abstract theory, but in its daily and most applauded practice. The intercourse between the sexes, and which, properly regulated, not only continues, but humanizes and adorns our natures, is the foundation of all the thousand romances, plays, and novels which are in the hands of everybody. Some of them lead to the confirmation of every virtuous principle; others, though with the same profession, address the imagination in a manner to lead the passions into dangerous excesses. But though the law does not nicely discriminate the various shades which distinguish these works from one another, so as that it suffers many to pass, through its liberal spirit, that upon principle might be suppressed, would it or does it tolerate, or does any decent man contend that it ought to pass by unpunished, libels of the most shameless obscenity, manifestly pointed to debauch innocence, and to blast and poison the morals of the rising generation? This is only another illustration to demonstrate the obvious distinction between the works of an author who fairly exercises the powers of his mind in investigating doctrinal points in the religion of any country, and him who attacks the rational existence of every religion, and brands with absurdity and folly the state which sanctions, and the obedient tools who cherish, the delusion. But this publication appears to me to be as mischievous and cruel in its probable effects, as it is manifestly illegal in its principles; because it strikes at the best, sometimes, alas! the only refuge and consolation amid the distresses and afflictions of the world. The poor and humble, whom it affects to pity, may be stabbed to the heart by it. They have more occasion for firm hopes beyond the grave than those who have greater comforts to render life delightful. I can conceive a distressed, but virtuous man, surrounded by children, looking up to him for bread when he has none to give them, sinking under the last day's labor, and unequal to the next, yet still looking up with confidence to the hour when all tears shall be wiped from the eyes of affliction, bearing the burden laid upon him by a mysterious Providence which he adores, and looking forward with exultation to the revealed promises of his Creator, when he shall be greater than the greatest, and happier than the happiest of mankind. What a change in such a mind might be wrought by such a merciless publication! Gentlemen, whether these remarks are the overcharged declamations of an accusing counsel, or the just reflections of a man anxious for the public freedom, which is best secured by the morals of a nation, will be best settled by an appeal to the passages in the work, that are selected in the indictment for your consideration and judgment. You are at liberty to connect them with every context and sequel, and to bestow upon them the mildest interpretation. [Here Mr. Erskine read and commented upon several of the selected passages.]

Gentlemen, it would be useless and disgusting to enumerate the other passages within the scope of the indictment. How any man can rationally vindicate the publication of such a book, in a country where the Christian religion is the very foundation of the law of the land, I am totally at a loss to conceive, and have no wish to discuss. How is a tribunal whose whole jurisdiction is founded upon the solemn belief and practice of what is denied as falsehood, and reprobated

as impiety, to deal with such an anomalous defense? Upon
what principle is it even offered to the court, whose authority
is contemned and mocked at? If the religion proposed to
be called in question is not previously adopted in belief, and
solemnly acted upon, what authority has the court to pass
any judgment at all of acquittal or condemnation? Why am
I now, or upon any other occasion, to submit to your lordship's authority? Why am I now, or at any time, to address
twelve of my equals, as I am now addressing you, with reverence and submission? Under what sanction are the witnesses to give their evidence, without which there can be no
trial? Under what obligations can I call upon you, the jury,
representing your country, to administer justice? Surely
upon no other than that you are sworn to administer it
under the oaths you have taken. The whole judicial fabric,
from the king's sovereign authority to the lowest office of
magistracy, has no other foundation. The whole is built,
both in form and substance, upon the same oath of every
one of its ministers, to do justice, " *as God shall help them
hereafter.*" What God? and what hereafter? That God,
undoubtedly, who has commanded kings to rule, and judges
to decree with justice; who has said to witnesses, not by the
voice of nature, but in revealed commandments, " *thou shalt
not bear false witness against thy neighbor*"; and who has
enforced obedience to them by the revelation of the unutterable blessings which shall attend their observances, and the
awful punishments which shall await upon their transgressions.

But it seems this course of reason, and the time and the
person are at last arrived, that are to dissipate the errors
which have overspread the past generations of ignorance!
The believers in Christianity are many, but it belongs to the
few that are wise to correct their credulity! Belief is an act
of reason; and superior reason may, therefore, dictate to the
weak. In running the mind along the numerous list of sincere and devout Christians, I cannot help lamenting that
Newton had not lived to this day, to have had his shallow-
ness filled up with this new flood of light. But the subject
is too awful for irony. I will speak plainly and directly.
Newton was a Christian! Newton, whose mind burst forth
from the fetters cast by nature upon our finite conceptions;

Newton, whose science was truth, and the foundation of whose knowledge of it was philosophy. Not those visionary and arrogant assumptions which too often usurp its name, but philosophy resting upon the basis of mathematics, which, like figures, cannot lie. Newton, who carried the line and rule to the utmost barriers of creation, and explored the principles by which, no doubt, all created matter is held together and exists. But this extraordinary man, in the mighty reach of his mind, overlooked, perhaps, the errors which a minuter investigation of the created things on this earth might have taught him of the essence of his Creator. What shall then be said of the great Mr. Boyle, who looked into the organic structure of all matter, even to the brute inanimate substances which the foot treads on? Such a man may be supposed to have been equally qualified with Mr. Paine to " look through nature, up to nature's God." Yet the result of all his contemplation was the most confirmed and devout belief in all which the other holds in contempt as despicable and driveling superstition. But this error might, perhaps, arise from a want of due attention to the foundations of human judgment, and the structure of that understanding which God has given us for the investigation of truth. Let that question be answered by Mr. Locke, who was to the highest pitch of devotion and adoration a Christian. Mr. Locke, whose office was to detect the errors of thinking, by going up to the fountains of thought, and to direct into the proper track of reasoning the devious mind of man, by showing him its whole process, from the first perceptions of sense to the last conclusions of ratiocination; putting a rein, besides, upon false opinion, by practical rules for the conduct of human judgment.

But these men were only deep thinkers, and lived in their closets, unaccustomed to the traffic of the world, and to the laws which practically regulate mankind. Gentlemen, in the place where you now sit to administer the justice of this great country, above a century ago the never-to-be-forgotten Sir Matthew Hale presided, whose faith in Christianity is an exalted commentary upon its truth and reason, and whose life was a glorious example of its fruits in man; administering human justice with a wisdom and purity drawn from the pure fountain of the Christian dispensation, which has been, and will be, in all ages, a subject of the highest reverence and admiration.

But it is said by Mr. Paine that the Christian fable is but the tale of the more ancient superstitions of the world, and may be easily detected by a proper understanding of the mythologies of the heathens. Did Milton understand those mythologies? Was he less versed than Mr. Paine in the superstitions of the world? No; they were the subject of his immortal song; and though shut out from all recurrence to them, he poured them forth from the stores of a memory rich with all that man ever knew, and laid them in their order as the illustration of that real and exalted faith, the unquestionable source of that fervid genius, which cast a sort of shade upon all the other works of man : —

> " He pass'd the bounds of flaming space,
>   Where angels tremble while they gaze;
>   He saw, till, blasted with excess of light,
>   He clos'd his eyes in endless night! "

But it was the light of the *body* only that was extinguished; "the celestial light shone inward," and enabled him to "justify the ways of God to man." The result of his thinking was, nevertheless, not the same as Mr. Paine's. The mysterious incarnation of our blessed Saviour, which the " Age of Reason" blasphemes in words so wholly unfit for the mouth of a Christian, or for the ear of a court of justice, that I dare not and will not give them utterance, Milton made the grand conclusion of "Paradise Lost," the rest of his finished labors, and the ultimate hope, expectation, and glory of the world : —

> " A virgin is his mother, but his sire
>   The power of the Most High: he shall ascend
>   The throne hereditary, and bound his reign
>   With earth's wide bounds, his glory with the heavens."

The immortal poet having thus put into the mouth of the angel the prophecy of man's redemption, follows it with that solemn and beautiful admonition, addressed in the poem to our great First Parent, but intended as an address to his posterity through all generations: —

> " This having learned, thou hast attained the sum
> Of wisdom: hope no higher, though all the stars
> Thou knew'st by name, and all th'ethereal powers,
> All secrets of the deep, all Nature's works,
> Or works of God in heaven, air, earth, or sea,
> And all the riches of this world enjoy'st,
> And all the rule one empire; only add
> Deeds to thy knowledge answerable, add faith,
> Add virtue, patience, temperance; add love,
> By name to come call'd Charity, the soul
> Of all the rest: then wilt thou not be loth
> To leave this Paradise, but shalt possess
> A paradise within thee, happier far."

Thus you find all that is great, or wise, or splendid, or illustrious among created beings—all the minds gifted beyond ordinary nature, if not inspired by their universal Author for the advancement and dignity of the world, though divided by distant ages, and by the clashing opinions distinguishing them from one another, yet joining, as it were, in one sublime chorus to celebrate the truths of Christianity, and laying upon its holy altars the never-fading offerings of their immortal wisdom.

Against all this concurring testimony, we find suddenly, from Mr. Paine, that the Bible teaches nothing but "lies, obscenity, cruelty, and injustice." Did the author or publisher ever read the sermon of Christ upon the Mount, in which the great principles of our faith and duty are summed up? Let us all but read and practise it, and lies, obscenity, cruelty, and injustice, and all human wickedness, would be banished from the world.

Gentlemen, there is but one consideration more, which I cannot possibly omit, because, I confess, it affects me very deeply. Mr. Paine has written largely on public liberty and government; and this last performance has, on that account, been more widely circulated, and principally among those who attached themselves from principle to his former works. This circumstance renders a public attack upon all revealed religion, from such a writer, infinitely more dangerous. The religious and moral sense of the people of Great Britain is the great anchor which alone can hold the vessel of the state amid the storms which agitate the world. If I could believe, for a moment, that the mass of the people were to be debauched from the principles of religion, which form the true basis of that humanity, charity, and benevolence that has been so long the national characteristic, instead of mixing myself, as I sometimes have done, in political reformations, I would rather retire to the uttermost corners of the earth to avoid their agitation; and would bear, not only the imperfections and abuses complained of in our own wise establishment, but even the worst government that ever existed in the world, rather than go to the work of reformation with a multitude set free from all the charities of Christianity, who had no sense of God's existence but from Mr. Paine's observation of nature, which the mass of mankind have no leisure to contemplate; nor any belief of future rewards and punishments to animate the good in the glorious pursuit of human happiness, nor to deter the wicked from destroying it even in its birth. But I know the people of England better. They are a religious people; and, with the blessing of God, as far as it is in my power, I will lend my aid to keep them so. I have no objections to the freest and most extended discussions upon doctrinal points of the Christian religion; and, though the law of England does not permit it, I do not dread the reasoned arguments of Deists against the existence of Christianity itself, because, as was said by its divine author, if it is of God, it will stand. An intellectual book, however erroneous, addressed to the intellectual world upon so profound and complicated a subject, can never work the mischief which this indictment is calculated to repress. Such works will only employ the minds of men enlightened by study in a deeper investigation of a subject well worthy of their profound and continued contemplation. The powers of the mind are given for human improvement in the progress of human existence. The changes produced by such reciprocations of lights and intelligences are certain in their progressions, and make their way imperceptibly, as conviction comes upon the world, by the final and irresistible power of truth. If Christianity be founded in falsehood, let us become Deists in this manner, and I am contented. But this book hath no such object and no such capacity; it presents no arguments to the wise and enlightened. On the contrary, it treats the faith and opinions of the wisest with the most shocking contempt, and stirs up men without the advantages of learning or sober thinking to a total disbelief of everything hitherto held sacred, and, consequently, to a rejection of all the laws and ordinances of the state, which stand only upon the assumption of their truth.

Gentlemen, I cannot conclude without expressing the deepest regret at all attacks upon the Christian religion by authors who profess to promote the civil liberties of the world. For under what other auspices than Christianity have the lost and subverted liberties of mankind in former ages been reasserted? By what zeal, but the warm zeal of devout Christians, have English liberties been redeemed and consecrated? Under what other sanctions, even in our own days, have liberty and happiness been extending and spreading to the uttermost corners of the earth? What work of civilization, what commonwealth of greatness, has the bald religion of nature ever established? We see, on the contrary, the nations that have no other light than that of nature to direct them, sunk in barbarism or slaves to arbitrary governments; while, since the Christian era, the great career of the world has been slowly, but clearly, advancing lighter at every step, from the awful prophecies of the Gospel, and leading, I trust, in the end, to universal and eternal happiness. Each generation of mankind can see but a few revolving links of this mighty and mysterious chain; but, by doing our several duties in our allotted stations, we are sure that we are fulfilling the purposes of our existence. You, I trust, will fulfill yours this day!

WILLIAM MAXWELL EVARTS

WHAT THE AGE OWES TO AMERICA

[William M. Evarts was born in Boston, Mass., 1818. He graduated at Yale in 1837, took a law course in Cambridge, and settled in New York. Here he began and here he carried on his practice through a long life, the events of which are chiefly the records of his successful conduct of important cases. From July 15, 1868, until the end of Johnson's term he served as attorney-general of the United States. In 1872 he was one of the counsel for the United States before the General Board of Arbitration to pass on the "Alabama" claims preferred by the United States against Great Britain for damage inflicted on American commerce during the Civil War.

He became secretary of state in the Hayes Cabinet in 1877, after serving as the advocate of the Republican party before the electoral commission in determining the results of that election. His last public office was as senator from New York from 1885 to 1891. He died in 1901. The speech given here was delivered in Philadelphia, July 4, 1876, at the Centennial Exposition, held in celebration of the one hundredth year of our independence.]

FELLOW-CITIZENS: The event which to-day we commemorate supplies its own reflections and enthusiasms and brings its own plaudits. They do not at all hang on the voice of the speaker nor do they greatly depend upon the contracts and associations of the place. The Declaration of American Independence was when it occurred a capital transaction in human affairs; as such it has kept its place in history; as such it will maintain itself while human interest in human institutions shall endure. The scene and the actors, for their profound impression upon the world at the time and ever since, have owed nothing to dramatic effects, nothing to epical exaggerations.

To the eye there was nothing wonderful, or vast, or splendid, or pathetic in the movement or the display. Imagination or art can give no sensible grace or decoration to the persons, the place, or the performance which made up the business of that day. The worth and the force that belong to the agents and the action rest wholly on the wisdom, the courage, and the faith that formed and executed the great design, and the potency and permanence of its operation upon the affairs of the world, which, as foreseen and legitimate consequences, followed.

The dignity of the act is the deliberate, circumspect, open, and serene performance by these men in the clear light of day, and by a concurrent purpose, of a civic duty, which embraced the greatest hazards to themselves and to all the people from whom they held this disputed discretion, but which to their sober judgments promised benefits to that people and their posterity from generation to generation exceeding these hazards and commensurate with its own fitness.

The question of their conduct is to be measured by the actual weight and pressure of the manifold considerations which surrounded the subject before them and by the abundant evidence that they comprehended their vastness and variety. By a voluntary and responsible choice they willed to do what was done and what without their will would not have been done.

Thus estimated, the illustrious act covers all who participated in it with its own renown and makes them forever conspicuous among men, as it is forever famous among events. And thus the signers of the Declaration of our independence " wrote their names where all nations should behold them and all time should not efface them." It was " in the course of human events " intrusted to them to determine whether the fulness of time had come when a nation should be born in a day. They declared the independence of a new nation in the sense in which men declare emancipation or declare war; the Declaration created what was declared.

Famous always among men are the founders of states, and fortunate above all others in such fame are these, our fathers, whose combined wisdom and courage began the great structure of our national existence, and laid sure the foundations of liberty and justice on which it rests. Fortunate, first, in the clearness of their title and in the world's acceptance of their rightful claim. Fortunate, next, in the enduring magnitude of the state they founded and the beneficence of its protection of the vast interests of human life and happiness, which have here had their home. Fortunate, again, in the admiring imitation of their work, which the institutions of the most powerful and most advanced nations more and more exhibit; and, last of all, fortunate in the full demonstration of our later time, that their work is adequate to withstand the most disastrous storms of human fortunes, and survives unwrecked, unshaken, and unharmed.

This day has now been celebrated by a great people at each recurrence of its anniversary for a hundred years, with every form of ostentatious joy, with every demonstration of respect and gratitude for the ancestral virtue which gave it its glory, and with the firmest faith that growing time should neither obscure its lustre nor reduce the ardor nor discredit the sincerity of its observance. A reverent spirit has explored the lives of the men who took part in the great transaction; has unfolded their characters and exhibited to an admiring posterity the purity of their motives; the sagacity, the bravery, the fortitude, and the perseverance which marked their conduct, and which secured the prosperity and permanence of their work.

Philosophy has divined the secrets of all this power and eloquence emblazoned the magnificence of its results. The heroic war which fought out the acquiescence of the Old World in the independence of the New; the manifold and masterly forms of noble character, and of patient and serene wisdom which the great influences of the times begat; the large and splendid scale on which these elevated purposes were wrought out and the majestic proportions to which they have been filled up; the unended line of eventful progress, casting ever backward a flood of light upon the sources of the original energy, and ever forward a promise and a prophecy of unexhausted power—all these have been made familiar to our people by the genius and the devotion of historians and orators.

The greatest statesmen of the Old World for this same period of one hundred years have traced the initial step in these events, looked into the nature of the institutions thus founded, weighed by the Old World wisdom and measured by recorded experience the probable fortunes of this new adventure on an unknown sea.   This circumspect and searching survey of our wide field of political and social experiment no doubt has brought them a diversity of judgment as to the past and of expectation as to the future.   But of the magnitude and the novelty and the power of the forces set at work by the event we commemorate no competent authorities have ever greatly differed.   The contemporary judgment of Burke is scarcely an over-statement of the European opinion of the immense import of American independence.   He declared: " A great revolution has happened—a revolution made, not by chopping and changing of power in any of the existing states, but by the appearance of a new state of a new species in a new part of the globe.   It has made as great a change in all the relations and balances and gravitations of power as the appearance of a new planet would in the system of the solar world."

It is easy to understand that the rupture between the colonies and the mother country might have worked a result of political independence that would have involved no such mighty consequences as are here so strongly announced by the most philosophic statesman of his age.   The resistance of the colonies, which came to a head in the revolt, was led in the name and for the maintenance of the liberties of Englishmen against parliamentary usurpation and a subversion of the British constitution.

A triumph of those liberties might have ended in an emancipation from the rule of the English Parliament and a continued submission to the scheme and system of the British monarchy, with an American parliament adjusted thereto upon the true principles of the English constitution.   Whether this new political establishment should have maintained loyalty to the British sovereign or should have been organized under a crown and throne of its own the transaction would then have had no other importance than such as belongs to a dismemberment of existing empire, but with preservation of existing institutions.   There would have been, to be sure, a " new state," but not " of a new species," and that it was "in a new part of the globe" would have gone far to make the dismemberment but a temporary and circumstantial disturbance in the old and settled order of things.

Indeed, the solidity and perpetuity of that order might have been greatly confirmed by this propagation of the model of the European monarchies on the boundless regions of this continent. It is precisely here that the Declaration of Independence has its immense importance. As a civil act, and by the people's decree, and not by the achievement of the army or through military motives, at the first stage of the conflict it assigned a new nationality with its own institutions as the civilly pre-ordained end to be fought for and secured. It did not leave it to an after-fruit of triumphant war, shaped and measured by military power, and conferred by the army of the people. This assured at the outset the supremacy of civil over military authority, the subordination of the army to the unarmed people.

This deliberative choice of the scope and goal of the Revolution made sure of two things which must have been always greatly in doubt if military reasons and events had held the mastery over the civil power. The first was that nothing less than the independence of the nation and its separation from the system of Europe would be attained if our arms were prosperous; and the second that the new nation would always be the mistress of its own institutions. This might not have been its fate had a triumphant army won the prize of independence, not as a task set for it by the people, and done in its service, but by its own might and held by its own title, and so to be shaped and dealt with by its own will.

There is the best reason to think that the Congress which declared our independence gave its chief solicitude, not to the hazards of military failure, not to the chance of miscarriage in the project of separation from England, but to the grave responsibility of the military success—of which they made no doubt—and as to what should replace as government to the new nation the monarchy of England, which they considered as gone to them forever from the date of the Declaration.

Nor did this Congress feel any uncertainty, either in disposition or expectation, that the natural and necessary result would preclude the formation of the new government out of any other materials than such as were to be found in society as established on this side of the Atlantic. These materials they foresaw were capable of and would tolerate only such political establishments as would maintain and perpetuate the equality and liberty always enjoyed in the several colonial communities. But all these limitations upon what was possible still left a large range of anxiety as to what was probable and might become actual.

One thing was too essential to be left uncertain, and the founders of this nation determined that there never should be a moment when the several communities of the different colonies should lose the character of component parts of one nation. By their plantation and growth up to the day of the Declaration of Independence they were subjects of one sovereignty, bound together in one political connection, parts of one country, under one constitution, with one destiny. Accordingly the Declaration by its very terms made the act of separation a dissolving by " one people " of " the political bands that have connected them with another," and the proclamation of the right and of the fact of independent nationality was " that these United Colonies are and of right ought to be free and independent states."

It was thus, that at one breath, " independence and union " were declared and established. The confirmation of the first by war, and of the second by civil wisdom, was but the execution of the single design which it is the glory of this great instrument of our national existence to have framed and announced. The recognition of our independence, first by France, and then by Great Britain, the closer union by the Articles of Confederation and the final unity by the federal constitution, were all but muniments of title of that "liberty and union, one and inseparable," which were proclaimed at this place and on this day one hundred years ago, which have been our possession from that moment hitherto, and which we surely avow shall be our possession forever.

What half a century ago was hopefully prophesied for our far future goes out to its fulfillment. The prophecy then uttered has become a truth—a realization.

" As the sun rises one Sabbath morning and travels westward from Newfoundland to the Oregon, he will behold the countless millions assembling, as if by a common impulse, in the temples with which every valley, mountain, and plain will be adorned. The morning psalm and the evening anthem will commence with the multitudes on the Atlantic coast, be sustained by the loud chorus of ten thousand times ten thousand in the valley of the Mississippi, and be prolonged by the thousands of thousands on the shores of the Pacific."

What remains but to search the spirit of the laws of the land as framed by, and modeled to, the popular government to which our fortunes were committed by the Declaration of Independence? I do not mean to examine the particular legislation, state, or general, by which the affairs of the people have been managed, sometimes wisely and well, at others feebly and ill, nor even the fundamental arrangement of political authority, or the critical treatment of great junctures in our policy and history. The hour and the occasion concur to preclude so intimate an inquiry.

The chief concern in this regard to us and to the rest of the world is, whether the proud trust, the profound radicalism, the wide benevolence which spoke in the Declaration, and were infused into the Constitution at the first, have been in good faith adhered to by the people, and whether now these principles supply the living forces which sustain and direct government and society.

He who doubts needs but to look around to find all things full of the original spirit, and testifying to its wisdom and strength. We have taken no steps backward, nor have we needed to seek other paths in our progress than those in which our feet were planted at the beginning. Weighty and manifold have been our obligations to the great nations of the earth, to their scholars, their philosophers, their men of genius and of science, to their skill, their taste, their invention, to their wealth, their arts, their industry. But in the institutions and methods of government; in civil prudence, courage, or policy; in statesmanship, in the art of " making of a small town a great city," in the adjustment of authority to liberty; in the concurrence of reason and strength in peace, of force and obedience in war; we have found nothing to recall us from the course of our fathers, nothing to add to our safety or aid our progress in it.

So far from this all modifications of European politics accept the popular principles of our system and tend to our model. The movements toward equality of representation, enlargement of the suffrage, and public education in England; the restoration of unity in Italy; the confederation of Germany under the lead of Prussia; the actual republic in France; the unsteady throne of Spain; the new liberties of Hungary; the constant gain to the people's share in government throughout all Europe; all tend one way, the way pointed out in the Declaration of Independence.

The care and zeal with which our people cherish and invigorate the primary supports and defences of their own sovereignty have all the unswerving force and confidence of instincts. The community and publicity of education at the charge and as an institution of the state is firmly embedded in the wants and desires of the people. Common schools are rapidly extending through the only part of the country which has been shut against them, and follow close upon the footsteps of its new liberty to enlighten the enfranchised race. Freedom of conscience easily stamps out the first sparkles of persecution and snaps as green withes the first bonds of spiritual domination. The sacred oracles of their religion the people wisely hold in their own keeping as the keys of religious liberty, and refuse to be beguiled by the voice of the wisest charmer into loosing their grasp.

Freedom from military power and the maintenance of that arm of the government in the people; a trust in their own adequacy as soldiers when their duty as citizens should need to take on that form of service to the state; these have gained new force by the experience of foreign and civil war, and a standing army is a remoter possibility for this nation in its present or prospective greatness than it was in the days of its small beginnings.

But in the freedom of the press and the universality of the suffrage as maintained and exercised to-day throughout the length and breadth of the land we find the most conspicuous and decisive evidence of the unspent force of the institutions of liberty, and the jealous guard of its principal defences.   These, indeed, are the great agencies and engines of the people's sovereignty.   They hold the same relations to the vast democracy of modern society that the persuasions of the orators and the personal voices of the assembly did in the narrow confines of the Grecian states.   The laws, the customs, the impulses, and sentiments of the people have given wider and wider range and license to the legislations of the press, multiplied and more frequent occasions for the exercise of the suffrage, larger and larger communication of its franchise.

The progress of a hundred years finds these prodigious activities in the fullest play—incessant and all powerful—indispensable in the habits of the people and impregnable in their affections.   The public service and their subordination to the public safety stand in their play upon one another, and in their freedom thus maintained.   Neither could long exist in true vigor in our system without the other.   Without the watchful, omnipresent, and indomitable energy of the press the suffrage would languish, would be subjugated by the corporate power of the legions of placemen which the administration of the affairs of a great nation imposes upon it, and fall a prey to that "vast patronage which," we are told, "distracted, corrupted, and finally subverted the Roman republic."

On the other hand, if the impressions of the press upon the opinions and passions of the people found no settled and ready mode of their working out through the frequent and peaceful suffrage, the people would be driven to satisfy their displeasure at government or their love of change to the coarse methods of barricades and batteries, by the force of arms, as it were.

We cannot then hesitate to declare that the original principles of equal society and popular government still inspire the laws, live in the habits of the people, and animate their purposes and their hopes.   These principles have not lost their spring or elasticity.   They have sufficed for all the methods of government in the past; we feel no fear for their adequacy in the future.   Released now from the tasks and burdens of the formative period, these principles and methods can be directed with undivided force to the everyday conduct of government, to the staple and steady virtues of administration.

The feebleness of crowding the statute-books with unexecuted laws, the danger of power outgrowing or evading responsibility, the rashness and fickleness of temporary expedients, the constant tendency by which parties decline into factions and end in conspiracies, all these mischiefs beset all governments and are part of the life of each generation. To deal with these evils, the tasks and burdens of the immediate future, the nation needs no other resources than the principles and the examples which our past history supply. These principles, these examples of our fathers, are the strength and the safety of our state to-day: Moribus antiquis, stat res Romana, virisque.

Unity, liberty, power, prosperity—these are our possessions to-day. Our territory is safe against foreign dangers; its completeness dissuades from further ambition to extend it, and its rounded symmetry discourages all attempts to dismember it. No division into greatly unequal parts would be tolerable to either. No imaginable union of interests or passions large enough to include one-half the country but must embrace much more. The madness of partition into numerous and feeble fragments could proceed only from the hopeless degradation of the people, and would form but an incident in the general ruin.

The spirit of the nation is at the highest—its triumph over the inborn, inbred perils of the Constitution has chased away all fears, justified all hopes, and with universal joy we greet this day. We have not proved unworthy of a great ancestry; we have had the virtue to uphold what they so wisely, so firmly established. With these proud possessions of the past, with powers matured, with principles settled, with habits formed, the nation passes as it were from preparatory growth to responsible development of character and the steady performance of duty. What labors await it, what trials shall attend it, what triumphs for human nature, what glory for itself, are prepared for this people in the coming century, we may not presume to foretell. "One generation passeth away and another generation cometh, but the earth abideth forever," and we reverently hope that these, our constituted liberties, shall be maintained to the unending line of our posterity and so long as the earth itself shall endure.

EDWARD EVERETT

THE HISTORY OF LIBERTY

[Edward Everett was born in Dorchester, Mass., in 1794. At ten years of age he entered the grammar school, and matriculated at Harvard in 1807. After graduating he studied divinity under President Kirkland, and was called to the pastorate of the Brattle Street Church, Boston. He was elected to Congress in 1825, as an independent, and retained his seat for ten years. He then became governor of Massachusetts, and was three times reelected. In 1840 he went abroad, and, upon the incoming of the Whig president, Harrison, was accredited to the Court of St. James's. With the change of administration in 1845 he retired and became president of Harvard College, which office he administered for three years. He interested himself in the founding of the Boston Public Library, to which he gave his entire collection of state papers, together with many books. After the death of Webster, in 1852, Everett held the office of secretary of state until the close of the administration. Afterwards he represented Massachusetts (1853–54) in the United States Senate. He died January 15, 1865. The following Fourth of July oration, delivered at Charlestown, Mass., in 1828, is a good example of the classic elegance of his oratorical style.]

THE event which we commemorate is all-important, not merely in our own annals, but in those of the world. The sententious English poet has declared that " the proper study of mankind is man," and of all inquiries of a temporal nature, the history of our fellow-beings is unquestionably among the most interesting. But not all the chapters of human history are alike important. The annals of our race have been filled up with incidents which concern not, or at least ought not to concern, the great company of mankind. History, as it has often been written, is the genealogy of princes, the field-book of conquerors; and the fortunes of our fellow-men have been treated only so far as they have been affected by the influence of the great masters and destroyers of our race. Such history is, I will not say a worthless study, for it is necessary for us to know the dark side as well as the bright side of our condition. But it is a melancholy study which fills the bosom of the philanthropist and the friend of liberty with sorrow.

But the history of Liberty—the history of men struggling to be free—the history of men who have acquired and are exercising their freedom—the history of those great movements in the world, by which liberty has been established and perpetuated, forms a subject which we cannot contemplate too closely. This is the real history of man, of the human family, of rational immortal beings.

This theme is one—the free of all climes and nations are themselves a people. Their annals are the history of freedom. Those who fell victims to their principles in the civil convulsions of the short-lived republics of Greece, or who sunk beneath the power of her invading foes; those who shed their blood for liberty amidst the ruins of the Roman Republic; the victims of Austrian tyranny in Switzerland and of Spanish tyranny in the Netherlands; the solitary champions or the united bands of high-minded and patriotic men who have, in any region or age, struggled and suffered in this great cause, belong to that people of the free whose fortunes and progress are the most noble theme man can contemplate.

The theme belongs to us. We inhabit a country which has been signalized in the great history of freedom. We live under forms of government more favorable to its diffusion than any the world has elsewhere known. A succession of incidents, of rare curiosity and almost mysterious connection, has marked out America as a great theater of political reform. Many circumstances stand recorded in our annals, connected with the assertion of human rights, which, were we not familiar with them, would fill even our own minds with amazement.

The theme belongs to the day. We celebrate the return of the day on which our separate national existence was declared—the day when the momentous experiment was commenced, by which the world, and posterity, and we ourselves were to be taught how far a nation of men can be trusted with self-government—how far life, liberty, and property are safe, and the progress of social improvement is secure, under the influence of laws made by those who are to obey them—the day when, for the first time in the world, a numerous people was ushered into the family of nations, organized on the principle of the political equality of all the citizens.

Let us then, fellow-citizens, devote the time which has been set apart for this portion of the duties of the day to a hasty review of the history of Liberty, especially to a contemplation of some of those astonishing incidents which preceded, accompanied, or have followed the settlement of America, and the establishment of our constitutions, and which plainly indicate a general tendency and cooperation of things towards the erection, in this country, of the great monitorial school of political freedom.

We hear much at school of the liberty of Greece and Rome—a great and complicated subject, which this is not the occasion to attempt to disentangle. True it is that we find, in the annals of both these nations, bright examples of public virtue—the record of faithful friends of their country—of strenuous foes of oppression at home or abroad—and admirable precedents of popular strength. But we nowhere find in them the account of a populous and extensive region, blessed with institutions securing the enjoyment and transmission of regulated liberty. In freedom, as in most other things, the ancient nations, while they made surprisingly close approaches to the truth, yet, for want of some one great and essential principle or instrument, they came utterly short of it in practice. They had profound and elegant scholars; but, for want of the art of printing, they could not send information out among the people, where alone it is of great use in reference to human happiness. Some of them ventured boldly out to sea, and possessed an aptitude for foreign commerce; yet, for want of the mariner's compass, they could not navigate distant seas, but crept for ages along the shores of the Mediterranean. In respect to freedom, they established popular governments in single cities; but, for want of the representative principle, they could not extend these institutions over a large and populous country. But as a large and populous country, generally speaking, can alone possess strength enough for self-defense, this want was fatal.

The freest of their cities accordingly fell a prey, sooner or later, either to a foreign invader or to domestic traitors.

In this way, liberty made no firm progress in the ancient states. It was a speculation of the philosopher and an experiment of the patriot, but not an established state of society. The patriots of Greece and Rome had indeed succeeded in enlightening the public mind on one of the cardinal points of freedom—the necessity of an elected executive. The name and the office of a king were long esteemed not only something to be rejected, but something rude and uncivilized, belonging to savage nations, ignorant of the rights of man, as understood in cultivated states. The word "tyrant," which originally meant no more than monarch, soon became with the Greeks synonymous with oppressor and despot, as it has continued to be ever since. When the first Cæsar made his encroachments on the liberties of Rome, the patriots even of that age boasted that they had—

> "heard their fathers say,
> There was a Brutus once, that would have brooked
> The eternal devil, to keep his state in Rome,
> As easily as a king."

So deeply rooted was this horror of the very name of king in the bosom of the Romans, that under their worst tyrants, and in the darkest days, the forms of the Republic were preserved. There was no name under Nero and Caligula for the office of monarch. The individual who filled the office was called Cæsar and Augustus, after the first and second of the line. The word "emperor" (imperator) implied no more than general. The offices of consul and tribune were kept up; although, if the choice did not fall, as it frequently did, on the emperor, it was conferred on his favorite general, and sometimes on his favorite horse. The Senate continued to meet, and affected to deliberate; and, in short, the Empire began and continued a pure military despotism, ingrafted, by a sort of permanent usurpation, on the forms and names of the ancient Republic. The spirit, indeed, of liberty had long since ceased to animate these ancient forms, and when the barbarous tribes of Central Asia and Northern Europe burst into the Roman Empire, they swept away the

poor remnant of these forms, and established upon their
ruins the system of feudal monarchy from which all modern
kingdoms are descended. Efforts were made in the Middle
Ages by the petty republics of Italy to regain the political
rights which a long proscription had wrested from them.
But the remedy of bloody civil wars between neighboring
cities was plainly more disastrous than the disease of subjection. The struggles of freedom in these little states resulted
much as they had done in Greece, exhibiting brilliant examples of individual character and short intervals of public
prosperity, but no permanent progress in the organization of
liberal governments.

At length a new era seemed to begin. The art of printing was invented. The capture of Constantinople by the
Turks drove the learned Greeks of that city into Italy, and
letters revived. A general agitation of public sentiment in
various parts of Europe ended in the religious Reformation.
A spirit of adventure had been awakened in the maritime
nations, projects of remote discovery were started, and the
signs of the times seemed to augur a great political regeneration. But, as if to blast this hope in its bud; as if to counter-
balance at once the operation of these springs of improvement;
as if to secure the permanence of the arbitrary institutions
which existed in every part of the continent at the moment
when it was most threatened, the last blow at the same time
was given to the remaining power of the great barons, the
sole check on the despotism of the monarch which the feudal
system provided was removed, and a new institution was
firmly established in Europe, prompt, efficient, and terrible
in its operation beyond anything which the modern world
had seen—I mean the system of standing armies; in other
words, a military force organized and paid to support the
king on his throne and retain the people in their subjection.

From this moment, the fate of freedom in Europe was
sealed. Something might be hoped from the amelioration
of manners in softening down the more barbarous parts of
political despotism, but nothing was to be expected in the form
of liberal institutions, founded on principle.

The ancient and the modern forms of political servitude
were thus combined. The Roman emperors, as I have hinted,

maintained themselves simply by military force, in nominal accordance with the forms of the Republic. Their power (to speak in modern terms) was no part of the constitution. The feudal sovereigns possessed a constitutional precedence in the state, which, after the diffusion of Christianity, they claimed by the grace of God; but their power, in point of fact, was circumscribed by that of their brother barons. With the firm establishment of standing armies was consummated a system of avowed despotism, paralyzing all expression of the popular will, existing by divine right, and unbalanced by any effectual check in the state. It needs but a glance at the state of Europe, in the beginning of the sixteenth century, to see that, notwithstanding the revival and diffusion of letters, the progress of the Reformation, and the improvement of the manners, the tone of the people, in the most enlightened countries, was more abject than it had been since the days of the Cæsars. The state of England certainly compared favorably with that of any other part of Europe; but who can patiently listen to the language with which Henry VIII. chides and Elizabeth scolds the lords and commons of the Parliament of Great Britain?

All hope of liberty then seemed lost; in Europe all hope was lost. A disastrous turn had been given to the general movement of things; and in the disclosure of the fatal secret of standing armies, the future political servitude of man was apparently decided.

But a change is destined to come over the face of things, as romantic in its origin as it is wonderful in its progress. All is not lost; on the contrary, all is saved, at the moment when all seemed involved in ruin. Let me just allude to the incidents connected with this change, as they have lately been described by an accomplished countryman, now beyond the sea.

About half a league from the little seaport of Palos, in the Province of Andalusia, in Spain, stands a convent dedicated to St. Mary. Some time in the year 1486, a poor, wayfaring stranger, accompanied by a small boy, makes his appearance on foot at the gate of this convent, and begs of the porter a little bread and water for his child. This friendless stranger is Columbus. Brought up in the hardy pur-

suit of a mariner—occasionally serving in the fleets of his
native country—with the burden of fifty years upon his
frame, the unprotected foreigner makes his suit to the sovereigns of Portugal and Spain. He tells them that the broad,
flat earth on which we tread is round; and he proposes, with
what seems a sacrilegious hand, to lift the veil which has
hung from the creation of the world over the bounds of the
ocean. He promises, by a western course, to reach the eastern
shores of Asia, the region of gold, diamonds, and spices; to
extend the sovereignty of Christian kings over realms and
nations hitherto unapproached and unknown; and, ultimately,
to perform a new crusade to the Holy Land, and ransom the
sepulchre of our Saviour with the new-found gold of the East.

Who shall believe the chimerical pretension? The
learned men examine it and pronounce it futile. The royal
pilots have ascertained by their own experience that it is
groundless. The priesthood have considered it, and have
pronounced that sentence, so terrific where the Inquisition
reigns, that it is a wicked heresy. The common sense and
popular feeling of men have been kindled into disdain and
indignation towards a project, which, by a strange, new chi-
mera, represented one-half of mankind walking with their feet
towards the other half.

Such is the reception which his proposal meets. For a
long time the great cause of humanity, depending on the
discovery of this fair continent, is involved in the fortitude,
perseverance, and spirit of the solitary stranger, already past
the time of life when the pulse of adventure beats full and
high. If, sinking beneath the indifference of the great, the
sneers of the wise, the enmity of the mass, and the persecution of a host of adversaries, high and low, he give up the
thankless pursuit of his noble vision, what a hope for mankind is blasted! But he does not sink. He shakes off his
enemies, as the lion shakes the dewdrops from his mane.
That consciousness of motive and of strength, which always
supports the man who is worthy to be supported, sustains
him in his hour of trial; and, at length, after years of expectation, importunity, and hope deferred, he launches forth
upon the unknown deep, to discover a new world under the
patronage of Ferdinand and Isabella.

The patronage of Ferdinand and Isabella! Let us dwell for a moment on the auspices under which our country was discovered. The patronage of Ferdinand and Isabella! Yes, doubtless, they have fitted out a convoy worthy the noble temper of the man and the grandeur of his project. Convinced at length that it is no day-dream of a heated visionary, the fortunate sovereigns of Castile and Aragon, returning from their triumph over the last of the Moors, and putting a victorious close to a war of seven centuries' duration, have no doubt prepared an expedition of well-appointed magnificence to go out upon this splendid search for other worlds. They have made ready, no doubt, their proudest galleon to waft the heroic adventurer upon his path of glory, with a whole armada of kindred spirits to accompany him.

Alas! from his ancient resort of Palos—which he first visited as a mendicant—in three frail barks, of which two were without decks, the great discoverer of America sails forth on the first voyage across the unexplored ocean! Such is the patronage of kings! A few years pass by; he discovers a new hemisphere; the wildest of his visions fade into insignificance before the reality of their fulfillment; he finds a new world for Castile and Leon, and comes back to Spain loaded with chains. Republics, it is said, are ungrateful. Such are the rewards of monarchies!

With this humble instrumentality did it please Providence to prepare the theater for those events by which a new dispensation of liberty was to be communicated to man. But much is yet to transpire before even the commencement can be made in the establishment of those institutions by which this great advance in human affairs was to be effected. The discovery of America had taken place under the auspices of the government most disposed for maritime adventure, and best enabled to extend a helping arm, such as it was, to the enterprise of the great discoverer. But it was not from the same quarter that the elements of liberty could be introduced into the New World. Causes, upon which I need not dwell, made it impossible that the great political reform should go forth from Spain. For this object, a new train of incidents was preparing in another quarter.

The only real advance which modern Europe had made

in freedom had been made in England. The cause of constitutional liberty in that country was persecuted, was subdued, but not annihilated, nor trampled out of being. From the choicest of its suffering champions were collected the brave band of emigrants who first went out on the second, the more precious voyage of discovery—the discovery of a land where liberty and its consequent blessings might be established.

A late English writer has permitted himself to say that the original establishment of the United States, and that of the colony of Botany Bay, were modeled nearly on the same plan. The meaning of this slanderous insinuation is that the United States was settled by deported convicts, as New South Wales has been settled by transported felons. It is doubtless true that at one period the English government was in the habit of condemning to hard labor, as servants in the colonies, a portion of those who had received the sentence of the law. If this practice makes it proper to compare America with Botany Bay, the same comparison might be made of England herself, before the practice of transportation began, and even now, inasmuch as a considerable number of convicts are at all times retained at home. In one sense, indeed, we might doubt whether the allegation were more of a reproach or a compliment. During the time that the colonization of America was going on most rapidly, some of the best citizens of England, if it be any part of good citizenship to resist oppression, were immured in her prisons of state or lying at the mercy of the law.

Such were some of the convicts by whom America was settled—men convicted of fearing God more than they feared man; of sacrificing property, ease, and all the comforts of life, to a sense of duty and to the dictates of conscience; men convicted of pure lives, brave hearts, and simple manners. The enterprise was led by Raleigh, the chivalrous convict, who unfortunately believed that his royal master had the heart of a man, and would not let a sentence of death, which had slumbered for sixteen years, revive and take effect after so long an interval of employment and favor. But *nullum tempus occurrit regi*. The felons who followed next were the heroic and long-suffering church of Robinson, at Leyden—Carver, Brewster, Bradford, Winslow, and their pious associates, convicted of worshiping God according to the dictates of their consciences, and of giving up all—country, property, and the tombs of their fathers—that they might do it unmolested. Not content with having driven the Puritans from her soil, England next enacted or put in force the oppressive laws which colonized Maryland with Catholics, and Pennsylvania with Quakers. Nor was it long before the American plantations were recruited by the Germans, convicted of inhabiting the Palatinate, when the merciless armies of Louis XIV. were turned into that devoted region, and by the Huguenots, convicted of holding what they deemed the simple truth of Christianity, when it pleased the mistress of Louis XIV. to be very zealous for the Catholic faith. These were followed, in the next century, by the Highlanders, convicted of the enormous crime, under a monarchical government, of loyalty to their hereditary prince on the plains of Culloden, and by the Irish, convicted of supporting the rights of their country against what they deemed an oppressive external power. Such are the convicts by whom America was settled!

In this way a fair representation of whatsoever was most valuable in European character—the resolute industry of one nation, the inventive skill and curious arts of another, the courage, conscience, principle, self-denial of all—was winnowed out, by the policy of the prevailing governments, as a precious seed wherewith to plant the American soil. By this singular coincidence of events, our country was constituted the great asylum of suffering virtue and oppressed humanity. It could now no longer be said—as it was of the Roman Empire—that mankind was shut up, as if in a vast prison house, from whence there was no escape. The political and ecclesiastical oppressors of the world allowed their persecution to find a limit at the shores of the Atlantic. They scarcely ever attempted to pursue their victims beyond its protecting waters. It is plain that in this way alone the design of Providence could be accomplished, which provided for one catholic school of freedom in the Western hemisphere. For it must not be a freedom of too sectional and peculiar a cast. On the stock of the English civilization, as the general basis, were to be ingrafted the language, the arts, and the tastes of the other civilized nations.   A tie of consanguinity must connect the members of every family of Europe with some portion of our happy land; so that in all their trials and disasters they may look safely beyond the ocean for a refuge.   The victims of power, of intolerance, of war, of disaster, in every other part of the world, must feel that they may find a kindred home within our limits. Kings, whom the perilous convulsions of the day have shaken from their thrones, must find a safe retreat; and the needy emigrant must at least not fail of his bread and water, were it only for the sake of the great discoverer, who was himself obliged to beg them.   On this corner-stone the temple of our freedom was laid from the first—

> " For here the exile met from every clime,
> And spoke in friendship every distant tongue;
> Men, from the blood of warring Europe sprung,
> Were here divided by the running brook."

This peculiarity of our population, which some have thought a misfortune, is in reality one of the happiest circumstances attending the settlement of the country.   It assures the exile from every part of Europe a kind reception from men of his own tongue and race.   Had we been the unmixed descendants of any one nation of Europe, we should have retained a moral and intellectual dependence on that nation, even after the dissolution of our political connection had taken place.   It was sufficient for the great purpose in view, that the earliest settlements were made by men who had fought the battles of liberty in England, and who brought with them the rudiments of constitutional freedom to a region where no deep-rooted proscriptions would prevent their development.   Instead of marring the symmetry of our social system, it is one of its most attractive and beautiful peculiarities, that, with the prominent qualities of the Anglo-Saxon character inherited from our English fathers, we have an admixture of almost everything that is valuable in the character of most of the other states of Europe.

Such was the first preparation for the great political reform, of which America was to be the theater. The colonies of England—of a country where the supremacy of laws and the constitution is best recognized—the North American colonies—were protected from the first against the introduction of the unmitigated despotism which prevailed in the Spanish settlements—the continuance of which, down to the moment of their late revolt, prevented the education of these provinces in the exercise of political rights, and in that way has thrown them into the revolution inexperienced and unprepared—victims, some of them, to a domestic anarchy scarcely less grievous than the foreign yoke they have thrown off. While, however, the settlers of America brought with them the principles and feelings, the political habits and temper, which defied the encroachment of arbitrary power, and made it necessary, when they were to be oppressed, that they should be oppressed under the forms of law, it was an unavoidable consequence of the state of things—a result, perhaps, of the very nature of a colonial government—that they should be thrown into a position of controversy with the mother country, and thus become familiar with the whole energetic doctrine and discipline of resistance. This formed and hardened the temper of the colonists, and trained them up to a spirit meet for the struggles of separation.

On the other hand, by what I had almost called an accidental circumstance, but one which ought rather to be considered as a leading incident in the great train of events connected with the establishment of constitutional freedom in this country, it came to pass that nearly all the colonies (founded as they were on the charters granted to corporate institutions in England, which had for their object the pursuit of the branches of industry and trade pertinent to a new plantation) adopted a regular representative system, by which as in ordinary civil corporations, the affairs of the community are decided by the will and the voices of its members, or those authorized by them. It was no device of the parent government which gave us our colonial assemblies. It was no refinement of philosophical statesmen to which we are indebted for our republican institutions of government. They grew up, as it were, by accident, on the simple foundation I have named. "A house of burgesses," says Hutchinson,

" broke out in Virginia in 1620;" and, " although there was no color for it in the charter of Massachusetts, a house of deputies appeared suddenly in 1634." " Lord Say," observes the same historian, " tempted the principal men of Massachusetts to make themselves and their heirs nobles and absolute governors of a new colony, but under this plan they could find no people to follow them."

At this early period, and in this simple, unpretending manner, was introduced to the world that greatest discovery in political science, or political practice, a representative republican system. " The discovery of the system of the representative republic," says M. de Chateaubriand, " is one of the greatest political events that ever occurred." But it is not one of the greatest, it is the very greatest, and combined with another principle, to which I shall presently advert, and which is also the invention of the United States, it marks an era in human affairs—a discovery in the great science of social life, compared with which everything else that terminates in the temporal interests of man, sinks into insignificance.

Thus, then, was the foundation laid, and thus was the preparation commenced, of the world's grand political regeneration. For about a century and a half this preparation was carried on. Without any of the temptations which drew the Spanish adventurers to Mexico and Peru, the colonies throve almost beyond example, and in the face of neglect, contempt, and persecution. Their numbers, in the substantial, middle classes of life, increased with regular rapidity. They had no materials out of which an aristocracy could be formed, and no great eleemosynary establishments to cause an influx of paupers. There was nothing but the rewards of labor and the hope of freedom.

But at length this hope, never adequately satisfied, began to turn into doubt and despair. The colonies had become too important to be overlooked; their government was a prerogative too important to be left in their own hands; and the legislation of the mother country decidedly assumed a form which announced to the patriots that the hour at length had come when the chains of the great discoverer were to be avenged, the sufferings of the first settlers to be compensated, and the long-deferred hopes of humanity to be fulfilled.

You need not, friends and fellow citizens, that I should dwell upon the incidents of the last great acts in the colonial drama. This very place was the scene of some of the earliest and the most memorable of them, and their recollection is a part of your inheritance of honor. In the early councils and first struggles of the great revolutionary enterprise, the citizens of this place were among the most prominent. The measures of resistance which were projected by the patriots of Charlestown were opposed by but one individual. An active cooperation existed between the political leaders in Boston and this place. The beacon light which was kindled in the towers of Christ Church in Boston, on the night of the eighteenth of April, 1775, was answered from the steeple of the church in which we are now assembled. The intrepid messenger who was sent forward to convey to Hancock and Adams the intelligence of the approach of the British troops was furnished with a horse, for his eventful errand, by a respected citizen of this place. At the close of the following momentous day, the British forces—the remnant of its disasters—found refuge, under the shades of night, upon the heights of Charlestown; and there, on the ever-memorable seventeenth of June, that great and costly sacrifice in the cause of freedom was consummated with fire and blood. Your hilltops were strewed with illustrious dead; your homes were wrapped in flames; the fair fruits of a century and a half of civilized culture were reduced to a heap of bloody ashes, and two thousand men, women, and children turned houseless on the world. With the exception of the ravages of the nineteenth of April, the chalice of woe and desolation was in this manner first presented to the lips of the citizens of Charlestown. Thus devoted, as it were, to the cause, it is no wonder that the spirit of the Revolution should have taken possession of their bosoms, and been transmitted to their children. The American who, in any part of the Union, could forget the scenes and the principles of the Revolution would thereby prove himself unworthy of the blessings which he enjoys; but the citizen of Charlestown who could be cold on this momentous theme, must hear a voice of reproach from the walls which were reared on the ashes of the seventeenth of June—a piercing cry from the very sods of yonder hill.

The Revolution was at length accomplished. The political separation of the country of Great Britain was effected, and it now remained to organize the liberty which had been reaped on bloody fields—to establish, in the place of the government whose yoke had been thrown off, a government at home, which should fulfil the great design of the Revolution and satisfy the demands of the friends of liberty at large. What manifold perils awaited the step! The danger was great that too little or too much would be done. Smarting under the oppressions of a distant government, whose spirit was alien to their feelings, there was great danger that the colonies in the act of declaring themselves sovereign and independent states would push to an extreme the prerogative of their separate independence, and refuse to admit any authority beyond the limits of each particular commonwealth. On the other hand, achieving their independence under the banners of the Continental army, ascribing, and justly, a large portion of their success to the personal qualities of the beloved Father of his Country, there was danger not less imminent that those who perceived the evils of the opposite extreme would be disposed to confer too much strength on one general government, and would, perhaps, even fancy the necessity of investing the hero of the Revolution, in form, with that sovereign power which his personal ascendency gave him in the hearts of his countrymen. Such and so critical was the alternative which the organization of the new government presented, and on the successful issue of which the entire benefit of this great movement in human affairs was to depend.

The first effort to solve the great problem was made in the course of the Revolution, and was without success. The Articles of Confederation verged to the extreme of a union too weak for its great purposes; and the moment the pressure of this war was withdrawn, the inadequacy of this first project of a government was felt. The United States found themselves overwhelmed with debt, without the means of paying it. Rich in the materials of an extensive commerce, they found their ports crowded with foreign ships, and themselves without the power to raise a revenue.   Abounding in all the elements of national wealth, they wanted resources to defray the ordinary expenses of government.

For a moment, and to the hasty observer, this last effort for the establishment of freedom had failed.   No fruit had sprung from this lavish expenditure of treasure and blood. We had changed the powerful protection of the mother country into a cold and jealous amity, if not into a slumbering hostility.   The oppressive principles against which our fathers had struggled were succeeded by more oppressive realities.   The burden of the British Navigation Act, as it operated on the colonies, was removed, but it was followed by the impossibility of protecting our shipping by a Navigation Act of our own.   A state of material prosperity, existing before the Revolution, was succeeded by universal exhaustion; and a high and indignant tone of militant patriotism by universal despondency.

It remained, then, to give its last great effort to all that had been done since the discovery of America for the establishment of the cause of liberty in the Western Hemisphere, and by another more deliberate effort to organize a government by which not only the present evils under which the country was suffering should be remedied, but the final design of Providence should be fulfilled.   Such was the task that devolved on the statesmen who convened at Philadelphia on the second day of May, 1787, in the Assembly of which General Washington was elected president, and over whose debates your townsman, Mr. Gorham, presided for two or three months as chairman of the Committee of the Whole, during the discussion of the plan of the Federal Constitution.

The very first step to be taken was one of pain and regret. The old Confederation was to be given up.   What misgivings and grief must not this preliminary sacrifice have occasioned to the patriotic members of the convention!   They were attached, and with reason, to its simple majesty.   It was weak then, but it had been strong enough to carry the colonies through the storms of the Revolution.   Some of the great men who led up the forlorn hope of their country in the hour of her direst peril, had died in its defense.   Could not a little inefficiency be pardoned to a Union with which France had made an alliance, and England had made peace? Could the proposed new government do more or better things than this had done? Who could give assurance, when the flag of the Old Thirteen was struck, that the hearts of the people could be rallied to another banner?

Such were the misgivings of some of the great men of that day—the Henrys, the Gerrys, and other eminent anti-federalists, to whose scruples it is time that justice should be done. They were the sagacious misgivings of wise men, the just forebodings of brave men, who were determined not to defraud posterity of the blessings for which they had all suffered, and for which some of them had fought.

The members of that convention, in going about the great work before them, deliberately laid aside the means by which all preceding legislators had aimed to accomplish a like work. In founding a strong and efficient government, adequate to the raising up of a powerful and prosperous people, their first step was to reject the institutions in which other governments traced their strength and prosperity, or had, at least, regarded as the necessary conditions of stability and order. The world had settled down into the belief that an hereditary monarch was necessary to give strength to the executive power. The framers of our Constitution provided for an elective chief magistrate, chosen every four years. Every other country had been betrayed into the admission of a distinction of ranks in society, under the absurd impression that privileged orders are necessary to the permanence of the social system. The framers of our Constitution established everything on the purely natural basis of a uniform equality of the elective franchise, to be exercised by all the citizens at fixed and short intervals. In other countries it had been thought necessary to constitute some one political center, towards which all political power should tend, and at which, in the last resort, it should be exercised. The framers of the Constitution devised a scheme of confederate and representative sovereign republics, united in a happy distribution of powers, which, reserving to the separate States all the political functions essential to local administrations and private justice, bestowed upon the general government those, and those only, required for the service of the whole.

Thus was completed the great revolutionary movement; thus was perfected that mature organization of a free system, destined, as we trust, to stand forever, as the exemplar of popular government; thus was discharged the duty of our fathers to themselves, to the country, and to the world.

The power of the example thus set up, in the eyes of the nations, was instantly and widely felt. It was immediately made visible to sagacious observers that a constitutional age had begun. It was in the nature of things that, where the former evil existed in its most inveterate form, the reaction should also be the most violent. Hence the dreadful excesses that marked the progress of the French Revolution, and, for a while, almost made the name of liberty odious. But it is not less in the nature of things that, when the most indisputable and enviable political blessings stand illustrated before the world—not merely in speculation and in theory, but in living practice and bright example—the nations of the earth, in proportion as they have eyes to see, and ears to hear, and hands to grasp, should insist on imitating the example. France clung to the hope of constitutional liberty through thirty years of appalling tribulation, and now enjoys the freest constitution in Europe. Spain, Portugal, the two Italian kingdoms, and several of the German states, have entered on the same path. Their progress has been and must be various, modified by circumstances, by the interests and passions of governments and men, and, in some cases, seemingly arrested. But their march is as sure as fate. If we believe at all in the political revival of Europe, there can be no really retrograde movement in this cause; and that which seems so in the revolutions of government is, like that of the heavenly bodies, a part of their eternal orbit.

There can be no retreat, for the great exemplar must stand, to convince the hesitating nations, under every reverse, that the reform they strive at is real, is practicable, is within their reach. Efforts at reform, by the power of action and reaction, may fluctuate; but there is an element of popular strength abroad in the world, stronger than forms and institutions, and daily growing in power. A public opinion of a new kind has arisen among men—the opinion of the civilized world. Springing into existence on the shores of our own continent, it has grown with our growth and strengthened with our strength, till now this moral giant, like that of the ancient poet, marches along the earth and across the ocean, but his front is among the stars. The course of the day does not weary, nor the darkness of the night arrest him. He grasps the pillars of the temple where Oppression sits enthroned, not groping and benighted, like the strong man of old, to be crushed, himself, beneath the fall, but trampling, in his strength, on the massy ruins.

Under the influence, I might almost say the unaided influence, of public opinion, formed and nourished by our example, three wonderful revolutions have broken out in a generation. That of France, not yet consummated, has left that country (which it found in a condition scarcely better than Turkey) in the possession of the blessings of a representative constitutional government. Another revolution has emancipated the American possessions of Spain, by an almost unassisted action of moral causes. Nothing but the strong sense of the age, that a government like that of Ferdinand ought not to subsist over regions like those which stretch to the South of us on the continent, could have sufficed to bring about their emancipation, against all the obstacles which the state of society among them opposes at present to regulated liberty and safe independence. When an eminent British statesman [Mr. Canning] said of the emancipation of these states, that " he had called into existence a new world in the West," he spoke as wisely as the artist who, having tipped the forks of a conductor with silver, should boast that he had created the lightning which it calls down from the clouds. But the greatest triumph of public opinion is the revolution of Greece. The spontaneous sense of the friends of liberty, at home and abroad—without armies, without navies, without concert, and acting only through the simple channels of ordinary communication, principally the press—has rallied the governments of Europe to this ancient and favored soil of freedom. Pledged to remain at peace, they have been driven by the force of public sentiment into the war. Leagued against the cause of revolution, as such, they have been compelled to send their armies and navies to fight the battles of revolt. Dignifying the barbarous oppressor of

Christian Greece with the title of " ancient and faithful ally," they have been constrained, by the outraged feelings of the civilized world, to burn up, in time of peace, the navy of their ally, with all his antiquity and all his fidelity; and to cast the broad shield of the Holy Alliance over a young and turbulent republic.

This bright prospect may be clouded in; the powers of Europe, which have reluctantly taken, may speedily abandon the field. Some inglorious composition may yet save the Ottoman Empire from dissolution, at the sacrifice of the liberty of Greece and the power of Europe. But such are not the indications of things. The prospect is fair that the political regeneration, which commenced in the West, is now going backward to resuscitate the once happy and long-deserted regions of the older world. The hope is not now chimerical, that those lovely islands, the flower of the Levant, —the shores of that renowned sea, around which all the associations of antiquity are concentrated—are again to be brought back to the sway of civilization and Christianity. Happily, the interest of the great powers of Europe seems to beckon them onward in the path of humanity. The half-deserted coasts of Syria and Egypt, the fertile but almost desolated archipelago, the empty shores of Africa, the granary of ancient Rome, seem to offer themselves as a ready refuge for the crowded, starving, discontented millions of Western Europe. No natural or political obstacle opposes itself to their occupation. France has long cast a wishful eye on Egypt. Napoleon derived the idea of his expedition, which was set down to the unchastened ambition of a revolutionary soldier, from a memoir found in the cabinet of Louis XIV. England has already laid her hand—an arbitrary, but a civilized and a Christian hand—on Malta; and the Ionian Isles, and Cyprus, Rhodes, and Claudia must soon follow. It is not beyond the reach of hope, that a representative republic may be established in Central Greece and the adjacent islands. In this way, and with the example of what has been done, it is not too much to anticipate that many generations will not pass, before the same benignant influence will revisit the awakened East, and thus fulfill, in the happiest sense, the vision of Columbus, by restoring a civilized population to the primitive seats of our holy faith.

Fellow-citizens, the eventful pages in the volume of human fortune are opening upon us with sublime rapidity of succession. It is two hundred years this summer since a few of that party who, in 1628, commenced in Salem the first settlement of Massachusetts, were sent by Governor Endicott to explore the spot where we stand. They found that one pioneer of the name of Walford had gone before them, and had planted himself among the numerous and warlike savages in this quarter. From them, the native lords of the soil, these first hardy adventurers derived their title to the lands on which they settled, and, in some degree, prepared the way by the arts of civilization and peace; for the main body of the colonists of Massachusetts came under Governor Winthrop, who, two years afterward, by a coincidence which you will think worth naming, arrived in Mystic River, and pitched his patriarchal tent on Ten Hills, upon the seventeenth day of June, 1630. Massachusetts at that moment consisted of six huts at Salem and one at this place. It seems but a span of time as the mind ranges over it. A venerable individual is living, at the seat of the first settlement, whose life covers one-half of the entire period; but what a destiny has been unfolded before our country! what events have crowded your annals! what scenes of thrilling interest and eternal glory have signalized the very spot where we stand!

In that unceasing march of things, which calls forward the successive generations of men to perform their part on the stage of life, we at length are summoned to appear. Our fathers have passed their hour of visitation—how worthily, let the growth and prosperity of our happy land and the security of our firesides attest. Or, if this appeal be too weak to move us, let the eloquent silence of yonder famous heights—let the column which is there rising in simple majesty—recall their venerable forms, as they toiled in the hasty trenches through the dreary watches of that night of expectation, heaving up the sods, where many of them lay in peace and honor before the following sun had set. The turn has come to us. The trial of adversity was theirs; the trial of prosperity is ours. Let us meet it as men who know their duty and prize their blessings. Our position is the most enviable, the most responsible, which men can fill. If this generation does its duty, the cause of constitutional freedom is safe. If we fail—if we fail, not only do we defraud our children of the inheritance which we received from our fathers, but we blast the hopes of the friends of liberty throughout our continent, throughout Europe, throughout the world, to the end of time.

History is not without her examples of hard-fought fields where the banner of liberty has floated triumphantly on the wildest storm of battle. She is without her examples of a people by whom the dear-bought treasure has been wisely employed and safely handed down. The eyes of the world are turned for that example to us. It is related by an ancient historian, of that Brutus who slew Cæsar, that he threw himself on his sword, after the disastrous battle of Philippi, with the bitter exclamation that he had followed virtue as a substance, but found it a name. It is not too much to say that there are, at this moment, noble spirits in the elder world, who are anxiously watching the practical operation of our institutions, to learn whether liberty, as they have been told, is a mockery, a pretense, a curse—or a blessing, for which it became them to brave the scaffold and the scimiter.

Let us then, as we assemble on the birthday of the nation, as we gather upon the green turf, once wet with precious blood—let us devote ourselves to the sacred cause of Constitutional Liberty! Let us abjure the interests and passions which divide the great family of American freemen! Let the rage of party spirit sleep to-day! Let us resolve that our children shall have cause to bless the memory of their fathers as we have cause to bless the memory of ours!

CHARLES JAMES FOX

ON THE REJECTION OF NAPOLEON'S OVERTURES

[Charles James Fox, an English statesman, was born in London in 1749. His irregular education included study at Oxford, and before he came of age he was elected to Parliament through family influence. His talents brought him prominence and he held many public offices. Throughout the American War of Independence he strenuously resisted the repressive policy of the British government and upheld the cause of the patriots under Washington. The struggle of his career was against Pitt, who came into power in 1784, and whose administration Fox assailed powerfully but ineffectually for years. The impeachment of Warren Hastings, the inauguration and development of the French Revolution, the circumstances attendant upon the establishment of the Regency in England, and the war against France, afforded Fox occasions for a display of his genius as an orator. But he was never able to gain the full confidence of his country, although he attained now and again the summit of popularity and was even appointed to a place in the ministry. After Pitt's death he was foreign secretary in the Grenville administration. He died in 1806. The speech that follows was an earnest reconsideration and review of the British Government's proposal to reject Napoleon's effort to establish peace, and was made in the House of Commons in 1800.]

AT so late an hour of the night, I am sure you will do me the justice to believe that I do not mean to go at length into the discussion of this great question. Exhausted as the attention of the House must be, and unaccustomed as I have been of late to attend in my place, nothing but a deep sense of my duty could have induced me to trouble you at all, and particularly to request your indulgence at such an hour.

Sir, my honorable and learned friend [Mr. Erskine] has truly said that the present is a new era in the war, and the right honorable gentleman opposite to me [Mr. Pitt] feels the justice of the remark; for by traveling back to the commencement of the war, and referring again to all the topics

and arguments which he has so often and so successfully
urged upon the House and by which he has drawn them on
to the support of his measures, he is forced to acknowledge
that, at the end of a seven years' conflict, we are come but to
a new era in the war, at which he thinks it necessary only to
press all his former arguments to induce us to persevere. All
the topics which have so often misled us—all the reasoning
which has so invariably failed—all the lofty predictions
which have so constantly been falsified by events—all the
hopes which have amused the sanguine, and all the assurances of the distress and weakness of the enemy which have
satisfied the unthinking, are again enumerated and advanced
as arguments for our continuing the war. What! at the end
of seven years of the most burdensome and the most calamitous struggle in which this country ever was engaged, are we
again to be amused with notions of finance, and calculations
of the exhausted resources of the enemy, as a ground of confidence and of hope? Gracious God! were we not told five
years ago that France was not only on the brink and in the
jaws of ruin, but that she was actually sunk into the gulf of
bankruptcy? Were we not told, as an unanswerable argument against treating, "that she could not hold out another
campaign—that nothing but peace could save her—that she
wanted only time to recruit her exhausted finances—that to
grant her repose was to grant her the means of again molest-
ing this country, and that we had nothing to do but persevere for a short time, in order to save ourselves forever from
the consequences of her ambition and her Jacobinism?"
What! after having gone on from year to year upon assurances like these, and after having seen the repeated refuta-
tions of every prediction, are we again to be gravely and
seriously assured that we have the same prospect of success
on the *same identical grounds?* And, without any other
argument or security, are we invited, at this new era of the
war, to conduct it upon principles which, if adopted and
acted upon, may make it eternal? If the right honorable
gentleman shall succeed in prevailing on Parliament and the
country to adopt the principles which he has advanced this
night, I see no possible termination to the contest. No man
can see an end to it; and upon the assurances and predic-

tions which have so uniformly failed, we are called upon not merely to refuse all negotiations, but to countenance principles and views as distant from wisdom and justice as they are in their nature wild and impracticable.

I must lament, sir, in common with every genuine friend of peace, the harsh and unconciliating language which ministers have held to the French, and which they have even made use of in their answer to a respectful offer of a negotiation.   Such language has ever been considered as extremely unwise, and has ever been reprobated by diplomatic men. I remember with pleasure the terms in which Lord Malmesbury, at Paris, in the year 1796, replied to expressions of this sort, used by M. de la Croix.   He justly said, "that offensive and injurious insinuations were only calculated to throw new obstacles in the way of accommodation, and that it was not by revolting reproaches nor by reciprocal invective that a sincere wish to accomplish the great work of pacification could be evinced."   Nothing could be more proper nor more wise than this language; and such ought ever to be the tone and conduct of men intrusted with the very important task of treating with a hostile nation.   Being a sincere friend to peace, I must say with Lord Malmesbury that it is not by reproaches and by invective that we can hope for a reconciliation; and I am convinced, in my own mind, that I speak the sense of this House, and if not of this House, certainly of a majority of the people of this country, when I lament that any unprovoked and unnecessary recriminations should be flung out, by which obstacles are put in the way of pacification.   I believe it is the prevailing sentiment of the people that we ought to abstain from harsh and insulting language; and in common with them, I must lament that both in the papers of Lord Grenville, and this night, such license has been given to invective and reproach.

For the same reason I must lament that the right honorable gentleman [Mr. Pitt] has thought proper to go at such length, and with such severity of minute investigation, into all the early circumstances of the war, which (whatever they were) are nothing to the present purpose, and ought not to influence the present feelings of the House.   I certainly shall not follow him through the whole of this tedious detail, though I do not agree with him in many of his assertions. I do not know what impression his narrative may make on other gentlemen; but I will tell him fairly and candidly, he has not convinced me. I continue to think, and until I see better grounds for changing my opinion than any that the right honorable gentleman has this night produced, I shall continue to think, and to say, plainly and explicitly, "that this country was the aggressor in the war." But with regard to Austria and Prussia—is there a man who, for one moment, can dispute that they were the aggressors? It will be vain for the right honorable gentleman to enter into long and plausible reasoning against the evidence of documents so clear, so decisive—so frequently, so thoroughly investigated. The unfortunate monarch, Louis XVI., himself, as well as those who were in his confidence, has borne decisive testimony to the fact that between him and the emperor [Leopold of Austria] there was an intimate correspondence and a perfect understanding. Do I mean by this that a positive treaty was entered into for the dismemberment of France? Certainly not. But no man can read the declarations which were made at Mantua as well as at Pilnitz, as they are given by M. Bertrand de Molville, without acknowledging that this was not merely an intention, but a *declaration* of an intention, on the part of the great powers of Germany, to interfere in the internal affairs of France, for the purpose of regulating the government against the opinion of the people. This, though not a plan for the partition of France, was, in the eye of reason and common-sense, an aggression against France. The right honorable gentleman denies that there was such a thing as a treaty of Pilnitz. Granted. But was there not a declaration which amounted to an act of hostile aggression? The two powers, the Emperor of Germany and the King of Prussia, made a public declaration that they were determined to employ their forces, in conjunction with those of the other sovereigns of Europe, "to put the King of France in a situation to establish, in perfect liberty, the foundations of a monarchical government equally agreeable to the rights of sovereigns and the welfare of the French." Whenever the other princes should agree to cooperate with them, "*then, and in that case,*" their majesties were determined to act promptly and by mutual consent, with the forces necessary to obtain the end proposed by all of them.   In the meantime, they declared that they would give orders for their troops to be ready for actual service." Now, I would ask gentlemen to lay their hands upon their hearts and say with candor what the true and fair construction of this declaration was—whether it was not a menace and an insult to France, since, in direct terms, it declared, that whenever the other powers should concur, they would attack France, then at peace with them, and then employed only in domestic and in internal regulations.   Let us suppose the case be that of Great Britain.   Will any gentleman say that if two of the great powers should make a public declaration that they were determined to make an attack on this kingdom as soon as circumstances should favor their intention; that they only waited for this occasion, and that in the meantime they would keep their forces ready for the purpose, it would not be considered by the Parliament and people of this country as a hostile aggression?   And is there any Englishman in existence who is such a friend to peace as to say that the nation could retain its honor and dignity if it should sit down under such a menace?   I know too well what is due to the national character of England to believe that there would be two opinions on the case, if thus put home to our own feelings and understandings.   We must, then, respect in others the indignation which such an act would excite in ourselves; and when we see it established on the most indisputable testimony, that both at Pilnitz and at Mantua declarations were made to this effect, it is idle to say that, as far as the Emperor and the King of Prussia were concerned, they were not the aggressors in the war.

"Oh! but the decree of the nineteenth of November, 1792." That, at least, the right honorable gentleman says, you must allow to be an act of aggression, not only against England, but against all the sovereigns of Europe.   I am not one of those, sir, who attach much interest to the general and indiscriminate provocations thrown out at random, like this resolution of the nineteenth of November, 1792.   I do not think it necessary to the dignity of any people to notice and to apply to themselves menaces without particular allusion, which are always unwise in the power which uses them, and which it is still more unwise to treat with seriousness. But if any such idle and general provocation to nations is given, either in insolence or in folly, by any government, it is a clear first principle that an *explanation* is the thing which a magnanimous nation, feeling itself aggrieved, ought to demand; and if an explanation be given which is not satisfactory, it ought clearly and distinctly to say so. There should be no ambiguity, no reserve, on the occasion. Now, we all know, from documents on our table, that M. Chauvelin [the French minister] did give an explanation of this silly decree. He declared, "in the name of his government, that it was never meant that the French government should favor insurrections; that the decree was applicable only to those people who, after having acquired their liberty by conquest, should demand the assistance of the Republic; but that France would respect not only the independence of England, but also that of her allies with whom she was not at war." This was the explanation of the offensive decree. "But this explanation was not satisfactory." Did you *say so* to M. Chauvelin? Did you tell him that you were not content with this explanation? and when you dismissed him afterward, on the death of the King [of France], did you say that this explanation was unsatisfactory? No. You did no such thing; and I contend that unless you demanded *further* explanations, and they were refused, you have no right to urge the decree of the nineteenth of November as an act of aggression. In all your conferences and correspondence with M. Chauvelin, did you hold out to him *what terms would satisfy you?* Did you give the French the power or the means of settling the misunderstanding which that decree, or any other of the points at issue, had created? I maintain that when a nation refuses to state to another the thing which would satisfy her, she shows that she is not actuated by a desire to preserve peace between them; and I aver that this was the case here. The Scheldt, for instance. You now say that the navigation of the Scheldt was one of your causes of complaint. Did you explain yourself on that subject? Did you make it one of the grounds for the dismissal of M. Chauvelin? Sir, I repeat it, that *a nation, to justify herself in appealing to the last solemn resort, ought to prove that she has taken every possible means, consistent with dignity, to demand the reparation and redress which would be satisfactory, and if she refuses to explain what would be satisfactory, she does not do her duty, nor exonerate herself from the charge of being the aggressor.*

But "France," it seems, "then declared war against us; and she was the aggressor, because the declaration came from her." Let us look at the circumstances of this transaction on both sides. Undoubtedly the declaration was made by them; but is a declaration the only thing which constitutes the commencement of a war? Do gentlemen recollect that, in consequence of a dispute about the commencement of war, respecting the capture of a number of ships, an article was inserted in our treaty with France, by which it was positively stipulated that in future, to prevent all disputes, the act of the *dismissal* of a minister from either of the two courts should be held and considered as tantamount to a declaration of war? I mention this, sir, because when we are idly employed in this retrospect of the origin of a war which has lasted so many years, instead of turning our eyes only to the contemplation of the means of putting an end to it, we seem disposed to overlook everything on our own parts, and to search only for grounds of imputation on the enemy. I almost think it an insult on the House to detain them with this sort of examination. Why, sir, if France was the aggressor, as the right honorable gentleman says she was *throughout*, did not Prussia call upon us for the stipulated number of troops, according to the article of the definitive treaty of alliance subsisting between us, by which, in case that either of the contracting parties was attacked, they had a right to demand the stipulated aid? And the same thing again may be asked when we were attacked. The right honorable gentleman might here accuse himself, indeed, of reserve; but it unfortunately happened that *at the time* the point was too clear on which side the aggression lay. Prussia was too sensible that the war could not entitle her to make the demand, and that it was not a case within the scope of the defensive treaty. This is evidence worth a volume of subsequent reasoning; for if, at the time when all the facts were present to their minds, they could not take advantage of existing treaties, and that too when the courts were on the most friendly terms with one another, it will be manifest to every thinking man that *they were sensible they were not authorized to make the demand.*

I really, sir, cannot think it necessary to follow the right honorable gentleman into all the minute details which he has thought proper to give us respecting the first aggression; but that Austria and Prussia were the aggressors, not a man in any country, who has ever given himself the trouble to think at all on the subject, can doubt. Nothing could be more hostile than their whole proceedings. Did they not declare to France, that it was her internal concerns, not her external proceedings, which provoked them to confederate against her? Look back to the proclamations with which they set out. Read the declarations which they made themselves to justify their appeal to arms. They did not pretend to fear her ambition—her conquests—her troubling her neighbors; but they accused her of new-modelling her own government. They said nothing of her aggressions abroad. They spoke only of her clubs and societies at Paris.

Sir, in all this I am not justifying the French; I am not trying to absolve them from blame, either in their internal or external policy. I think, on the contrary, that their successive rulers have been as bad and as execrable, in various instances, as any of the most despotic and unprincipled governments that the world ever saw. I think it impossible, sir, that it should have been otherwise. It was not to be expected that the French, when once engaged in foreign wars, should not endeavor to spread destruction around them, and to form plans of aggrandizement and plunder on every side. Men bred in the school of the House of Bourbon could not be expected to act otherwise. They could not have lived so long under their ancient masters without imbibing the restless ambition, the perfidy, and the insatiable spirit of the race. They have imitated the practice of their great prototype, and, through their whole career of mischiefs and of crimes, have done no more than servilely trace the steps of their own Louis XIV. If they have overrun countries and ravaged them, they have done it upon Bourbon principles; if they have ruined and dethroned sovereigns, it is entirely after the Bourbon manner; if they have even fraternized with the people of foreign countries, and pretended to make their cause their own, they have only faithfully followed the Bourbon example. They have constantly had Louis, the Grand Monarque, in their eye. But it may be said, that this example was long ago, and that we ought not to refer to a period so distant. True, it is a remote period applied to the man, but not so of the principle. The principle was never extinct; nor has its operation been suspended in France, except, perhaps, for a short interval, during the administration of Cardinal Fleury; and my complaint against the Republic of France is, not that she has generated new crimes —not that she has promulgated new mischief—but that she has adopted and acted upon the principles which have been so fatal to Europe under the practice of the House of Bourbon. It is said that wherever the French have gone they have introduced revolution—they have sought for the means of disturbing neighboring states, and have not been content with mere conquest. What is this but adopting the ingenious scheme of Louis XIV.? He was not content with merely overrunning a state. Whenever he came into a new territory, he established what he called his chamber of claims, a most convenient device, by which he inquired whether the conquered country or province had any dormant or disputed claims—any cause of complaint—any unsettled demand upon any other state or province—upon which he might wage war upon such state, thereby discover again ground for new devastation, and gratify his ambition by new acquisitions. What have the republicans done more atrocious, more Jacobinical than this? Louis went to war with Holland. His pretext was, that Holland had not treated him with sufficient *respect*. A very just and proper cause for war indeed!

This, sir, leads me to an example which I think seasonable, and worthy the attention of his Majesty's ministers. When our Charles II., as a short exception to the policy of his reign, made the triple alliance for the protection of Europe, and particularly of Holland, against the ambition of Louis XIV., what was the conduct of that great, virtuous, and most able statesman, M. de Witt, when the confederates came to deliberate upon the terms upon which they should treat with the French monarch? When it was said that he had made unprincipled conquests, and that he ought to be forced to surrender them all, what was the language of that great and wise man? " No," said he; " I think we ought not to look back to the origin of the war so much as the means of putting an end to it. If you had united in time to prevent these conquests, well; but now that he has made them, he stands upon the ground of conquest, and we must agree to treat with him, not with reference to the origin of the conquest, but with regard to his present posture. He has those places, and some of them we must be content to give up as the means of peace; for conquest will always successfully set up its claims to indemnification." Such was the language of this minister, who was the ornament of his time; and such, in my mind, ought to be the language of statesmen, with regard to the French, at this day; and the same ought to have been said at the formation of the confederacy. It was true that the French had overrun Savoy; but they had overrun it upon Bourbon principles; and, having gained this and other conquests before the confederacy was formed, they ought to have treated with her rather for future security than for past correction. States in possession, whether monarchical or republican, will claim indemnity in proportion to their success; and it will never so much be inquired by what right they gained possession as by what means they can be prevented from enlarging their depredations. Such is the safe practice of the world; and such ought to have been the conduct of the powers when the reduction of Savoy made them coalesce. The right honorable gentleman may know more of the secret particulars of their overrunning Savoy than I do; but certainly, as they have come to my knowledge, it was a most Bourbon-like act. A great and justly celebrated historian, I mean Mr. Hume, a writer certainly estimable in many particulars, but who is a childish lover of princes, talks of Louis XIV. in very magnificent terms. But he says of him, that, though he managed his enterprises with great skill and bravery, he was unfortunate in this, *that he never got a good and fair pretense for war.* This he reckons among his misfortunes. Can we say more of the republican French? In seizing on Savoy I think they made use of the words "*convénances morales et physiques.*" These were her reasons. A most Bourbon-like phrase. And I therefore contend that as we never scrupled to treat with the princes of the House of Bourbon on account of their rapacity, their thirst of conquest, their violation of treaties, their perfidy, and their restless spirit, so I contend we ought not to refuse to treat with their republican imitators.

Ministers could not pretend ignorance of the unprincipled manner in which the French had seized on Savoy. The Sardinian minister complained of the aggression, and yet no stir was made about it. The courts of Europe stood by and saw the outrage; and our ministers saw it. The right honorable gentleman will in vain, therefore, exert his power to persuade me of the interest he takes in the preservation of the rights of nations, since, at the moment when an interference might have been made with effect, no step was taken, no remonstrance made, no mediation negotiated, to stop the career of conquest. All the pretended and hypocritical sensibility " for the rights of nations, and for social order," with which we have since been stunned, cannot impose upon those who will take the trouble to look back to the period when this sensibility ought to have roused us into seasonable exertion. At that time, however, the right honorable gentleman makes it his boast that he was prevented, by a sense of neutrality, from taking any measures of precaution on the subject. I do not give the right honorable gentleman much credit for his spirit of neutrality on the occasion. It flowed from the sense of the country at the time, the great majority of which was clearly and decidedly against all interruptions being given to the French in their desire of regulating their own internal government.

But this neutrality, which respected only the internal rights of the French, and from which the people of England would never have departed but for the impolitic and hypocritical cant which was set up to arouse their jealousy and alarm their fears, was very different from the great principle of political prudence which ought to have actuated the councils of the nation, on seeing the first steps of France toward a career of external conquest. My opinion is, that when the unfortunate King of France offered to us, in the letter delivered by M. Chauvelin and M. Talleyrand, and even entreated us to mediate between him and the allied powers of Austria and Prussia, they [the ministers] ought to have accepted the offer, and exerted their influence to save Europe from the consequence of a system which was then beginning to manifest itself. It was, at least, a question of prudence; and as we had never refused to treat and to mediate with the old princes on account of their ambition or their perfidy, we ought to have been equally ready now, when the same principles were acted upon by other men. I must doubt the sensibility which could be so cold and so indifferent at the proper moment for its activity. I fear that there were at that moment the germs of ambition rising in the mind of the right honorable gentleman, and that he was beginning, like others, to entertain hopes that something might be obtained out of the coming confusion. What but such a sentiment could have prevented him from overlooking the fair occasion that was offered for preventing the calamities with which Europe was threatened? What but some such interested principle could have made him forego the truly honorable task, by which his administration would have displayed its magnanimity and its power? But for some such feeling, would not this country, both in wisdom and in dignity, have interfered, and, in conjunction with the other powers, have said to France: " You ask for a mediation. We will mediate with candor and sincerity, but we will at the same time declare to you our apprehensions. We do not trust to your assertion of a determination to avoid all foreign conquest, and that you are desirous only of settling your own constitution, because your language is contradicted by experience and the evidence of facts. You are Frenchmen, and you cannot so soon have forgotten and thrown off the Bourbon principles in which you were educated. You have already imitated the bad practice of your princes. You have seized on Savoy without a color of right. But here we take our stand. Thus far you have gone, and we cannot help it; but you must go no farther. We will tell you distinctly what we shall consider as an attack on the balance and the security of Europe; and, as the condition of our interference, we will tell you also the securities that we think essential to the general repose." This ought to have been the language of his Majesty's ministers when their mediation was solicited; and something of this kind they evidently thought of when they sent the instructions to St. Petersburg which they have mentioned this night, but upon which they never acted. Having not done so, I say they have no right to talk now about the violated rights of Europe, about the aggression of the French, and about the origin of the war in which this country was so suddenly afterward plunged. Instead of this, what did they do? They hung back; they avoided explanation; they gave the French no means of satisfying them; and I repeat my proposition—when there is a question of peace and war between two nations, *that government finds herself in the wrong which refuses to state with clearness and precision what she should consider as a satisfaction and a pledge of peace.*

Sir, if I understand the true precepts of the Christian religion, as set forth in the New Testament, I must be permitted to say that there is no such thing as a rule or doctrine by which we are directed, or can be justified, in waging a war for religion. The idea is subversive of the very foundations upon which it stands, which are those of peace and good-will among men. Religion never was and never can be a justifiable cause of war; but it has been too often grossly used as the pretext and the apology for the most unprincipled wars.

I have already said, and I repeat it, that the conduct of the French to foreign nations cannot be justified. They have given great cause of offense, but certainly not to all countries alike. The right honorable gentlemen opposite to me have made an indiscriminate catalogue of all the countries which the French have offended, and, in their eagerness to throw odium on the nation, have taken no pains to investigate the sources of their several quarrels. I will not detain you, sir, by entering into the long detail which has been given of their aggressions and their violences; but let me mention Sardinia as one instance which has been strongly insisted upon. Did the French attack Sardinia when at peace with her? No such thing. The King of Sardinia had accepted of a subsidy from Great Britain; and Sardinia

was, to all intents and purposes, a belligerent power. Several
other instances might be mentioned; but though, perhaps,
in the majority of instances, the French may be unjustifiable,
is this the moment for us to dwell upon these enormities—
to waste our time and inflame our passions by criminating
and recriminating upon each other? There is no end to
such a war. I have somewhere read, I think in Sir Walter
Raleigh's "History of the World," of a most bloody and
fatal battle which was fought by two opposite armies, in
which almost all the combatants on both sides were killed,
"because," says the historian, "though they had offensive
weapons on both sides, they had none for defense." So,
in this war of words, if we are to use only offensive weapons
—if we are to indulge only in invective and abuse, the contest must be eternal.

If this war of reproach and invective is to be counte-
nanced, may not the French with equal reason complain of
the outrages and horrors committed by the powers opposed
to them? If we must not treat with the French on account
of the iniquity of their former transactions, ought we not to
be as scrupulous of connecting ourselves with other powers
equally criminal? Surely, sir, if we must be thus rigid in
scrutinizing the conduct of an enemy, we ought to be equally
careful in not committing ourselves, our honor, and our
safety, with an ally who has manifested the same want of
respect for the rights of other nations. Surely, if it is material to know the character of a power with whom you are
about only to treat for peace, it is more material to know the
character of allies with whom you are about to enter into
the closest connection of friendship, and for whose exertions
you are about to pay. Now, sir, what was the conduct of
your own allies to Poland? Is there a single atrocity of the
French, in Italy, in Switzerland, in Egypt, if you please,
more unprincipled and inhuman than that of Russia, Austria,
and Prussia, in Poland? What has there been in the conduct
of the French to foreign powers; what in the violation of
solemn treaties; what in the plunder, devastation, and dismemberment of unoffending countries; what in the horrors
and murders perpetrated upon the subdued victims of their
rage in any district which they have overrun, worse than the

conduct of those three great powers in the miserable, devoted, and trampled-on kingdom of Poland, and who have been, or are, our allies in this war for religion and social order, and the rights of nations? "Oh, but you regretted the partition of Poland!" Yes, regretted! you regretted the violence, and that is all you did. You united yourselves with the actors; you, in fact, by your acquiescence, confirmed the atrocity. But they are your allies; and though they overran and divided Poland, there was nothing, perhaps, in the manner of doing it which stamped it with peculiar infamy and disgrace. The hero of Poland [Suwarroff], perhaps, was merciful and mild! He was "as much superior to Bonaparte in bravery, and in the discipline which he maintained, as he was superior in virtue and humanity!" He was animated by the purest principles of Christianity, and was restrained in his career by the benevolent precepts which it inculcates. Was he? Let unfortunate Warsaw, and the miserable inhabitants of the suburb of Praga in particular, tell! What do we understand to have been the conduct of this magnanimous hero, with whom, it seems, Bonaparte is not to be compared? He entered the suburb of Praga, the most populous suburb of Warsaw, and there he let his soldiery loose on the miserable, unarmed, and unresisting people. Men, women, and children, nay, infants at the breast, were doomed to one indiscriminate massacre! Thousands of them were inhumanly, wantonly butchered! And for what? Because they had dared to join in a wish to meliorate their own condition as a people, and to improve their constitution, which had been confessed by their own sovereign to be in want of amendment. And such is the hero upon whom the cause of religion and social order is to repose! And such is the man whom we praise for his discipline and his virtue, and whom we hold out as our boast and our dependence; while the conduct of Bonaparte unfits him to be even treated with as an enemy!

But the behavior of the French toward Switzerland raises all the indignation of the right honorable gentleman, and inflames his eloquence. I admire the indignation which he expresses, and I think he felt it, in speaking of this country, so dear and so congenial to every man who loves the sacred name of liberty. "He who loves Liberty," says the right honorable gentleman, "thought himself at home on the favored and happy mountains of Switzerland, where she seemed to have taken up her abode under a sort of implied compact, among all other states, that she should not be disturbed in this her chosen asylum." I admire the eloquence of the right honorable gentleman in speaking of this country of liberty and peace, to which every man would desire, once in his life at least, to make a pilgrimage! But who, let me ask him, first proposed to the Swiss people to *depart from the neutrality*, which was their chief projection, and to join the confederacy against the French? I aver that a noble relation of mine [Lord Robert Fitzgerald], then the Minister of England to the Swiss Cantons, was instructed, in direct terms, to propose to the Swiss, by an official note, to break from the safe line they had laid down for themselves, and to tell them, in such a contest neutrality was criminal. I know that noble lord too well, though I have not been in habits of intercourse with him of late, from the employments in which he has been engaged, to suspect that he would have presented such a paper without the express instructions of his court, or that he would have gone beyond those instructions.

But was it only to Switzerland that this sort of language was held? What was our language also to Tuscany and Genoa? An honorable gentleman [Mr. Canning] has denied the authenticity of a pretended letter which has been circulated, and ascribed to Lord Harvey. He says it is all a fable and a forgery. Be it so; but is it also a fable that Lord Harvey did speak in terms to the Grand Duke, which he considered as offensive and insulting? I cannot tell, for I was not present; but was it not, and is it not believed? Is it a fable that Lord Harvey went into the closet of the Grand Duke, laid his watch on the table and demanded, in a peremptory manner, that he should, within a certain number of minutes (I think I have heard within a quarter of an hour), determine, aye or no, to dismiss the French minister, and order him out of his dominions, with the menace, that if he did not, the English fleet should bombard Leghorn? Will the honorable gentleman deny this also? I certainly do not know it from my own knowledge; but I know that persons of the first credit, then at Florence, have stated these facts, and that they have never been contradicted. It is true, that upon the Grand Duke's complaint of this indignity, Lord Harvey was recalled; but was the *principle* recalled? was the mission recalled? Did not ministers persist in the demand which Lord Harvey had made, perhaps ungraciously? and was not the Grand Duke forced, in consequence, to dismiss the French minister? and did they not drive him to enter into an unwilling war with the republic? It is true that he afterward made his peace, and that, having done so, he was treated severely and unjustly by the French; but what do I conclude from all this, but that we have no right to be scrupulous, we who have violated the respect due to peaceable powers ourselves, in this war, which, more than any other that ever afflicted human nature, has been distinguished by the greatest number of disgusting and outrageous insults by the great to the smaller powers? And I infer from this, also, that the instances not being confined to the French, but having been perpetrated by every one of the allies, and by England as much as by others, we have no right, either in personal character or from our own deportment, to refuse to treat with the French on this ground. Need I speak of your conduct to Genoa also? Perhaps the note delivered by Mr. Drake was also a forgery. Perhaps the blockade of the port never took place. It is impossible to deny the facts, which were so glaring at the time. It is a painful thing to me, sir, to be obliged to go back to these unfortunate periods of the history of this war, and of the conduct of this country; but I am forced to the task by the use which has been made of the atrocities of the French as an argument against negotiation. I think I have said enough to prove that if the French have been guilty, we have not been innocent. Nothing but determined incredulity can make us deaf and blind to our own acts, when we are so ready to yield an assent to all the reproaches which are thrown out on the enemy, and upon which reproaches we are gravely told to continue the war.

"But the French," it seems, "have behaved ill everywhere. They seized on Venice, which had preserved the most exact neutrality, or rather," as it is hinted, "had manifested symptoms of friendship to them." I agree with the right honorable gentleman, it was an abominable act. I am not the apologist, much less the advocate, of their iniquities; neither will I countenance them in their pretenses for the injustice. I do not think that much regard is to be paid to the charges which a triumphant soldiery bring on the conduct of a people whom they have overrun. Pretenses for outrage will never be wanting to the strong when they wish to trample on the weak; but when we accuse the French of having seized on Venice, after stipulating for its neutrality, and guaranteeing its independence, we should also remember the excuse that they made for the violence, namely, that their troops had been attacked and murdered. I say I am always incredulous about such excuses; but I think it fair to hear whatever can be alleged on the other side. We cannot take one side of a story only. Candor demands that we should examine the whole before we make up our minds on the guilt. I cannot think it quite fair to state the view of the subject of one party as indisputable fact, without even mentioning what the other party has to say for itself. But, sir, is this all? Though the perfidy of the French to the Venetians be clear and pal-pable, was it worse in morals, in principle, and in example, than the conduct of Austria? My honorable friend [Mr. Whitbread] properly asked: " Is not the receiver as bad as the thief?" If the French seized on the territory of Venice, did not the Austrians agree to receive it? " But this," it seems, " is not the same thing." It is quite in the nature and within the rule of diplomatic morality for Austria to receive the country which was thus seized upon unjustly. " The emperor took it as a compensation. It was his by barter. He was not answerable for the guilt by which it was obtained." What is this, sir, but the false and abominable reasoning with which we have been so often disgusted on the subject of the slave trade? Just in the same manner have I heard a noto-rious wholesale dealer in this inhuman traffic justify his abominable trade. "I am not guilty of the horrible crime of tearing that mother from her infants; that husband from his wife; of depopulating that village; of depriving that family of its sons, the support of their aged parents! No, thank Heaven! I am not guilty of this horror. I only bought them in the fair way of trade. They were brought to the market; they had been guilty of crimes, or they had been made prisoners of war; they were accused of witchcraft, of obi, or of some other sort of sorcery; and they were brought to me for sale. I gave a valuable consideration for them. But God forbid that I should have stained my soul with the guilt of dragging them from their friends and families!" Such has been the precious defense of the slave trade, and such is the argument set up for Austria in this instance of Venice. "I did not commit the crime of trampling on the independence of Venice; I did not seize on the city; I gave a quid pro quo. It was a matter of barter and indemnity; I gave half a million of human beings to be put under the yoke of France in another district, and I had these people turned over to me in return! This, sir, is the defense of Austria, and under such detestable sophistry is the infernal traffic in human flesh, whether in white or black, to be continued, and even justified! At no time has that diabolical traffic been carried to a greater length than during the present war, and that by England herself, as well as Austria and Russia.

"But France," it seems, " has roused all the nations of Europe against her "; and the long catalogue has been read to you, to prove that she must have been atrocious to provoke them all. Is it true, sir, that she has roused them all? It does not say much for the address of his Majesty's ministers, if this be the case. What, sir! have all your negotiations, all your declamation, all your money, been squandered in vain? Have you not succeeded in stirring the indignation, and engaging the assistance, of a single power? But you do yourselves injustice. Between the crimes of France and your money the rage *has* been excited, and full as much is due to your seductions as to her atrocities. My honorable and learned friend [Mr. Erskine] was correct, therefore, in his argument; for you cannot take both sides of the case; you cannot accuse France of having provoked all Europe, and at the same time claim the merit of having roused all Europe to join you.

You talk, sir, of your allies. I wish to know who your allies are? Russia is one of them, I suppose. Did France attack Russia? Has the *magnanimous* Paul taken the field for social order and religion, or on account of personal aggression? The Emperor of Russia has declared himself Grand Master of Malta, though his religion is as opposite to that of the Knights as ours is; and he is as much considered a heretic by the Church of Rome as we are. The King of Great Britain might, with as much reason and propriety, declare himself the head of the order of the Chartreuse monks. Not content with taking to himself the commandery of this institution of Malta, Paul has even created a married man a knight, contrary to all the most sacred rules and regulations of the order; and yet this ally of ours is fighting for religion! So much for his religion. Let us see his regard for social order! How does he show his abhorrence of the principles of the French, in their violation of the rights of other nations? What has been his conduct to Denmark? He says to her: "You have seditious clubs at Copenhagen; no Danish vessel shall therefore enter the ports of Russia!" He holds a still more despotic language to Hamburg. He threatens to lay an embargo on her trade; and he forces her to surrender up men who are claimed by the French as their citizens, whether truly or not I do not inquire. He threatens her with his own vengeance if she refuse, and subjects her to that of the French if she comply. And what has been his conduct to Spain? He first sends away the Spanish minister from St. Petersburg, and then complains, as a great insult, that his minister was dismissed from Madrid! This is one of our allies; and he has declared that the object for which he has taken up arms is to replace the ancient race of the House of Bourbon on the throne of France, and that he does this for the cause of religion and social order! Such is the respect for religion and social order which he himself displays, and such are the examples of it with which we coalesce.

No man regrets, sir, more than I do, the enormities that France has committed; but how do they bear upon the question as it at present stands? Are we forever to deprive ourselves of the benefits of peace because France has perpetrated acts of injustice? Sir, we cannot acquit ourselves upon such ground. We *have* negotiated. With the knowledge of these acts of injustice and disorder, we have treated with her twice; yet the right honorable gentleman cannot enter into negotiation with her again; and it is worth while to attend to the reasons that he gives for refusing her offer. The Revolution itself is no more an objection now than it was in the year 1796, when he did negotiate. For the government of France at that time was surely as unstable as it is at present.

But you say you have not refused to treat. You have stated a case in which you will be ready immediately to enter into a negotiation, viz., the restoration of the House of Bourbon. But you deny that this is a sine qua non; and in your nonsensical language, which I do not understand, you talk of "limited possibilities," which may induce you to treat without the restoration of the House of Bourbon. But do you state what they are? Now, sir, I say, that if you put one case upon which you declare that you are willing to treat immediately, and say that there are other possible cases which may induce you to treat hereafter, without mentioning what these possible cases are, you do state a sine qua non of immediate treaty. Suppose I have an estate to sell, and I say my demand is £1,000 for it. For that sum I will sell the estate immediately. To be sure, there may be other terms upon which I may be willing to part with it; but I mention nothing of them. The £1,000 is the only condition that I state at the time. Will any gentleman assert that I do not make the £1,000 the sine qua non of the immediate sale? Thus you say the restoration of the Bourbons is not the only possible ground; but you give no other. This is your project. Do you demand a counter project? Do you follow your own rule? Do you not do the thing of which you complained in the enemy? You seemed to be afraid of receiving another proposition; and, by confining yourselves to this one point, you make it in fact, though not in terms, your sine qua non.

But the right honorable gentleman, in his speech, does what the official note avoids. He finds there the convenient words, "experience and the evidence of facts." Upon these he goes into detail; and in order to convince the House that new evidence is required, he reverts to all the earliest acts and crimes of the Revolution; to all the atrocities of all the governments that have passed away; and he contends that he must have experience that these foul crimes are repented of, and that a purer and a better system is adopted in France, by which he may be sure that she will be capable of maintaining the relations of peace and amity. Sir, these are not conciliatory words; nor is this a practicable ground to gain experience. Does he think it possible that evidence of a peaceable demeanor can be obtained in war? What does he mean to say to the French consul? "Until you shall, in *war*, behave yourself in a *peaceable* manner, I will not treat with you!" Is there not in this something extremely ridiculous? In duels, indeed, we have often heard of such language. Two gentlemen go out and fight, when, having discharged their pistols at one another, it is not unusual for one of them to say to the other: "Now I am satisfied. I see that you are a man of honor, and we are friends again." There is something, by-the-by, ridiculous even here. But between nations it is more than ridiculous. It is criminal. It is a ground which no principle can justify, and which is as impracticable as it is impious. That two nations should be set on to *beat* one another into friendship is too abominable even for the fiction of romance; but for a statesman seriously and gravely to lay it down as a system upon which he means to act is monstrous. What can we say of such a test as he means to put the French government to, but that it is hopeless? It is in the nature of war to inflame animosity; to exasperate, not to soothe; to widen, not to approximate. So long as this is to be acted upon, I say it is in vain to hope that we can have the evidence which we require.

The right honorable gentleman, however, thinks otherwise; and he points out four distinct possible cases, besides the reestablishment of the Bourbon family, in which he would agree to treat with the French.

(1.) "If Bonaparte shall conduct himself so as to convince him that he has abandoned the principles which were objectionable in his predecessors, and that he will be actuated by a more moderate system." I ask you, sir, if this is likely to be ascertained in war. It is the nature of war not to allay, but to inflame the passions; and it is not by the invective and abuse which have been thrown upon him and his government, nor by the continued irritations which war is sure to give, that the virtues of moderation and forbearance are to be nourished.

(2.) "If, contrary to the expectations of ministers, the people of France shall show a disposition to acquiesce in the government of Bonaparte." Does the right honorable gentleman mean to say, that because it is a usurpation on the part of the present chief, that therefore the people are not likely to acquiesce in it? I have not time, sir, to discuss the question of this usurpation, or whether it is likely to be permanent; but I certainly have not so good an opinion of the French, nor of any people, as to believe that it will be short-lived, *merely* because it was a usurpation, and because it is a system of military despotism. Cromwell was a usurper; and in many points there may be found a resemblance between him and the present Chief Consul of France. There is no doubt but that, on several occasions of his life, Cromwell's sincerity may be questioned, particularly in his self-denying ordinance, in his affected piety, and other things; but would it not have been insanity in France and Spain to refuse to treat with him because he was a usurper or wanted candor? No, sir, these are not the maxims by which governments are actuated. They do not inquire so much into the means by which power may have been acquired, as into the fact of where the power resides. The people did acquiesce in the government of Cromwell. But it may be said that the splendor of his talents, the vigor of his administration, the high tone with which he spoke to foreign nations, the success of his arms, and the character which he gave to the English name, induced the nation to acquiesce in his usurpation; and that we must not try Bonaparte by his example. Will it be said that Bonaparte is not a man of great abilities? Will it be said that he has not, by his victories, thrown a splendor over even the violence of the Revolution, and that he does not conciliate the French people by the high and lofty tone in which he speaks to foreign nations? Are not the French, then, as likely as the English in the case of Cromwell, to acquiesce in his government? If they should do so, the right honorable gentleman may find that this possible predicament may fail him. He may find that though one power may make war, it requires two to make peace. He may find that

Bonaparte was as insincere as himself in the proposition which he made; and in his turn he may come forward and say: "I have no occasion now for concealment. It is true that, in the beginning of the year 1800, I offered to treat, not because I wished for peace, but because the people of France wished for it; and besides, my old resources being exhausted, and there being no means of carrying on the war without ' a new and solid system of finance,' I pretended to treat, because I wished to procure the unanimous assent of the French people to this ' new and solid system of finance.' Did you think I was in earnest? You were deceived. I now throw off the mask. I have gained my point, and I reject your offers with scorn." Is it not a very possible case that he may use this language? Is it not within the right honorable gentleman's *knowledge of human nature?* But even if this should not be the case, will not the very test which you require, the acquiescence of the people of France in his government, give him an advantage-ground in the negotiation which he does not now possess? Is it quite sure that when he finds himself safe in his seat, he will treat on the same terms as at present, and that you will get a better peace some time hence than you might reasonably hope to obtain at this moment? Will he not have one interest less to do it, and do you not overlook a favorable occasion, for a chance which is exceedingly doubtful? These are the considerations which I would urge to his Majesty's ministers against the dangerous experiment of waiting for the acquiescence of the people of France.

(3.) "If the allies of this country shall be less successful than they have every reason to expect they will be in stirring up the people of France against Bonaparte, and in the further prosecution of the war." And,

(4.) "If the pressure of the war should be heavier upon us than it would be convenient for us to continue to bear." These are the other two possible emergencies in which the right honorable gentleman would treat even with Bonaparte. Sir, I have often blamed the right honorable gentleman for being disingenuous and insincere. On the present occasion I certainly cannot charge him with any such thing. He has made to-night a most honest confession. He is open and candid. He tells Bonaparte fairly what he has to expect. "I mean," says he, "to do everything in my power to raise up the people of France against you; I have engaged a number of allies, and our combined efforts shall be used to excite insurrection and civil war in France. I will strive to murder you, or to get you sent away. If I succeed, well; but if I fail, then I will treat with you. My resources being exhausted, even my 'solid system of finance' having failed to supply me with the means of keeping together my allies, and of feeding the discontents I have excited in France, then you may expect to see me renounce my high tone, my attachment to the House of Bourbon, my abhorrence of your crimes, my alarm at your principles; for then I shall be ready to own that, on the balance and comparison of circumstances, there will be less danger in concluding a peace than in the continuance of war!" Is this politic language for one state to hold to another? And what sort of peace does the right honorable gentleman expect to receive in that case? Does he think that Bonaparte would grant to baffled insolence, to humiliated pride, to disappointment, and to imbecility the same terms which he would be ready to give now? The right honorable gentleman cannot have forgotten what he said on another occasion:

> "Potuit quæ plurima virtus
> Esse, fuit. Toto certatum est corpore regni."

He would then have to repeat his words, but with a different application. He would have to say: "All our efforts are vain. We have exhausted our strength. Our designs are impracticable, and we must sue to you for peace."

Sir, what is the question to-night? We are called upon to support ministers in refusing a frank, candid, and respectful offer of negotiation, and to countenance them in continuing the war. Now I would put the question in another way. Suppose that ministers had been inclined to adopt the line of conduct which they pursued in 1796 and 1797, and that to-night instead of a question on a war address, it had been an address to his Majesty to thank him for accepting the overture, and for opening a negotiation to treat for peace, I ask the gentlemen opposite—I appeal to the whole five

hundred and fifty-eight representatives of the people—to lay
their hands upon their hearts and to say whether they would
not have cordially voted for such an address. Would they,
or would they not? Yes, sir, if the address had breathed a
spirit of peace, your benches would have resounded with re-
joicings, and with praises of a measure that was likely to
bring back the blessings of tranquility. On the present occasion, then, I ask for the vote of no gentlemen but of those
who, in the secret confession of their conscience, admit at
this instant, while they hear me, that they would have cheerfully and heartily voted with the minister for an address
directly the reverse of the one proposed. If every such gentleman were to vote with me, I should be this night in the
greatest majority that ever I had the honor to vote with in
this House. I do not know that the right honorable gentleman would find, even on the benches around him, a single
individual who would not vote with me. I am sure he would
not find many. I do not know that in this House I could
single out the individual who would think himself bound by
consistency to vote against the right honorable gentleman on
an address for negotiation. There may be some, but they
are very few. I do know, indeed, one most honorable man
in another place, whose purity and integrity I respect, though
I lament the opinion he has formed on this subject, who
would think himself bound, from the uniform consistency
of his life, to vote against an address for negotiation. Earl
Fitzwilliam would, I verily believe, do so. He would feel
himself bound, from the previous votes he has given, to declare his objection to all treaty. But I own I do not know
more in either House of Parliament. There may be others,
but I do not know them. What, then, is the House of Commons come to, when, notwithstanding their support given to
the right honorable gentleman in 1796 and 1797 on his entering into negotiation; notwithstanding their inward conviction that they would vote with him this moment for the same
measure —— who, after supporting the minister in his negotiation for a solid system of finance, can now bring themselves
to countenance his abandonment of the ground he took, and
to support him in refusing all negotiation? What will be
said of gentlemen who shall vote in this way, and yet feel,

in their consciences, that they would have, with infinitely more readiness, voted the other?

Sir, we have heard to-night a great many most acrimonious invectives against Bonaparte, against all the course of his conduct, and against the unprincipled manner in which he seized upon the reins of government. I will not make his defense. I think all this sort of invective, which is used only to inflame the passions of this House and of the country, exceedingly ill-timed, and very impolitic. But I say I will not make his defense. I am not sufficiently in possession of materials upon which to form an opinion on the character and conduct of this extraordinary man. On his arrival in France, he found the government in a very unsettled state, and the whole affairs of the Republic deranged, crippled, and involved. He thought it necessary to reform the government; and he did reform it, just in the way in which a military man may be expected to carry on a reform. He seized on the whole authority for himself. It will not be expected from me that I should either approve of or apologize for such an act. I am certainly not for reforming governments by such expedients; but how this House can be so violently indignant at the idea of military despotism is, I own, a little singular, when I see the composure with which it can observe it nearer home; nay, when I see it regard it as a frame of government most peculiarly suited to the exercise of free opinion, on a subject the most important of any that can engage the attention of a people. Was it not the system which was so *happily* and so *advantageously* established of late, all over Ireland, and which even now the government may, at its pleasure, proclaim over the whole of that kingdom? Are not the persons and property of the people left, in many districts, at this moment, to the entire will of military commanders? and is not this held out as peculiarly proper and advantageous, at a time when the people of Ireland are freely, and with unbiassed judgments, to discuss the most interesting question of a legislative union? Notwithstanding the existence of martial law, so far do we think Ireland from being enslaved, that we presume it precisely the period and the circumstances under which she may best declare her free opinion? Now really, sir, I cannot think that gentlemen who talk in this way about Ireland can, with a good grace, rail at military despotism in France.

But it seems "Bonaparte has broken his oaths. He has violated his oath of fidelity to the constitution of the third year." Sir, I am not one of those who hold that any such oaths ought ever to be exacted. They are seldom or ever of any effect; and I am not for sporting with a thing so sacred as an oath. I think it would be good to lay aside all such oaths. Who ever heard that, in revolutions, the oath of fidelity to the former government was ever regarded, or even that, when violated, it was imputed to the persons as a crime? In times of revolution, men who take up arms are called rebels. If they fail, they are adjudged to be traitors; but who before ever heard of their being perjured? On the restoration of King Charles II., those who had taken up arms for the Commonwealth were stigmatized as rebels and traitors, but not as men forsworn. Was the Earl of Devonshire charged with being perjured, on account of the allegiance he had sworn to the House of Stuart, and the part he took in those struggles which preceded and brought about the Revolution? The violation of oaths of allegiance was never imputed to the people of England, and will never be imputed to any people. But who brings up the question of oaths? He who strives to make twenty-four millions of persons violate the oaths they have taken to their present constitution, and who desires to reestablish the House of Bourbon by such violation of their vows. I put it so, sir, because, if the question of oaths be of the least consequence, it is equal on both sides! He who desires the whole people of France to perjure themselves, and who hopes for success in his project only upon their doing so, surely cannot make it a charge against Bonaparte that he has done the same!

"Ah! but Bonaparte has declared it as his opinion that the two governments of Great Britain and of France cannot exist together. After the treaty of Campo Formio, he sent two confidential persons, Berthier and Monge, to the Directory, to say so in his name." Well, and what is there in this absurd and puerile assertion, if it were ever made? Has not the right honorable gentleman, in this House, said the same thing? In this at least they resemble one another! They have both made use of this assertion; and I believe that these two illustrious persons are the only two on earth who think it! But let us turn the tables. We ought to put ourselves at times in the place of the enemy, if we are desirous of really examining with candor and fairness the dispute between us. How may they not interpret the speeches of ministers and their friends, in both Houses of the British Parliament? If we are to be told of the idle speech of Berthier and Monge, may they not also bring up speeches, in which it has not been merely hinted, but broadly asserted, that the two constitutions of England and France could not exist together? May not these offenses and charges be reciprocated without end? Are we ever to go on in this miserable squabble about words? Are we still, as we happen to be successful on the one side or the other, to bring up these impotent accusations, insults, and provocations against each other; and only when we are beaten and unfortunate, to think of treating? Oh! pity the condition of man, gracious God, and save us from such a system of malevolence, in which all our old and venerated prejudices are to be done away with, and by which we are to be taught to consider war as the natural state of man, and peace but as a dangerous and difficult extremity!

Sir, this temper must be corrected. It is a diabolical spirit, and would lead to an interminable war. Our history is full of instances that, where we have overlooked a proffered occasion to treat, we have uniformly suffered by delay. At what time did we ever profit by obstinately persevering in war? We accepted at Ryswick the terms we refused five years before, and the same peace which was concluded at Utrecht might have been obtained at Gertruydenberg; and as to security from the future machinations or ambition of the French, I ask you what security you ever had or could have? Did the different treaties made with Louis XIV. serve to tie up his hands, to restrain his ambition, or to stifle his restless spirit? At what time, in old or in recent periods, could you safely repose on the honor, forbearance, and moderation of the French government? Was there *ever* an idea of refusing to treat because the peace might be afterward insecure? The peace of 1763 was not accompanied with securities; and it was no sooner made than the French court began, as usual, its intrigues. And what security did the right honorable gentleman exact at the peace of 1783, in which he was engaged? Were we rendered secure by that peace? The right honorable gentleman knows well that, soon after that peace, the French formed a plan, in conjunction with the Dutch, of attacking our India possessions, of raising up the native powers against us, and of driving us out of India; as they were more recently desirous of doing, only with this difference, that the cabinet of France formerly entered into this project in a moment of profound peace, and when they conceived us to be lulled into a perfect security. After making the peace of 1783, the right honorable gentleman and his friends went out, and I, among others, came into office. Suppose, sir, that we had taken up the jealousy upon which the right honorable gentleman now acts, and had refused to ratify the peace which he had made. Suppose that we had said—No! France is acting a perfidious part; we see no security for England in this treaty; they want only a respite in order to attack us again in an important part of our dominions, and we ought not to confirm the treaty. I ask you, Would the right honorable gentleman have supported us in this refusal? I say that upon his present reasoning he ought. But I put it fairly to him, would he have supported us in refusing to ratify the treaty upon such a pretense? He certainly ought not, and I am sure he would not; but the course of reasoning which he now assumes would have justified his taking such a ground. On the contrary, I am persuaded that he would have said: " This security is a refinement upon jealousy. You have security, the only security that you can ever expect to get. It is the present interest of France to make peace. She will keep it if it be her interest. She will break it if it be her interest. Such is the state of nations; and you have nothing but your own vigilance for your security."

" It is not the interest of Bonaparte," it seems, " sincerely to enter into a negotiation, or, if he should even make peace, sincerely to keep it." But how are we to decide upon his sincerity? By refusing to treat with him? Surely, if we mean to discover his sincerity, we ought to hear the propo-

sitions which he desires to make. " But peace would be unfriendly to his system of military despotism." Sir, I hear a
great deal about the short-lived nature of military despotism.
I wish the history of the world would bear gentlemen out in
this description of it. Was not the government erected by
Augustus Cæsar a military despotism? and yet it endured
for six or seven hundred years. Military despotism, unfortunately, is too likely in its nature to be permanent, and it is
not true that it depends on the life of the first usurper.
Though half of the Roman emperors were murdered, yet the
military despotism went on; and so it would be, I fear, in
France. If Bonaparte should disappear from the scene, to
make room, perhaps, for Berthier, or any other general, what
difference would that make in the quality of French despotism, or in our relation to the country? We may as safely
treat with a Bonaparte, or with any of his successors, be they
whom they may, as we could with a Louis XVI., a Louis
XVII., or a Louis XVIII. There is no difference but in the
name. Where the power essentially resides, thither we ought
to go for peace.

But, sir, if we are to reason on the fact, I should think that
it is the interest of Bonaparte to make peace. A lover of
military glory, as that general must necessarily be, may he
not think that his measure of glory is full; that it may be
tarnished by a reverse of fortune, and can hardly be increased
by any new laurels? He must feel that, in the situation to
which he is now raised, he can no longer depend on his own
fortune, his own genius, and his own talents, for a continuance
of his success. He must be under the necessity of employing
other generals, whose misconduct or incapacity might en-
danger his power, or whose triumphs even might affect the
interest which he holds in the opinion of the French. Peace,
then, would secure to him what he has achieved, and fix the
inconstancy of fortune. But this will not be his only motive.
He must see that France also requires a respite—a breathing
interval, to recruit her wasted strength. To procure her this
respite, would be, perhaps, the attainment of more solid glory,
as well as the means of acquiring more solid power, than anything which he can hope to gain from arms, and from the
proudest triumphs. May he not, then, be zealous to secure

this fame, perhaps, that is worth acquiring? Nay, granting that his soul may still burn with the thirst of military exploits, is it not likely that he is disposed to yield to the feelings of the French people, and to consolidate his power by consulting their interests? I have a right to argue in this way when suppositions of his insincerity are reasoned upon on the other side. Sir, these aspersions are, in truth, always idle, and even mischievous. I have been too long accustomed to hear imputations and calumnies thrown out upon great and honorable characters to be much influenced by them. My honorable and learned friend [Mr. Erskine] has paid this night a most just, deserved, and eloquent tribute of applause to the memory of that great and unparalleled character, who is so recently lost to the world. I must, like him, beg leave to dwell a moment on the venerable GEORGE WASHINGTON, though I know that it is impossible for me to bestow anything like adequate praise on a character which gave us, more than any other human being, the example of a perfect man; yet, good, great, and unexampled as General Washington was, I can remember the time when he was not better spoken of in this House than Bonaparte is at present. The right honorable gentleman who opened this debate [Mr. Dundas] may remember in what terms of disdain, or virulence, even of contempt, General Washington was spoken of by gentlemen on that side of the House. Does he not recollect with what marks of indignation any member was stigmatized as an enemy to his country who mentioned with common respect the name of General Washington? If a negotiation had then been proposed to be opened with that great man, what would have been said? Would you treat with a rebel, a traitor? What an example would you not give by such an act? I do not know whether the right honorable gentleman may not yet possess some of his old prejudices on the subject. I hope not; I hope by this time we are all convinced that a republican government, like that of America, may exist without danger or injury to social order, or to established monarchies. They have happily shown that they can maintain the relations of peace and amity with other states. They have shown, too, that they are alive to the feelings of honor; but they do not lose sight of plain good sense and discretion.

They have not refused to negotiate with the French, and they have accordingly the hopes of a speedy termination of every difference. We cry up their conduct, but we do not imitate it. At the beginning of the struggle we were told that the French were setting up a set of wild and impracticable theories, and that we ought not to be misled by them; that they were phantoms with which we could not grapple. Now we are told that we must not treat, because, out of the lottery, Bonaparte has drawn such a prize as military despotism. Is military despotism a theory? One would think that that is one of the practical things which ministers might understand, and to which *they* would have no particular objection. But what is our present conduct founded on but a theory, and that a most wild and ridiculous theory? For what are we fighting? Not for a principle; not for security; not for conquest; but merely for an experiment and a speculation, to discover whether a gentleman at Paris may not turn out a better man than we now take him to be.

Sir, I wish the atrocities of which we hear so much, and which I abhor as much as any man, were, indeed, unexampled. I fear that they do not belong exclusively to the French. When the right honorable gentleman speaks of the extraordinary successes of the last campaign, he does not mention the horrors by which some of these successes were accompanied. Naples, for instance, has been, among others, what is called *delivered;* and yet, if I am rightly informed, it has been stained and polluted by murders so ferocious, and by cruelties of every kind so abhorrent, that the heart shudders at the recital. It has been said not only that the miserable victims of the rage and brutality of the fanatics were savagely murdered, but that in many instances their flesh was eaten and devoured by the cannibals, who are the advocates and the instruments of social order! Nay, England is not totally exempt from reproach, if the rumors which are circulated be true. I will mention a fact, to give ministers the opportunity, if it be false, to wipe away the stain that it must otherwise affix on the British name. It is said that a party of the republican inhabitants of Naples took shelter in the fortress of the Castel de Uovo. They were besieged by a detachment from the royal army, to whom they refused to

surrender; but demanded that a British officer should be
brought forward, and to him they capitulated.   They made
terms with him under the sanction of the British name.   It
was agreed that their persons and property should be safe,
and that they should be conveyed to Toulon.   They were
accordingly put on board a vessel; but before they sailed
their property was confiscated, numbers of them taken out,
thrown into dungeons, and some of them, I understand, notwithstanding the British guaranty, actually executed!

Where, then, sir, is this war, which on every side is pregnant with such horrors, to be carried?   Where is it to stop?
Not till we establish the House of Bourbon!   And this you
cherish the hope of doing, because you have had a successful campaign.   Why, sir, before this you have had a successful campaign.   The situation of the allies, with all they have
gained, is surely not to be compared now to what it was
when you had taken Valenciennes, Quesnoy, Condé, etc.,
which induced some gentlemen in this House to prepare
themselves for a march to Paris.   With all that you have
gained, you surely will not say that the prospect is brighter
now than it was then.   What have you gained but the recov-
ery of a part of what you before lost?   One campaign is successful to you, another to them; and in this way, animated
by the vindictive passions of revenge, hatred, and rancor,
which are infinitely more flagitious, even, than those of ambition and the thirst of power, you may go on forever, as,
with such black incentives, I see no end to human misery.

And all this without an intelligible motive!   All this because you may gain a better peace a year or two hence!   So
that we are called upon to go on merely as a speculation.
We must keep Bonaparte for some time longer at war, as a
state of probation.   Gracious God, sir! is war a state of probation?   Is peace a rash system?   Is it dangerous for nations
to live in amity with each other?   Are your vigilance, your
policy, your common powers of observation, to be extinguished by putting an end to the horrors of war?   Cannot
this state of probation be as well undergone without adding
to the catalogue of human sufferings?   " But we must *pause!* "
What! must the bowels of Great Britain be torn out—her
best blood be spilled—her treasure wasted—that you may

make an experiment? Put yourselves, O, that you would put yourselves in the field of battle, and learn to judge of the sort of horrors that you excite! In former wars a man might, at least, have some feeling, some interest, that served to balance in his mind the impressions which a scene of carnage and of death must inflict. If a man had been present at the battle of Blenheim, for instance, and had inquired the motive of the battle, there was not a soldier engaged who could not have satisfied his curiosity, and even, perhaps, allayed his feelings. They were fighting, they knew, to repress the uncontrolled ambition of the Grand Monarque. But if a man were present now at a field of slaughter, and were to inquire for what they were fighting, "Fighting!" would be the answer; "they are not fighting; they are *pausing*." "Why is that man expiring? Why is that other writhing with agony? What means this implacable fury?" The answer must be: "You are quite wrong, sir; you deceive yourself—they are not fighting—do not disturb them—they are merely *pausing!* This man is not expiring with agony —that man is not dead—he is only *pausing!* Lord help you, sir! they are not angry with one another; they have now no cause of quarrel; but their country thinks that there should be a *pause*. All that you see, sir, is nothing like fighting—there is no harm, nor cruelty, nor bloodshed in it whatever; it is nothing more than a *political pause!* It is merely to try an experiment—to see whether Bonaparte will not behave himself better than heretofore; and in the meantime we have agreed to a *pause*, in pure friendship!" And is this the way, sirs, that you are to show yourselves the advocates of order? You take up a system calculated to uncivilize the world—to destroy order—to trample on religion—to stifle in the heart, not merely the generosity of noble sentiment, but the affections of social nature; and in the prosecution of this system you spread terror and devastation all around you.

Sir, I have done. I have told you my opinion. I think you ought to have given a civil, clear, and explicit answer to the overture which was fairly and handsomely made you. If you were desirous that the negotiation should have included all your allies, as the means of bringing about a gen-

eral peace, you should have told Bonaparte so. But I believe
you were afraid of his agreeing to the proposal. You took
that method before. Ay, but you say the people were
anxious for peace in 1797. I say they are friends to peace
now; and I am confident that you will one day acknowledge
it. Believe me, they are friends to peace; although by the
laws which you have made, restraining the expression of the
sense of the people, public opinion cannot now be heard as
loudly and unequivocally as heretofore. But I will not go
into the internal state of this country. It is too afflicting to
the heart to see the strides which have been made by means
of, and under the miserable pretext of, this war, against liberty of every kind, both of power of speech and of writing,
and to observe in another kingdom the rapid approaches to
that military despotism which we affect to make an argument
against peace. I know, sir, that public opinion, if it could
be collected, would be for peace, as much now as in 1797;
and that it is only by public opinion, and not by a sense of
their duty, or by the inclination of their minds, that ministers
will be brought, if ever, to give us peace.

I conclude, sir, with repeating what I said before: I ask
for no gentleman's vote who would have reprobated the compliance of ministers with the proposition of the French government. I ask for no gentleman's support to-night who
would have voted against ministers, if they had come down
and proposed to enter into a negotiation with the French.
But I have a right to ask, and in honor, in consistency, in
conscience, I have a right to expect, the vote of every honorable gentleman who would have voted with ministers in an
address to his Majesty, diametrically opposite to the motion
of this night.

WILLIAM PIERCE FRYE

THE REPUBLICAN PARTY

[William Pierce Frye, an American statesman, was born in Maine in 1831. He graduated at Bowdoin College and immediately took up the study and practice of law, in which his success was assured in a very short time. He made his first appearance in politics as a young man, when the newly formed Republican party secured his devoted allegiance. Elected to the Maine legislature, he made himself one of the party leaders, and was sent to Congress in 1871, where he held a seat in the House of Representatives for ten years. He was promoted to the National Senate in 1881. He has been continuously reelected ever since. His activities during this long public career have been manifold. He was chairman of the Commerce Committee of the Senate, was chosen President pro tem of that body when Vice-President Hobart died, was on the Peace Commission that went to Paris to end the war with Spain, and has been acting chairman of the very important Senate Committee on foreign relations. The speech that follows was made at a banquet in New York city, in 1895, in response to a toast to the Republican party.]

MR. PRESIDENT: My theme is as broad as an ocean, my time as narrow as a frith. The Republican party's past would make a magnificent picture, but I can only give it a few touches, leaving the filling out to the imagination of these banqueters.

We received the country from the Democratic party in 1861 and restored it to them in 1893. Through this period we could not do our perfect work, because we were handicapped by a Democratic House half of the time; but fortunately they could only cripple us in the race, and were powerless to capture the laurels won. The fact remains that the marvelous progress made by this Republic during these thirty years has been accomplished under Republican legislation.

What of that progress?

I have stood by the shore of the ocean in the night time and seen the full-orbed moon rise from the waters, and as it rose higher and higher, cast across the sea a gleaming, glittering, magnificent pathway of light, narrow where it began, but broadening out in glory and beauty as it stretched away towards me.   Such a pathway, so splendid, so ever broadening in purpose and achievement, has been that trodden by the Republican party.   Its first great and beneficent gift was Abraham Lincoln, and from then to now it has held in generous hand the horn of plenty.

We received the Republic from the Democratic party disrupted—eleven states in open rebellion, a terrible war inaugurated : we restored it to them in peace at home and abroad, the states reunited, ten more added to the sisterhood, with a possibility of a union more thoroughly cemented than ever before.   We received it from them with a bankrupt treasury and an impaired credit: we restored it to them with a credit second to that of no nation on earth.   We received it from them dishonored by slavery: we restored it to them without a slave within its borders and with an amendment to the Constitution prohibiting it forever.   We received it, if not despised by the peoples of the earth, disregarded: we restored it to them, the most powerful of them all.

Regard this growth of power a moment.   Shortly after it came under our guardianship, England joined France in an attempt to create a monarchy in Mexico to be a perpetual menace to us, and before the war was fairly over England deserted France, France deserted Maximilian, Maximilian became a saint, and monarchy a myth.   England unhesitatingly fitted out, armed, and manned cruisers to prey on our commerce.   When the war was over, President Grant demanded redress for the wrong.   England disregarded the demand.   Then the President in a message to the people asked the sufferers from those cruisers to send in their claims, saying that he would collect them.   Then England submitted to arbitration, paid fifteen and a half millions of dollars damages, and apologized for the wrong.

Later on Germany seized the Samoan Islands, dethroned and deported Malietoa, our friend; but when the indignant voice of our people was heard, she asked for a consultation, restored Malietoa, and agreed to help perpetuate the independence of the islands.

Now a member of the English Parliament, indorsed by a majority of his colleagues, is urging upon our government the propriety of a treaty, providing that all disturbing questions between the two nations shall be submitted to arbitration. Would she have thought of this thirty years ago?

When we received it from them, in all industrial enterprises, Great Britain was almost out of our sight. When we restored it to them we had distanced her in the race and could see her only by looking backward through the dust raised by the wheels of our own magnificent progress.

We received it from them with thirty millions of people : we restored it to them with about seventy millions. We received it from them worth sixteen billions of dollars : we restored it to them worth over sixty billions. We received it from them in dishonor : we restored it to them in honor. We received it in weakness : we restored it in strength.

The year 1892 was, I suppose, the banner year of the Republic. Every man who sought work found it, with better wages, and of greater purchasing power than ever before known in the world. Every mill-wheel was revolving, every spindle singing, every furnace fire burning. The volume of business was enormous; our foreign trade greater than ever before known in our history. Compare 1861 with 1892, and the achievements of the Republican party are disclosed.

What of its present? We are only lookers on in Venice, that sad, silent, and solemn city of the sea. We are not disturbed by the noise of traffic, the song of the spindles, or the roar of the furnace fires. We hear the cry of the hungry, and the tramp of millions of men hunting for work they cannot find. Every now and then comes from the Treasury a hoarse cry for help, never the same in cadence of tone, but ever the same in results. It falls upon the heedless ears of a dazed and entirely demoralized Democratic majority. What has happened? In November, 1892, the people, in a fit of madness, had restored, for the first time since the days of James Buchanan, the Democratic party to full power, had given it the presidency and both houses of Congress, had

afforded it the opportunity to work out its own sweet will.
Why they did it no man can say. The Athenians banished
Aristides, weary with hearing him called " The Just." It
may be the people were tired of the name of " Grand Old
Party." The very shadow of this party as it fell over the
land in that November produced gloom, doubt, and dismay.

Damocles, at the festal board of the tyrant Dionysius,
surrounded by everything to gratify the taste, looked up and
saw a gleaming sword suspended just over him by a single
hair. He dared not reach out for food or wine, lest even a
motion of the hand should break the hair and death be his.
Our people saw suspended over them the threats of the
Democratic platform, and paralysis held them in its grasp.
Though our natural resources were as abundant as ever, our
workmen as intelligent and willing, our business men as
sagacious and enterprising, no one dared move lest destruction should follow. A fearful financial panic was upon us,
followed by a terrible business depression—neither one
necessarily the cause or effect of the other, but both caused
by Democracy, soon to be in power.

The substance of the party was even worse than its
shadow. They had solemnly declared in their platform that
protection was unconstitutional, that in making their tariff
they would disregard the difference in wages abroad and here,
that they would radically change the policy under which all
of our industries had been so marvelously prospered. And
now, assembled in Congress, they had the power. What
could have been expected other than business paralysis?
They entered upon their program with a stupidity utterly
amazing. They carried it out and finally passed a tariff law
which had not the approval of any Democrat or Republican,
which the President declared to be an outrage, and piteously
cried, " How can we face the American people with a law so
full of unjust discriminations as this?" which no intelligent
man in America favored, and every foreign power applauded.
What mountain ever so labored and brought forth such a
mouse?

What shall be our future? At the very first opportunity
the people, realizing their stupendous blunder, fully appre-
ciating the utter incapacity of the Democratic party for

government, like a cyclone swept them from power so far as was possible. In November, 1896, they will complete the work, and the Republican party will elect their President and control both Houses.

With power comes responsibility. We shall be confronted with grave questions of labor, of immigration, of currency, of tariff, of foreign policy. Shall we be equal to the emergencies? We have never failed in solving even graver questions than these in the past, and shall not falter in the future. The currency question may confront us in the very next Congress. The people must remember that while we have the apparent power in the Senate, it is not the real, and we shall still be handicapped until the election of '96.

I have no time to discuss financial problems now, nor is a dinner party the fitting occasion; but I believe our party may be relied upon never to legislate any one currency which shall be inferior to any other, knowing well that the inferior would expel the superior, and that the average man, the wage worker, would pay the penalty and not the rich. Nor do I believe the party will ever consent to any currency which shall not be maintained at a parity with the world's measure of value.

It will deal with the protective tariff, for it believes that the verdict of the people in November, 1893, was an indorsement of its policy; and it believes that the marvelous prosperity of the last thirty years was its legitimate fruit. Its doctrine is that all things, other than luxuries, we use and cannot produce shall be admitted free; that as to all products of foreign countries competing with our own there shall be a duty equivalent to the difference in the wages paid there and here. It will legislate on those lines. On them the McKinley law was constructed—in my opinion, take it all in all, the best tariff law ever enacted. The Sheffield (England) "Telegram" said of it:—

"The promoters of the McKinley tariff meant it to push forward the policy of America for Americans. One method of realizing it was to keep all work within their own dominions. The country was to be made self-supplying; what could be produced at home was not to be bought abroad. That was the keynote of the McKinley scheme, and it is working out the idea of its designers with the precision and effectiveness of a machine."

It was thoroughly efficient, though handicapped by the election of a tremendous Democratic majority in the November following the October when it took effect. It transferred the manufacture of over sixty-five million dollars worth of iron and steel, of cotton, wool, and silk, from foreign countries to our own, and never increased to our people the price of a single product a cent. It transferred some industries entire. It, in fact, gave us the year 1892, with all its wealth of prosperity.

Give our party a single decade of uncrippled control of the government, and it will illustrate the beneficence of its administration. We will lift our treasury from bankruptcy; raise sufficient revenue, without resorting to an odious income tax, to meet all current expenses with an annual surplus adequate for all extraordinary expenditures; keep the gold reserve intact, and instead of increasing the national debt in a time of peace, gradually extinguish it.

We will not yield to any crazy populistic clamors or adopt any cranky schemes of finance, but will give to our people a sound currency, each dollar of which shall be equal in value to every other dollar. We will restore the wages of 1892, and in doing that increase the purchasing power of our people billions of dollars. We will restore confidence, revive hope, inspire courage, so that every wheel shall be set in motion, every furnace fire shall be rekindled, every man have employment who seeks it, the volume of business be enormously increased, our railroads relieved from the hands of receivers, and confidence given to their securities. We will legislate in the interest of our merchant marine, revive, if possible, our foreign carrying trade, stop the paying to England of one hundred and fifty millions in gold annually for transporting our own exports and imports, and restore our flag to the seas.

We will increase our White Squadron of armed ships until they shall command the respect of the world. We will care for our coast defenses, and insure safety to our seaboard cities.

We will construct the Nicaragua Canal, and realize the dream of the centuries in the marriage of the two great oceans.

We will annex the Hawaiian Islands; improve and fortify Pearl Harbor; lay a cable to our coast, and then with Russia dominate and control the North Pacific.

Our foreign policy shall be American.

LEON GAMBETTA

ADDRESS TO THE DELEGATES FROM ALSACE

[Leon Gambetta, a French statesman of marked eloquence, was born
in Cahors, in the South of France, in 1838. Though of Jewish descent,
his immediate forbears were residents of Italy. He became a lawyer
in Paris, and while defending a political prisoner made a speech against
the empire of the third Napoleon that won him celebrity. He was
elected deputy in 1869 to the Corps Legislatif on a radical platform,
opposed the war with Germany, and on the fall of the empire proclaimed
the third French republic, becoming a member of the government of
national defense. He escaped from Paris in a balloon during the siege
of the capital by the German armies, assumed what amounted to a dictatorship, but relinquished power when order was assured, and founded
a newspaper to disseminate his republican principles. Repeatedly
elected to the Chamber of Deputies, of which he became president,
Gambetta was the soul of republican France, which he more than once
saved by his energy and eloquence. He died in 1882. The following
speech was delivered in 1873, on receiving a bronze statuette from his
admirers in Alsace ; the second speech was made at Belleville in 1878.]

ON receiving from your hands this testimonial of the
indissoluble bonds of solidarity which unite to each
other the various members of the great French family—for
the moment, alas, separated as you say—I know not which
feeling touches me more poignantly, the sentiment of gratitude or that of grief.

It is truly terrible to think that it is on the day on which
we are negotiating, for a golden price, — hard and necessary
results of our defeats the evacuation of our departments, — to
think that this lesson, this last exhortation, are given us by
you. I feel all the grief which you experience in being
obliged to count, to weigh, to postpone your hopes. I realize that you have need, as we have, to tell yourselves that
you will not give way to it. I well know that you are right
in repeating to yourselves that constancy is one of the qualities of your race. Ah ! it is from that very circumstance

that our dear Alsace was particularly necessary to French unity. She represented among us, by the side of that mobility and lightness, which, unfortunately, at certain moments mar our national character, she represented, I say, an invincible energy. And on this great pathway of invasion she was always found the first and the last to defend the fatherland!

It is for that reason, that as long as she returns not to the family, we may justly say there is neither a France nor a Europe.

But the hour is serious and full of difficulties, and it is greatly to be feared that if we give ear only to things which excite our patriotism and to bitter remembrances which recall us to impossible struggles, to the sentiment of our isolation in the world, to the memory of the weaknesses which have overwhelmed us—we shall go to some extreme, and compromise a cause which we might better serve.

Yes, in our present meeting, what ought to be reported and repeated to the constituents who have chosen me — who have saluted in me, the last one to protest, and to defend their rights and their honor, — is by no means a word of excitement or enthusiasm, but rather a message of resignation, albeit of active resignation.

We must take account of the state of France, we must look it squarely in the face. At the present hour the Republic, which you associate and always have associated not only with the defense of the fatherland, but also with her upraising and regeneration, the Republic, I say, claims the allegiance of some from necessity, of others from interest, and, of the generality of sensible people, from sentiments of patriotism.

People in France are beginning to understand that all that has happened is the result of successive monarchies, and that it would be wrong to hold the latest of the despotisms through which we have passed responsible for everything. The evil dates far backward, and from the first day when the Republic succumbed to the sabre of a soldier. Other *régimes* have followed, which have done nothing to purify and uplift the national heart and keep it on a level with events.

It is on this account, gentlemen, that we can truly say that the republican sentiment is a veritably national one, because it testifies that all the monarchy has done in this country, even in a liberal sense, all its tentative remedies, all its half measures, were equivocal and weakened the national sentiment, in that they were done for the benefit of a class, leaving others outside; and were not addressed to the whole country. Thus they blighted in the bud all patriotism. So when it became necessary for all to be patriots, sad to say, many failed in their duty.

To-day, under the stress of events and the great struggles of which we have been the victims, France has learned —so, at least, we may believe from recent and decisive manifestations—that the Republic is henceforward to be regarded as the common pledge of the rebirth of our nation's material and moral forces.

This great result could only have been obtained by means of reserve and prudence. The Republic could gain intellectual assent, conciliate interests, make progress in the general conscience, only by means of moderation among republicans, by proving to the majority of the indifferent, that only in this way is the spirit of order, of civil peace, and of progress peacefully and rationally to be obtained.

This demonstration is now merely commencing. We must follow it up, continue it. Especially must tardy convictions be made absolute. These have assisted us for some time, but in their turn may confirm the convictions of others, on which we have not counted, and which, gradually, under the influence of a continuous republican agitation, are transformed and enlarged, and become the general convictions of all.

We are favored by the circumstances of the hour. I do not mean that we ought to count on this to do everything, but we must take account of the fact and use it to solicit from all the spirit of concord, the spirit of union, and above all, the spirit of resignation and sacrifice. Ah! it is indeed cruel to ask of these brothers, harshly abandoned, the spirit of sacrifice and resignation, and yet it is of these that we make the supreme demand that they will not harass the country in her travail of reconstruction. And just as yours has been the section in which the greatest numbers have taken arms for the national defense, just as you have given your children and your gold, just as you have borne for the longest period, bullets, fire, bombs, and the exactions of the enemy, so during this unhappy peace you must give to France the example of a population able to preserve its sentiments without rushing to extremes, without provoking an intervention.

You owe to the Mother Country the supreme consolation of learning that, however impotent you may be to aid her, your heart is unconquerably attached to her. And I know you will exhibit towards your fatherland this consolation, this resignation; because, whatever may be the ardor of your sentiments, you have never made anything but a French cause out of your Alsatian cause. And it is in this very way that you have given a true proof of patriotism, putting aside in the greatest measure your personal interests for the cause of France. France ought to make requital to you for these great and noble sentiments. If she were so forgetful and impious as not to have constantly before her eyes the picture of your Alsace, bleeding and mutilated, oh, then you would be right to despair! But have no fear, so long as there is in France a National Party. And be sure that this National Party is now being formed anew and reconstituted. The true spirit of France seized and delivered over to the enemy by the Second Empire is to-day enlightened. From all sides publications let us know the *rôle* which our populations have played, and it is manifest that France has been much more disheartened than beaten, much more surprised than conquered. And the very moment the real state of events is made clear, the conscience of the country is reborn. You see the beginning of a great work, legitimate although melancholy, the work of ensuring and stigmatizing those who have deserved it. I hope that you will aid in the infliction of necessary penalties.

At the same time with the country all the parties reunite in demanding the punishment of the crime of "contempt of France" beneath the walls of Metz, and you see coming into our ranks true patriots, men who without hesitating, without discussing, have done their duty and have been true heroes of the army of the Loire.

Ah! how strongly those who struggled felt that there was no other resource, and no other honor for France, than to make the flag of the Republic the flag of the nation. There was something in this spectacle to urge us to retire within ourselves and to seek by starting fresh, by yielding to a new impulse, to impress the French mind, whatever the true means of restoring our moral and scientific greatness, financial probity, and military strength. And when we have in all the work-yards of construction rebuilt France piece by piece, do you believe that this will be ignored by Europe, and that nations will fail to think twice before approving and ratifying the outrageous gospel of force? Do you believe that that barbarous and Gothic axiom that might makes right will remain inscribed in the annals of international law? No! No!

If an ill-omened silence has greeted such a theory, it is because France was cast down. But there is not another country in Europe that does not think France should renew herself. They are not thinking of assisting her—they have not arrived at that—to that position our best wishers and those who sympathize with us the most desire for her. We have not received, and we shall not for a long time receive, either aid or cooperation, but the sentiment of the neighboring nations is plainly seen. They feel that the storm may not have spent all its strength on us, and that it may visit other countries and strike other peoples. The sentiment of general self-preservation is springing up. They are looking from France, and they see the occidental world empty.

Let us show our strength to those who are examining our morality, our internal power, and avoid displaying, as we have till now too often done, the spectacle of dynastic quarrels or dissension about chimeras.

Let us give this pledge to Europe, that we have no other aim than to take all the time necessary to arrive at that moral and material position where there is no need of drawing the sword, where people yield to right all that is her due, because they feel that there is force behind.

But let us neither be unduly elated, nor depressed by discouragement.

Let us take to the letter—and this is a reflection that you

will permit me to make in the presence of this bronze group which you have been so good as to offer me—let us take to the letter the thought which has animated the artist and the patriot. As this mother, who, extending her hand over the body of her fallen son, and feeling her bosom pressed by her babe, as yet too feeble to bear arms, counts only on the future, let us take the only course worthy of people truly animated by a wise and steadfast purpose. Let us not talk of revenge or speak rash words. Let us collect ourselves. Let us ever work to acquire that quality which we lack, that quality of which you have so admirably spoken—patience that nothing discourages, tenacity which wears out even time itself.

Then, gentlemen, when we have undergone this necessary renovation, time enough will have passed to bring about changes in the world around us. For this world which surrounds us is not, even now, in a very enviable situation. The din of arms, because it has ceased in France, has not ceased elsewhere.

One need not travel very far among his neighbors to perceive that on all sides preparations are being made, that the match is lighted. The only activity that prevails amid the operations of governments is military activity.

I do not say that from this we should draw delusive inferences. We should simply understand that the true program for every good Frenchman is, above all, to discipline himself at home, to devote himself to making of each citizen a soldier, and, if it be possible, an educated man, and leaving the rest to come to us in the process of our national growth.

Our enemies have given us examples on this point, which you know better than we do. For you, dwelling just on the frontiers, between them and us, have derived from intercourse with them a greater intellectual culture, have learnt the application of scientific ideas to promote the interests of practical life, at the same time that you still possess that fire, that energy, that vigor, which are characteristic of the French race.

It is with you and like you that we wish to labor, without letting ourselves be turned from our end by monarchical conspiracies. You can repeat to your brothers of Alsace that there is nothing to be feared from that quarter. That fear would be of a nature singularly alarming to your patriotic hopes. And again I say, gentlemen, now that sophists on all sides are declaring that if we remain a Republic we shall lack alliances outside and that we shall find no cooperation nor aid in the governments of Europe, again I say that if there be a *régime*, a system of government which has above all a horror of the spirit of conquest and annexation, it is the Republican. Any other political combination than the Republic would lead to civil war and foreign occupation. And we should have but one passion, one aim—to get rid of that. We ought to repeat the cry of Italy, " Out with the foreigners!"

Be persuaded, be sure, that under a government which is resolved to follow a truly national policy you can wait and need never despair.

As for me, you know the sentiments I have avowed to you ; you know how completely I am yours. I have no other ambition than to remain faithful to the charge you have given me, and which I shall consider as the law and honor of my life.

Let those among you, gentlemen, who have the sorrowful honor of rejoining your compatriots of Alsace, say that after I had seen you I could not find in my heart a single word which would express, as I would have it do, the profound gratitude that I feel toward you.

ON THE CONSTITUTIONAL LAWS

IN all the difficulties of political life, since the day when you opened its doors to me, I have never forgotten, never ceased to bear in mind the debt I owe to you, my first electors. Good and bad fortune are alike impotent to break the bonds that unite us. This union, gentlemen, we did not, if you recall, lightly contract, and since your thoughts have been called to that memory so dear to me, the beginning of our common political life, I shall try to recall, in a word, that which has bound us together from the time you were willing to cast your eyes on the man who is now before you.

We began by settling in advance, after free discussion, the conditions and stipulations that were to unite us. It was an example for all France, an example which was not lost, but which has not been sufficiently generalized. But the idea was just and good. It had birth here. It has grown. It will be developed in the future; so, gentlemen, by the accidents and revolutions of politics, I always love to come back to this spot. It is among you that I find the best encouragements, the strongest support amid the difficulties, the truest consolations amid the bitternesses, of public life. Do you wish to know the cause of my presence this evening? Citizens, I have come to ask those who were my first constituents: Does the contract still hold?

Gentlemen, your applause touches and moves me, and now I may add that I have not come here merely to seek inspirations of force and authority, I have come also—I say it with the only pride compatible with the dignity of a republican—to seek my reward.

My dear fellow citizens, they may say, may write, may murmur, against the men of the republican party, accusations the most absurd and the most stupid, whose contradiction would only gratify their vanity. They may also, in a style more or less elegant and polite, say that we are abandoning the principles on which we base our origins, that the moderation, wisdom, and calculating spirit which we have introduced into our political method are misjudged and misunderstood. They may represent our party as comprising all sorts of political adventurers, ready to separate from those to whom they really owe their existence. They may say that we are *petroleurs*, that we are hypocrites, Italians brought up in the school of Machiavelli, Cæsarians, Orleanists. I believe, gentlemen, that there is only one way for a public man to answer these accusations, and that way I take. It is to come back constantly before his constituents, before his natural judges, to explain to them his policy, his whole policy, without reservations or restrictions, in order to judge, by the reception of his statements, whether or not his constituents deem that he has remained faithful to his first engagements, whether or not he has, in his speeches and his acts, interpreted their thoughts and expressed their will.

Since our last meeting what has happened? After recalling briefly the events of the last two years we shall be enabled to see what is the present situation. We shall be
enabled to pass judgment upon it. And taking account of
the perils and alarms by which the present situation is encom-
passed, we shall together inquire what remedies, what resolutions, what measures ought to be employed, to attain finally
that result, without which there is neither a future for the
country, nor social peace, nor internal nor external politics,
nor government for France. That result, dear fellow citizens,
you know. It is a Republic, definitely founded, and placed
above all the contests of parties and all the attacks of faction.

Let us cast a glance over this period of two years, at
once so near to us and yet so dead.

We have seen, since our last meeting, an audacious,
shameless, attempt to restore that monarchy styled "legitimate." Before the repulsion manifested by public opinion,
before the shudder of unquiet and horror which shook
France to its deepest foundations, the restoration of the
monarchy either from exhaustion, fear, or impotence, miser-
ably miscarried. It miscarried because it was contrary,
absolutely contrary, to the national genius. Nobody in
France wanted the restoration of the monarchy, neither the
peasant, whose terror it is, nor the workingman, who has
never concealed his aversion for it, nor the army whose flag
it suppresses, symbol of its glory and honor:—nobody
wanted it. And so, gentlemen, how can any one be astonished that even he who is at the head of the state, the first
magistrate of the country, should have pronounced the
significant word, which shall remain as the death warrant of
the monarchy? He said that at the first attempt to bring
about a restoration, the chassepots would go off of themselves, and so the monarchy went back into the shade.

Nevertheless, the plotters did not consider themselves
beaten. They tried to introduce another monarchy. It was
difficult to manage it at the time. Not that men of title were
lacking, not that there was any deficiency of courtiers, not
that there was any want of adroit adherents, all ready to
present it to the country as a means of deliverance and
renewal, but because—[Interruptions]. I was saying, gen-

tlemen, that after the final repulse of the legitimate monarchy another monarchy was held in reserve, that things were not pushed to any overt attempt, but on the contrary the projected attempt was carefully masked, and although events pass very quickly, you have not yet forgotten the name of that combination, as odd as it was inexplicable and which was to serve as a screen to the projects then planned, and was called the "Septennat." The "Septennat" eventually rejoined in the realm of nothingness, from which no one ought to draw it, a dream indulged by the partisan of traditional royalty. That hybrid and nameless government lasted long enough, however, to chill the confidence and arrest the activity of the nation. It lasted long enough to bring to light the men and the party, whose existence constituted the most shameful as well as the most sinister peril that could threaten France.

Yes, gentlemen, statesmen of light character, prodigal of hatred, desperate, and seeing only one means of escape from that trend of the country, growing each day stronger, which drove them to a republic, these men did not fear to drag from its shame and its ignominy all that remained of the faction of December, and to draw it forth under the eyes of all France, which was astounded at so much audacity and stupidity. Gentlemen, although certain persons thought so, that combination was calculated to inspire France with horror and not to drag her toward their constitutional monarchy prepared and disguised under their Byzantine Septennat; it was above all a means of checking the republican party, which was every day growing in the country. But, gentlemen, these clever persons were not of the size to take the field with their new collaborators, any more than to resist such accomplices and dominate them. And it was promptly seen that in the association of parties, detesting each other, there was one which became more menacing every day, because it was the most unscrupulous and the most impudent. The danger was great and fears were justifiable. Conspiracy was felt everywhere. The most complete revelations were soon to be placed before the eyes of France and of the Assembly. That day, gentlemen, it must be said, a beam of patriotism flashed into honest minds an

impulse of political decency, and national honor took possession of the Assembly at Versailles, and, as always, appeal
was made to the only force that, in this country, can repel
the cutthroats of despotism.   Appeal was made to the Republic.   It became possible to form a majority of honest folk,
of devoted citizens.   Some of them made real sacrifices of
opinion, and others concessions of position, while others
consented to defer the immediate realization of their political
schemes.   Gentlemen, the truth must be spoken, it was from
horror of Cæsarism—that hideous leprosy which threatens
anew to overrun France, it was to make an end of that deadly
and irritating provisional state, which poisons the very
sources of national life, that it was decided to listen to the
voice of universal suffrage.   At the approach of peril, illusions were dispelled, eyes were opened, men of good will
and of good faith entrusted themselves to the democracy
and to its spirit and the Republic was made.   Oh, I know
all that may be said.   I know that when people have the
right, when they are in possession of political truth, when
they possess just principles, it would be good and fine, great
and advantageous, never to permit them, in political action,
to be hindered or restrained.   I know that above all the
dearest and noblest task would be to salute truth and justice
in all their splendor and all their majesty.   Yes, my fellow
citizens, we should be happy, were we never compelled to
palter with difficulties, nor yet with principles.   But societies
do not commence in the ideal.   The creations of man come
not to absolute perfection, nor even to a better state, at a
single bound.   Progress is the work of time and patience.
The way is long, it is sown with perils and sacrifices, it is
strewn with martyrs.   And who, then, among those who
know the nature of man, the conditions of society, the annals
of history, has ever flattered himself that he was able, before
dying, to greet the appearance of complete and absolute
truth among men?

No! No! Let us pursue our task, contribute our devoted
services, increase, even by a little, the patrimony bequeathed
us by our ancestors.   Let us bring our tribute to that treasury transmitted to us not only from the French Revolution,
but from the time there has been a people breathing, work-

ing, suffering, struggling for rights and liberty, on the soil of our great and unhappy country; from the ocean to the Rhine, from the Alps to the Pyrenees.   Have liberty, democracy, justice, and progress ever been awaited by this glorious and unfortunate people of France, and greeted in fugitive moments as lightning amid the storm?   Could we desire anything better, amid the many difficulties through which we are passing, than to have on our side right, legality, and as much as possible, the respect of magistrates for the principles we represent—and assure to this French Revolution, of whose conquests they are shamelessly trying to deprive us, a legal, defined, definitive *régime*, sheltered from the force and the vicissitudes of fortune?   Gentlemen, what have we obtained at last?   We have brought it about that all Frenchmen—all without exception as well as those at the head of the state as the last subordinate agents—willingly yield to our ideas, our principles, our government (under penalty of forfeiture and treason), respect and obedience.

We were in a position of perturbation and fatigue, and threatened by external dangers, from whlch we demanded relief.   For, gentlemen, let us never forget that, in spite of her crippled condition, France remains still an object of envy and covetousness in the world.   We had to get out of a fearful dilemma, an inextricable difficulty.   The peril was extreme. What part were we to take?   Well, gentlemen, reflect,—as for your children, they will never forget it—there was a day when, under the inspiration of a patriotism enlightened by the dangers to which France was exposed, men invested with the mandates of their fellow citizens joined together and made a solemn compact with the Republic, to assure peace abroad and at home.

The constitution had been made, but had not been much discussed.   Offices were organized, without being very minutely and analytically examined and arranged.   It was all quickly done, and yet do you know what happened? The work is better perhaps than the circumstances that produced it, and if we are willing to appropriate that work and make it our own, to examine it, to make use of it, and above all to understand it so that we may properly apply it, it may well happen that this constitution which our opponents feared even more than they abused it, which our friends do not yet sufficiently understand, should offer to the republican democracy the best instrument for enfranchisement and liberation that has ever been put into our hands.

Gentlemen, if you like, we will take to pieces this mechanism, examine together what it contains, and what can be made of it, for the greatest good of France and of the democracy.

You know that the constitution is short. It contains two laws and three chapters. It contains a chamber of deputies elected by direct universal suffrage. It has a president of the Republic, chosen by the chamber of deputies and by the second chamber which I will explain presently, a second chamber which composes the third delegation of power and is called the senate.

Note first that the powers of the president of the Republic have a good origin. His powers are not authorized by the universal suffrage of all the nation, and no one thinks of supposing that the first magistrate, the guardian and servant of the law, is superior to or preeminent over the representatives of the country who make the law. The president shall no longer be a sort of lieutenant general of an empire or monarchy. He can no longer have the same facilities that were granted so lightly and so rashly to—not his predecessor, but to the predecessor of his predecessor. Elective at stated times, obliged to register the will of the assembly and to promulgate the laws they make, responsible to them if he attack the fundamental laws of the country; he is in fact a president, and not a monarch in expectation, nor a prince getting ready to don the Cæsarian purple. His situation, though a modest one, yet is so high that the authority in his hands is worthy of France which he represents, and of the law, which he is charged to execute.

But let us speak of the senate, and it is evidently the desire of you all to learn the nature of that senate which has just been given to us. I say, first and foremost, that there is nothing to misapprehend from it, and that those who first had the idea of constituting a senate desired, from the origin, to create a citadel for the spirit of reaction, to organize in it a sort of last refuge for those dispossessed or rejected by universal suffrage. It is not doubtful that, in the spirit of all

legislators—I specify one no more than another—the first
thought which presided at the organization of the legislative
power into two chambers was a thought of resistance against
the republican democracy. But we must see if those who
had that thought realized it. We must inquire if, being by
hazard themselves imbued, and more deeply than they believed, with the democratic spirit that palpitates throughout
the whole country, and desiring to create a chamber of resistance, they did not organize a power essentially democratic
in its origin, in its tendencies, in its future. Gentlemen, that
is my conviction, and I shall try to prove it.

A senate, you are aware, is an institution which originated
far back in the annals of men.

There have been senates in all the countries of Europe,
in the most diverse latitudes, under the most varied and
opposing *régimes*, in antiquity and in modern times. Among
these political bodies there are those which have left glorious memories of skill and power, of tradition and of security,
in the development of a great national policy. I point to the
senate of Rome and that of the Venetian Republic. Side by
side with these historic senates we must place the upper
chambers, which have been, and are still, the representatives
of fortune, birth, great estates, and established churches.
These upper chambers, chambers of lords, of peers, of
seigneurs, played a great part at certain epochs; but at
present, without going into the details of the causes, they
are objects of a certain disfavor, even in England, on the
classic soil where they had their birth.

In France we have had not senates, because one cannot
call by that name the assemblies or collections of men that
the First and Second Empire gathered at the Luxembourg, but
we have had the chambers of peers. Those chambers, which
contained certainly all that the *élite* of the dominating classes
had of culture, brilliance, or influence, have passed away
after many vicissitudes, after casting from time to time great
luster on the tribune, but giving no support, no solidity to
the institutions among which they existed, enjoying no pres-
tige, displaying no force in the days of danger, and languishing in moments of peril, without the necessity even of running
away from popular anger.

Our legislators of to-day, with their heads full of these memories, and somewhat disturbed also about the political future of a certain number of them, considered the senate as a supreme hope, as a refuge against the disdain of the masses, that is, everybody—that is, of France. Convinced as they were that France did not appreciate them according to their merit, they said that no one could better serve them than themselves. And it was with that intention that they procured for themselves a senate. But this senate, in which they wished to install themselves as majestically as possible, they first dreamt of forming by direct vote, then of having its members vicariously nominated by a supreme electoral college, sufficiently dosed, sorted, prepared, and armed with rights so reduced and imperceptible, that it would have been a veritable homeopathic dilution of universal suffrage. These different combinations only appeared in order to vanquish; as soon as they were presented on the tribune such a burst of laughter arose that no one saw either the orator or his project. It was thus that we got rid of those successive concocted senates in which those gentlemen might surely have installed themselves. But as some method had to be found to establish something which resembled an upper-chamber, a senate was created, which is to-day the law of the land, which we ought to respect by that title, and all the more in that it must be considered the anchor of safety on which the ship of state relies. The Republic, as my dear friend Blanchet has just told you, has passed from the de facto state to the de jure, the legal state of the country. That is a word which we ought to repeat without ceasing. That is an idea whose conception, consequences, and bearing should be made to penetrate even to the last ranks of universal suffrage. It means that everywhere, in the most distant villages of France, it is known that the Republic is the law of France, and all who oppose it are factionists and deserve to be treated as the worst of revolutionists, because they raise their hands against the edifice which alone can shelter present and future generations from the catastrophes which still threaten us.

These few words seem necessary to anticipate all unexact comments upon your meeting; not that I care for comments, but it is good, when occasion arises, to prove to all that, with you, only reason and good sense are admissible, and that in all our encounters we have never said anything short of the truth or beyond it. I say, then, that if our new allies go down with us to the electoral arena against the common enemy—Cæsarism—the composition of the senate will be the better for it. It will be our part to give them a legitimate place, a place proportionate to their number, to their merit, and to the services that they shall be able to render to the Republic and to France. And therefore, gentlemen, if that supreme resource of reaction, a senate oligarchical and almost factious, baffles the adversaries of republican institution, I tell you we shall truly be able then to enter upon the era of industry, of growth, of improvement, and of progress. We shall have solved the political problem, and shall not employ all our days in mere theories, which is the worst of things when reforms do not soon follow. And we shall be able to take up for consideration questions near to our heart, discussing those which are timely and reserving the others, proceeding always with order, with precision, and with security. Gentlemen, I do not offer a program here. Nothing is more sterile than an empty program, and nothing would be more rash on my part. My program for the moment is yours and I sum it up in a single word, a word which will give an answer both to alarms at home and anxieties abroad.

Dear fellow citizens, I would like to come to see you and talk together as accidents occur and necessities arise, to consider in common our duties, our rights, and our mutual interests. But one thing sustains me when I am far from you, when I am among my colleagues and municipal counselors, those friends of "the Left" and of the "extreme Left," between whom I make no distinction; one idea sustains us all. It is that the people of Paris are, above all, the people of France, and most clearly and most quickly understand the *rôle* of their representatives and mandatories.

Again: We never hesitate to take sides positively and resolutely as soon as questions are put before us, because we have the conviction that we love Paris as it would be loved and that we understand it as it would be understood. We are all so filled with its spirit that, although we may err, our mistakes are shared with you. Our successes and our errors are in common, as is our devotion to the Republic and to France, and our faith in the future. Now before finishing, this is what I ask. When you disperse to your workshops, to your meetings, and to your families, say that we came here to explain the constitution and that this constitution must not be disparaged. Say that the senate must not be made light of, but on the contrary must be taken seriously, and preparation made to combat those of our adversaries who would take possession of that institution. Say that the senate is not like other senates, and that you understand now what to expect of the *rôle* for which democracy destines it and of the part it must play. Say also that, if you are willing to work, you will make of it a chamber with democratic attributes, which shall endow France with a new political spirit, and put into communication all parts of the nation, which is in need of the cooperation of all her children. The result will be something unhoped for and not realized for twenty-four years past. At a given moment, in four or five months perhaps, France shall be permitted to speak by the voice of her hamlets, her villages, her towns, her cities, throughout her whole territory. Yes. It is more than twenty years since France has presented a similar spectacle. At the dawn of our Revolution all the communes of France spoke and made known their complaints. That was the period of complaints. To-day is the period of rights. Well, let the communes speak, let them make known their will, and when France thus assembled, thus consulted, recalling the federation of '90, shall have spoken, who in this whole country will not bow his head and obey?

You must bear in mind, my dear fellow citizens, that institutions go nearly always higher and further than one is apt to think. Among these is the institution of the senate, and I repeat, what I said in the beginning, it is worth more than the circumstances and the men that produced it. Only it must be put into practice, it must also be loved. One never serves well save where one loves, and that is why you are such good servants of democracy. That is why I ask you to greet with me the dawn of this Republic, which it will be your part, I hope, to make as great and glorious as we have always wished it to be.

JAMES ABRAM GARFIELD

ON THE RESTORATION OF THE SOUTH

[James Abram Garfield, twentieth president of the United States, was born at Orange, Cuyahoga Co., Ohio, in 1831. He taught school at eighteen, and began his college course at Williams when he was twenty-two. In two years he received his diploma ; and in the eight years following he made the most extraordinary advances, becoming in turn a college president, a state senator of Ohio, a major-general of the army, and a member of the National House of Representatives. He entered military service in 1861, and in 1863 he became chief of staff to General Rosecrans and later he was appointed by President Lincoln a major-general of the United States Army, "for gallant and meritorious conduct in the battle of Chickamauga." In 1880 he was elected President of the United States. Four months after his inauguration, on July 2, 1881, he was shot by an assassin, at the railway station in Washington, and died September 19 of the same year. The following speech was delivered in the House of Representatives, in 1866, soon after the close of the civil war.]

GIBBON has recorded an incident which may serve to illustrate the influence of slavery in this country. The Christians of Alexandria, under the lead of Theophilus, their bishop, resolved, as a means of overthrowing Egyptian idolatry, to demolish the temple of Serapis and erect on its ruins a church in honor of the Christian martyrs.

"The colossal statue of Serapis was involved in the ruin of his temple and religion. . . . It was confidently affirmed that, if any impious hand should dare to violate the majesty of the god, the heavens and the earth should instantly return to their original chaos. An intrepid soldier, animated by zeal, and armed with a weighty battle-axe, ascended the ladder, and even the Christian multitude expected with some anxiety the event of the combat. He aimed a vigorous stroke against the cheek of Serapis: the cheek fell to the ground; the thunder was still silent, and both the heavens and the earth continued to preserve their accustomed order and tranquillity. The victorious soldier repeated his blows: the huge idol was overthrown and broken in pieces; and the limbs of Serapis were ignominiously dragged through the streets of Alexandria. His mangled carcass was burnt in the amphitheater amidst the shouts of the populace; and many persons attributed their conversion to this discovery of the impotence of their tutelar deity."

So sat slavery in this republic. The temple of the Rebellion was its sanctuary, and seven million rebels were its devoted worshipers. Our loyal millions resolved to overthrow both the temple and its idol. On the first day of January, 1863, Abraham Lincoln struck the grim god on the cheek, and the faithless and unbelieving among us expected to see the fabric of our institutions dissolve into chaos because their idol had been smitten. He struck it again; Congress and the states repeated the blow, and its unsightly carcass lies rotting in our streets. The sun shines in the heavens brighter than before. Let us remove the carcass and leave not a vestige of the monster. We shall never have done that, until we declare that all men shall be consulted in regard to the disposition of their lives, liberty, and property.

Is this Congress brave enough and virtuous enough to apply that principle to every citizen, whatever be the color of his skin? The spirit of our government demands that there shall be no rigid, horizontal strata running across our political society, through which some classes of citizen may never pass up to the surface; but it shall be rather like the ocean, where every drop can seek the surface and glisten in the sun. Until we are true enough and brave enough to declare that in this country the humblest, the lowest, the meanest of our citizens shall not be prevented from passing to the highest place he is worthy to attain, we shall never realize freedom in all its glorious meanings. I do not expect we can realize this result immediately; it may be impossible to realize it very soon; but let us keep our eyes fixed in that direction, and march toward that goal.

There is a second great fact which we must recognize, namely, that the seven million white men lately in rebellion now stand waiting to have their case adjudged—to have it determined what their status shall be in this government. Shall they be held under military power? Shall they be governed by deputies appointed by the Executive? or shall they again resume the functions of self-government in the Union?—are some of the questions growing out of this second fact.

I will proceed to state, in a few words, what seems to me necessary for the practical settlement of this question. In view of the events of the war, and the peculiar and novel situation of the parties and interests concerned; in view of the powers conferred upon us by the Constitution and the laws of war; and in view of the solemn obligations which rest upon us to maintain the freedom, security, and peace of all the citizens of the Republic—I inquire, what practical measures can we adopt best calculated to reach the desired result? It appears to me, sir, that we should take action in regard to persons and in regard to states.

In reference to persons, we must see to it that, hereafter, personal liberty and personal rights are placed in the keeping of the nation; that the right to life, liberty, and property shall be guaranteed to the citizen in reality, as it now is in the words of the Constitution, and no longer be left to the caprice of mobs or the contingencies of local legislation. If our Constitution does not now afford all the powers necessary to that end, we must ask the people to add to them. We must give full force and effect to the provision that " no person shall be deprived of life, liberty, or property without due process of law." We must make it as true in fact as it is in law, that " The citizens of each state shall be entitled to all privileges and immunities of citizens in the several states." We must make American citizenship the shield that protects every citizen, on every foot of our soil. The bill now before the House is one of the means for reaching this desirable result.

What shall be done with the states lately in rebellion? How shall we discharge our duty toward them? I shall hail with joy the day when all shall be again in their places, loyally obedient and fully represented by loyal men. Are they now entitled to admission? Are they worthy of so great confidence? To my mind, Mr. Speaker, the prima facie evidence is against them; the burden of proof rests on each of them to show whether it is fit again to enter the Federal circle in full communion of privileges. We are sitting as a general court of the nation. They are to appear at the bar of the Republic, and show cause why they should be brought in. I say the burden of proof is upon their shoulders. When we knew them last they were hurling the lightnings of war against us; they were starving our soldiers whom they held as prisoners of war in their dungeons; they were burning our towns; they were hating the Union above all things, and were bound by bloody oaths to destroy it. Thus stood the case when Congress adjourned ten months ago. They must give us proof, strong as holy writ, that they have washed their hands and are worthy to be trusted. No rumors of change; no Delphic oracle, telling beautiful tales of peace and restoration; no gentle declarations like those that we hear from the other side of this chamber, that the people of the South " have accepted the results of war," will suffice. I know they have accepted the results of war— as Buckner accepted them at Fort Donelson, as Pemberton accepted them at Vicksburg, as Lee accepted them last April in Virginia.

I hasten to say, Mr. Speaker, that I do not expect seven million men to change their hearts—to love what they hated and hate what they loved—on the issue of a battle. Nor are we set up as a judge over their beliefs, their loves, or their hatreds. Our duty is to demand that before we admit them they shall give us sufficient assurance that, whatever they may think, believe, or wish, their actions in the future shall be such as loyal men can approve. What have they done to give us that assurance?

I hold in my hand, Mr. Speaker, a proclamation issued a few days since by Benjamin G. Humphreys, late a general in the rebel army, now the so-called Governor of Mississippi, which will illustrate the spirit in which it is desired to administer the affairs of reorganized Mississippi. He says:

"Whereas, section 6 of an act of the Legislature of the State of Mississippi, entitled, ' An act authorizing the issuance of treasury notes as advance upon cotton, approved December 19, 1861,' provides that when-

ever the present blockade of the ports of the Confederate states shall be
removed .   .   .

" Now, therefore, I, Benjamin G. Humphreys, governor of the state of
Mississippi, by virtue of the authority vested in me by the constitution
and laws of said state, do hereby proclaim that the blockade of the ports
of the Confederate states has been removed ; and I do require all persons
to whom advances have been made to deliver the number of bales of
cotton upon which they have received an advance, in accordance with
their respective receipts on file in the auditor's office, within ninety days
from the date of this proclamation."

Now, what does that mean? It means that he recognizes
as valid the acts of the Legislature of the late rebel state of
Mississippi, and of the Confederate states, and bases his
proclamation thereon.   This proclamation reached us only a
few days ago.   And yet there are members of this House
who ask us to admit the representatives of Mississippi at
once !

Now, Mr. Speaker, in the neighboring state of Virginia a
law has lately been passed which declares certain negroes
vagrants, and provides that as a penalty they may be sold into
slavery.   Major-General Terry, on the twenty-fourth of January, issued his military order nullifying that law.   Is that a
civil government in which the military authorities abrogate the
laws?   Are the men who make such laws worthy of our
confidence?   I say again, the case is against them, the burden of proof is on their shoulders.   They must purge themselves before I can consent to let them in.

How stands the case in Tennessee, the least treasonable
of all?   In a letter addressed to yourself, Mr. Speaker, under
date of January 15, 1866, after pleading for the admission of
the delegation from that state, Governor Brownlow says:

" Not a man south of Tennessee should be admitted until those states
manifest less of the spirit of rebellion, and elect a more loyal set of men,
men who can take the congressional test oath, which but few of those
elected can do.

" If the removal of the Federal troops from Tennessee must necessarily
follow upon the admission of our congressional delegation to their seats,
why, then, and in that case, the loyal men of Tennessee beg to be without representatives in Congress.   But our members can be admitted, and
a military force retained sufficient to govern and control the rebellious.

I tell you, and through you all whom it may concern, that without a law to disfranchise rebels and a force to carry out the provisions of that law, this state will pass into the hands of the rebels, and a terrible state of affairs is bound to follow. Union men will be driven from the state, forced to sacrifice what they have, and seek homes elsewhere. And yet Tennessee is in a much better condition than any of the other revolted states, and affords a stronger loyal population.

"Those who suppose the South is 'reconstructed,' and that her people cheerfully accept the results of war, are fearfully deceived. The whole South is full of the spirit of rebellion, and the people are growing more bitter and insolent every day. Rebel newspapers are springing up all over the South, and speaking out in terms of bitterness and reproach against the government of the United States. These papers lead the people, and at the same time reflect their feelings and sentiments. Of the twenty-one papers in Tennessee, fourteen are decidedly rebel, out-spoken and undisguised, some of them pretending to acquiesce in the existing state of affairs. In all the vacancies occurring in our Legislature, even with our franchise law in force, rebels are invariably returned in battle fighting against the United States forces; and yet I tell you that Tennessee is in a better condition than any other revolted state.

"Others will give you a more favorable account. I cannot in justice to myself and the truth. I think I know the Southern people. I have lived fifty-eight years in the South of choice, and two at the North of necessity."

In view of these facts we await further proofs.

But, sir, there is a duty laid upon us by the Constitution. That duty is declared in these words: "The United States shall guarantee to every state in this Union a republican form of government." What does that mean? Read the twenty-first and forty-third numbers of the "Federalist," and you will understand what the fathers of the Constitution meant when they put this clause into our organic law. With wonderful foresight, amounting almost to prophecy, they appear to have foreseen just such a contingency as the one that has arisen. Madison said that an insurrection might arise too powerful to be suppressed by the local authorities, and Congress must have authority to put it down and to see that no usurping government shall be erected on the ruins of a state.

What is a republican form of government? When the Union was formed the free colored people were not a tenth of the population of any state.   Now all black men are free citizens, and "we are asked," as the lamented Henry Winter Davis has so clearly stated it, "to recognize as republican such despotisms as these: in North Carolina 631,000 citizens will ostracize 331,000 citizens; in Virginia 719,000 citizens ostracize 533,000 citizens; in Alabama 596,000 citizens will ostracize 437,000 citizens; in Louisiana 357,000 citizens will ostracize 350,000 citizens; in Mississippi 353,000 citizens will ostracize 436,000 citizens; in South Carolina 291,000 citizens will ostracize 411,000 citizens."

We are asked to guarantee all these as republican governments!   Gentlemen upon the other side of the House ask us to let such shameless despotisms as these be represented here as republican states.   I venture to assert that a more monstrous proposition was never before made to an American Congress.

I am therefore in favor of the amendment to the Constitution that passed the House yesterday, to reform the basis of representation.   I could have wished that it had been more thorough and searching in its terms.   I took it as the best we could get, but I say here, before this House, that I will never, so long as I have any voice in political affairs, rest satisfied until the way is opened by which these colored citizens, so soon as they are worthy, shall be lifted to the full rights of citizenship.   I will not be factious in my action here.   If I cannot to-day get all I desire, I will try again to-morrow, securing all that can be obtained to-day.   But so long as I have any voice or vote here, it shall aid in giving the suffrage to every citizen qualified, by intelligence, to exercise it.

Mr. Speaker, I know of nothing more dangerous to a republic than to put into its very midst four million people stripped of the rights of citizenship, robbed of the right of representation, but bound to pay taxes to the government. If they can endure it, we cannot.   The murderer is to be pitied more than the murdered man; the robber more than the robbed; and we who defraud four million citizens of their rights are injuring ourselves vastly more than we are injuring those whom we defraud.   I say that the inequality of rights before the law, which is now a part of our system,

is more dangerous to us than to the black man whom it dis-
franchises.   It is like a foreign substance in the body, a
thorn in the flesh; it will wound and disease the body politic.

I remember that this question of suffrage caused one of
the greatest civil wars in the history of Rome.   Ninety years
before Christ, when Rome was near the climax of her glory,
just before the dawn of the Augustan age, twelve peoples of
Italy, to whom the franchise was denied, rose in rebellion
against Rome; and after three years and ten months of
bloody war they compelled Rome to make her first capitulation for three hundred years.   For three hundred years the
Roman eagle had been carried triumphantly over every battle-
field; but when iron Rome, with all her pride and glory, met
men who were fighting for the right of suffrage, she was compelled to succumb, and give the ballot to the twelve peoples
to save herself from dissolution.   Let us learn wisdom from
that lesson, and extend the suffrage to people who may one
day bring us more disaster than foreign or domestic war has
yet done.

I must refer for a moment to the proposition of Mr.
Deming, who asks us to embed in the imperishable bulwarks
of the Constitution an amendment that will forbid secession
in the future.   I want no such change of the Constitution.
The rebels never had, by the Constitution, the right to
secede.   If we have not settled that question by war, it can
never be settled by a court.   The court of war is higher than
any other tribunal.   As the governor of Ohio has so well
said, "These things have been decided in the dread court
of last resort for peoples and nations.   By as much as the
shock of armed hosts is more grand than the intellectual tilt
of lawyers, as the God of battles is a more awful judge than
any earthly court, by so much does the dignity of this
contest and the finality of this decision exceed that of any
human tribunal."   I care not what provision might be in the
Constitution; if any states of this Union desire to rebel and
break up the Union, and are able to do it, they will do it in
spite of the Constitution.   All I want, therefore, is so to
amend our Constitution and administer our laws as to secure
liberty and loyalty among the citizens of the rebel states.

I am not among those who believe that all men in the

South are enemies in the eye of the law.   Their property
was "enemy's property" when it was transported and used
contrary to the laws of the government, but all are not
therefore enemies of the government.   Judge Sprague, in
the Amy Warwick case, distinctly declared that they were
only enemies in a technical sense; and in reference to
property, Justice Nelson, in 1862, declared distinctly that
men who resided within the limits of the rebellious states
were not therefore to be considered as enemies.   He distinctly declared that the question of their property being
enemy's property depended upon the use made of it.   If the
attempt was made to take and transport the property in
opposition to law, then it fell under the technical category
of enemy's property, and not otherwise.   I take it for
granted that the farm of Andrew Johnson, in Tennessee, was
never enemy's property.   If he had undertaken to violate
the revenue laws in the use of his property it would have
become such.

I remember that the long range of mountains stretching
from Western Virginia, through Tennessee and Georgia, to
the sand-hills of Mississippi, stood like a promontory in the
fiery ruin with which the Rebellion had involved the Republic.
I remember that East Tennessee, with its loyal thousands,
stood like a rock in the sea of treason.   I remember that
thirty-five thousand brave men from Tennessee stood beside
us in putting down the Rebellion.   They are not enemies of
the country, and never were; and it is cruelly wicked, by
any fiction of the law, to call them so.   To those patriotic
men of Tennessee, let me say, I want you to show that there
is behind you a loyal state government, based on the will of
loyal people, and that districts of loyal constituents have sent
you here.   When you do that, you shall have my vote in
favor of your admission.   But the burden of proof is on your
shoulders.

Mr. Speaker, let us learn a lesson from the dealings of
God with the Jewish nation.   When his chosen people, led by
the pillar of cloud and fire, had crossed the Red Sea and
traversed the gloomy wilderness with its thundering Sinai,
its bloody battles, disastrous defeats, and glorious victories
—when near the end of their perilous pilgrimage they lis-

tened to the last words of blessing and warning from their
great leader, before he was buried with immortal honors by
the angel of the Lord—when at last the victorious host,
sadly joyful, stood on the banks of the Jordan, their enemies
drowned in the sea or slain in the wilderness—they paused,
and having reviewed the history of God's dealings with them,
made solemn preparation to pass over and possess the land
of promise.   By the command of God, given through Moses
and enforced by his great successor, the ark of the covenant,
containing the tables of the law and the sacred memorial of
their pilgrimage, was borne by chosen men two thousand
cubits in advance of the people.   On the farther shore stood
Ebal and Gerizim, the mounts of cursing and blessing, from
which, in the hearing of all the people, were pronounced the
curses of God against injustice and disobedience, and his
blessing upon justice and obedience.   On the shore, between
the mountains and in the midst of the people, a monument
was erected, and on it were written the words of the law,
"to be a memorial unto the children of Israel for ever and
ever."

Let us learn wisdom from this illustrious example.   We
have passed the Red Sea of slaughter; our garments are yet
wet with its crimson spray.   We have crossed the fearful
wilderness of war, and have left our three hundred thousand
heroes to sleep beside the dead enemies of the Republic.
We have heard the voice of God amid the thunders of battle commanding us to wash our hands of iniquity—to " proclaim liberty throughout the land unto all the inhabitants
thereof."   When we spurned his counsels we were defeated,
and the gulfs of ruin yawned before us.   When we obeyed
his voice, he gave us victory.   And now, at last, we have
reached the confines of the wilderness.   Before us is the land
of promise, the land of hope, the land of peace, filled with
possibilities of greatness and glory too vast for the grasp of
the imagination.   Are we worthy to enter it?   On what condition may it be ours to enjoy and transmit it to our children's
children?   Let us pause and make deliberate and solemn
preparation.   Let us as representatives of the people, whose
servants we are, bear in advance the sacred ark of republican
liberty, with its tables of the law inscribed with the " irre-

versible guaranties" of liberty.   Let us here build a monument on which shall be written, not only the curses of the
law against treason, disloyalty, and oppression, but also an
everlasting covenant of peace and blessing with loyalty, liberty, and obedience; and all the people will say, Amen!

WILLIAM LLOYD GARRISON

ON THE DEATH OF JOHN BROWN

[William Lloyd Garrison was born in Newburyport, Mass., in 1804. He began life by editing the Newburyport "Free Press," in which appeared the earliest poems of John G. Whittier. He next engaged in newspaper ventures at Boston, and later at Bennington, Vt., until he finally joined Benjamin Lundy in the publication of an anti-slavery journal called "Genius of Universal Emancipation." Starting as a public advocate, he was imprisoned for denouncing the domestic slave trade in Baltimore; but upon his release he resumed the work of agitation both by popular lectures and by means of "The Liberator," a journal he established in Boston in 1831. In 1834 the American Anti-Slavery Society was formed in Philadelphia and adopted the principles which Garrison formulated. In 1844 the non-political wing of the anti-slavery party, headed by Mr. Garrison, went so far as to repudiate the Constitution, because under it the system of slavery found sanction. During the long anti-slavery struggle he made two visits to England, where he was enthusiastically received by the abolitionists of that country. After his death, which occurred in New York city in 1879, a bronze statue was erected to his memory by the city of Boston. The speech given here was made in Boston, in 1859, two months after John Brown was hanged near Harper's Ferry for inciting negroes to revolt against slavery.]

GOD forbid that we should any longer continue the accomplices of thieves and robbers, of men-stealers and women-whippers! We must join together in the name of freedom. As for the Union—where is it and what is it? In one half of it no man can exercise freedom of speech or the press—no man can utter the words of Washington, of Jeffersen, of Patrick Henry—except at the peril of his life; and Northern men are everywhere hunted and driven from the South, if they are supposed to cherish the sentiment of freedom in their bosoms. We are living under an awful despotism—that of a brutal slave oligarchy. And they threaten to leave us, if we do not continue to do their evil work, as we have hitherto done it, and go down in the dust before them! Would to heaven they would go! It would only be the paupers clearing out from the town, would it not? But, no, they do not mean to go; they mean to cling to you and they mean to subdue you. But will you be subdued? I tell you our work is the dissolution of this slavery-cursed Union, if we would have a fragment of our liberties left to us! Surely between freemen, who believe in exact justice and impartial liberty, and slaveholders, who are for cleaving down all human rights at a blow, it is not possible there should be any Union whatever. " How can two walk together except they be agreed ? " The slaveholder with his hands dripping in blood—will I make a compact with him? The man who plunders cradles—will I say to him: "Brother, let us walk together in unity?" The man who, to gratify his lust or his anger, scourges woman with the lash till the soil is red with her blood—will I say to him: "Give me your hand; let us form a glorious Union" ? No, never—never! There can be no union between us. "What concord hath Christ with Belial?" What union has freedom with slavery? Let us tell the inexorable and remorseless tyrants of the South that their conditions hitherto imposed upon us, whereby we are morally responsible for the existence of slavery, are horribly inhuman and wicked, and we cannot carry them out for the sake of their evil company.

By the dissolution of the Union we shall give the finishing blow to the slave system; and then God will make it possible for us to form a true, vital, enduring, all-embracing Union, from the Atlantic to the Pacific—one God to be worshiped, one Saviour to be revered, one policy to be carried out—freedom everywhere to all the people, without regard to complexion or race—and the blessing of God resting upon us all! I want to see that glorious day! Now the South is full of tribulation and terror and despair, going down to irretrievable bankruptcy, and fearing each bush an officer! Would to God it might all pass away like a hideous dream! And how easily it might be! What is it that God requires of the South, to remove every root of bitterness, to allay every fear, to fill her borders with prosperity? But one simple act of justice, without violence and convulsion, without danger and hazard. It is this: " Undo the heavy bur-

dens, break every yoke, and let the oppressed go free!"
Then shall thy light break forth as the morning, and thy
darkness shall be as the noonday.   Then shalt thou call and
the Lord shall answer; thou shalt cry, and he shall say:
"Here I am."   "And they that shall be of thee shall build
the old waste places; thou shalt raise up the foundations of
many generations; and thou shalt be called the repairer of
the breach, the restorer of paths to dwell in."

How simple and how glorious!   It is the complete solution of all the difficulties in the case.   Oh, that the South
may be wise before it is too late, and give heed to the word
of the Lord!   But whether she will hear or forbear, let us
renew our pledges to the cause of bleeding humanity, and
spare no effort to make this truly the land of the free and
the refuge of the oppressed!

> " Onward, then, ye fearless band,
>   Heart to heart, and hand to hand;
>   Yours shall be the Christian stand,
>   Or the martyr's grave."

WILLIAM EWART GLADSTONE

ON DOMESTIC AND FOREIGN AFFAIRS

[William Ewart Gladstone, four times premier of Great Britain, was born in Liverpool in 1809. He graduated at Oxford and almost immediately entered Parliament. In 1868 he became premier, after being a brilliant leader of the Opposition. He disestablished the Irish Church, carried an Irish land bill, abolished the purchase of army commissions, and reformed the suffrage. He was superseded in 1874, but returned to power in 1880, and resigned in 1885. In the next year, however, he was recalled to the premiership, only to suffer defeat later on the Home Rule Bill. He continued to lead his following in the House of Commons until 1892, when he carried the elections. His Home Rule Bill was passed by a narow margin the following year, but the House of Lords rejected the measure by a large majority. Gladstone vacated the pre-miership in 1894. In 1895 he retired, after sitting sixty years in the House of Commons. He died in 1898. The following address, relating to the domestic and foreign policy of Great Britain in his own time, was delivered at West Calder, Scotland, November 27, 1879. Mr. John Morley's masterly biography of Gladstone appeared in 1903.]

IN addressing you to-day, as in addressing like audiences assembled for a like purpose in other places of the county, I am warmed by the enthusiastic welcome which you have been pleased in every quarter and in every form to accord to me. I am, on the other hand, daunted when I recollect, first of all, what large demands I have to make on your patience; and secondly, how inadequate are my powers, and how inadequate almost any amount of time you can grant me, to set forth worthily the whole of the case which ought to be laid before you in connection with the coming election.

To-day, gentlemen, as I know that many among you are interested in the land, and as I feel that what is termed " agricultural distress " is at the present moment a topic too serious to be omitted from our consideration, I shall say some words upon the subject of that agricultural distress, and particularly, because in connection with it there have arisen in some quarters of the country proposals, which have received a countenance far beyond their deserts, to reverse or to compromise the work which it took us one whole generation to achieve, and to revert to the mischievous, obstructive, and impoverishing system of protection.   Gentlemen, I speak of agricultural distress as a matter now undoubtedly serious. Let none of us withhold our sympathy from the farmer, the cultivator of the soil, in the struggle he has to undergo.   His struggle is a struggle of competition with the United States. But I do not fully explain the case when I say the United States.   It is not with the entire United States, it is with the Western portion of these states—that portion remote from the seaboard; and I wish in the first place, gentlemen, to state to you all a fact of very great interest and importance, as it seems to me, relating to and defining the point at which the competition of the Western states of America is most severely felt.   I have in my hand a letter received recently from one well known, and honorably known, in Scotland—Mr. Lyon Playfair, who has recently been a traveller in the United States, and who, as you well know, is as well qualified as any man upon earth for accurate and careful investigation.   The point, gentlemen, at which the competition of the Western states of America is most severely felt is in the Eastern states of America.   Whatever be agricultural distress in Scotland, whatever it be, where undoubtedly it is more felt, in England, it is greater by much in the Eastern states of America.   In the states of New England the soil has been to some extent exhausted by careless methods of agriculture, and these, gentlemen, are the greatest of all the enemies with which the farmer has to contend.

But the foundation of the statement I make, that the Eastern states of America are those that most feel the competition of the West, is to be found in facts—in this fact above all, that not only they are not in America, as we are here, talking about the shortness of the annual returns, and in some places having much said on the subject of rents, and of temporary remission or of permanent reduction.   That is not the state of things; they have actually got to this point, that the capital values of land, as tested by sales in the market, have undergone an enormous diminution. Now I will tell you something that actually happened, on the authority of my friend Mr. Playfair. I will tell you something that has happened in one of the New England states—not, recollect, in a desert or a remote country—in an old cultivated country, and near one of the towns of these states, a town that has the honorable name of Wellesley.

Mr. Playfair tells me this: Three weeks ago—that is to say, about the first of this month, so you will see my information is tolerably recent—three weeks ago a friend of Mr. Playfair bought a farm near Wellesley for $33 an acre, for £6 12s. an acre—agricultural land, remember, in an old settled country. That is the present condition of agricultural property in the old states of New England. I think by the simple recital of that fact I have tolerably well established my case, for you have not come in England, and you have not come in Scotland, to the point at which agricultural land is to be had—not wild land, but improved and old cultivated land—is to be had for the price of £6 12s. an acre. He mentions that this is by no means a strange case, an isolated case, that it fairly represented the average transactions that have been going on; and he says that in that region the ordinary price of agricultural land at the present time is from $20 to $50 an acre, or from £4 to £10. In New York the soil is better, and the population is greater; but even in the state of New York land ranges for agricultural purposes from $50 to $100, that is to say, from £10 to £20 an acre.

I think those of you, gentlemen, who are farmers will perhaps derive some comfort from perceiving that if the pressure here is heavy the pressure elsewhere and the pressure nearer to the seat of this very abundant production is greater and far greater still.

It is most interesting to consider, however, what this pressure is. There has been developed in the astonishing progressive power of the United States—there has been developed a faculty of producing corn for the subsistence of man, with a rapidity and to an extent unknown in the experience of mankind. There is nothing like it in history. Do not let us conceal, gentlemen, from ourselves the fact; I

shall not stand the worse with any of you who are farmers if
I at once avow that this greater and comparatively immense
abundance of the prime article of subsistence for mankind is
a great blessing vouchsafed by Providence to mankind. In
part I believe that the cheapness has been increased by
special causes. The lands from which the great abundance
of American wheat comes are very thinly peopled as yet.
They will become more thickly peopled, and as they become
more thickly peopled a larger proportion of their produce
will be wanted for home consumption and less of it will come
to you, and at a higher price. Again, if we are rightly
informed, the price of American wheat has been unnaturally
reduced by the extraordinary depression, in recent times, of
trade in America, and especially of the mineral trades, upon
which many railroads are dependent in America, and with
which these railroads are connected in America in a degree
and manner that in this country we know but little of. With
a revival of trade in America it is to be expected that the
freights of corn will increase, and all other freights, because
the employment of the railroads will be a great deal more
abundant, and they will not be content to carry corn at nominal rates. In some respects, therefore, you may expect a
mitigation of the pressure, but in other respects it is likely
to continue.

Nay, the prime minister is reported as having not long
ago said—and he ought to have the best information on this
subject, nor am I going to impeach in the main what he
stated—he gave it to be understood that there was about to
be a development of corn production in Canada which would
entirely throw into the shade this corn production in the
United States. Well, that certainly was very cold comfort,
as far as the British agriculturist is concerned, because he
did not say—he could not say—that the corn production of
the United States was to fall off, but there was to be added
an enormous corn production from Manitoba, the great
province which forms now a part of the Canada Dominion.
There is no doubt, I believe, that it is a correct expectation
that vast or very large quantities of corn will proceed from that
province, and therefore we have to look forward to a state of
things in which, for a considerable time to come, large quan-

tities of wheat will be forthcoming from America, probably larger quantities, and perhaps frequently at lower prices than those at which the corn-producing and corn-exporting districts of Europe have commonly been able to supply us. Now that I believe to be, gentlemen, upon the whole, not an unfair representation of the state of things.

How are you to meet that state of things? What are your fair claims? I will tell you. In my opinion your fair claims are, in the main, two. One is to be allowed to purchase every article that you require in the cheapest market, and have no needless burden laid upon anything that comes to you and can assist you in the cultivation of your land. But that claim has been conceded and fulfilled.

I do not know whether there is an object, an instrument, a tool of any kind, an auxiliary of any kind, that you want for the business of the farmer, which you do not buy at this moment in the cheapest market. But beyond that, you want to be relieved from every unjust and unnecessary legislative restraint. I say every unnecessary legislative restraint, because taxation, gentlemen, is unfortunately a restraint upon us all, but we cannot say that it is always unnecessary, and we cannot say that it is always unjust. Yesterday I ventured to state—and I will therefore not now return to the subject —a number of matters connected with the state of legislation in which it appears to me to be of vital importance, both to the agricultural interest and to the entire community, that the occupiers and cultivators of the land of this country should be relieved from restraints under the operation of which they now suffer considerably. Beyond those two great heads, gentlemen, what you have to look to, I believe, is your own energy, your own energy of thought and action, and your care not to undertake to pay rents greater than, in reasonable calculation, you think you can afford. I am by no means sure, though I speak subject to the correction of higher authority—I am by no means sure that in Scotland within the last fifteen or twenty years something of a speculative character has not entered into rents, and particularly, perhaps, into the rents of hill farms. I remember hearing of the augmentations which were taking place, I believe, all over Scotland—I verified the fact in a number of counties—

about twelve or fourteen years ago, in the rents of hill farms which I confess impressed me with the idea that the high prices that were then ruling, and ruling increasingly from year to year, for meat and wool, were perhaps for once leading the wary and shrewd Scottish agriculturist a little beyond the mark in the rents he undertook to pay. But it is not this only which may press. It is, more broadly, in a serious and manful struggle that you are engaged, in which you will have to exert yourselves to the utmost, in which you will have a right to claim everything that the legislature can do for you; and I hope it may perhaps possibly be my privilege and honor to assist in procuring for you some of those provisions of necessary liberation from restraint; but beyond that, it is your own energies, of thought and action, to which you will have to trust.

Now, gentlemen, having said thus much, my next duty is to warn you against quack remedies, against delusive remedies, against the quack remedies that there are plenty of people found to propose, not so much in Scotland as in England; for, gentlemen, from Mid-Lothian at present we are speaking to England as well as to Scotland. Let me give a friendly warning from this northern quarter to the agriculturist of England not to be deluded by those who call themselves his friends in a degree of special and superior excellence, and who have been too much given to delude him in other times; not to be deluded into hoping relief from sources from which it can never come. Now, gentlemen, there are three of these remedies. The first of them, gentlemen, I will not call a quack remedy at all, but I will speak of it notwithstanding in the tone of rational and dispassionate discussion. I am not now so much upon the controversial portion of the land question—a field which, Heaven knows, is wide enough—as I am upon matters of deep and universal interest to us in our economic and social condition. There are some gentlemen, and there are persons for whom I for one have very great respect, who think that the difficulties of our agriculture may be got over by a fundamental change in the land-holding system of this country.

I do not mean, now pray observe, a change as to the law

of entail and settlement, and all those restraints which, I hope, were tolerably well disposed of yesterday at Dalkeith; but I mean those who think that if you can cut up the land, or a large part of it, into a multitude of small properties, that of itself will solve the difficulty, and start everybody on a career of prosperity.

Now, gentlemen, to a proposal of that kind, I, for one, am not going to object upon the ground that it would be inconsistent with the privileges of landed proprietors. In my opinion, if it is known to be for the welfare of the community at large, the legislature is perfectly entitled to buy out the landed proprietors. It is not intended probably to confiscate the property of a landed proprietor more than the property of any other man; but the state is perfectly entitled, if it please, to buy out the landed proprietors as it may think fit, for the purpose of dividing the property into small lots. I don't wish to recommend it, because I will show you the doubts that, to my mind, hang about that proposal; but I admit that in principle no objection can be taken. Those persons who possess large portions of the spaces of the earth are not altogether in the same position as the possessors of mere personalty; that personalty does not impose the same limitations upon the action and industry of man, and upon the well-being of the community, as does the possession of land; and, therefore, I freely own that compulsory expropriation is a thing which for an adequate public object is in itself admissible and so far sound in principle.

Now, gentlemen, this idea about small proprietors, however, is one which very large bodies and parties in this country treat with the utmost contempt; and they are accustomed to point to France, and say: "Look at France." In France you have got 5,000,000—I am not quite sure whether it is 5,000,000 or even more; I do not wish to be beyond the mark in anything—you have 5,000,000 of small proprietors, and you do not produce in France as many bushels of wheat per acre as you do in England. Well, now I am going to point out to you a very remarkable fact with regard to the condition of France. I will not say that France produces—for I believe it does not produce—as many bushels of wheat per acre as England does, but I should like to know whether the wheat of France is produced mainly upon the small properties of France. I believe that the wheat of France is produced mainly upon the large properties of France, and I have not any doubt that the large properties of England are, upon the whole, better cultivated and more capital is put into the land than in the large properties of France. But it is fair that justice should be done to what is called the peasant proprietary. Peasant proprietary is an excellent thing, if it can be had, in many points of view. It interests an enormous number of the people in the soil of the country, and in the stability of its institutions and its laws. But now look at the effect that it has upon the progressive value of the land—and I am going to give you a very few figures which I will endeavor to relieve from all complication, lest I should unnecessarily weary you. But what will you think when I tell you that the agricultural value of France—the taxable income derived from the land, and therefore the income of the proprietors of that land—has advanced during our lifetime far more rapidly than that of England? When I say England I believe the same thing is applicable to Scotland, certainly to Ireland; but I shall take England for my test, because the difference between England and Scotland, though great, does not touch the principle; and because it so happens that we have some means of illustration from former times for England which are not equally applicable for all the three kingdoms.

Here is the state of the case. I will not go back any further than 1851. I might go back much further; it would only strengthen my case. But for 1851 I have a statement made by French official authority of the agricultural income of France, as well as the income of other real property, viz., houses. In 1851 the agricultural income of France was £76,000,000. It was greater in 1851 than the whole income from land and houses together had been in 1821. This is a tolerable evidence of progress; but I will not enter into the detail of it, because I have no means of dividing the two—the house income and the land income—for the earlier year, namely, 1821. In 1851 it was £76,000,000—the agricultural income; and in 1864 it had risen from £76,000,000 to £106,000,000. That is to say, in the space of thirteen years the increase of agricultural values in France—annual values—was no less than forty per cent., or three per cent. per annum. Now I go to England. Wishing to be quite accurate, I shall limit myself to that with respect to which we have positive figures. In England the agricultural income in 1813–14 was £37,000,000; in 1842 it was £42,000,000, and that year is the one I will take as my starting-point. I have given you the years 1851 to 1864 in France. I could only give you those thirteen years with a certainty that I was not misleading you, and I believe I have kept within the mark. I believe I might have put my case more strongly for France.

In 1842, then, the agricultural income of England was £42,000,000; in 1876 it was £52,000,000—that is to say, while the agricultural income of France increased forty per cent. in thirteen years, the agricultural income of England increased twenty per cent. in thirty-four years. The increase in France was three per cent. per annum; the increase in England was about one-half or three-fifths per cent. per annum. Now, gentlemen, I wish this justice to be done to a system where peasant proprietary prevails. It is of great importance. And will you allow me, you who are Scotch agriculturists, to assure you that I speak to you not only with the respect which is due from a candidate to a constituency, but with the deference which is due from a man knowing very little of agricultural matters to those who know a great deal? And there is one point at which the considerations that I have been opening up, and this rapid increase of the value of the soil in France, bear upon our discussions. Let me try to explain it. I believe myself that the operation of economic laws is what in the main dictates the distribution of landed property in this country. I doubt if those economic laws will allow it to remain cut up into a multitude of small properties like the small properties of France. As to small holdings, I am one of those who attach the utmost value to them. I say that in the Lothians—I say that in the portion of the country where almost beyond any other large holdings prevail—in some parts of which large holdings exclusively are to be found—I attach the utmost value to them. But it is not on that point I am going to dwell, for we have no time for what is unnecessary.   What I do wish very respectfully to submit to you, gentlemen, is this.   When you see this vast increase of the agricultural value of France, you know at once it is perfectly certain that it has not been upon the large properties of France, which, if anything, are inferior in cultivation to the large properties of England.   It has been upon those very peasant-properties which some people are so ready to decry.   What do the peasant-properties mean?   They mean what, in France, is called the small cultivation—that is to say, cultivation of superior articles, pursued upon a small scale—cultivation of flowers, cultivation of trees and shrubs, cultivation of fruits of every kind, and all that, in fact, which rises above the ordinary character of farming produce, and rather approaches the produce of the gardener.

Gentlemen, I cannot help having this belief, that, among other means of meeting the difficulties in which we may be placed, our destiny is that a great deal more attention will have to be given than heretofore by the agriculturalists of England, and perhaps even by the agriculturalists of Scotland, to the production of fruits, of vegetables, of flowers, of all that variety of objects which are sure to find a market in a rich and wealthy country like this, but which have hitherto been consigned almost exclusively to garden production. You know that in Scotland, in Aberdeenshire—and I am told also in Perthshire—a great example of this kind has been set in the cultivation of strawberries—the cultivation of strawberries is carried on over hundreds of acres at once.   I am ashamed, gentlemen, to go further into this matter, as if I was attempting to instruct you.   I am sure you will take my hint as a respectful hint—I am sure you will take it as a friendly hint.   I do not believe that the large properties of this country, generally or universally, can or will be broken up into small ones.   I do not believe that the land of this country will be owned, as a general rule, by those who cultivate it.   I believe we shall continue to have, as we have had, a class of landlords and a class of cultivators, but I most earnestly desire to see—not only to see the relations of those classes to one another harmonious and sound, their interests never brought into conflict; but I desire to see both flourish-

WILLIAM EWART GLADSTONE

ing and prospering, and the soil of my country producing, as far as may be, under the influence of capital and skill, every variety of product which may give an abundant livelihood to those who live upon it. I say, therefore, gentlemen, and I say it with all respect, I hope for a good deal from the small culture, the culture in use among the small proprietors of France; but I do not look to a fundamental change in the distribution of landed property in this country as a remedy for agricultural distress.

But I go on to another remedy which is proposed, and I do it with a great deal less of respect; nay, I now come to the region of what I have presumed to call quack remedies. There is a quack remedy which is called Reciprocity, and this quack remedy is under the special protection of quack doctors, and among the quack doctors, I am sorry to say, there appear to be some in very high station indeed; and if I am rightly informed, no less a person than her Majesty's Secretary of State for Foreign Affairs has been moving about the country, and indicating a very considerable expectation that possibly by reciprocity agricultural distress will be relieved. Let me test, gentlemen, the efficacy of this quack remedy for your, in some places, agricultural pressure, and generally distress—the pressure that has been upon you, the struggle in which you are engaged. Pray watch its operation; pray note what is said by the advocates of reciprocity. They always say, "We are the soundest and best free-traders. We recommend reciprocity because it is the truly effectual method of bringing about free trade. At present America imposes enormous duties upon our cotton goods and upon our iron goods. Put reciprocity into play, and America will become a free-trading country". Very well, gentlemen, how would that operate upon you agriculturists in particular? Why, it would operate thus: If your condition is to be regretted in certain particulars, and capable of amendment, I beg you to cast an eye of sympathy upon the condition of the American agriculturist. It has been very well said, and very truly said—though it is a smart antithesis—the American agriculturist has got to buy everything that he wants at prices which are fixed in Washington by the legislation of America, but he has got to sell everything that he produces

at prices which are fixed in Liverpool—fixed by the free
competition of the world.   How would you like that, gentlemen—to have protective prices to pay for everything that
you use—for your manures, for your animals, for your implements, for all your farming stock, and at the same time to
have to sell what you produce in the free and open market
of the world?   But bring reciprocity into play, and then, if
reciprocity doctors are right, the Americans will remove all
their protective duties, and the American farmer, instead of
producing, as he does now, under the disadvantage, and the
heavy disadvantage, of having to pay protective prices for
everything that constitutes his farming stock, will have all
his tools, and implements, and manures, and everything else
purchased in the free, open market of the world at free-trade
prices.   So he will be able to produce his corn to compete
with you even cheaper than he does now.   So much for
reciprocity considered as a cure for distress.   I am not
going to consider it now in any other point of view.

But, gentlemen, there is another set of men who are
bolder still, and who are not for reciprocity; who are not
content with that milder form of quackery, but who recommend a reversion, pure and simple, to what I may fairly call,
I think, the exploded doctrine of protection.   And upon
this, gentlemen, I think it necessary, if you will allow me, to
say to you a few words, because it is a very serious matter,
and it is all the more serious because her Majesty's government—I do not scruple to say—are coquetting with the subject in a way which is not right.   They are tampering with
it; they are playing with it.   A protective speech was made
in the House of Commons, in a debate last year, by Mr.
Chaplin, on the part of what is called " the agricultural interest."   Mr. Chaplin did not use the word " protection," but
what he did say was this : he said he demanded that the malt
tax should be abolished, and the revenue supplied by a tax
upon foreign barley or some other foreign commodity.
Well, if he has a measure of that kind in his pocket, I don't
ask him to affix the word " protection " to it.   I can do that for
myself.   Not a word of rebuke, gentlemen, was uttered to
the doctrines of Mr. Chaplin.   He was complimented upon
the ability of his speech and the well-chosen terms of his

motion.   Some of the members of her Majesty's government
—the minor members of her Majesty's government—the
humbler luminaries of that great constellation—have been
going about the country and telling their farming constituents that they think the time has come when a return to protection might very wisely be tried.   But, gentlemen, what
delusions have been practiced upon the unfortunate British
farmer!   When we go back for twenty years, what is now
called the Tory party was never heard of as the Tory party.
It was always heard of as the party of protection.   As long
as the chiefs of the protective party were not in office, as
long as they were irresponsible, they recommended themselves to the good-will of the farmer as protectionists, and
said they would set him up and put his interests on a firm
foundation through protection.   We brought them into office
in the year 1852.   I gave with pleasure a vote that assisted
to bring them into office.   I thought bringing them into
office was the only way of putting their professions to the
test.   They came into office, and before they had been six
months in office they had thrown protection to the winds.
And that is the way in which the British farmer's expectations are treated by those who claim for themselves in the
special sense the designation of his friends.

It is exactly the same with the malt tax.   Gentlemen,
what is done with the malt tax?   The malt tax is held by
them to be a great grievance on the British farmer.   Whenever a Liberal government is in office, from time to time
they have a great muster from all parts of the country to
vote for the abolition of the malt tax.   But when a Tory
government comes into office, the abolition of the malt tax
is totally forgotten; and we have now had six years of a
Tory government without a word said, as far as I can recollect—and my friend in the chair could correct me if I were
wrong—without a motion made, or a vote taken, on the subject of the malt tax.   The malt tax, great and important as
it is, is small in reference to protection.   Gentlemen, it is a
very serious matter indeed if we ought to go back to protection, because how did we come out of protection to free
trade?   We came out of it by a struggle which in its crisis
threatened to convulse the country, which occupied Parlia-

ments, upon which elections turned, which took up twenty years of our legislative life, which broke up parties. In a word, it effected a change so serious, that if, after the manner in which we effected that change, it be right that we should go back upon our steps, then all I can say is, that we must lose that which has ever been one of the most honorable distinctions of British legislation in the general estimation of the world—that British legislation, if it moves slowly, always moves in one direction—that we never go back upon our steps.

But are we such children that, after spending twenty years—as I may say from 1840 to 1860—in breaking down the huge fabric of protection, in 1879 we are seriously to set about building it up again? If that be right, gentlemen, let it be done, but it will involve on our part a most humiliating confession. In my opinion it is not right. Protection, however, let me point out, now is asked for in two forms, and I am next going to quote Lord Beaconsfield for the purpose of expressing my concurrence with him.

Mostly, I am bound to say, as far as my knowledge goes, protection has not been asked for by the agricultural interest, certainly not by the farmers of Scotland.

It has been asked for by certain injudicious cliques and classes of persons connected with other industries—connected with some manufacturing industries. They want to have duties laid upon manufactures.

But here Lord Beaconsfield said—and I cordially agree with him—that he would be no party to the institution of a system in which protection was to be given to manufactures, and to be refused to agriculture.

That one-sided protection I deem to be totally intolerable, and I reject it even at the threshold as unworthy of a word of examination or discussion.

But let us go on to two-sided protection, and see whether that is any better—that is to say, protection in the shape of duties on manufactures, and protection in the shape of duties upon corn, duties upon meat, duties upon butter and cheese and eggs, and everything that can be produced from the land. Now, gentlemen, in order to see whether we can here find a remedy for our difficulties, I prefer to speculation and mere abstract argument the method of reverting to experience. Experience will give us very distinct lessons upon this matter. We have the power, gentlemen, of going back to the time when protection was in full and unchecked force, and of examining the effect which it produced upon the wealth of the country. How, will you say, do I mean to test that wealth? I mean to test that wealth by the exports of the country, and I will tell you why: because your prosperity depends upon the wealth of your customers—that is to say, upon their capacity to buy what you produce. And who are your customers? Your customers are the industrial population of the country, who produce what we export and send all over the world. Consequently, when exports increase, your customers are doing a large business, are growing wealthy, are putting money in their pockets, and are able to take that money out of their pockets in order to fill their stomachs with what you produce. When, on the contrary, exports do not increase, your customers are poor, your prices go down, as you have felt within the last few years, in the price of meat, for example, and in other things, and your condition is proportionally depressed. Now, gentlemen, down to the year 1842 no profane hand had been laid upon the august fabric of protection. For recollect that the farmers' friends always told us that it was a very august fabric, and that if you pulled it down it would involve the ruin of the country. That, you remember, was the commonplace of every Tory speech delivered from a country hustings to a farming constituency. But before 1842 another agency had come into force, which gave new life in a very considerable degree to the industry of the country, and that was the agency of railways, of improved communication, which shortened distance and cheapened transit, and effected in that way an enormous economical gain and addition to the wealth of the country. Therefore, in order to see what we owe to our friend protection, I won't allow that friend to take credit for what was done by railways in improving the wealth of the country. I will go to the time when I may say there were virtually no railways—that is the time before 1830. Now, gentlemen, here are the official facts which I shall lay before you in the simplest form, and, remember, using round numbers.   I do that because, although round numbers cannot be absolutely accurate, they are easy for the memory to take in, and they involve no material error, no falsification of the case.   In the year 1800, gentlemen, the exports of British produce were thirty-nine and a half millions sterling in value. The population at that time—no, I won't speak of the exact figure of the population, because I have not got it for the three kingdoms.   In the years 1826 to 1830—that is, after a medium period of eight-and-twenty years—the average of our exports for those five years, which had been thirty-nine and a half millions in 1800, was thirty-seven millions.   It is fair to admit that in 1800 the currency was somewhat less sound, and therefore I am quite willing to admit that the thirty-seven millions probably meant as much in value as the thirty-nine and a half millions; but substantially, gentlemen, the trade of the country was stationary, practically stationary, under protection.   The condition of the people grew, if possible, rather worse than better.   The wealth of the country was nearly stationary.   But now I show you what protection produced; that it made no addition, it gave no onward movement to the profits of those who are your customers.   But on these profits you depend: because, under all circumstances, gentlemen, this, I think, nobody will dispute—a considerable portion of what the Englishman or the Scotchman produces will, some way or other, find its way down his throat.

What has been the case, gentlemen, since we cast off the superstition of protection, since we discarded the imposture of protection?   I will tell you what happened between 1830, when there were no railways, and 1842, when no change, no important change, had been made as to protection, but when the railway system was in operation, hardly in Scotland, but in England to a very great extent, to a very considerable extent upon the main lines of communication.   The exports which in 1830 had been somewhere about £37,000,000, between 1840 and 1842 showed an average amount of £50,000,000.   That seems due, gentlemen, to the agency of railways; and I wish you to bear in mind the increasing benefit now derived from that agency, in order that I may not claim any undue credit for freedom of trade. From 1842, gentlemen, onward, the successive stages of free trade began;

in 1842, in 1845, in 1846, in 1853, and again in 1860, the
large measures were carried which have completely reformed
your customs tariff, and reduced it from a taxation of twelve
hundred articles to a taxation of, I think, less than twelve.

Now, under the system of protection, the export trade
of the country, the wealth and the power of the manufacturing and producing classes to purchase your agricultural
products, did not increase at all. In the time when railways
began to be in operation, but before free trade, the exports
of the country increased, as I have shown you, by £13,000,-
000 in somewhere about thirteen years—that is to say, taking it roughly, at the rate of £1,000,000 a year.

But since 1842, and down to the present time, we have
had, along with railways, always increasing their benefits—
we have had the successive adoption of free-trade measures;
and what has been the state of the export business of the
country? It has risen in this degree, that that which from
1840 to 1842 averaged £50,000,000, from 1873 to 1878
averaged £218,000,000. Instead of increasing, as it had
done between 1830 and 1842, when railways only were at
work, at the rate of £1,000,000 a year—instead of remaining stagnant as it did when the country was under protection
pure and simple, with no augmentation of the export trade
to enlarge the means of those who buy your products, the
total growth in a period of thirty-five years was no less than
£168,000,000, or, taking it roughly, a growth in the export
trade of the country to the extent of between £4,000,000 and
£5,000,000 a year. But, gentlemen, you know the fact.
You know very well that while restriction was in force you
did not get the prices that you have been getting for the last
twenty years. The price of wheat has been much the same
as it had been before. The price of oats is a better price
than was to be had on the average of protective times. But
the price, with the exception of wheat, of almost every agricultural commodity, the price of wool, the price of meat, the
price of cheese, the price of everything that the soil produces, has been largely increased in a market free and open
to the world; because, while the artificial advantage which
you got through protection, as it was supposed to be an
advantage, was removed, you were brought into that free and

open market, and the energy of free trade so enlarged the buying capacity of your customers, that they were willing and able to give you, and did give you, a great deal more for your meat, your wool, and your products in general, than you would ever have got under the system of protection. Gentlemen, if that be true—and it cannot, I believe, be impeached or impugned—if that be true, I don't think I need further discuss the matter, especially when so many other matters have to be discussed.

I will therefore ask you again to cross the seas with me. I see that the time is flying onward, and, gentlemen, it is very hard upon you to be so much vexed upon the subject of policy abroad. You think generally, and I think, that your domestic affairs are quite enough to call for all your attention. There was a saying of an ancient Greek orator, who, unfortunately, very much undervalued what we generally call the better portion of the community—namely, women; he made a very disrespectful observation, which I am going to quote, not for the purpose of concurring with it, but for the purpose of an illustration.

Pericles, the great Athenian statesman, said with regard to women, their greatest merit was to be never heard of.

Now, what Pericles untruly said of women, I am very much disposed to say of foreign affairs—their great merit would be to be never heard of. Unfortunately, instead of being never heard of, they are always heard of, and you hear almost of nothing else; and I can't promise you, gentlemen, that you will be relieved from this everlasting din, because the consequences of an unwise meddling with foreign affairs are consequences that will for some time necessarily continue to trouble you, and that will find their way to your pockets in the shape of increased taxation.

Gentlemen, with that apology I ask you again to go with me beyond the seas. And as I wish to do full justice, I will tell you what I think to be the right principles of foreign policy; and then, as far as your patience and my strength will permit, I will, at any rate for a short time, illustrate those right principles by some of the departures from them that have taken place of late years. I first give you, gentlemen, what I think the right principles of foreign policy.

The first thing is to foster the strength of the empire by just legislation and economy at home, thereby producing two of the great elements of national power—namely, wealth, which is a physical element, and union and contentment, which are moral elements—and to reserve the strength of the empire, to reserve the expenditure of that strength, for great and worthy occasions abroad. Here is my first principle of foreign policy: good government at home.

My second principle of foreign policy is this: that its aim ought to be to preserve to the nations of the world—and especially, were it but for shame, when we recollect the sacred name we bear as Christians, especially to the Christian nations of the world—the blessings of peace. That is my second principle.

My third principle is this: Even, gentlemen, when you do a good thing, you may do it in so bad a way that you may entirely spoil the beneficial effect; and if we were to make ourselves the apostles of peace in the sense of conveying to the minds of other nations that we thought ourselves more entitled to an opinion on that subject than they are, or to deny their rights—well, very likely we should destroy the whole value of our doctrines. In my opinion the third sound principle is this: to strive to cultivate and maintain, aye, to the very uttermost, what is called the concert of Europe; to keep the powers of Europe in union together. And why? Because by keeping all in union together you neutralize, and fetter, and bind up the selfish aims of each. I am not here to flatter either England or any of them. They have selfish aims, as, unfortunately, we in late years have too sadly shown that we too have had selfish aims; but their common action is fatal to selfish aims. Common action means common objects; and the only objects for which you can unite together the powers of Europe are objects connected with the common good of them all. That, gentlemen, is my third principle of foreign policy.

My fourth principle is: that you should avoid needless and entangling engagements. You may boast about them, you may brag about them, you may say you are procuring consideration for the country. You may say that an Englishman can now hold up his head among the nations.

You may say that he is not in the hands of a Liberal ministry, who thought of nothing but pounds, shillings, and pence. But what does all this come to, gentlemen? It comes to this, that you are increasing your engagements without increasing your strength; and if you increase engagements without increasing strength, you diminish strength, you abolish strength; you really reduce the empire and do not increase it. You render it less capable of performing its duties; you render it an inheritance less precious to hand on to future generations.

My fifth principle is this, gentlemen: to acknowledge the equal rights of all nations. You may sympathize with one nation more than another. Nay, you must sympathize in certain circumstances with one nation more than another. You sympathize most with those nations, as a rule, with which you have the closest connection in language, in blood, and in religion, or whose circumstances at the time seem to give the strongest claim to sympathy. But in point of right all are equal, and you have no right to set up a system under which one of them is to be placed under moral suspicion or espionage, or to be made the constant subject of invective. If you do that, but especially if you claim for yourself a superiority, a pharisaical superiority over the whole of them, then I say you may talk about your patriotism if you please, but you are a misjudging friend of your country, and in undermining the basis of the esteem and respect of other people for your country you are in reality inflicting the severest injury upon it. I have now given you, gentlemen, five principles of foreign policy. Let me give you a sixth, and then I have done.

And that sixth is: that in my opinion foreign policy, subject to all the limitations that I have described, the foreign policy of England should always be inspired by the love of freedom. There should be a sympathy with freedom, a desire to give it scope, founded not upon visionary ideas, but upon the long experience of many generations within the shores of this happy isle, that in freedom you lay the firmest foundations both of loyalty and order; the firmest foundations for the development of individual character, and the best provision for the happiness of the nation at large. In the foreign policy of this country the name of Canning ever will be honored. The name of Russell ever will be honored. The name of Palmerston ever will be honored by those who recollect the erection of the kingdom of Belgium and the union of the disjoined provinces of Italy. It is that sympathy, not a sympathy with disorder, but, on the contrary, founded upon the deepest and most profound love of order —it is that sympathy which in my opinion ought to be the very atmosphere in which a foreign secretary of England ought to live and to move.

Gentlemen, it is impossible for me to do more to-day than to attempt very slight illustrations of those principles. But in uttering those principles I have put myself in a position in which no one is entitled to tell me—you will hear me out in what I say—that I simply object to the acts of others, and lay down no rules of action myself. I am not only prepared to show what are the rules of action which in my judgment are the right rules, but I am prepared to apply them, nor will I shrink from their application. I will take, gentlemen, the name which, most of all others, is associated with suspicion, and with alarm, and with hatred in the minds of many Englishmen. I will take the name of Russia, and at once I will tell you what I think about Russia, and how I am prepared as a member of Parliament to proceed in anything that respects Russia. You have heard me, gentlemen, denounced sometimes, I believe, as a Russian spy, sometimes as a Russian agent, sometimes as perhaps a Russian fool, which is not so bad, but still not very desirable. But, gentlemen, when you come to evidence, the worst thing that I have ever seen quoted out of any speech or writing of mine about Russia is that I did one day say, or I believe I wrote, these terrible words: I recommended Englishmen to imitate Russia in her good deeds. Was not that a terrible proposition? I cannot recede from it. I think we ought to imitate Russia in her good deeds, and if the good deeds be few, I am sorry for it, but I am not the less disposed on that account to imitate them when they come. I will now tell you what I think just about Russia.

I make it one of my charges against the foreign policy of her Majesty's government, that, while they have completely estranged from this country—let us not conceal the fact—the feelings of a nation of eighty millions, for that is the number of the subjects of the Russian empire—while they have contrived completely to estrange the feelings of that nation, they have aggrandized the power of Russia. They have aggrandized the power of Russia in two ways, which I will state with perfect distinctness. They have augmented her territory. Before the European powers met at Berlin, Lord Salisbury met with Count Schouvaloff, and Lord Salisbury agreed that, unless he could convince Russia by his arguments in the open Congress of Berlin, he would support the restoration to the despotic power of Russia of that country north of the Danube which at the moment constituted a portion of the free state of Roumania. Why, gentlemen, what had been done by the Liberal government, which forsooth, attended to nothing but pounds, shillings, and pence? The Liberal government had driven Russia back from the Danube. Russia, which was a Danubian power before the Crimean War, lost this position on the Danube by the Crimean War; and the Tory government, which has been incensing and inflaming you against Russia, yet nevertheless, by binding itself beforehand to support, when the judgment was taken, the restoration of that country to Russia, has aggrandized the power of Russia.

It further aggrandized the power of Russia in Armenia; but I would not dwell upon that matter if it were not for a very strange circumstance. You know that an Armenian province was given to Russia after the war, but about that I own to you I have very much less feeling of objection. I have objected from the first, vehemently, and in every form, to the granting of territory on the Danube to Russia, and carrying back the population of a certain country from a free state to a despotic state; but with regard to the transfer of a certain portion of the Armenian people from the government of Turkey to the government of Russia, I must own that I contemplate that transfer with much greater equanimity. I have no fear myself of the territorial extensions of Russia, in Asia, no fear of them whatever. I think the fears are no better than an old woman's fears. And I don't wish to encourage her aggressive tendencies in Asia, or anywhere

else. But I admit it may be, and probably is, the case that
there is some benefit attending upon the transfer of a portion of Armenia from Turkey to Russia.

But here is a very strange fact. You know that that
portion of Armenia includes the port of Batoum. Lord
Salisbury has lately stated to the country that, by the Treaty
of Berlin, the port of Batoum is to be only a commercial
port. If the Treaty of Berlin stated that it was to be only a
commercial port, which of course could not be made an
arsenal, that fact would be very important. But happily,
gentlemen, although treaties are concealed from us nowadays
as long and as often as is possible, the Treaty of Berlin is an
open instrument. We can consult it for ourselves; and
when we consult the Treaty of Berlin, we find it states
that Batoum shall be essentially a commercial port, but
not that it shall be only a commercial port. Why, gentlemen, Leith is essentially a commercial port, but there is
nothing to prevent the people of this country, if in their
wisdom or their folly they should think fit, from constituting
Leith as a great naval arsenal or fortification; and there is
nothing to prevent the Emperor of Russia, while leaving to
Batoum a character that shall be essentially commercial, from
joining with that another character that is not in the slightest
degree excluded by the treaty, and making it as much as he
pleases a port of military defense. Therefore, I challenge
the assertion of Lord Salisbury; and as Lord Salisbury is
fond of writing letters to the " Times " to bring the Duke of
Argyll to book, he perhaps will be kind enough to write
another letter to the " Times," and tell in what clause of the
Treaty of Berlin he finds it written that the port of Batoum
shall be only a commercial port. For the present, I simply
leave it on record that he has misrepresented the Treaty of
Berlin.

With respect to Russia, I take two views of the position
of Russia. The position of Russia in Central Asia I believe
to be one that has, in the main, been forced upon her against
her will. She has been compelled—and this is the impartial
opinion of the world—she has been compelled to extend her
frontier southward in Central Asia by causes in some degree
analogous to, but certainly more stringent and imperative

than, the causes which have commonly led us to extend, in a
far more important manner, our frontier in India; and I
think it, gentlemen, much to the credit of the late government, much to the honor of Lord Clarendon and Lord Gran-
ville, that, when we were in office, we made a covenant with
Russia, in which Russia bound herself to exercise no influence or interference whatever in Afghanistan, we, on the
other hand, making known our desire that Afghanistan
should continue free and independent. Both the powers
acted with uniform strictness and fidelity upon this engage-
ment until the day when we were removed from office. But
Russia, gentlemen, has another position—her position in
respect to Turkey; and here it is that I have complained of
the government for aggrandizing the power of Russia; it is
on this point that I most complain.

The policy of her Majesty's government was a policy of
repelling and repudiating the Slavonic population of Turkey-
in-Europe, and of declining to make England the advocate
for their interests. Nay, more, she became in their view the
advocate of the interests opposed to theirs. Indeed, she
was rather the decided advocate of Turkey; and now Turkey
is full of loud complaints—and complaints, I must say, not
unjust—that we allured her on to her ruin; that we gave the
Turks a right to believe that we should support them; that
our ambassadors, Sir Henry Elliot and Sir Austin Layard,
both of them said we had most vital interests in maintaining
Turkey as it was, and consequently the Turks thought if we
had vital interests, we should certainly defend them; and
they were thereby lured on into that ruinous, cruel, and
destructive war with Russia. But by our conduct to the
Slavonic populations we alienated those populations from us.
We made our name odious among them. They had every
disposition to sympathize with us, every disposition to confide in us. They are, as a people, desirous of freedom,
desirous of self-government, with no aggressive views, but
hating the idea of being absorbed in a huge despotic empire
like Russia. But when they found that we, and the other
powers of Europe under our unfortunate guidance, declined
to become in any manner their champions in defence of the
rights of life, of property, and of female honor—when they

found that there was no call which could find its way to the
heart of England through its government, or to the hearts of
other powers, and that Russia alone was disposed to fight for
them, why naturally they said Russia is our friend. We
have done everything, gentlemen, in our power to drive these
populations into the arms of Russia. If Russia has aggressive dispositions in the direction of Turkey—and I think it
probable that she may have them—it is we who have laid the
ground upon which Russia may make her march to the
south—we who have taught the Bulgarians, the Servians, the
Roumanians, the Montenegrins, that there is one power in
Europe, and only one, which is ready to support in act and
by the sword her professions of sympathy with the oppressed
populations of Turkey. That power is Russia, and how can
you blame these people if, in such circumstances, they are
disposed to say, Russia is our friend? But why did we make
them say it? Simply because of the policy of the government, not because of the wishes of the people of this country.
Gentlemen, this is the most dangerous form of aggrandizing
Russia. If Russia is aggressive anywhere, if Russia is formidable anywhere, it is by movements toward the south, it is
by schemes for acquiring command of the Straits or of Constantinople; and there is no way by which you can possibly
so much assist her in giving reality to these designs, as by
inducing and disposing the populations of these provinces,
who are now in virtual possession of them, to look upon Russia as their champion and their friend, to look upon England
as their disguised, perhaps, but yet real and effective enemy.

Why, now, gentlemen, I have said that I think it not unreasonable either to believe, or at any rate to admit it to be
possible, that Russia has aggressive designs in the east of
Europe. I do not mean immediate aggressive designs. I do
not believe that the Emperor of Russia is a man of aggressive schemes or policy. It is that, looking to that question
in the long run, looking at what has happened, and what
may happen in ten or twenty years, in one generation, in two
generations, it is highly probable that in some circumstances
Russia may develop aggressive tendencies toward the south.

Perhaps you will say I am here guilty of the same injustice to Russia that I have been deprecating, because I say

that we ought not to adopt the method of condemning anybody without cause, and setting up exceptional principles in proscription of a particular nation. Gentlemen, I will explain to you in a moment the principle upon which I act, and the grounds upon which I form my judgment. They are simply these grounds: I look at the position of Russia, the geographical position of Russia relatively to Turkey. I look at the comparative strength of the two empires; I look at the importance of the Dardanelles and the Bosphorus as an exit and a channel for the military and commercial marine of Russia to the Mediterranean; and what I say to myself is this: If the United Kingdom were in the same position relatively to Turkey which Russia holds upon the map of the globe, I feel quite sure that we should be very apt indeed both to entertain and to execute aggressive designs upon Turkey. Gentlemen, I will go further, and will frankly own to you that I believe if we, instead of happily inhabiting this island, had been in the possession of the Russian territory, and in the circumstances of the Russian people, we should most likely have eaten up Turkey long ago. And consequently, in saying that Russia ought to be vigilantly watched in that quarter, I am only applying to her the rule which in parallel circumstances I feel convinced ought to be applied, and would be justly applied, to judgments upon our own country.

Gentlemen, there is only one other point on which I must still say a few words to you, although there are a great many upon which I have a great many words yet to say somewhere or other.

Of all the principles, gentlemen, of foreign policy which I have enumerated, that to which I attach the greatest value is the principle of the equality of nations; because, without recognizing that principle, there is no such thing as public right, and without public international right there is no instrument available for settling the transactions of mankind except material force. Consequently the principle of equality among nations lies, in my opinion, at the very basis and root of a Christian civilization, and when that principle is compromised or abandoned, with it must depart our hopes of tranquillity and of progress for mankind.

I am sorry to say, gentlemen, that I feel it my absolute duty to make this charge against the foreign policy under which we have lived for the last two years, since the resignation of Lord Derby. It has been a foreign policy, in my opinion, wholly, or to a perilous extent, unregardful of public right, and it has been founded upon the basis of a false, I think an arrogant and a dangerous, assumption, although I do not question its being made conscientiously and for what was believed the advantage of the country—an untrue, arrogant, and dangerous assumption that we are entitled to assume for ourselves some dignity, which we should also be entitled to withhold from others, and to claim on our own part authority to do things which we would not permit to be done by others. For example, when Russia was going to the Congress at Berlin, we said: " Your Treaty of San Stefano is of no value. It is an act between you and Turkey; but the concerns of Turkey by the Treaty of Paris are the concerns of Europe at large. We insist upon it that the whole of your Treaty of San Stefano shall be submitted to the Congress at Berlin, that they may judge how far to open it in each and every one of its points, because the concerns of Turkey are the common concerns of the powers of Europe acting in concert."

Having asserted that principle to the world, what did we do? These two things, gentlemen: secretly, without the knowledge of Parliament, without even the forms of official procedure, Lord Salisbury met Count Schouvaloff in London, and agreed with him upon the terms on which the two powers together should be bound in honor to one another to act upon all the most important points when they came before the Congress at Berlin. Having alleged against Russia that she should not be allowed to settle Turkish affairs with Turkey, because they were but two powers, and these affairs were the common affairs of Europe, and of European interest, we then got Count Schouvaloff into a private room, and on the part of England and Russia, they being but two powers, we settled a large number of the most important of these affairs in utter contempt and derogation of the very principle for which the government had been contending for months before, for which they had asked Parliament to grant a sum of £6,000,000, for which they had spent that £6,000,000 in needless and mischievous armaments. That which we would not allow Russia to do with Turkey, because we pleaded the rights of Europe, we ourselves did with Russia, in contempt of the rights of Europe. Nor was that all, gentlemen. That act was done, I think, on one of the last days of May, in the year 1878, and the document was published, made known to the world, made known to the Congress at Berlin, to its infinite astonishment, unless I am very greatly misinformed.

But that was not all. Nearly at the same time we performed the same operation in another quarter. We objected to a treaty between Russia and Turkey as having no authority, though that treaty was made in the light of day—namely, to the Treaty of San Stefano; and what did we do? We went not in the light of day, but in the darkness of the night —not in the knowledge and cognizance of other powers, all of whom would have had the faculty and means of watching all along, and of preparing and taking their own objections and shaping their own policy—not in the light of day, but in the darkness of the night, we sent the ambassador of England in Constantinople to the minister of Turkey and there he framed, even while the Congress of Berlin was sitting to determine these matters of common interest, he framed that which is too famous, shall I say, or rather too notorious, as the Anglo-Turkish Convention.

Gentlemen, it is said, and said truly, that truth beats fiction; that what happens in fact from time to time is of a character so daring, so strange, that if the novelist were to imagine it and put it upon his pages, the whole world would reject it from its improbability. And that is the case of the Anglo-Turkish Convention. For who would have believed it possible that we should assert before the world the principle that Europe only could deal with the affairs of the Turkish empire, and should ask Parliament for six millions to support us in asserting that principle, should send ministers to Berlin who declared that unless that principle was acted upon they would go to war with the material that Parliament had placed in their hands, and should at the same time be concluding a separate agreement with Turkey, under which those matters of European jurisdiction were coolly transferred to English jurisdiction; and the whole matter was sealed with the worthless bribe of the possession and administration of the island of Cyprus! I said, gentlemen, the worthless bribe of the island of Cyprus, and that is the truth. It is worthless for our purposes—not worthless in itself; an island of resources, an island of natural capabilities, provided they are allowed to develop themselves in the course of circumstances, without violent and unprincipled methods of action. But Cyprus was not thought to be worthless by those who accepted it as a bribe. On the contrary, you were told that it was to secure the road to India; you were told that it was to be the site of an arsenal very cheaply made, and more valuable than Malta; you were told that it was to revive trade. And a multitude of companies were formed, and sent agents and capital to Cyprus, and some of them, I fear, grievously burned their fingers there. I am not going to dwell upon that now. What I have in view is not the particular merits of Cyprus, but the illustration that I have given you in the case of the agreement of Lord Salisbury with Count Schouvaloff, and in the case of the Anglo-Turkish Convention, of the manner in which we have asserted for ourselves a principle that we had denied to others—namely, the principle of overriding the European authority of the Treaty of Paris, and taking the matters which that treaty gave to Europe into our own separate jurisdiction.

Now, gentlemen, I am sorry to find that that which I call the pharisaical assertion of our own superiority has found its way alike into the practice, and seemingly into the theories, of the government. I am not going to assert anything which is not known, but the prime minister has said that there is one day in the year—namely, the ninth of November, Lord Mayor's day—on which the language of sense and truth is to be heard amidst the surrounding din of idle rumors generated and fledged in the brains of irresponsible scribes. I do not agree, gentlemen, in that panegyric upon the ninth of November. I am much more apt to compare the ninth of November—certainly a well-known day in the year—but as to some of the speeches that have lately been made upon it I am very much disposed to compare it with another day in the year, well known to British tradition, and that other day in the year is the first of April. But, gentlemen, on that day the prime minister, speaking out—I do not question for a moment his own sincere opinion—made what I think one of the most unhappy and ominous allusions ever made by a minister of this country. He quoted certain words, easily rendered as "Empire and Liberty"—words (he said) of a Roman states-man, words descriptive of the state of Rome—and he quoted them as words which were capable of legitimate application to the position and circumstances of England. I join issue with the prime minister upon that subject, and I affirm that nothing can be more fundamentally unsound, more practi-cally ruinous, than the establishment of Roman analogies for the guidance of British policy. What, gentlemen, was Rome? Rome was indeed an imperial state; you may tell me—I know not, I cannot read the counsels of Providence —a state having a mission to subdue the world, but a state whose very basis it was to deny the equal rights, to proscribe the independent existence of other nations. That, gentle-men, was the Roman idea. It has been partially and not ill described in three lines of a translation from Virgil by our great poet Dryden, which runs as follows:—

> " O Rome! 't is thine alone with awful sway
> To rule mankind, and make the world obey,
> Disposing peace and war thine own majestic way."

We are told to fall back upon this example. No doubt the word "Empire" was qualified with the word "Liberty." But what did the two words "Liberty" and "Empire" mean in a Roman mouth? They meant simply this: "Lib-erty for ourselves, Empire over the rest of mankind."

I do not think, gentlemen, that this ministry, or any other ministry, is going to place us in the position of Rome. What I object to is the revival of the idea. I care not how feebly, I care not even how, from a philosophic or historical point of view, how ridiculous the attempt at this revival may be. I say it indicates an intention—I say it indicates a frame of mind, and the frame of mind, unfortunately, I find, has been consistent with the policy of which I have given you some illustrations—the policy of denying to others the rights that

we claim ourselves.   No doubt, gentlemen, Rome may have
had its work to do, and Rome did its work.   But modern
times have brought a different state of things.   Modern times
have established a sisterhood of nations, equal, independent,
each of them built up under that legitimate defense which
public law affords to every nation, living within its own
borders, and seeking to perform its own affairs; but if one
thing more than another has been detestable to Europe, it
has been the appearance upon the stage from time to time
of men who, even in the times of the Christian civilization,
have been thought to aim at universal dominion.   It was
this aggressive disposition on the part of Louis XIV., King
of France, that led your forefathers, gentlemen, freely to
spend their blood and treasure in a cause not immediately
their own, and to struggle against the method of policy
which, having Paris for its center, seemed to aim at an universal monarchy.

It was the very same thing, a century and a half later,
which was the charge launched, and justly launched, against
Napoleon, that under his dominion France was not content
even with her extended limits, but Germany, and Italy, and
Spain, apparently without any limit to this pestilent and pernicious process, were to be brought under the dominion or
influence of France, and national equality was to be trampled
under foot, and national rights denied.   For that reason,
England in the struggle almost exhausted herself, greatly
impoverished her people, brought upon herself, and Scotland too, the consequences of a debt that nearly crushed
their energies, and poured forth their best blood without
limit, in order to resist and put down these intolerable pretensions.

Gentlemen, it is but in a pale and weak and almost
despicable miniature that such ideas are now set up, but you
will observe that the poison lies—that the poison and the
mischief lie—in the principle and not the scale.

It is the opposite principle which, I say, has been compromised by the action of the ministry, and which I call
upon you, and upon any who choose to hear my views, to
vindicate when the day of our election comes; I mean the
sound and the sacred principle that Christendom is formed

of a band of nations who are united to one another in the bonds of right; that they are without distinction of great and small; there is an absolute equality between them—the same sacredness defends the narrow limits of Belgium as attaches to the extended frontiers of Russia, or Germany, or France. I hold that he who by act or word brings that principle into peril or disparagement, however honest his intentions may be, places himself in the position of one inflicting—I won't say intending to inflict—I ascribe nothing of the sort—but inflicting injury upon his own country, and endangering the peace and all the most fundamental interests of Christian society.

HENRY GRATTAN

AGAINST ENGLISH IMPERIALISM

[Henry Grattan, an Irish statesman and orator, was born at Dublin in 1746. He was educated at Trinity College, Dublin. The ambition of Grattan's life was to excel in oratory, and to the realization of this ambition he sacrificed every other worldly consideration, even success at the Irish bar, to which he was called at twenty-two. In 1775 he entered the Irish Parliament, allied himself with the anti-English party, and was hailed as its leader as soon as he had finished a series of effective speeches. Grattan in the Imperial Parliament, to which he was returned in 1806, strove for Catholic Emancipation, as he had previously opposed the legislative union with Great Britain, and he aimed at a national solidarity of Ireland that would disregard narrow sectarian or partisan lines. He died in 1820. The following speech is a patriotic appeal for the legislative independence of Ireland, and was delivered in the Irish parliament in 1780 on the occasion of moving the " Declaration of Right."]

I HAVE entreated an attendance on this day, that you might, in the most public manner, deny the claim of the British Parliament to make law for Ireland, and lift up your hands against it.

If I had lived when the Act, passed in the ninth year of William's reign, took away the woolen manufacture, or when the Act passed in the sixth year of the reign of George the First declared this country to be dependent, and subject to laws to be enacted by the Parliament of England, I should have made a covenant with my own conscience to seize the first moment of rescuing my country from the ignominy of such acts of power; or, if I had a son, I should have administered to him an oath that he would consider himself a person separate and set apart for the discharge of so important a duty; upon the same principle am I now come to move a Declaration of Right, the first moment occurring, since my time, in which such a declaration could be made with any chance of success, and without aggravation of oppression.

Sir, it must appear to every person that, notwithstanding the import of sugar and export of woolens, the people of this country are not satisfied—something remains: the greater work is behind; the public heart is not well at ease. To promulgate our satisfaction; to stop the throats of millions with the votes of Parliament; to preach homilies to the volunteers; to utter invectives against the people under pretence of affectionate advice, is an attempt weak, suspicious, and inflammatory.

You cannot dictate to those whose sense you are entrusted to represent; your ancestors, who sat within these walls, lost to Ireland trade and liberty; you, by the assistance of the people, have recovered trade, you still owe the kingdom liberty; she calls upon you to restore it.

The ground of public discontent seems to be, "we have gotten commerce, but not freedom": the same power which took away the export of woolens and the export of glass may take them away again; the repeal is partial, and the ground of repeal is upon a principle of expediency.

Sir, expedient is a word of appropriated and tyrannical import; expedient is an ill-omened word, selected to express the reservation of authority, while the exercise is mitigated; expedient is the ill-omened expression of the Repeal of the American Stamp Act. England thought it expedient to repeal that law; happy had it been for mankind, if, when she withdrew the exercise, she had not reserved the right! To that reservation she owes the loss of her American empire, at the expense of millions, and America the seeking of liberty through a sea of bloodshed. The repeal of the woolen act, similarly circumstanced, pointed against the principle of our liberty, present relaxation, — but tyranny in reserve, — may be a subject for illumination to a populace, or a pretence for apostacy to a courtier, but cannot be the subject of settled satisfaction to a freeborn, an intelligent, and an injured community. It is therefore they consider the free trade as a trade de facto, not de jure, a license to trade under the Parliament of England, not a free trade under the charters of Ireland, as a tribute to her strength; to maintain which she must continue in a state of armed preparation, dreading the approach of a general peace, and attributing all she

holds dear to the calamitous condition of the British interest
in every quarter of the globe. This dissatisfaction, founded
upon a consideration of the liberty we have lost, is increased
when they consider the opportunity they are losing; for if
this nation, after the death-wound given to her freedom, had
fallen on her knees in anguish, and besought the Almighty
to frame an occasion in which a weak and injured people
might recover their rights, prayer could not have asked, nor
God have furnished, a moment more opportune for the restoration of liberty than this in which I have the honor to address
you.

England now smarts under the lesson of the American
war; the doctrine of imperial legislature she feels to be pernicious; the revenues and monopolies annexed to it she has
found to be untenable, she lost the power to enforce it; her
enemies are a host, pouring upon her from all quarters of the
earth; her armies are dispersed; the sea is not hers; she
has no minister, no ally, no admiral, none in whom she long
confides, and no general whom she has not disgraced; the
balance of her fate is in the hands of Ireland; you are not
only her last connection, you are the only nation in Europe
that is not her enemy. Besides, there does, of late, a certain
damp and spurious supineness overcast her arms and councils,
miraculous as that vigor which has lately inspirited yours;
for with you everything is the reverse: never was there a
Parliament in Ireland so possessed of the confidence of the
people; you are the greatest political assembly now sitting
in the world; you are at the head of an immense army; nor
do we only possess an unconquerable force, but a certain
unquenchable public fire, which has touched all ranks of
men like a visitation.

Turn to the growth and spring of your country, and behold and admire it; where do you find a nation, who, upon
whatever concerns the rights of mankind, expresses herself
with more truth or force, perspicuity or justice? not the set
phrase of scholastic men, not the tame unreality of court addresses, not the vulgar raving of a rabble, but the genuine
speech of liberty, and the unsophisticated oratory of a free
nation!

See her military ardor, expressed not only in 40,000

men, conducted by instinct as they were raised by inspiration, but manifested in the zeal and promptitude of every young member of the growing community. Let corruption tremble; let the enemy, foreign or domestic, tremble; but let the friends of liberty rejoice at these means of safety and this hour of redemption. Yes, there does exist an enlightened sense of rights, a young appetite for freedom, a solid strength, and a rapid fire, which not only put a declaration of right within your power, but put it out of your power to decline one. Eighteen counties are at your bar: they stand there with the compact of Henry, with the charter of John, and with all the passions of the people. " Our lives are at your service, but our liberties—we received them from God; we will not resign them to man." Speaking to you thus, if you repulse these petitioners, you abdicate the privileges of Parliament, forfeit the rights of the kingdom, repudiate the instruction of your constituents, bilge the sense of your country, palsy the enthusiasm of the people, and reject that good which not a minister, not a Lord North, not a Lord Buckinghamshire, not a Lord Hillsborough, but a certain providential conjuncture, or rather the hand of God, seems to extend to you. Nor are we only prompted to this when we consider our strength; we are challenged to it when we look to Great Britain. The people of that country are now waiting to hear the Parliament of Ireland speak on the subject of their liberty; it begins to be made a question in England whether the principal persons wish to be free; it was the delicacy of former parliaments to be silent on the subject of commercial restrictions, lest they should show a knowledge of the fact, and not a sense of the violation; you have spoken out, you have shown a knowledge of the fact, and not a sense of the violation. On the contrary, you have returned thanks for a partial repeal made on a principle of power; you have returned thanks as for a favor, and your exultation has brought your charters as well as your spirit into question, and tends to shake to her foundation your title to liberty: thus you do not leave your rights where you found them. You have done too much not to do more; you have gone too far not to go on; you have brought yourselves into that situation, in which you must silently abdicate the rights of your country or publicly restore them. It is very true you may feed your manufacturers, and landed gentlemen may get their rents, and you may export woolen, and may load a vessel with baize, serges, and kerseys, and you may bring back again directly from the plantations sugar, indigo, specklewood, beetle-root, and panellas. But liberty, the foundation of trade, the charters of the land, the independency of Parliament, the securing, crowning, and the consummation of everything, are yet to come. Without them the work is imperfect, the foundation is wanting, the capital is wanting, trade is not free, Ireland is a colony without the benefit of a charter, and you are a provincial synod without the privileges of a parliament.

I read Lord North's proposition; I wish to be satisfied, but I am controlled by a paper, I will not call it a law, it is the sixth of George the First. [The paper was read.] I will ask the gentlemen of the long robe is this the law? I ask them whether it is not practice? I appeal to the judges of the land, whether they are not in a course of declaring that the Parliament of Great Britain, naming Ireland, binds her. I appeal to the magistrates of justice, whether they do not, from time to time, execute certain acts of the British Parliament. I appeal to the officers of the army, whether they do not fine, confine, and execute their fellow-subjects by virtue of the Mutiny Act, an act of the British Parliament; and I appeal to this House whether a country so circumstanced is free. Where is the freedom of trade? Where is the security of property? Where is the liberty of the people? I here, in this Declamatory Act, see my country proclaimed a slave! I see every man in this house enrolled a slave! I see the judges of the realm, the oracles of the law, borne down by an unauthorized foreign power, by the authority of the British Parliament against the law! I see the magistrates prostrate, and I see Parliament witness of these infringements, and silent (silent or employed to preach moderation to the people whose liberties it will not restore)! I therefore say, with the voice of 3,000,000 of people, that, notwithstanding the import of sugar, beetle-wood and panellas, and the export of woolens and kerseys, nothing is safe, satisfactory, or honorable, nothing except a declaration of right. What! are you, with 3,000,000 of men at your back, with charters in one hand and arms in the other, afraid to say you are a free people? Are you, the greatest House of Commons that ever sat in Ireland, that wants but this one act to equal that English House of Commons that passed the Petition of Right, or that other that passed the Declaration of Right, are you afraid to tell that British Parliament you are a free people? Are the cities and the instructing counties who have breathed a spirit that would have done honor to old Rome when Rome did honor to mankind, are they to be free by connivance? Are the military associations, those bodies whose origin, progress, and deportment have transcended, equaled at least, anything in modern or ancient story—is the vast line of northern army—are they to be free by connivance? What man will settle among you? Where is the use of the Naturalization Bill? What man will settle among you? Who will leave a land of liberty and a settled government for a kingdom controlled by the parliament of another country, whose liberty is a thing by stealth, whose trade a thing by permission, whose judges deny her charters, whose parliament leaves everything at random; where the chance of freedom depends upon the hope that the jury shall despise the judge stating a British act, or a rabble stop the magistrate executing it, rescue your abdicated privileges, and save the constitution by trampling on the government, by anarchy and confusion?

But I shall be told that these are groundless jealousies, and that in the principal cities, and in more than one-half of the counties of the kingdom, are misguided men, raising those groundless jealousies. Sir, let me become, on this occasion, the people's advocate and your historian; the people of this country were possessed of a code of liberty similar to that of Great Britain, but lost it through the weakness of the kingdom and the pusillanimity of its leaders. Having lost our liberty by the usurpation of the British Parliament, no wonder we became a prey to her ministers; and they did plunder us with all the hands of all the harpies, for a series of years, in every shape of power, terrifying our people with the thunder of Great Britain, and bribing our leaders with the rapine of Ireland. The kingdom became a plantation, her Parliament, deprived of its privileges, fell into contempt; and, with the legislature, the law, the spirit of liberty, with her forms, vanished.   If a war broke out, as in 1778, and an occasion occurred to restore liberty and restrain rapine, Parliament declined the opportunity; but with an active servility and trembling loyalty, gave and granted, without regard to the treasure we had left or the rights we had lost.   If a partial separation was made upon a principle of expediency, Parliament did not receive it with the tranquil dignity of an august assembly, but with the alacrity of slaves.

The principal individuals, possessed of great property but no independency, corrupted by their extravagance, or enslaved by their following a species of English factor against an Irish people, more afraid of the people of Ireland than the tyranny of England, proceeded to that excess that they opposed every proposition to lessen profusion, extend trade, or promote liberty; they did more, they supported a measure which, at one blow, put an end to all trade; they did more, they brought you to a condition which they themselves did unanimously acknowledge a state of impending ruin; they did this, talking as they are now talking, arguing against trade as they now argue against liberty, threatening the people of Ireland with the power of the British nation, and imploring them to rest satisfied with the ruins of their trade, as they now implore them to remain satisfied with the wreck of their constitution.

The people thus admonished, starving in a land of plenty, the victim of two parliaments, of one that stopped their trade, the other that fed on their constitution, inhabiting a country where industry was forbid, or towns swarming with begging manufacturers, and being obliged to take into their own hands that part of government which consists in protecting the subject, had recourse to two measures which, in their origin, progress, and consequence, are the most extraordinary to be found in any age or in any country—viz., a commercial and a military association.   The consequence of these measures was instant; the enemy that hung on your shores departed, the Parliament asked for a free trade, and the British nation granted the trade, but withheld the freedom.   The people of Ireland are, therefore, not satisfied; they ask for a constitution; they have the authority of the wisest men in this House for what they now demand. What have these walls, for this last century, resounded? The usurpation of the British Parliament, and the interference of the privy council. Have we taught the people to complain, and do we now condemn their insatiability, because they desire us to remove such grievances, at a time in which nothing can oppose them, except the very men by whom these grievances were acknowledged?

Sir, we may hope to dazzle with illumination, and we may sicken with addresses, but the public imagination will never rest, nor will her heart be well at ease—never! so long as the Parliament of England exercises or claims a legislation over this country; so long as this shall be the case, that very free trade, otherwise a perpetual attachment, will be the cause of new discontent; it will create a pride to feel the indignity of bondage; it will furnish a strength to bite your chain, and the liberty withheld will poison the good communicated.

The British minister mistakes the Irish character; had he intended to make Ireland a slave, he should have kept her a beggar; there is no middle policy; win her heart by the restoration of her right, or cut off the nation's right hand; greatly emancipate, or fundamentally destroy. We may talk plausibly to England, but so long as she exercises a power to bind this country, so long are the nations in a state of war; the claims of the one go against the liberty of the other, and the sentiments of the latter go to oppose those claims to the last drop of her blood. The English opposition, therefore, are right; mere trade will not satisfy Ireland —they judge of us by other great nations, by the nation whose political life has been a struggle for liberty; they judge of us with a true knowledge of, and just deference for, our character—that a country enlightened as Ireland, chartered as Ireland, armed as Ireland, and injured as Ireland, will be satisfied with nothing less than liberty.

I admire that public-spirited merchant (Alderman Horan) who spread consternation at the custom-house, and, despising the example which great men afforded, determined to try the question, and tendered for entry what the British Parliament prohibits the subject to export, some articles of silk, and sought at his private risk the liberty of his country; with him I am convinced it is necessary to agitate the question of right.   In vain will you endeavor to keep it back, the passion is too natural, the sentiment is too irresistible; the question comes on of its own vitality—you must reinstate the laws.

There is no objection to this resolution, except fears. I have examined your fears; I pronounce them to be frivolous.   I might deny that the British nation was attached to the idea of binding Ireland; I might deny that England was a tyrant at heart; and I might call to witness the odium of North and the popularity of Chatham, her support of Holland, her contributions to Corsica, and the charters communicated to Ireland: but ministers have traduced England to debase Ireland; and politicians, like priests, represent the power they serve as diabolical, to possess with superstitious fears the victim whom they design to plunder.   If England is a tyrant, it is you who have made her so; it is the slave that makes the tyrant, and then murmurs at the master whom he himself has constituted.   I do allow, on the subject of commerce, England was jealous in the extreme, and I do say it was commercial jealousy, it was the spirit of monopoly (the woolen trade, and the act of navigation had made her tenacious of a comprehensive legislative authority), and having now ceded that monopoly, there is nothing in the way of your liberty except your own corruption and pusillanimity; and nothing can prevent your being free except yourselves. It is not in the disposition of England; it is not in the interest of England; it is not in her arms.   What! can 8,000,-000 of Englishmen, opposed to 20,000,000 of French, to 7,000,000 of Spanish, to 3,000,000 of Americans, reject the alliance of 3,000,000 in Ireland?   Can 8,000,000 of British men, thus outnumbered by foes, take upon their shoulders the expense of an expedition to enslave you?   Will Great Britain, a wise and magnanimous country, thus tutored by experience and wasted by war, the French navy riding her Channel, send an army to Ireland, to levy no tax, to enforce no law, to answer no end whatsoever, except to spoliate the charters of Ireland and enforce a barren oppression?   What! has England lost thirteen provinces?   has she reconciled herself to this loss, and will she not be reconciled to the liberty of Ireland? Take notice, that the very constitution which I move you to declare, Great Britain herself offered to America; it is a very instructive proceeding in the British history. In 1778 a commission went out, with powers to cede to the thirteen provinces of America, totally and radically, the legislative authority claimed over her by the British Parliament, and the commissioners, pursuant to their powers, did offer to all or any of the American states the total surrender of the legislative authority of the British Parliament. I will read you their letter to the Congress. [Here the letter was read, surrendering the power as aforesaid.] What! has England offered this to the resistance of America, and will she refuse it to the loyalty of Ireland? Your fears then are nothing but an habitual subjugation of mind; that subjugation of mind which made you, at first, tremble at every great measure of safety; which made the principal men amongst us conceive the commercial association would be a war; that fear, which made them imagine the military association had a tendency to treason, which made them think a short money-bill would be a public convulsion; and yet these measures have not only proved to be useful, but are held to be moderate, and the Parliament that adopted them praised, not for its unanimity only, but for its temper also. You now wonder that you submitted for so many years to the loss of the woolen trade and the deprivation of the glass trade; raised above your former abject state in commerce, you are ashamed at your past pusillanimity; so when you have summoned a boldness which shall assert the liberties of your country—raised by the act, and reinvested, as you will be, in the glory of your ancient rights and privileges, you will be surprised at yourselves, who have so long submitted to their violation. Moderation is but a relative term; for nations, like men, are only safe in proportion to the spirit they put forth, and the proud contemplation with which they survey themselves. Conceive yourselves a plantation, ridden by an oppressive government, and everything you have done is but a fortunate frenzy; conceive yourselves to be what you are, a great, a growing, and a proud nation, and a declaration of right is no more than the safe exercise of your indubitable authority.

But though you do not hazard disturbance by agreeing to this resolution, you do most exceedingly hazard tranquillity by rejecting it. Do not imagine that the question will be over when this motion shall be negatived. No; it will recur in a vast variety of shapes and diversity of places. Your constituents have instructed you in great numbers, with a powerful uniformity of sentiment, and in a style not the less awful because full of respect. They will find resources in their own virtue, if they have found none in yours. Public pride and conscious liberty, wounded by repulse, will find ways and means of vindication. You are in that situation in which every man, every hour of the day, may shake the pillars of the state; every court may swarm with the question of right; every quay and wharf with prohibited goods: what shall the judges, what the commissioners, do upon this occasion? Shall they comply with the laws of Ireland, and against the claims of England, and stand firm where you have capitulated? Shall they, on the other hand, not comply, and shall they persist to act against the law? Will you punish them if they do so? Will you proceed against them for not showing a spirit superior to your own? On the other hand, will you not punish them? Will you leave liberty to be trampled on by those men? Will you bring them and yourselves, all constituted orders, executive power, judicial power, and parliamentary authority, into a state of odium, impotence, and contempt; transferring the task of defending public right into the hands of the populace, and leaving it to the judges to break the laws, and to the people to assert them? Such would be the consequence of false moderation, of irritating timidity, of inflammatory palliatives, of the weak and corrupt hope of compromising with the court, before you have emancipated the country.

I have answered the only semblance of a solid reason against the motion; I will remove some lesser pretences, some minor impediments; for instance, first, that we have a resolution of the same kind already on our journals, it will be said; but how often was the great charter confirmed? not more frequently than your rights have been violated. Is one solitary resolution, declaratory of your right, sufficient for a country whose history, from the beginning unto the end, has been a course of violation? The fact is, every new breach is a reason for a new repair; every new infringement should be a new declaration; lest charters should be overwhelmed with precedents to their prejudice, a nation's right obliterated, and the people themselves lose the memory of their own freedom.

I shall hear of ingratitude: I name the argument to despise it and the men who make use of it: I know the men who use it are not grateful, they are insatiate; they are public extortioners, who would stop the tide of public prosperity and turn it to the channel of their own emolument: I know of no species of gratitude which should prevent my country from being free, no gratitude which should oblige Ireland to be the slave of England. In cases of robbery and usurpation, nothing is an object of gratitude except the thing stolen, the charter spoliated. A nation's liberty cannot, like her treasures, be meted and parcelled out in gratitude; no man can be grateful or liberal of his conscience, nor woman of her honor, nor nation of her liberty: there are certain unimpartable, inherent, invaluable properties not to be alienated from the person, whether body politic or body natural. With the same contempt do I treat that charge which says that Ireland is insatiable; saying that Ireland asks nothing but that which Great Britain has robbed her of, her rights and privileges; to say that Ireland will not be satisfied with liberty, because she is not satisfied with slavery, is folly. I laugh at that man who supposes that Ireland will not be content with a free trade and a free constitution; and would any man advise her to be content with less?

I shall be told that we hazard the modification of the law of Poynings and the Judges' Bill, and the Habeas Corpus Bill, and the Nullum Tempus Bill; but I ask, have you been for years begging for these little things, and have not you yet been able to obtain them? and have you been contending against a little body of eighty men in Privy Council assembled, convocating themselves into the image of a parliament and ministering your high office? and have you been contending against one man, an humble individual, to you a leviathan—the English attorney-general—who advises in the case of Irish bills, and exercises legislation in his own person, and makes your parliamentary deliberations a blank by altering your bills or suppressing them? and have you not yet been able to conquer this little monster? Do you wish to know the reason? I will tell you: because you have not been a parliament, nor your country a people. Do you wish to know the remedy?—be a parliament, become a nation, and these things will follow in the train of your consequences. I shall be told that titles are shaken, being vested by force of English acts; but in answer to that, I observe, time may be a title, acquiescence a title, forfeiture a title, but an English act of parliament certainly cannot: it is an authority which, if a judge would charge, no jury would find, and which all the electors in Ireland have already disclaimed unequivocally, cordially, and universally. Sir, this is a good argument for an act of title, but no argument against a declaration of right. My friend who sits above me (Mr. Yelverton) has a Bill of Confirmation; we do not come unprepared to Parliament. I am not come to shake property, but to confirm property and restore freedom. The nation begins to form; we are moulding into a people; freedom asserted, property secured, and the army (a mercenary band) likely to be restrained by law. Never was such a revolution accomplished in so short a time, and with such public tranquillity. In what situation would those men who call themselves friends of the constitution and of government have left you? They would have left you without a title, as they state it, to your estates, without an assertion of your constitution, or a law for your army; and this state of unexampled private and public insecurity, this anarchy raging in the kingdom for eighteen months, these mock moderators would have had the presumption to call peace.

I shall be told that the judges will not be swayed by the resolution of this House. Sir, that the judges will not be borne down by the resolutions of Parliament, not founded in law, I am willing to believe; but the resolutions of this House, founded in law, they will respect most exceedingly. I shall always rejoice at the independent spirit of the distributors of the law, but must lament that hitherto they have given no such symptom. The judges of the British nation, when they adjudicated against the laws of that country, pleaded precedent and the prostration and profligacy of a long tribe of subservient predecessors, and were punished. The judges of Ireland, if they should be called upon, and should plead sad necessity, the thraldom of the times, and, above all, the silent fears of Parliament, they no doubt will be excused: but when your declarations shall have protected them from their fears; when you shall have emboldened the judges to declare the law according to the charter, I make no doubt they will do their duty; and your resolution, not making a new law, but giving new life to the old ones, will be secretly felt and inwardly acknowledged, and there will not be a judge who will not perceive, to the innermost recess of his tribunal, the truth of your charters, and the vigor of your justice.

The same laws, the same charters, communicate to both kingdoms, Great Britain and Ireland, the same rights and privileges; and one privilege above them all is that communicated by Magna Charta, by the 25th of Edward the Third, and by a multitude of other statutes, "not to be bound by any act except made with the archbishops, bishops, earls, barons, and freemen of the community," viz., of the parliament of the realm. On this right of exclusive legislation are founded the Petition of Right, Bill of Right, Revolution, and Act of Settlement. The king has no other title to his crown than that which you have to your liberty; both are founded, the throne and your freedom, upon the right vested in the subjects to resist by arms, notwithstanding their oaths of allegiance, any authority attempting to impose acts of power as laws, whether that authority be one man or a host, the second James or the British Parliament!

Every argument for the House of Hanover is equally an argument for the liberties of Ireland: the Act of Settlement is an act of rebellion, or the declaratory statute of the 6th of George the First an act of usurpation; for both cannot be by law.

I do not refer to doubtful history, but to living record; to common charters; to the interpretation England has put upon these charters—an interpretation not made by words only, but crowned by arms; to the revolution she had formed upon them, to the king she had deposed, and to the king she has established; and, above all, to the oath of allegiance solemnly plighted to the House of Stuart, and afterwards set aside, in the instance of a grave and moral people absolved by virtue of these very charters.

And as anything less than liberty is inadequate to Ireland, so is it dangerous to Great Britain. We are too near the British nation, we are too conversant with her history, we are too much fired by her example, to be anything less than her equal; anything less, we should be her bitterest enemies—an enemy to that power which smote us with her mace, and to that constitution from whose blessings we were excluded; to be ground as we have been by the British nation, bound by her Parliament, plundered by her crown, threatened by her enemies, insulted with her protection, while we returned thanks for her condescension, is a system of meanness and misery which has expired in our determination, as I hope it has in her magnanimity.

There is no policy left for Great Britain but to cherish the remains of her empire, and do justice to a country which is determined to do justice to herself, certain that she gives nothing equal to what she received from us when we gave her Ireland.

With regard to this country, England must resort to the free principles of government, and must forego that legislative power which she has exercised to do mischief to herself; she must go back to freedom, which, as it is the foundation of her constitution, so is it the main pillar of her empire; it is not merely the connection of the crown, it is a constitutional annexation, an alliance of liberty, which is the true meaning and mystery of the sisterhood, and will make both countries one arm and one soul, replenishing from time to time, in their immortal connection, the vital spirit of law and liberty from the lamp of each other's light; thus combined by the ties of common interest, equal trade and equal liberty, the constitution of both countries may become immortal, a new and milder empire may arise from the errors of the old, and the British nation assume once more her natural station—the head of mankind.

That there are precedents against us I allow—acts of power I would call them, not precedent; and I answer the

English pleading such precedents, as they answered their kings when they urged precedents against the liberty of England. Such things are the weakness of the times; the tyranny of one side, the feebleness of the other, the law of neither; we will not be bound by them; or rather, in the words of the declaration of right, "no doing judgment, proceeding, or anywise to the contrary, shall be brought into precedent or example." Do not then tolerate a power—the power of the British Parliament over this land, which has no foundation in utility, or necessity, or empire, or the laws of England, or the laws of Ireland, or the laws of nature, or the laws of God—do not suffer it to have a duration in your mind.

Do not tolerate that power which blasted you for a century, that power which shattered your loom, banished your manufactures, dishonored your peerage, and stopped the growth of your people; do not, I say, be bribed by an export of wool, or an import of sugar, and permit that power which has thus withered the land to remain in your country and have existence in your pusillanimity.

Do not suffer the arrogance of England to imagine a surviving hope in the fears of Ireland; do not send the people to their own resolves for liberty, passing by the tribunals of justice and the high court of Parliament; neither imagine that, by any formation of apology, you can palliate such a commission to your hearts, still less to your children, who will sting you with their curses in your grave for having interposed between them and their Maker, robbing them of an immense occasion, and losing an opportunity which you did not create, and can never restore.

Hereafter, when these things shall be history, your age of thraldom and poverty, your sudden resurrection, commercial redress, and miraculous armament, shall the historian stop at liberty, and observe—that here the principal men among us fell into mimic trances of gratitude—they were awed by a weak ministry, and bribed by an empty treasury—and when liberty was within their grasp, and the temple opened her folding doors, and the arms of the people clanged, and the zeal of the nation urged and encouraged them on, that they fell down, and were prostituted at the threshold?

I might, as a constituent, come to your bar and demand my liberty. I do call upon you, by the laws of the land and their violation, by the instruction of eighteen counties, by the arms, inspiration, and providence of the present moment, tell us the rule by which we shall go—assert the law of Ireland—declare the liberty of the land.

I will not be answered by a public lie, in the shape of an amendment; neither, speaking for the subjects' freedom, am I to hear of faction. I wish for nothing but to breathe, in this our island, in common with my fellow-subjects, the air of liberty. I have no ambition unless it be the ambition to break your chain, and contemplate your glory. I never will be satisfied so long as the meanest cottager in Ireland has a link of the British chain clanking to his rags; he may be naked, he shall not be in irons; and I do see the time is at hand, the spirit is gone forth, the declaration is planted; and though great men should apostatize, yet the cause will live; and though the public speaker should die, yet the immortal fire shall outlast the organ which conveyed it, and the breath of liberty, like the word of the holy man, will not die with the prophet, but survive him.

I shall move you, "That the King's most excellent Majesty, and the Lords and Commons of Ireland, are the only power competent to make laws to bind Ireland."

ALEXANDER HAMILTON

ON THE EXPEDIENCY OF ADOPTING THE FEDERAL CONSTITUTION

[Alexander Hamilton, statesman and publicist, was born in the West Indian Island of Nevis, January 11, 1757. In 1776, being nineteen, he forsook his studies at King's College, now Columbia, New York, and entered the army, served at Long Island and White Plains, and finally was taken on Washington's staff, ranking as lieutenant-colonel. In 1782 he was sent to Congress by New York State, and his first work was an effort to relieve the condition of the national currency. Through his influence New York State was represented in the Constitutional Convention, and he helped to frame the document under which the union of states was effected. He wrote more than half the papers of the " Federalist,"which was intended to contravene the prevalent reluctance to ratification. He subsequently became secretary of the treasury in Washington's cabinet. When the presidency fell to John Adams he retired to private life, resuming the practice of his profession in New York. He was killed in a duel with Aaron Burr, July 11, 1804. The speech that follows, urging the adoption of the Constitution, was delivered before the Constitutional Convention at New York, June 24, 1788.]

I AM persuaded, Mr. Chairman, that I in my turn shall be indulged in addressing the committee. We all, in equal sincerity, profess to be anxious for the establishment of a republican government on a safe and solid basis. It is the object of the wishes of every honest man in the United States, and I presume that I shall not be disbelieved when I declare that it is an object of all others the nearest and most dear to my own heart. The means of accomplishing this great purpose has become the most important study which can interest mankind. It is our duty to examine all those means with peculiar attention, and to choose the best and most effectual. It is our duty to draw from nature, from reason, from examples, the best principles of policy, and to pursue and apply them in the formation of our government. We should contemplate and compare the systems, which in this examination come under our view; distinguish, with a careful eye, the defects and excellencies of each, and discarding the former, incorporate the latter, as far as circumstances will admit, into our Constitution. If we pursue a different course and neglect this duty we shall probably disappoint the expectations of our country and of the world.

In the commencement of a revolution, which received its birth from the usurpations of tyranny, nothing was more natural than that the public mind should be influenced by an extreme spirit of jealousy. To resist these encroachments, and to nourish this spirit, was the great object of all our public and private institutions. The zeal for liberty became predominant and excessive. In forming our confederation, this passion alone seemed to actuate us, and we appear to have had no other view than to secure ourselves from despotism. The object certainly was a valuable one, and deserved our utmost attention. But, sir, there is another object equally important, and which our enthusiasm rendered us little capable of regarding: I mean a principle of strength and stability in the organization of our government, and vigor in its operations. This purpose can never be accomplished but by the establishment of some select body, formed peculiarly upon this principle. There are few positions more demonstrable than that there should be in every republic some permanent body to correct the prejudices, check the intemperate passions, and regulate the fluctuations of a popular assembly. It is evident that a body instituted for these purposes must be so formed as to exclude as much as possible from its own character those infirmities and that mutability which it is designed to remedy. It is therefore necessary that it should be small, that it should hold its authority during a considerable period, and that it should have such an independence in the exercise of its powers as will divest it as much as possible of local prejudices. It should be so formed as to be the center of political knowledge, to pursue always a steady line of conduct, and to reduce every irregular propensity to system. Without this establishment we may make experiments without end, but shall never have an efficient government.

It is an unquestionable truth, that the body of the people in every country desire sincerely its prosperity; but it is equally unquestionable that they do not possess the discernment and stability necessary for systematic government. To deny that they are frequently led into the grossest errors by misinformation and passion would be a flattery which their own good sense must despise. That branch of administration especially which involves our political relations with foreign states, a community will ever be incompetent to. These truths are not often held up in public assemblies; but they cannot be unknown to any who hears me. From these principles it follows that there ought to be two distinct bodies in our government: one, which shall be immediately constituted by and peculiarly represent the people, and possess all the popular features; another, formed upon the principle and for the purposes before explained. Such considerations as these induced the convention who formed your state constitution, to institute a senate upon the present plan. The history of ancient and modern republics had taught them that many of the evils which these republics had suffered arose from the want of a certain balance and mutual control indispensable to a wise administration; they were convinced that popular assemblies are frequently misguided by ignorance, by sudden impulses, and the intrigues of ambitious men; and that some firm barrier against these operations was necessary; they, therefore, instituted your senate, and the benefits we have experienced have fully justified their conceptions.

Gentlemen in their reasoning have placed the interests of the several states and those of the United States in contrast; this is not a fair view of the subject; they must necessarily be involved in each other. What we apprehend is, that some sinister prejudice, or some prevailing passion, may assume the form of a genuine interest. The influence of these is as powerful as the most permanent conviction of the public good; and against this influence we ought to provide. The local interests of a state ought in every case to give way to the interests of the Union; for when a sacrifice of one or the other is necessary, the former becomes only an apparent, partial interest, and should yield, on the principle that the small good ought never to oppose the great one. When you assemble from your several counties in the Legislature, were every member to be guided only by the apparent interests of his county, government would be impracticable. There must be a perpetual accommodation and sacrifice of local advantages to general expediency; but the spirit of a mere popular assembly would rarely be actuated by this important principle. It is therefore absolutely necessary that the Senate should be so formed as to be unbiased by false conceptions of the real interests or undue attachment to the apparent good of their several states.

Gentlemen indulge too many unreasonable apprehensions of danger to the state governments; they seem to suppose that the moment you put men into a national council they become corrupt and tyrannical, and lose all their affection for their fellow citizens. But can we imagine that the senators will ever be so insensible of their own advantage as to sacrifice the genuine interest of their constituents? The state governments are essentially necessary to the form and spirit of the general system. As long, therefore, as Congress has a full conviction of this necessity, they must, even upon principles purely national, have as firm an attachment to the one as to the other. This conviction can never leave them, unless they become madmen. While the Constitution continues to be read and its principle known, the states must, by every rational man, be considered as essential, component parts of the Union; and therefore the idea of sacrificing the former to the latter is wholly inadmissible.

The objectors do not advert to the natural strength and resources of state governments, which will ever give them an important superiority over the general government. If we compare the nature of their different powers, or the means of popular influence which each possesses, we shall find the advantage entirely on the side of the states. This consideration, important as it is, seems to have been little attended to. The aggregate number of representatives throughout the states may be two thousand. Their personal influence will, therefore, be proportionably more extensive than that of one or two hundred men in Congress. The state establishments of civil and military officers of every description, infinitely

ALEXANDER HAMILTON

Photogravure after a painting

surpassing in number any possible correspondent establishments in the general government, will create such an extent and complication of attachments as will ever secure the predilection and support of the people. Whenever, therefore, Congress shall meditate any infringement of the state constitutions, the great body of the people will naturally take part with their domestic representatives. Can the general government withstand such a united opposition? Will the people suffer themselves to be stripped of their privileges? Will they suffer their legislatures to be reduced to a shadow and a name? The idea is shocking to common sense.

From the circumstances already explained, and many others which might be mentioned, results a complicated, irresistible check, which must ever support the existence and importance of the state governments. The danger, if any exists, flows from an opposite source. The probable evil is, that the general government will be too dependent on the state legislatures, too much governed by their prejudices, and too obsequious to their humors; that the states, with every power in their hands, will make encroachments on the national authority, till the Union is weakened and dissolved.

Every member must have been struck with an observation of a gentleman from Albany. "Do what you will," says he, "local prejudices and opinions will go into the government." What! shall we then form a constitution to cherish and strengthen these prejudices? Shall we confirm the distemper, instead of remedying it? It is undeniable that there must be a control somewhere. Either the general interest is to control the particular interests, or the contrary. If the former, then certainly the government ought to be so framed as to render the power of control efficient to all intents and purposes; if the latter, a striking absurdity follows; the controlling powers must be as numerous as the varying interests, and the operations of the government must therefore cease; for the moment you accommodate these different interests, which is the only way to set the government in motion, you establish a controlling power. Thus, whatever constitutional provisions are made to the contrary, every government will be at last driven to the necessity of subjecting the partial to the universal interest. The gentlemen ought always, in their

reasoning, to distinguish between the real, genuine good of
a state, and the opinions and prejudices which may prevail
respecting it; the latter may be opposed to the general
good, and consequently ought to be sacrificed; the former
is so involved in it, that it never can be sacrificed.

There are certain social principles in human nature from
which we may draw the most solid conclusions with respect
to the conduct of individuals and of communities. We love
our families more than our neighbors; we love our neighbors
more than our countrymen in general. The human affections,
like the solar heat, lose their intensity as they depart from
the center, and become languid in proportion to the expansion of the circle on which they act. On these principles,
the attachment of the individual will be first and forever
secured by the state governments; they will be a mutual
protection and support. Another source of influence, which
has already been pointed out, is the various official connections in the states. Gentlemen endeavor to evade the force
of this by saying that these offices will be insignificant. This
is by no means true. The state officers will ever be important, because they are necessary and useful. Their powers
are such as are extremely interesting to the people; such as
affect their property, their liberty, and life.

What is more important than the administration of justice
and the execution of the civil and criminal laws? Can the
state governments become insignificant while they have the
power of raising money independently and without control?
If they are really useful, if they are calculated to promote
the essential interests of the people, they must have their
confidence and support. The states can never lose their
powers till the whole people of America are robbed of
their liberties. These must go together; they must support
each other, or meet one common fate. On the gentleman's
principle, we may safely trust the state governments, though
we have no means of resisting them; but we cannot confide
in the national government, though we have an effectual
constitutional guard against every encroachment. This is
the essence of their argument, and it is false and fallacious
beyond conception.

With regard to the jurisdiction of the two governments, I

shall certainly admit that the Constitution ought to be so formed as not to prevent the states from providing for their own existence; and I maintain that it is so formed, and that their power of providing for themselves is sufficiently established. This is conceded by one gentleman, and in the next breath the concession is retracted. He says Congress has but one exclusive right in taxation — that of duties on imports; certainly, then, their other powers are only concurrent. But to take off the force of this obvious conclusion he immediately says that the laws of the United States are supreme; and that where there is one supreme there cannot be a concurrent authority; and further, that where the laws of the Union are supreme, those of the states must be subordinate; because there cannot be two supremes. This is curious sophistry. That two supreme powers cannot act together is false. They are inconsistent only when they are aimed at each other or at one indivisible object. The laws of the United States are supreme as to all their proper, constitutional objects; the laws of the states are supreme in the same way. These supreme laws may act on different objects without clashing; or they may operate on different parts of the same common object with perfect harmony. Suppose both governments should lay a tax of a penny on a certain article; has not each an independent and uncontrollable power to collect its own tax? The meaning of the maxim, there cannot be two supremes, is simply this — two powers cannot be supreme over each other. This meaning is entirely perverted by the gentlemen. But, it is said, disputes between collectors are to be referred to the federal courts. This is again wandering in the field of conjecture. But suppose the fact is certain; is it not to be presumed that they will express the true meaning of the Constitution and the laws? Will they not be bound to consider the concurrent jurisdiction; to declare that both the taxes shall have equal operation; that both the powers, in that respect, are sovereign and co-extensive? If they transgress their duty, we are to hope that they will be punished. Sir, we cannot reason from probabilities alone. When we leave common-sense, and give ourselves up to conjecture, there can be no certainty, no security in our reasonings.

I imagine I have stated to the committee abundant reasons to prove the entire safety of the state governments and of the people. I would go into a more minute consideration of the nature of the concurrent jurisdiction and the operation of the laws in relation to revenue, but at present I feel too much indisposed to proceed. I shall, with leave of the committee, improve another opportunity of expressing to them more fully my ideas on this point. I wish the committee to remember that the Constitution under examination is framed upon truly republican principles; and that, as it is expressly designed to provide for the common protection and the general welfare of the United States, it must be utterly repugnant to this Constitution to subvert the state governments or oppress the people.

JOHN HANCOCK

THE BOSTON MASSACRE

[John Hancock, an American statesman, noted as the first signer of the Declaration of Independence and also for his fearless and eloquent power of address, was born in Massachusetts in 1737. He was the son of a clergyman and completed his education at Harvard. Long before differences arose with the mother country, Hancock warmly espoused the patriot cause, and particularly distinguished himself at the obsequies of the victims of the Boston Massacre by an ardent speech. A few years later he was president of the Congress called to discuss colonial grievances. The British endeavored to affect his arrest, but were frustrated. When a general "pardon" was issued by the British military commander, Hancock's name was exempted from it. When the Continental Congress met in 1775 Hancock was made its President. He retained this dangerous honor for two years. During the War of Independence he led the Massachusetts militia and was for a time governor of his State, an office he also held after independence had been won. He died in 1793. On March 5, 1774, in Boston, he delivered the following oration in memory of the citizens who were killed by the British in the Boston massacre in 1770.]

THE attentive gravity, the venerable appearance of this crowded audience; the dignity which I behold in the countenances of so many in this great assembly; the solemnity of the occasion upon which we have met together, joined to a consideration of the part I am to take in the important business of this day, fill me with an awe hitherto unknown, and heighten the sense which I have ever had, of my unworthiness to fill this sacred desk. But, allured by the call of some of my respected fellow citizens, with whose request it is always my greatest pleasure to comply, I almost forgot my want of ability to perform what they required. In this situation I find my only support in assuring myself that a generous people will not severely censure what they know was well intended, though its want of merit should prevent their being able to applaud it. And I pray that my sincere

attachment to the interest of my country, and the hearty detestation of every design formed against her liberties, may
be admitted as some apology for my appearance in this
place.

I have always, from my earliest youth, rejoiced in the
felicity of my fellow men; and have ever considered it as the
indispensable duty of every member of society to promote,
as far as in him lies, the prosperity of every individual, but
more especially of the community to which he belongs; and
also, as a faithful subject of the state, to use his utmost endeavors to detect, and having detected, strenuously to oppose
every traitorous plot which its enemies may devise for its
destruction. Security to the persons and properties of the
governed is so obviously the design and end of civil government, that to attempt a logical proof of it would be like
burning tapers at noonday, to assist the sun in enlightening
the world; and it cannot be either virtuous or honorable to
attempt to support a government of which this is not the
great and principal basis; and it is to the last degree vicious
and infamous to attempt to support a government which
manifestly tends to render the persons and properties of the
governed insecure. Some boast of being friends to government; I am a friend to righteous government, to a government founded upon the principles of reason and justice; but
I glory in publicly avowing my eternal enmity to tyranny.
Is the present system, which the British administration have
adopted for the government of the colonies, a righteous government—or is it tyranny? Here suffer me to ask (and
would to Heaven there could be an answer), What tenderness,
what regard, respect, or consideration has Great Britain
shown, in her late transactions, for the security of the persons or properties of the inhabitants of the colonies? Or
rather what has she omitted doing to destroy that security?
She has declared that she has ever had, and of right
ought ever to have, full power to make laws of sufficient
validity to bind the colonies in all cases whatever. She
has exercised this pretended right by imposing a tax upon
us without our consent; and lest we should show some reluctance at parting with our property, her fleets and armies
are sent to enforce her mad pretensions. The town of

Boston, ever faithful to the British Crown, has been invested by a British fleet; the troops of George III. have crossed the wide Atlantic, not to engage an enemy, but to assist a band of traitors in trampling on the rights and liberties of his most loyal subjects in America—those rights and liberties which as a father he ought ever to regard, and as a king he is bound in honor to defend from violation, even at the risk of his own life.

Let not the history of the illustrious House of Brunswick inform posterity that a king, descended from that glorious monarch, George II., once sent his British subjects to conquer and enslave his subjects in America. But be perpetual infamy entailed upon that villain who dared to advise his master to such execrable measures; for it was easy to foresee the consequences which so naturally followed upon sending troops into America, to enforce obedience to acts of the British Parliament, which neither God nor man ever empowered them to make. It was reasonable to expect that troops, who knew the errand they were sent upon, would treat the people whom they were to subjugate, with a cruelty and haughtiness which too often buries the honorable character of a soldier in the disgraceful name of an unfeeling ruffian. The troops, upon their first arrival, took possession of our senate house, and pointed their cannon against the judgment hall, and even continued them there whilst the supreme court of judicature for this province was actually sitting to decide upon the lives and fortunes of the king's subjects. Our streets nightly resounded with the noise of riot and debauchery; our peaceful citizens were hourly exposed to shameful insults, and often felt the effects of their violence and outrage. But this was not all: as though they thought it not enough to violate our civil rights, they endeavored to deprive us of the enjoyment of our religious privileges, to vitiate our morals, and thereby render us deserving of destruction. Hence the rude din of arms which broke in upon your solemn devotions in your temples, on that day hallowed by Heaven, and set apart by God himself for his peculiar worship. Hence impious oaths and blasphemies so often tortured your unaccustomed ear. Hence all the arts which idleness and luxury could invent were used to betray our youth of one sex into extravagance and effeminacy, and of the other to infamy and ruin; and did they not succeed but too well? Did not a reverence for religion sensibly decay? Did not our infants almost learn to lisp out curses before they knew their horrid import? Did not our youth forget they were Americans, and regardless of the admonitions of the wise and aged, servilely copy from their tyrants those vices which finally must overthrow the empire of Great Britain? And must I be compelled to acknowledge that even the noblest, fairest part of all the lower creation did not entirely escape the cursed snare? When virtue has once erected her throne within the female breast, it is upon so solid a basis that nothing is able to expel the heavenly inhabitant. But have there not been some, few, indeed, I hope, whose youth and inexperience have rendered them a prey to wretches, whom, upon the least reflection, they would have despised and hated as foes to God and their country? I fear there have been some such unhappy instances, or why have I seen an honest father clothed with shame? or why a virtuous mother drowned in tears?

But I forbear, and come reluctantly to the transactions of that dismal night, when in such quick succession we felt the extremes of grief, astonishment, and rage; when Heaven in anger, for a dreadful moment, suffered hell to take the reins; when Satan with his chosen band opened the sluices of New England's blood, and sacrilegiously polluted our land with the dead bodies of her guiltless sons! Let this sad tale of death never be told without a tear; let not the heaving bosom cease to burn with a manly indignation at the barbarous story through the long tracts of future time; let every parent tell the shameful story to his listening children until tears of pity glisten in their eyes, and boiling passions shake their tender frames; and whilst the anniversary of that ill-fated night is kept a jubilee in the grim court of pandemonium, let all America join in one common prayer to Heaven, that the inhuman, unprovoked murders of the fifth of March, 1770, planned by Hillsborough, and a knot of treacherous knaves in Boston, and executed by the cruel hand of Preston and his sanguinary coadjutors, may ever stand in history without a parallel. But what, my countrymen, withheld the ready arm of vengeance from executing instant justice on the vile assassins? Perhaps you feared promiscuous carnage might ensue, and that the innocent might share the fate of those who had performed the infernal deed. But were not all guilty? Were you not too tender of the lives of those who came to fix a yoke on your necks? But I must not too severely blame a fault, which great souls only can commit. May that magnificence of spirit which scorns the low pursuits of malice, may that generous compassion which often preserves from ruin, even a guilty villain, forever actuate the noble bosoms of Americans! But let not the miscreant host vainly imagine that we feared their arms. No, them we despised; we dread nothing but slavery. Death is the creature of a poltroon's brains; 'tis immortality to sacrifice ourselves for the salvation of our country. We fear not death. That gloomy night, the pale-faced moon, and the affrighted stars that hurried through the sky, can witness that we fear not death. Our hearts which, at the recollection, glow with rage that four revolving years have scarcely taught us to restrain, can witness that we fear not death; and happy it is for those who dared to insult us, that their naked bones are not now piled up an everlasting monument of Massachusetts' bravery. But they retired, they fled, and in that flight they found their only safety. We then expected that the hand of public justice would soon inflict that punishment upon the murderers which, by the laws of God and man, they had incurred. But let the unbiased pen of a Robertson, or perhaps of some equally famed American, conduct this trial before the great tribunal of succeeding generations. And though the murderers may escape the just resentment of an enraged people; though drowsy justice, intoxicated by the poisonous draught prepared for her cup, still nods upon her rotten seat, yet be assured, such complicated crimes will meet their due reward. Tell me, ye bloody butchers! ye villains high and low! ye wretches who contrived, as well as you who executed the inhuman deed! do you not feel the goads and stings of conscious guilt pierce through your savage bosoms? Though some of you may think yourselves exalted to a height that bids defiance to human justice; and others shroud yourselves beneath the mask of hypocrisy, and build your hopes of safety on the low arts of cunning, chicanery, and falsehood;

yet do you not sometimes feel the gnawings of that worm which never dies? Do not the injured shades of Maverick, Gray, Caldwell, Attucks, and Carr, attend you in your solitary walks; arrest you even in the midst of your debaucheries, and fill even your dreams with terror? But if the unappeased manes of the dead should not disturb their murderers, yet surely even your obdurate hearts must shrink, and your guilty blood must chill within your rigid veins, when you behold the miserable Monk, the wretched victim of your savage cruelty. Observe his tottering knees, which scarce sustain his wasted body; look on his haggard eyes; mark well the death-like paleness on his fallen cheek, and tell me, does not the sight plant daggers in your souls? Unhappy Monk! cut off, in the gay morn of manhood, from all the joys which sweeten life, doomed to drag on a pitiful existence, without even a hope to taste the pleasures of returning health! Yet, Monk, thou livest not in vain; thou livest a warning to thy country, which sympathizes with thee in thy sufferings; thou livest an affecting, an alarming instance of the unbounded violence which lust of power, assisted by a standing army, can lead a traitor to commit.

For us he bled, and now languishes. The wounds, by which he is tortured to a lingering death, were aimed at our country! Surely the meek-eyed Charity can never behold such sufferings with indifference. Nor can her lenient hand forbear to pour oil and wine into these wounds, and to assuage, at least, what it cannot heal.

Patriotism is ever united with humanity and compassion. This noble affection, which impels us to sacrifice everything dear, even life itself, to our country, involves in it a common sympathy and tenderness for every citizen, and must ever have a particular feeling for one who suffers in a public cause. Thoroughly persuaded of this, I need not add a word to engage your compassion and bounty towards a fellow citizen, who, with long-protracted anguish, falls a victim to the relentless rage of our common enemies.

Ye dark designing knaves, ye murderers, parricides! how dare you tread upon the earth, which has drunk in the blood of slaughtered innocents, shed by your wicked hands? How dare you breathe that air which wafted to the ear of Heaven

the groans of those who fell a sacrifice to your accursed
ambition? But if the laboring earth doth not expand her
jaws; if the air you breathe is not commissioned to be the
minister of death; yet, hear it and tremble! The eye of
Heaven penetrates the darkest chambers of the soul, traces
the leading clue through all the labyrinths which your industrious folly has devised; and you, however you may have
screened yourselves from human eyes, must be arraigned,
must lift your hands, red with the blood of those whose
death you have procured, at the tremendous bar of God!

But I gladly quit the gloomy theme of death, and leave
you to improve the thought of that important day, when our
naked souls must stand before that Being, from whom nothing can be hid. I would not dwell too long upon the horrid
effects which have already followed from quartering regular
troops in this town. Let our misfortunes teach posterity to
guard against such evils for the future. Standing armies are
sometimes (I would by no means say generally, much less
universally) composed of persons who have rendered themselves unfit to live in civil society; who have no other
motives of conduct than those which a desire of the present
gratification of their passions suggests; who have no property
in any country; men who have given up their own liberties,
and envy those who enjoy liberty; who are equally indifferent
to the glory of a George or a Louis; who, for the addition
of one penny a day to their wages, would desert from the
Christian cross, and fight under the crescent of the Turkish
sultan. From such men as these, what has not a state to
fear? With such as these, usurping Cæsar passed the
Rubicon; with such as these, he humbled mighty Rome,
and forced the mistress of the world to own a master in a
traitor. These are the men whom sceptred robbers now
employ to frustrate the designs of God, and render vain the
bounties which his gracious hand pours indiscriminately upon
his creatures. By these, the miserable slaves in Turkey,
Persia, and many other extensive countries are rendered
truly wretched, though their air is salubrious and their soil
luxuriously fertile. By these, France and Spain, though
blessed by nature with all that administers to the convenience
of life, have been reduced to that contemptible state in which

they now appear; and by these, Britain—but if I was possessed of the gift of prophecy, I dare not, except by divine
command, unfold the leaves on which the destiny of that
once powerful kingdom is inscribed.

But since standing armies are so hurtful to a state, perhaps my countrymen may demand some substitute, some
other means of rendering us secure against the incursions of
a foreign enemy. But can you be one moment at a loss?
Will not a well-disciplined militia afford you ample security
against foreign foes? We want not courage; it is discipline
alone in which we are exceeded by the most formidable
troops that ever trod the earth. Surely our hearts flutter no
more at the sound of war than did those of the immortal
band of Persia, the Macedonian phalanx, the invincible
Roman legions, the Turkish janissaries, the *gendarmes* of
France, or the well-known grenadiers of Britain. A well-
disciplined militia is a safe, an honorable guard to a community like this, whose inhabitants are by nature brave, and
are laudably tenacious of that freedom in which they were
born. From a well-regulated militia we have nothing to
fear; their interest is the same with that of the state. When
a country is invaded, the militia are ready to appear in its
defense; they march into the field with that fortitude which
a consciousness of the justice of their cause inspires; they
do not jeopard their lives for a master who considers them
only as the instruments of his ambition, and whom they
regard only as the daily dispenser of the scanty pittance of
bread and water. No, they fight for their houses, their lands,
for their wives, their children; for all who claim the tenderest
names, and are held dearest in their hearts; they fight pro
aris et focis, for their liberty, and for themselves, and for
their God. And let it not offend if I say that no militia ever
appeared in more flourishing condition than that of this
province now doth, and pardon me if I say of this town in
particular. I mean not to boast; I would not excite envy,
but manly emulation. We have all one common cause; let
it, therefore, be our only contest, who shall most contribute
to the security of the liberties of America. And may the
same kind Providence which has watched over this country
from her infant state still enable us to defeat our enemies. I

cannot here forbear noticing the signal manner in which the designs of those who wish not well to us have been discovered. The dark deeds of a treacherous cabal have been brought to public view. You now know the serpents who, whilst cherished in your bosoms, were darting their envenomed stings into the vitals of the Constitution. But the representatives of the people have fixed a mark on these ungrateful monsters, which, though it may not make them so secure as Cain of old, yet renders them at least as infamous. Indeed, it would be affrontive to the tutelar deity of this country, even to despair of saving it from all the snares which human policy can lay.

True it is, that the British ministry have annexed a salary to the office of the governor of this province, to be paid out of a revenue, raised in America, without our consent. They have attempted to render our courts of justice the instruments of extending the authority of acts of the British Parliament over this colony, by making the judges dependent on the British administration for their support. But this people will never be enslaved with their eyes open. The moment they knew that the governor was not such a governor as the charter of the province points out, he lost his power of hurting them. They were alarmed; they suspected him—have guarded against him, and he has found that a wise and a brave people, when they know their danger, are fruitful in expedients to escape it.

The courts of judicature, also, so far lost their dignity, by being supposed to be under an undue influence, that our representatives thought it absolutely necessary to resolve that they were bound to declare that they would not receive any other salary besides that which the general court should grant them; and if they did not make this declaration, that it would be the duty of the House to impeach them.

Great expectations were also formed from the artful scheme of allowing the East India Company to export tea to America upon their own account. This certainly, had it succeeded, would have effected the purpose of the contrivers, and gratified the most sanguine wishes of our adversaries. We soon should have found our trade in the hands of foreigners, and taxes imposed on everything which we consumed; nor would it have been strange if, in a few years, a company in London should have purchased an exclusive right of trading to America. But their plot was soon discovered. The people soon were aware of the poison which, with so much craft and subtilty, had been concealed. Loss and disgrace ensued; and perhaps this long-concerted masterpiece of policy may issue in the total disuse of tea in this country, which will eventually be the saving of the lives and the estates of thousands. Yet while we rejoice that the adversary has not hitherto prevailed against us, let us by no means put off the harness. Restless malice and disappointed ambition will still suggest new measures to our inveterate enemies. Therefore, let us also be ready to take the field whenever danger calls; let us be united and strengthen the hands of each other by promoting a general union among us. Much has been done by the committees of correspondence, for this and the other towns of this province, towards uniting the inhabitants; let them still go on and prosper. Much has been done by the committees of correspondence for the Houses of Assembly, in this and our sister colonies, for uniting the inhabitants of the whole continent for the security of their common interest. May success ever attend their generous endeavors. But permit me here to suggest a general congress of deputies, from the several Houses of Assembly on the continent, as the most effectual method of establishing such a union as the present posture of our affairs requires. At such a congress, a firm foundation may be laid for the security of our rights and liberties; a system may be formed for our common safety, by a strict adherence to which we shall be able to frustrate any attempts to overthrow our Constitution; restore peace and harmony to America, and secure honor and wealth to Great Britain, even against the inclinations of her ministers, whose duty it is to study her welfare; and we shall also free ourselves from those unmannerly pillagers who impudently tell us that they are licensed by an act of the British Parliament to thrust their dirty hands into the pockets of every American. But I trust the happy time will come when, with the besom of destruction, those noxious vermin will be swept forever from the streets of Boston.

Surely you never will tamely suffer this country to be a den of thieves. Remember, my friends, from whom you sprang. Let not a meanness of spirit, unknown to those whom you boast of as your fathers, excite a thought to the dishonor of your mothers. I conjure you, by all that is dear, by all that is honorable, by all that is sacred, not only that ye pray, but that ye act; that, if necessary, ye fight, and even die, for the prosperity of our Jerusalem. Break in sunder, with noble disdain, the bonds with which the Philistines have bound you. Suffer not yourselves to be betrayed by the soft arts of luxury and effeminacy into the pit digged for your destruction. Despise the glare of wealth. That people who pay greater respect to a wealthy villain than to an honest, upright man in poverty, almost deserve to be enslaved; they plainly show that wealth, however it may be acquired, is, in their esteem, to be preferred to virtue.

But I thank God that America abounds in men who are superior to all temptation, whom nothing can divert from a steady pursuit of the interest of their country; who are at once its ornament and safeguard. And sure I am I should not incur your displeasure, if I paid a respect so justly due to their much honored characters, in this place. But when I name an Adams, such a numerous host of fellow patriots rush upon my mind, that I fear it would take up too much of your time should I attempt to call over the illustrious roll. But your grateful hearts will point you to the men; and their revered names, in all succeeding time, shall grace the annals of America. From them let us, my friends, take example; from them let us catch the divine enthusiasm; and feel, each for himself, the godlike pleasure of diffusing happiness on all around us; of delivering the oppressed from the iron grasp of tyranny; of changing the hoarse complaints and bitter moans of wretched slaves into those cheerful songs which freedom and contentment must inspire. There is a heartfelt satisfaction in reflecting on our exertions for the public weal, which all the sufferings an enraged tyrant can inflict will never take away; which the ingratitude and reproaches of those whom we have saved from ruin cannot rob us of. The virtuous asserter of the rights of mankind merits a reward, which even a want of success in his endeavors to save his country, the heaviest misfortune which can befall a genuine patriot, cannot entirely prevent him from receiving.

I have the most animating confidence that the present noble struggle for liberty will terminate gloriously for America. And let us play the man for our God, and for the cities of our God; while we are using the means in our power, let us humbly commit our righteous cause to the great Lord of the universe, who loveth righteousness and hateth iniquity. And having secured the approbation of our hearts by a faithful and unwearied discharge of our duty to our country, let us joyfully leave our concerns in the hands of Him who raiseth up and pulleth down the empires and kingdoms of the world as he pleases; and with cheerful submission to his sovereign will, devoutly say, " Although the fig-tree shall not blossom, neither shall fruit be in the vines; the labor of the olive shall fail, and the field shall yield no meat; the flock shall be cut off from the fold, and there shall be no herd in the stalls: yet we will rejoice in the Lord, we will joy in the God of our salvation."

BENJAMIN HARRISON

INAUGURAL ADDRESS

[Benjamin Harrison, twenty-third President of the United States, was born at North Bend, Ohio, in 1833. He was fourth in descent from a signer of the Declaration of Independence, his grandfather was the ninth President of the United States, and his father twice a member of Congress. As a political speaker he first appeared in the campaign of 1856. In August, 1862, he was commissioned second lieutenant of volunteers, recruited a company of the 70th Indiana infantry, and was in active service until June, 1865, when, having the brevet rank of brigadier-general, he was mustered out. In 1876 he was Republican candidate for governor of Indiana, but failed of election. In the year 1881 he was elected to the United States Senate, where he remained till 1887, and became known as one of the ablest debaters of that body. He was elected to the U. S. presidency in 1888. He was renominated for the office in 1892, but failed of election. He died at Indianapolis in 1901. His inaugural address was delivered at Washington, March 4, 1889.]

THERE is no constitutional or legal requirement that the President shall take the oath of office in the presence of the people, but there is so manifest an appropriateness in the public induction to office of the chief executive officer of the nation that from the beginning of the government the people, to whose service the official oath consecrates the officer, have been called to witness the solemn ceremonial. The oath taken in the presence of the people becomes a mutual covenant. The officer covenants to serve the whole body of the people by a faithful execution of the laws, so that they may be the unfailing defense and security of those who respect and observe them, and that neither wealth, station, nor the power of combinations shall be able to evade their just penalties or to wrest them from a beneficent public purpose to serve the ends of cruelty or selfishness.

My promise is spoken; yours unspoken, but not the less real and solemn. The people of every state have here their representatives. Surely I do not misinterpret the spirit of the occasion when I assume that the whole body of the people covenant with me and with each other to-day to support and defend the Constitution and the union of the states, to yield willing obedience to all the laws and each to every other citizen his equal civil and political rights. Entering thus solemnly into covenant with each other, we may reverently invoke and confidently expect the favor and help of Almighty God—that he will give to me wisdom, strength, and fidelity, and to our people a spirit of fraternity and a love of righteousness and peace.

This occasion derives peculiar interest from the fact that the presidential term, which begins this day, is the twenty-sixth under our Constitution. The first inauguration of President Washington took place in New York, where Congress was then sitting, on the thirtieth day of April, 1789, having been deferred by reason of delays attending the organization of Congress and the canvass of the electoral vote. Our people have already worthily observed the centennials of the Declaration of Independence, of the battle of Yorktown, and of the adoption of the Constitution, and will shortly celebrate in New York the institution of the second great department of our constitutional scheme of government. When the centennial of the institution of the judicial department, by the organization of the Supreme Court, shall have been suitably observed, as I trust it will be, our nation will have fully entered its second century.

I will not attempt to note the marvelous, and, in great part, happy contrasts between our country as it steps over the threshold into its second century of organized existence under the Constitution, and that weak but wisely ordered young nation that looked undauntedly down the first century, when all its years stretched out before it.

Our people will not fail at this time to recall the incidents which accompanied the institution of government under the Constitution, or to find inspiration and guidance in the teachings and example of Washington and his great associates, and hope and courage in the contrast which thirty-eight populous and prosperous states offer to the thirteen states, weak in everything except courage and the love of liberty, that then fringed our Atlantic seaboard.

The territory of Dakota has now a population greater than any of the original states (except Virginia), and greater than the aggregate of five of the smaller states in 1790. The center of population when our national capital was located was east of Baltimore, and it was argued by many well-informed persons that it would move eastward rather than westward; yet in 1880 it was found to be near Cincinnati, and the new census about to be taken will show another stride to the westward. That which was the body has come to be only the rich fringe of the nation's robe. But our growth has not been limited to territory, population, and aggregate wealth, marvelous as it has been in each of those directions. The masses of our people are better fed, clothed, and housed than their fathers were. The facilities for popular education have been vastly enlarged and more generally diffused.

The virtues of courage and patriotism have given recent proof of their continued presence and increasing power in the hearts and over the lives of our people. The •influences of religion have been multiplied and strengthened. The sweet offices of charity have greatly increased. The virtue of temperance is held in higher estimation. We have not attained an ideal condition. Not all of our people are happy and prosperous; not all of them are virtuous and law-abiding. But on the whole, the opportunities offered to the individual to secure the comforts of life are better than are found elsewhere, and largely better than they were here one hundred years ago.

The surrender of a large measure of sovereignty to the general government, effected by the adoption of the Constitution, was not accomplished until the suggestions of reason were strongly reinforced by the more imperative voice of experience. The divergent interests of peace speedily demanded a " more perfect Union." The merchant, the shipmaster, and the manufacturer discovered and disclosed to our statesmen and to the people that commercial emancipation must be added to the political freedom

which had been so bravely won. The commercial policy of
the mother country had not relaxed any of its hard and
oppressive features. To hold in check the development of
our commercial marine, to prevent or retard the establishment and growth of manufactures in the states, and so to
secure the American market for their shops and the carrying
trade for their ships, was the policy of European statesmen,
and was pursued with the most selfish vigor.

Petitions poured in upon Congress urging the imposition
of discriminating duties that should encourage the production of needed things at home. The patriotism of the people,
which no longer found a field of exercise in war, was energetically directed to the duty of equipping the young Republic for the defense of its independence by making its
people self-dependent. Societies for the promotion of home
manufactures and for encouraging the use of domestics in
the dress of the people were organized in many of the states.
The revival at the end of the century of the same patriotic
interest in the preservation and development of domestic
industries and the defense of our working people against
injurious foreign competition is an incident worthy of attention. It is not a departure but a return that we have witnessed. The protective policy had then its opponents. The
argument was made, as now, that its benefits inured to particular classes or sections.

If the question became in any sense or at any time
sectional, it was only because slavery existed in some of the
states. But for this there was no reason why the cotton-
producing states should not have led or walked abreast with
the New England states in the production of cotton fabrics.
There was this reason only why the states that divide with
Pennsylvania the mineral treasures of the great southeastern
and central mountain ranges should have been so tardy in
bringing to the smelting furnace and to the mill the coal and
iron from their near opposing hillsides. Mill fires were
lighted at the funeral pile of slavery. The Emancipation
Proclamation was heard in the depths of the earth as well as
in the sky; men were made free, and material things became
our better servants.

The sectional element has happily been eliminated from

the tariff discussion. We have no longer states that are necessarily only planting states. None are excluded from achieving that diversification of pursuits among the people which brings wealth and contentment. The cotton plantation will not be less valuable when the product is spun in the country town by operatives whose necessities call for diversified crops and create a home demand for garden and agricultural products. Every new mine, furnace, and factory is an extension of the productive capacity of the state, more real and valuable than added territory.

Shall the prejudices and paralysis of slavery continue to hang upon the skirts of progress? How long will those who rejoice that slavery no longer exists cherish or tolerate the incapacities it put upon their communities? I look hopefully to the continuance of our protective system and to the consequent development of manufacturing and mining enterprises in the states hitherto wholly given to agriculture as a potent influence in the perfect unification of our people. The men who have invested their capital in these enterprises, the farmers who have felt the benefit of their neighborhood, and the men who work in shop or field, will not fail to find and to defend a community of interest.

Is it not quite possible that the farmers and the promoters of the great mining and manufacturing enterprises which have recently been established in the South may yet find that the free ballot of the workingman, without distinction of race, is needed for their defense as well as for his own? I do not doubt that if those men in the South who now accept the tariff views of Clay and the constitutional expositions of Webster would courageously avow and defend their real convictions, they would not find it difficult, by friendly instruction and cooperation, to make the black man their efficient and safe ally, not only in establishing correct principles in our national administration, but in preserving for their local communities the benefits of social order and economical and honest government. At least until the good offices of kindness and education have been fairly tried, the contrary conclusion cannot be plausibly urged.

I have altogether rejected the suggestion of a special executive policy for any section of our country. It is the duty of the executive to administer and enforce in the methods and by the instrumentalities pointed out and provided by the constitution all the laws enacted by Congress. These laws are general, and their administration should be uniform and equal. As a citizen may not elect what laws he will obey, neither may the executive elect which he will enforce. The duty to obey and to execute embraces the Constitution in its entirety and the whole code of laws enacted under it. The evil example of permitting individuals, corporations, or communities to nullify the laws because they cross some selfish or local interest or prejudice is full of danger, not only to the nation at large, but much more to those who use this pernicious expedient to escape their just obligations or to obtain an unjust advantage over others. They will presently themselves be compelled to appeal to the law for protection, and those who would use the law as a defense must not deny that use of it to others.

If our great corporations would more scrupulously observe their legal limitations and duties, they would have less cause to complain of the unlawful limitations of their rights or of violent interference with their operations. The community that by concert, open or secret, among its citizens, denies to a portion of its members their plain rights under the law, has severed the only safe bond of social order and prosperity. The evil works from a bad center both ways. It demoralizes those who practice it, and destroys the faith of those who suffer by it in the efficiency of the law as a safe protector. The man in whose breast that faith has been darkened is naturally the subject of dangerous and uncanny suggestions. Those who use unlawful methods, if moved by no higher motive than the selfishness that prompted them, may well stop and inquire what is to be the end of this.

An unlawful expedient cannot become a permanent condition of government. If the educated and influential classes in a community either practice or connive at the systematic violation of laws that seem to them to cross their convenience, what can they expect when the lesson that convenience or a supposed class interest is a sufficient cause for lawlessness has been well learned by the ignorant classes? A community where law is the rule of conduct and where courts, not mobs, execute its penalties, is the only attractive field for business investments and honest labor.

Our naturalization laws should be so amended as to make the inquiry into the character and good disposition of persons applying for citizenship more careful and searching. Our existing laws have been in their administration an unimpressive and often an unintelligible form. We accept the man as a citizen without any knowledge of his fitness, and he assumes the duties of citizenship without any knowledge as to what they are. The privileges of American citizenship ·are so great and its duties so grave that we may well insist upon a good knowledge of every person applying for citizenship and a good knowledge by him of our institutions. We should not cease to be hospitable to immigration, but we should cease to be careless as to the character of it. There are men of all races, even the best, whose coming is necessarily a burden upon our public revenues or a threat to social order. These should be identified and excluded.

We have happily maintained a policy of avoiding all interference with European affairs. We have been only interested spectators of their contentions in diplomacy and in war, ready to use our friendly offices to promote peace, but never obtruding our advice and never attempting unfairly to coin the distresses of other powers into commercial advantage to ourselves. We have a just right to expect that our European policy will be the American policy of European courts.

It is so manifestly incompatible with those precautions for our peace and safety, which all the great powers habitually observe and enforce in matters affecting them, that a shorter waterway between our eastern and western seaboards should be dominated by any European government, that we may confidently expect that such a purpose will not be entertained by any friendly power.

We shall in the future, as in the past, use every endeavor to maintain and enlarge our friendly relations with all the great powers, but they will not expect us to look kindly upon any project that would leave us subject to the dangers of a hostile observation or environment. We have not sought to dominate or to absorb any of our weaker neighbors, but rather to aid and encourage them to establish free and stable governments resting upon the consent of their own people. We have a clear right to expect, therefore, that no European government will seek to establish colonial dependencies upon the territory of these independent American states. That which a sense of justice restrains us from seeking, they may be reasonably expected willingly to forego.

But it must not be assumed that our interests are so exclusively American that our entire inattention to any events that may transpire elsewhere can be taken for granted. Our citizens, domiciled for purposes of trade in all countries and in many of the islands of the sea, demand and will have our adequate care in their personal and commercial rights. The necessities of our navy require convenient coaling stations and dock and harbor privileges. These and other trading privileges we will feel free to obtain only by means that do not in any degree partake of coercion, however feeble the government from which we ask such concessions. But having fairly obtained them by methods and for purposes entirely consistent with the most friendly disposition toward all other powers, our consent will be necessary to any modification or impairment of the concession.

We shall neither fail to respect the flag of any friendly nation, or the just rights of its citizens, nor to exact the like treatment for our own. Calmness, justice, and consideration should characterize our diplomacy. The offices of an intelligent diplomacy or of friendly arbitration in proper cases should be adequate to the peaceful adjustment of all international difficulties. By such methods we will make our contribution to the world's peace, which no nation values more highly, and avoid the opprobrium which must fall upon the nation that ruthlessly breaks it.

The duty devolved by law upon the President to nominate, and by and with the advice and consent of the Senate to appoint all public officers whose appointment is not otherwise provided for in the Constitution or by act of Congress, has become very burdensome, and its wise and efficient discharge full of difficulty. The civil list is so large that a personal knowledge of any large number of the applicants is impossible. The President must rely upon the representation of others, and these are often made inconsiderately and without any just sense of responsibility. I have a right, I think, to insist that those who volunteer or are invited to give advice as to appointments shall exercise consideration and fidelity. A high sense of duty and an ambition to improve the service should characterize all public officers.

There are many ways in which the convenience and comfort of those who have business with our public offices may be promoted by a thoughtful and obliging officer, and I shall expect those whom I may appoint to justify their selection by a conspicuous efficiency in the discharge of their duties. Honorable party service will certainly not be esteemed by me a disqualification for public office, but it will in no case be allowed to serve as a shield of official negligence, incompetency, or delinquency. It is entirely creditable to seek public office by proper methods and with proper motives, and all applicants will be treated with consideration; but I shall need, and the heads of departments will need, time for inquiry and deliberation. Persistent importunity will not, therefore, be the best support of an application for office. Heads of departments, bureaus, and all other public officers having any duty connected therewith will be expected to enforce the civil service law fully and without evasion. Beyond this obvious duty I hope to do something more to advance the reform of the civil service. The ideal, or even my own ideal, I shall probably not attain. Retrospect will be a safer basis of judgment than promises. We shall not, however, I am sure, be able to put our civil service upon a nonpartisan basis until we have secured an incumbency that fair-minded men of the opposition will approve for impartiality and integrity. As the number of such in the civil list is increased, removals from office will diminish.

While a treasury surplus is not the greatest evil, it is a serious evil. Our revenue should be ample to meet the ordinary annual demands upon our treasury, with a sufficient margin for those extraordinary but scarcely less imperative demands which arise now and then. Expenditure should always be made with economy, and only upon public necessity. Wastefulness, profligacy, or favoritism in public expenditure is criminal. But there is nothing in the condition of our country or of our people to suggest that anything presently necessary to the public prosperity, security, or honor should be unduly postponed.

It will be the duty of Congress wisely to forecast and estimate these extraordinary demands, and, having added them to our ordinary expenditures, to so adjust our revenue laws that no considerable annual surplus will remain. We will fortunately be able to apply to the redemption of the public debt any small and unforeseen excess of revenue. This is better than to reduce our income below our necessary expenditures, with the resulting choice between another change of our revenue laws and an increase of the public debt. It is quite possible, I am sure, to effect the necessary reduction in our revenues without breaking down our protective tariff or seriously injuring any domestic industry.

The construction of a sufficient number of modern warships and of their necessary armament should progress as rapidly as is consistent with care and perfection in plans and workmanship. The spirit, courage, and skill of our naval officers and seamen have many times in our history given to weak ships and inefficient guns a rating greatly beyond that of the naval list. That they will again do so upon occasion, I do not doubt; but they ought not, by premeditation or neglect, to be left to the risks and exigencies of an unequal combat. We should encourage the establishment of American steamship lines. The exchanges of commerce demand stated, reliable, and rapid means of communication; and until these are provided, the development of our trade with the states lying south of us is impossible.

Our pension laws should give more adequate and discriminating relief to the Union soldiers and sailors and to their widows and orphans. Such occasions as this should remind us that we owe everything to their valor and sacrifice.

It is a subject of congratulation that there is a near prospect of the admission into the Union of the Dakotas and Montana and Washington territories. This act of justice has been unreasonably delayed in the case of some of them. The people who have settled these territories are intelligent, enterprising, and patriotic, and the accession of these new states will add strength to the nation. It is due to the settlers in the territories who have availed themselves of the invitations of our land laws to make homes upon the public domain that their titles should be speedily adjusted and their honest entries confirmed by patent.

It is very gratifying to observe the general interest now being manifested in the reform of our election laws. Those who have been for years calling attention to the pressing necessity of throwing about the ballot box and about the elector further safeguards, in order that our elections might not only be free and pure, but might clearly appear to be so, will welcome the accession of any who did not so soon discover the need of reform. The National Congress has not as yet taken control of elections in that case over which the Constitution gives it jurisdiction, but has accepted and adopted the election laws of the several states, provided penalties for their violation and a method of supervision. Only the inefficiency of the state law or an unfair partisan administration of them could suggest a departure from this policy.

It was clear, however, in the contemplation of the framers of the Constitution, that such an exigency might arise, and provision was wisely made for it. The freedom of the ballot is a condition of our national life, and no power vested in Congress or in the Executive to secure or perpetuate it should remain unused upon occasion. The people of all the congressional districts have an equal interest that the election in each shall truly express the views and wishes of a majority of the qualified electors residing within it. The results of such elections are not local, and the insistence of electors residing in other districts that they shall be pure and free does not savor at all of impertinence.

If in any of the states the public security is thought to be threatened by ignorance among the electors, the obvious remedy is education. The sympathy and help of our people will not be withheld from any community struggling with special embarrassments or difficulties connected with the suffrage, if the remedies proposed proceed upon lawful lines and are promoted by just and honorable methods. How shall those who practice election frauds recover that respect for the sanctity of the ballot which is the first condition and obligation of good citizenship? The man who has come to regard the ballot box as a juggler's hat has renounced his allegiance.

Let us exalt patriotism and moderate our party contentions. Let those who would die for the flag on the field of battle give a better proof of their patriotism and a higher glory to their country by promoting fraternity and justice. A party success that is achieved by unfair methods or by practices that partake of revolution is hurtful and evanescent, even from a party standpoint. We should hold our differing opinions in mutual respect, and, having submitted them to the arbitrament of the ballot, should accept an adverse judgment with the same respect that we would have demanded of our opponents if the decision had been in our favor.

No other people have a government more worthy of their respect and love, or a land so magnificent in extent, so pleasant to look upon, and so full of generous suggestion to enterprise and labor. God has placed upon our head a diadem, and has laid at our feet power and wealth beyond definition or calculation. But we must not forget that we take these gifts upon the condition that justice and mercy shall hold the reins of power, and that the upward avenues of hope shall be free to all the people.

I do not mistrust the future. Dangers have been in frequent ambush along our path, but we have uncovered and vanquished them all. Passion has swept some of our communities, but only to give us a new demonstration that the great body of our people are stable, patriotic, and law-abiding. No political party can long pursue advantage at the expense of public honor, or by rude and indecent methods, without protest and fatal disaffection in its own body. The peaceful agencies of commerce are more fully revealing the necessary unity of all our communities, and the increasing intercourse of our people is promoting mutual respect. We shall find unalloyed pleasure in the revelation which our next census will make of the swift development of the great resources of some of the states. Each state will bring its generous contribution to the great aggregate of the nation's increase. And when the harvests from the fields, the cattle from the hills, and the ores of the earth shall have been weighed, counted, and valued, we will turn from them all to crown with the highest honor the state that has most promoted education, virtue, justice, and patriotism among its people.

JOHN HAY

ON WILLIAM McKINLEY

John Hay, LL.D., *littérateur*, diplomatist and statesman, was born in
Indiana in 1838. Twenty years later he graduated from Brown University. He entered as a student the law office of Abraham Lincoln, and
was in due time admitted to the bar, but when Lincoln became President
he made young Hay his private secretary. A long and brilliant diplomatic career eventually opened for John Hay, by his appointment as
secretary of legation in Paris. Later he held the same post in Vienna
and in Madrid. He returned to his native land in 1870, and devoted
himself to literature. In 1879 he became first assistant secretary of state.
In 1897 President McKinley sent Mr. Hay to the Court of St. James with
the rank of ambassador, only to recall him in about a year and place
him at the head of the cabinet as secretary of state. President Roosevelt would not consent, when he assumed office, to the retirement of
the secretary, so he continues (1903) to fill that important post. Mr.
Hay has written a number of poems, ballads and other interesting works
of an historical and biographical character. Secretary Hay's eloquent
tribute to the memory of the third of our martyred Presidents was
delivered in Washington, February 27, 1902.]

FOR the third time the Congress of the United States are
assembled to commemorate the life and the death of a
President slain by the hand of an assassin. The attention of
the future historian will be attracted to the features which
reappear with startling sameness in all three of these awful
crimes: the uselessness, the utter lack of consequence of the
act; the obscurity, the insignificance of the criminal; the
blamelessness—so far as in our sphere of existence the best
of men may be held blameless—of the victim. Not one of
our murdered Presidents had an enemy in the world; they
were all of such preeminent purity of life that no pretext
could be given for the attack of passional crime; they were
all men of democratic instincts, who could never have offended the most jealous advocates of equality; they were of
kindly and generous nature, to whom wrong or injustice was
impossible; of moderate fortune, whose slender means nobody

could envy. They were men of austere virtue, of tender heart, of eminent abilities, which they had devoted with single minds to the good of the Republic. If ever men walked before God and man without blame, it was these three rulers of our people. The only temptation to attack their lives offered was their gentle radiance—to eyes hating the light that was offense enough.

The stupid uselessness of such an infamy affronts the common sense of the world. One can conceive how the death of a dictator may change the political conditions of an empire; how the extinction of a narrowing line of kings may bring in an alien dynasty. But in a well-ordered republic like ours, the ruler may fall, but the state feels no tremor. Our beloved and revered leader is gone—but the natural process of our laws provides us a successor, identical in purpose and ideals, nourished by the same teachings, inspired by the same principles, pledged by tender affection as well as by high loyalty to carry to completion the immense task committed to his hands, and to smite with iron severity every manifestation of that hideous crime which his mild predecessor, with his dying breath, forgave. The sayings of celestial wisdom have no date; the words that reach us, over two thousand years, out of the darkest hour of gloom the world has ever known, are true to the life to-day: "They know not what they do." The blow struck at our dear friend and ruler was as deadly as blind hate could make it; but the blow struck at anarchy was deadlier still.

What a world of insoluble problems such an event excites in the mind! Not merely in its personal but in its public aspects it presents a paradox not to be comprehended. Under a system of government so free and so impartial that we recognize its existence only by its benefactions; under a social order so purely democratic that classes cannot exist in it, affording opportunities so universal that even conditions are as changing as the winds, where the laborer of to-day is the capitalist of to-morrow; under laws which are the result of ages of evolution, so uniform and so beneficent that the President has just the same rights and privileges as the artisan —we see the same hellish growth of hatred and murder which dogs equally the footsteps of benevolent monarchs and blood-stained despots. How many countries can join with us in the community of a kindred sorrow! I will not speak of those distant regions where assassination enters into the daily life of government. But among the nations bound to us by the ties of familiar intercourse—who can forget that wise and high-minded autocrat who had earned the proud title of the Liberator? that enlightened and magnanimous citizen whom France still mourns? that brave and chivalrous King of Italy who only lived for his people? and, saddest of all, that lovely and sorrowing empress, whose harmless life could hardly have excited the animosity of a demon? Against that devilish spirit nothing avails—neither virtue, nor patriotism, nor age, nor youth, nor conscience, nor pity. We cannot even say that education is a sufficient safeguard against this baleful evil—for most of the wretches whose crimes have so shocked humanity in recent years are men not unlettered, who have gone from the common schools through murder to the scaffold.

Our minds cannot discern the origin nor conceive the extent of wickedness so perverse and so cruel; but this does not exempt us from the duty of trying to control and counteract it. We do not understand what electricity is, whence it comes or what its hidden properties may be. But we know it as a mighty force for good or evil—and so with the painful toil of years, men of learning and skill have labored to store and to subjugate it, to neutralize, and even to employ its destructive energies. This problem of anarchy is dark and intricate, but it ought to be within the compass of democratic government—although no sane mind can fathom the mysteries of these untracked and orbitless natures—to guard against their aberrations, to take away from them the hope of escape, the long luxury of scandalous days in court, the unwholesome sympathy of hysterical degenerates, and so by degrees to make the crime not worth committing, even to these abnormal and distorted souls.

It would be presumptuous for me in this presence to suggest the details of remedial legislation for a malady so malignant. That task may safely be left to the skill and patience of the National Congress, which have never been found unequal to any such emergency. The country believes

that the memory of three murdered comrades of yours—all
of whose voices still haunt these walls—will be a sufficient
inspiration to enable you to solve even this abstruse and painful problem, which has dimmed so many pages of history
with blood and with tears.

Before an audience less sympathetic than this I should not
dare to speak of that great career which we have met to
commemorate. But we are all his friends, and friends do not
criticise each other's words about an open grave. I thank
you for the honor you have done me in inviting me here, and
not less for the kind forbearance I know I shall have from
you in my most inadequate efforts to speak of him worthily.

The life of William McKinley was, from his birth to his
death, typically American. There is no environment, I
should say, anywhere else in the world which could produce
just such a character. He was born into that way of life
which elsewhere is called the middle class, but which in this
country is so nearly universal as to make of other classes an
almost negligible quantity. He was neither rich nor poor,
neither proud nor humble; he knew no hunger he was not
sure of satisfying, no luxury which could enervate mind or
body. His parents were sober, God-fearing people; intelligent and upright, without pretension and without humility.
He grew up in the company of boys like himself: wholesome, honest, self-respecting. They looked down on nobody; they never felt it possible they could be looked down
upon. Their houses were the homes of probity, piety,
patriotism. They learned in the admirable school readers of
fifty years ago the lessons of heroic and splendid life which
have come down from the past. They read in their weekly
newspapers the story of the world's progress, in which they
were eager to take part, and of the sins and wrongs of civilization, with which they burned to do battle. It was a serious
and thoughtful time. The boys of that day felt dimly, but
deeply, that days of sharp struggle and high achievement
were before them. They looked at life with the wondering
yet resolute eyes of a young esquire in his vigil of arms.
They felt a time was coming when to them should be addressed
the stern admonition of the Apostle, "Quit you like men;
be strong."

It is not easy to give to those of a later generation any clear idea of that extraordinary spiritual awakening which passed over the country at the first red signal fires of the Civil War. It was not our earliest apocalypse: a hundred years before the nation had been revealed to itself, when after long discussion and much searching of heart the people of the colonies had resolved that to live without liberty was worse than to die, and had therefore wagered in the solemn game of war "their lives, their fortunes, and their sacred honor." In a stress of heat and labor unutterable, the country had been hammered and welded together; but thereafter for nearly a century there had been nothing in our life to touch the innermost fountain of feeling and devotion. We had had rumors of wars—even wars we had had, not without sacrifices and glory—but nothing which went to the vital self-consciousness of the country, nothing which challenged the nation's right to live. But in 1860 the nation was going down into the Valley of Decision. The question which had been debated on thousands of platforms, which had been discussed in countless publications, which, thundered from innumerable pulpits, had caused in their congregations the bitter strife and dissension to which only cases of conscience can give rise, was everywhere pressing for solution. And not merely in the various channels of publicity was it alive and clamorous. About every fireside in the land, in the conversation of friends and neighbors, and, deeper still, in the secret of millions of human hearts, the battle of opinion was waging; and all men felt and saw—with more or less clearness—that an answer to the importunate question, Shall the nation live? was due, and not to be denied. And I do not mean that in the North alone there was this austere wrestling with conscience. In the South as well, below all the effervescence and excitement of a people perhaps more given to eloquent speech than we were, there was the profound agony of question and answer, the summons to decide whether honor and freedom did not call them to revolution and war. It is easy for partisanship to say that the one side was right and that the other was wrong. It is still easier for an indolent magnanimity to say that both were right. Perhaps in the wide view of ethics one is always right to follow his conscience, though it lead him to disaster and death. But history is inexorable. She takes no account of sentiment and intention; and in her cold and luminous eyes that side is right which fights in harmony with the stars in their courses. The men are right through whose efforts and struggles the world is helped onward, and humanity moves to a higher level and a brighter day.

The men who are living to-day and who were young in 1860 will never forget the glory and glamour that filled the earth and the sky when the long twilight of doubt and uncertainty was ending and the time of action had come. A speech by Abraham Lincoln was an event not only of high moral significance, but of far-reaching importance; the drilling of a militia company by Ellsworth attracted national attention; the fluttering of the flag in the clear sky drew tears from the eyes of young men. Patriotism, which had been a rhetorical expression, became a passionate emotion, in which instinct, logic, and feeling were fused. The country was worth saving; it could be saved only by fire; no sacrifice was too great; the young men of the country were ready for the sacrifice; come weal, come woe, they were ready.

At seventeen years of age William McKinley heard this summons of his country. He was the sort of youth to whom a military life in ordinary times would possess no attractions. His nature was far different from that of the ordinary soldier. He had other dreams of life, its prizes and pleasures, than that of marches and battles. But to his mind there was no choice or question. The banner floating in the morning breeze was the beckoning gesture of his country. The thrilling notes of the trumpet called *him*—him and none other —into the ranks. His portrait in his first uniform is familiar to you all—the short, stocky figure; the quiet, thoughtful face; the deep, dark eyes. It is the face of a lad who could not stay at home when he thought he was needed in the field. He was of the stuff of which good soldiers are made. Had he been ten years older he would have entered at the head of a company and come out at the head of a division. But he did what he could. He enlisted as a private; he learned to obey. His serious, sensible ways, his prompt, alert efficiency soon attracted the attention of his superiors.

He was so faithful in little things: they gave him more and more to do. He was untiring in camp and on the march; swift, cool, and fearless in fight. He left the army with field rank when the war ended, breveted by President Lincoln for gallantry in battle.

In coming years when men seek to draw the moral of our great Civil War, nothing will seem to them so admirable in all the history of our two magnificent armies as the way in which the war came to a close. When the Confederate army saw the time had come, they acknowledged the pitiless logic of facts and ceased fighting. When the army of the Union saw it was no longer needed, without a murmur or question, making no terms, asking no return, in the flush of victory and fullness of might it laid down its arms and melted back into the mass of peaceful citizens. There is no event, since the nation was born, which has so proved its solid capacity for self-government. Both sections share equally in that crown of glory. They had held a debate of incomparable importance and had fought it out with equal energy. A conclusion had been reached—and it is to the everlasting honor of both sides that they each knew when the war was over and the hour of a lasting peace had struck. We may admire the desperate daring of others who prefer annihilation to compromise, but the palm of common sense, and, I will say, of enlightened patriotism, belongs to the men like Grant and Lee, who knew when they had fought enough, for honor and for country.

William McKinley, one of that sensible million of men, gladly laid down his sword and betook himself to his books. He quickly made up the time lost in soldiering. He attacked his Blackstone as he would have done a hostile entrenchment; finding the range of a country law library too narrow, he went to the Albany Law School, where he worked energetically with brilliant success; was admitted to the bar and settled down to practice—a breveted veteran of twenty-four— in the quiet town of Canton, now and henceforward forever famous as the scene of his life and his place of sepulture. Here many blessings awaited him: high repute, professional success, and a domestic affection so pure, so devoted and stainless, that future poets, seeking an ideal of Christian marriage, will find in it a theme worthy of their songs. This is a subject to which the lightest allusion seems profanation; but it is impossible to speak of William McKinley without remembering that no truer, tenderer knight to his chosen lady ever lived among mortal men. If to the spirits of the just made perfect is permitted the consciousness of earthly things, we may be sure that his faithful soul is now watching over that gentle sufferer who counts the long hours in their shattered home in the desolate splendor of his fame.

A man possessing the qualities with which nature had endowed McKinley seeks political activity as naturally as a growing plant seeks light and air. A wholesome ambition; a rare power of making friends and keeping them; a faith, which may be called religious, in his country and its institutions; and, flowing from this, a belief that a man could do no nobler work than to serve such a country—these were the elements in his character that drew him irresistibly into public life. He had from the beginning a remarkable equipment; a manner of singular grace and charm; a voice of ringing quality and great carrying power—vast as were the crowds that gathered about him, he reached their utmost fringe without apparent effort. He had an extraordinary power of marshaling and presenting significant facts, so as to bring conviction to the average mind. His range of reading was not wide; he read only what he might some day find useful, and what he read his memory held like brass. Those who knew him well in those early days can never forget the consummate skill and power with which he would select a few pointed facts, and, blow upon blow, would hammer them into the attention of great assemblages in Ohio, as Jael drove the nail into the head of the Canaanite captain. He was not often impassioned; he rarely resorted to the aid of wit or humor; yet I never saw his equal in controlling and convincing a popular audience by sheer appeal to their reason and intelligence. He did not flatter or cajole them, but there was an implied compliment in the serious and sober tone in which he addressed them. He seemed one of them; in heart and feeling he *was* one of them. Each workingman in a great crowd might say: That is the sort of man I would like to be, and under more favoring circumstances might have been. He had the divine gift of sympathy, which, though given only to the elect, makes all men their friends.

So it came naturally about that in 1876—the beginning of the second century of the Republic—he began, by an election to Congress, his political career. Thereafter for fourteen years this chamber was his home. I use the word advisedly. Nowhere in the world was he so in harmony with his environment as here; nowhere else did his mind work with such full consciousness of its powers. The air of debate was native to him; here he drank delight of battle with his peers. In after days, when he drove by this stately pile, or when on rare occasions his duty called him here, he greeted his old haunts with the affectionate zest of a child of the house; during all the last ten years of his life, filled as they were with activity and glory, he never ceased to be homesick for this hall. When he came to the presidency, there was not a day when his Congressional service was not of use to him. Probably no other President has been in such full and cordial communion with Congress, if we may except Lincoln alone. McKinley knew the legislative body thoroughly, its composition, its methods, its habits of thought. He had the profoundest respect for its authority and an inflexible belief in the ultimate rectitude of its purposes. Our history shows how surely an Executive courts disaster and ruin by assuming an attitude of hostility or distrust to the Legislature; and, on the other hand, McKinley's frank and sincere trust and confidence in Congress were repaid by prompt and loyal support and cooperation. During his entire term of office this mutual trust and regard—so essential to the public welfare—was never shadowed by a single cloud.

He was a Republican. He could not be anything else. A Union soldier grafted upon a Clay Whig, he necessarily believed in the " American system " — in protection to home industries; in a strong, aggressive nationality; in a liberal construction of the Constitution. What any self-reliant nation might rightly do, he felt this nation had power to do, if required by the common welfare and not prohibited by our written charter.

Following the natural bent of his mind, he devoted

himself to questions of finance and revenue, to the essentials of the national housekeeping. He took high rank in the House from the beginning. His readiness in debate, his mastery of every subject he handled, the bright and amiable light he shed about him, and above all the unfailing courtesy and good will with which he treated friend and foe alike— one of the surest signatures of a nature born to great destinies — made his service in the House a pathway of unbroken success and brought him at last to the all-important post of Chairman of Ways and Means and leader of the majority. Of the famous revenue act which, in that capacity, he framed and carried through Congress, it is not my purpose here and now to speak. The embers of the controversy in the midst of which that law had its troubled being are yet too warm to be handled on a day like this. I may only say that it was never sufficiently tested to prove the praises of its friends or the criticism of its opponents. After a brief existence it passed away, for a time, in the storm that swept the Republicans out of power. McKinley also passed through a brief zone of shadow; his Congressional district having been rearranged for that purpose by a hostile legislature.

Some one has said it is easy to love our enemies; they help us so much more than our friends. The people whose malevolent skill had turned McKinley out of Congress deserved well of him and of the Republic. Never was Nemesis more swift and energetic. The Republicans of Ohio were saved the trouble of choosing a governor—the other side had chosen one for them. A year after McKinley left Congress he was made governor of Ohio, and two years later he was reelected, each time by majorities unhoped for and overwhelming. He came to fill a space in the public eye which obscured a great portion of the field of vision. In two national conventions the presidency seemed within his reach. But he had gone there in the interest of others, and his honor forbade any dalliance with temptation. So his nay was nay—delivered with a tone and gesture there was no denying. His hour was not yet come.

There was, however, no long delay. He became, from year to year, the most prominent politician and orator in the country. Passionately devoted to the principles of his party, he was always ready to do anything, to go anywhere, to proclaim its ideas and to support its candidates. His face and his voice became familiar to millions of our people; and wherever they were seen and heard, men became his partisans. His face was cast in a classic mould; you see faces like it in antique marble in the galleries of the Vatican and in the portraits of the great cardinal-statesmen of Italy; his voice was the voice of the perfect orator—ringing, vibrating, tireless, persuading by its very sound, by its accent of sincere conviction. So prudent and so guarded were all his utterances, so lofty his courtesy, that he never embarrassed his friends, and never offended his opponents. For several months before the Republican national convention met in 1896 it was evident to all who had eyes to see that Mr. McKinley was the only probable candidate of his party. Other names were mentioned, of the highest rank in ability, character, and popularity; they were supported by powerful combinations; but the nomination of McKinley as against the field was inevitable.

The campaign he made will be always memorable in our political annals. He and his friends had thought that the issue for the year was the distinctive and historic difference between the two parties on the subject of the tariff. To this wager of battle the discussions of the previous four years distinctly pointed. But no sooner had the two parties made their nominations than it became evident that the opposing candidate declined to accept the field of discussion chosen by the Republicans, and proposed to put forward as the main issue the free coinage of silver. McKinley at once accepted this challenge, and taking the battle for protection as already won, went with energy into the discussion of the theories presented by his opponents. He had wisely concluded not to leave his home during the canvass, thus avoiding a proceeding which has always been of sinister augury in our politics; but from the front porch of his modest house in Canton he daily addressed the delegations which came from every part of the country to greet him in a series of speeches so strong, so varied, so pertinent, so full of facts briefly set forth, of theories embodied in a single phrase, that they formed the hourly text for the other speakers of his party, and give probably the most convincing proof we have of his surprising fertility of resource and flexibility of mind. All this was done without anxiety or strain. I remember a day I spent with him during that busy summer. He had made nineteen speeches the day before; that day he made many. But in the intervals of these addresses he sat in his study and talked, with nerves as quiet and a mind as free from care as if we had been spending a holiday at the seaside or among the hills.

When he came to the presidency he confronted a situation of the utmost difficulty, which might well have appalled a man of less serene and tranquil self-confidence. There had been a state of profound commercial and industrial depression, from which his friends had said his election would relieve the country. Our relations with the outside world left much to be desired. The feeling between the Northern and Southern sections of the Union was lacking in the cordiality which was necessary to the welfare of both. Hawaii had asked for annexation and had been rejected by the preceding administration. There was a state of things in the Caribbean which could not permanently endure. Our neighbor's house was on fire, and there were grave doubts as to our rights and duties on the premises. A man either weak or rash, either irresolute or headstrong, might have brought ruin on himself and incalculable harm to the country.

Again I crave the pardon of those who differ with me, if, against all my intentions, I happen to say a word which may seem to them unbefitting the place and hour. But I am here to give the opinion which his friends entertained of President McKinley, of course claiming no immunity from criticism in what I shall say. I believe, then, that the verdict of history will be that he met all these grave questions with perfect valor and incomparable ability; that in grappling with them he rose to the full height of a great occasion, in a manner which redounded to the lasting benefit of the country and to his own immortal honor.

The least desirable form of glory to a man of his habitual mood and temper—that of successful war—was nevertheless conferred upon him by uncontrollable events. He felt the conflict must come; he deplored its necessity; he strained almost to breaking his relations with his friends, in order, first— if it might be—to prevent and then to postpone it to the latest possible moment. But when the die was cast, he labored with the utmost energy and ardor, and with an intelligence in military matters which showed how much of the soldier still survived in the mature statesman to push forward the war to a decisive close. War was an anguish to him; he wanted it short and conclusive. His merciful zeal communicated itself to his subordinates, and the war, so long dreaded, whose consequences were so momentous, ended in a hundred days.

Mr. Stedman, the dean of our poets, has called him "Augmenter of the State." It is a noble title; if justly conferred, it ranks him among the few whose names may be placed definitely and forever in charge of the historic muse. Under his rule Hawaii has come to us, and Tutuila; Porto Rico and the vast archipelago of the East. Cuba is free. Our position in the Caribbean is assured beyond the possibility of future question. The doctrine called by the name of Monroe, so long derided and denied by alien publicists, evokes now no challenge or contradiction when uttered to the world. It has become an international truism. Our sister republics to the south of us are convinced that we desire only their peace and prosperity. Europe knows that we cherish no dreams but those of world-wide commerce, the benefit of which shall be to all nations. The state is augmented, but it threatens no nation under heaven. As to those regions which have come under the shadow of our flag, the possibility of their being damaged by such a change of circumstances was in the view of McKinley a thing unthinkable. To believe that we could not administer them to their advantage was to turn infidel to our American faith of more than a hundred years.

In dealing with foreign powers he will take rank with the greatest of our diplomatists. It was a world of which he had little special knowledge before coming to the presidency. But his marvelous adaptability was in nothing more remarkable than in the firm grasp he immediately displayed in international relations. In preparing for war and in the restoration of peace he was alike adroit, courteous, and far-sighted. When a sudden emergency declared itself, as in China, in a state of things of which our history furnished no precedent and international law no safe and certain precept, he hesitated not a moment to take the course marked out for him by considerations of humanity and the national interests. Even while the legations were fighting for their lives against bands of infuriated fanatics, he decided that we were at peace with China; and while that conclusion did not hinder him from taking the most energetic measures to rescue our imperilled citizens, it enabled him to maintain close and friendly relations with the wise and heroic viceroys of the south, whose resolute stand saved that ancient empire from anarchy and spoliation. He disposed of every question as it arose with a promptness and clarity of vision that astonished his advisers, and he never had occasion to review a judgment or reverse a decision.

By patience, by firmness, by sheer reasonableness, he improved our understanding with all the great powers of the world, and rightly gained the blessing which belongs to the peacemakers.

But the achievements of the nation in war and diplomacy are thrown in the shade by the vast economical developments which took place during Mr. McKinley's administration. Up to the time of his first election the country was suffering from a long period of depression, the reasons of which I will not try to seek. But from the moment the ballots were counted that betokened his advent to power a great and momentous movement in advance declared itself along all the lines of industry and commerce. In the very month of his inauguration steel rails began to be sold at eighteen dollars a ton—one of the most significant facts of modern times. It meant that American industries had adjusted themselves to the long depression—that through the power of the race to organize and combine, stimulated by the conditions then prevailing, and perhaps by the prospect of legislation favorable to industry, America had begun to undersell the rest of the world. The movement went on without ceasing. The President and his party kept the pledges of their platform and their canvass. The Dingley bill was speedily framed and set in operation. All industries responded to the new stimulus, and American trade set out on its new crusade, not to conquer the world, but to trade with it on terms advantageous to all concerned. I will not weary you with statistics; but one or two words seem necessary to show how the acts of McKinley as President kept pace with his professions as candidate. His four years of administration were costly; we carried on a war which, though brief, was expensive. Although we borrowed two hundred millions and paid our own expenses, without asking for indemnity, the effective reduction of the debt now exceeds the total of the war bonds. We pay six millions less in interest than we did before the war and no bond of the United States yields the holder two per cent. on its market value. So much for the government credit; and we have five hundred and forty-six millions of gross gold in the treasury.

But, coming to the development of our trade in the four McKinley years, we seem to be entering the realm of fable. In the last fiscal year our excess of exports over imports was $664,592,826. In the last four years it was $2,354,442,213. These figures are so stupendous that they mean little to a careless reader—but consider! The excess of exports over imports for the whole preceding period from 1790 to 1897 —from Washington to McKinley—was only $356,808,822.

The most extravagant promises made by the sanguine McKinley advocates five years ago are left out of sight by these sober facts. The "debtor nation" has become the chief creditor nation. The financial center of the world, which required thousands of years to journey from the Euphrates to the Thames and the Seine, seems passing to the Hudson between daybreak and dark.

I will not waste your time by explaining that I do not invoke for any man the credit of this vast result. The captain cannot claim that it is he who drives the mighty steamship over the tumbling billows of the trackless deep; but praise is justly due him if he has made the best of her tremendous powers, if he has read aright the currents of the sea and the lessons of the stars. And we should be ungrateful if in this hour of prodigious prosperity we should fail to remember that William McKinley with sublime faith foresaw it, with indomitable courage labored for it, put his whole heart and mind into the work of bringing it about; that it was his voice which, in dark hours, rang out, heralding the coming light, as over the twilight waters of the Nile the mystic cry of Memnon announced the dawn to Egypt, waking from sleep.

Among the most agreeable incidents of the President's term of office were the two journeys he made to the South. The moral reunion of the sections—so long and so ardently desired by him—had been initiated by the Spanish war, when the veterans of both sides, and their sons, had marched shoulder to shoulder together under the same banner. The President in these journeys sought, with more than usual eloquence and pathos, to create a sentiment which should end forever the ancient feud. He was too good a politician to expect any results in the way of votes in his favor, and he accomplished none. But for all that, the good seed did not fall on barren ground. In the warm and chivalrous hearts of that generous people the echo of his cordial and brotherly words will linger long, and his name will be cherished in many a household where even yet the Lost Cause is worshiped.

Mr. McKinley was reelected by an overwhelming majority. There had been little doubt of the result among well-informed people; but when it was known, a profound feeling of relief and renewal of trust were evident among the leaders of capital and of industry, not only in this country, but everywhere. They felt that the immediate future was secure, and that trade and commerce might safely push forward in every field of effort and enterprise. He inspired universal confidence, which is the life-blood of the commercial system of the world. It began frequently to be said that such a state of things ought to continue; one after another, men of prominence said that the President was his own best successor. He paid little attention to these suggestions until they were repeated by some of his nearest friends. Then he saw that one of the most cherished traditions of our public life was in danger. The generation which has seen the prophecy of the Papal throne—*Non videbis annos Petri*—twice contradicted by the longevity of holy men was in peril of forgetting the unwritten law of our Republic: Thou shalt not exceed the years of Washington. The President saw it was time to speak, and in his characteristic manner he spoke, briefly, but enough. Where the lightning strikes there is no need of iteration. From that hour no one dreamed of doubting his purpose of retiring at the end of his second term, and it will be long before another such lesson is required.

He felt that the harvest time was come, to garner in the fruits of so much planting and culture, and he was determined that nothing he might do or say should be liable to the reproach of a personal interest. Let us say frankly he was a party man; he believed the policies advocated by him and his friends counted for much in the country's progress and prosperity. He hoped in his second term to accomplish substantial results in the development and affirmation of those policies. I spent a day with him shortly before he started on his fateful journey to Buffalo. Never had I seen him higher in hope and patriotic confidence. He was as sure of the future of his country as the Psalmist who cried, "Glorious things are spoken of thee, thou City of God." He was gratified to the heart that we had arranged a treaty which gave us a free hand in the Isthmus. In fancy he saw the canal already built and the argosies of the world passing through it in peace and amity. He saw in the immense evolution of American trade the fulfilment of all his dreams, the reward of all his labors. He was—I need not say— an ardent protectionist, never more sincere and devoted than during those last days of his life. He regarded reciprocity as the bulwark of protection—not a breach, but a fulfilment of the law. The treaties which for four years had been preparing under his personal supervision he regarded as ancillary to the general scheme. He was opposed to any revolutionary plan of change in the existing legislation; he was careful to point out that everything he had done was in faithful compliance with the law itself.

In that mood of high hope, of generous expectation, he went to Buffalo, and there, on the threshold of eternity, he delivered that memorable speech, worthy for its loftiness of tone, its blameless morality, its breadth of view, to be regarded as his testament to the nation. Through all his pride of country and his joy of its success runs the note of solemn warning, as in Kipling's noble hymn, "Lest we forget."

"Our capacity to produce has developed so enormously and our products have so multiplied that the problem of more markets requires our urgent and immediate attention. Only a broad and enlightened policy will keep what we have. No other policy will get more. In these times of marvelous business energy and gain we ought to be looking to the future, strengthening the weak places in our industrial and commercial systems, that we may be ready for any storm or strain.

"By sensible trade arrangements which will not interrupt our home production we shall extend the outlets for our increasing surplus. A system which provides a mutual exchange of commodities is manifestly essential to the continued and healthful growth of our export trade. We must not repose in fancied security that we can forever sell everything and buy little or nothing. If such a thing were possible, it would not be best for us or for those with whom we deal. . . . Reciprocity is the natural outgrowth of our wonderful industrial development under the domestic policy now firmly established. . . . The period of exclusiveness is past. The expansion of our trade and commerce is the pressing problem. Commercial wars are unprofitable. A policy of good will and friendly trade relations will prevent reprisals. Reciprocity treaties are in harmony with the spirit of the times; measures of retaliation are not."

I wish I had time to read the whole of this wise and weighty speech; nothing I might say could give such a picture of the President's mind and character. His years of apprenticeship had been served. He stood that day past master of the art of statesmanship. He had nothing more to ask of the people. He owed them nothing but truth and faithful service. His mind and heart were purged of the temptations which beset all men engaged in the struggle to survive. In view of the revelation of his nature vouchsafed to us that day, and the fate which impended over him, we can only say in deep affection and solemn awe, "Blessed are the pure in heart, for they shall see God." Even for that vision he was not unworthy.

He had not long to wait. The next day sped the bolt of doom, and for a week after—in an agony of dread broken by illusive glimpses of hope that our prayers might be answered—the nation waited for the end. Nothing in the glorious life that we saw gradually waning was more admirable and exemplary than its close. The gentle humanity of his words, when he saw his assailant in danger of summary vengeance, "Don't let them hurt him; " his chivalrous care that the news should be broken gently to his wife; the fine courtesy with which he apologized for the damage which his death would bring to the great exhibition; and the heroic resignation of his final words, "It is God's way. His will, not ours, be done," were all the instinctive expressions of a nature so lofty and so pure that pride in its nobility at once softened and enhanced the nation's sense of loss. The Republic grieved over such a son—but is proud forever of having produced him. After all, in spite of its tragic ending, his life was extraordinarily happy. He had, all his days, troops of friends, the cheer of fame and fruitful labor; and he became at last—

> " On fortune's crowning slope,
> The pillar of a people's hope,
> The center of a world's desire."

He was fortunate even in his untimely death, for an event so tragical called the world imperatively to the immediate study of his life and character, and thus anticipated the sure praises of posterity.

Every young and growing people has to meet, at moments, the problems of its destiny. Whether the question comes, as in Thebes, from a sphinx, symbol of the hostile forces of omnipotent nature, who punishes with instant death our failure to understand her meaning; or whether it comes, as in Jerusalem, from the Lord of Hosts, who commands the building of his temple, it comes always with the warning that the past is past, and experience vain. " Your fathers, where are they? and the prophets, do they live forever? " The fathers are dead; the prophets are silent; the questions are new, and have no answer but in time.

When the horny outside case which protects the infancy of a chrysalis nation suddenly bursts, and, in a single abrupt shock, it finds itself floating on wings which had not existed before, whose strength it has never tested, among dangers it cannot foresee, and is without experience to measure, every motion is a problem, and every hesitation may be an error. The past gives no clew to the future. The fathers, where are they? and the prophets, do they live forever? We are ourselves the fathers! We are our ourselves the prophets! The questions that are put to us we must answer without delay, without help—for the sphinx allows no one to pass.

At such moments we may be humbly grateful to have had leaders simple in mind, clear in vision—as far as human vision can safely extend—penetrating in knowledge of men, supple and flexible under the strains and pressures of society, instinct with the energy of new life and untried strength, cautious, calm, and, above all, gifted in a supreme degree with the most surely victorious of all political virtues—the genius of infinite patience.

The obvious elements which enter into the fame of a public man are few and by no means recondite. The man who fills a great station in a period of change, who leads his country successfully through a time of crisis; who, by his power of persuading and controlling others, has been able to command the best thought of his age, so as to leave his country in a moral or material condition in advance of where he found it—such a man's position in history is secure. If, in addition to this, his written or spoken words possess the subtle qualities which carry them far and lodge them in men's hearts; and, more than all, if his utterances and actions, while informed with a lofty morality, are yet tinged with the glow of human sympathy, the fame of such a man will shine like a beacon through the mists of ages—an object of reverence, of imitation, and of love. It should be to us an occasion of solemn pride that in the three great crises of our history such a man was not denied us. The moral value to a nation of a renown such as Washington's and Lincoln's and McKinley's is beyond all computation. No loftier ideal can be held up to the emulation of ingenuous youth. With such examples we cannot be wholly ignoble. Grateful as we may be for what they did, let us be still more grateful for what they were. While our daily being, our public policies, still feel the influence of their work, let us pray that in our spirits their lives may be voluble, calling us upward and onward.

There is not one of us but feels prouder of his native land because the august figure of Washington presided over its beginnings; no one but vows it a tenderer love because Lincoln poured out his blood for it; no one but must feel his devotion for his country renewed and kindled when he remembers how McKinley loved, revered, and served it, showed in his life how a citizen should live, and in his last hour taught us how a gentleman could die.

ROBERT YOUNG HAYNE

ON FOOTE'S RESOLUTION

[Robert Young Hayne, an American statesman, was born in South Carolina in 1791. Having studied law for some years, he was admitted to the bar, but suspended his practice to serve in the War of 1812. After that experience he was sent to the State Legislature, where he made himself prominent, and was chosen speaker of the House and later attorney-general of South Carolina. In 1823 he was elected to the United States Senate, where his abilities singled him out from the first. His chief principles were opposition to a protective tariff and belief in the right of a State to secede from the Union. The states' rights doctrine was never urged with more graceful and more impressive eloquence than Hayne urged it in his famous encounter with Webster. Two years after the close of this memorable episode, Hayne headed the South Carolina State convention committee that brought in the nullification ordinance. This fact secured his election as governor of the state, and while filling the executive office he came into collision with President Jackson. Governor Hayne actually prepared to resist the Federal government with armed force, but the matter was smoothed over by the Clay compromise. Hayne died in 1839. The following speech referring to the policy advocated by Samuel A. Foote, a Senator from Connecticut, regarding the sale of public lands, was delivered in the United States Senate, and drew forth the famous reply of Mr. Webster in 1830.]

MR. PRESIDENT : Little did I expect to be called upon to meet such an argument as was yesterday urged by the gentleman from Massachusetts (Mr. Webster). Sir, I question no man's opinions; I impeach no man's motives; I charged no party, or state, or section of country with hostility to any other, but ventured, as I thought, in a becoming spirit, to put forth my own sentiments in relation to a great national question of public policy. Such was my course. The gentleman from Missouri (Mr. Benton), it is true, had charged upon the Eastern states an early and continued hostility toward the West, and referred to a number of historical facts and documents in support of that charge. Now, sir, how have these different arguments been met? The honorable gentleman from Massachusetts, after deliberating a whole night upon his course, comes into this chamber to vindicate New England; and instead of taking up his issue with the gentleman from Missouri, on the charges which *he had preferred*, chooses to consider me as the author of those charges, and losing sight entirely of that gentleman, selects me as his adversary, and pours out all the vials of his mighty wrath upon my devoted head. Nor is he willing to stop there. He goes on to assail the institutions and policy of the South, and calls in question the principles and conduct of the state which I have the honor to represent. When I find a gentleman of mature age and experience, of acknowledged talents and profound sagacity, pursuing a course like this, declining the contest offered from the West, and making war upon the unoffending South, I must believe, I am bound to believe, he has some object in view which he has not ventured to disclose. Mr. President, why is this? Has the gentleman discovered in former controversies with the gentleman from Missouri that he is overmatched by that senator? And does he hope for an easy victory over a more feeble adversary? Has the gentleman's distempered fancy been disturbed by gloomy forebodings of "new alliances to be formed," at which he hinted? Has the ghost of the murdered coalition come back, like the ghost of Banquo, to " sear the eyeballs " of the gentleman, and will not down at his bidding? Are dark visions of broken hopes, and honors lost forever, still floating before his heated imagination? Sir, if it be his object to thrust me between the gentleman from Missouri and himself, in order to rescue the East from the contest it has provoked with the West, he shall not be gratified. Sir, I will not be dragged into the defense of my friend from Missouri. The South shall not be forced into a conflict not its own. The gentleman from Missouri is able to fight his own battles. The gallant West needs no aid from the South to repel any attack which may be made upon them from any quarter. Let the gentleman from Massachusetts controvert the facts and arguments of the gentleman from Missouri, if he can—and if he win the victory, let him wear the honors; I shall not deprive him of his laurels.

Sir, any one acquainted with the history of parties in this country will recognize in the points now in dispute between the senator from Massachusetts and myself the very grounds which have, from the beginning, divided the two great parties in this country, and which (call these parties by what names you will, and *amalgamate* them as you may) will divide them forever. The true distinction between those parties is laid down in a celebrated manifesto issued by the convention of the Federalists of Massachusetts, assembled in Boston, in February, 1824, on the occasion of organizing a party opposition to the reelection of Governor Eustis. The gentleman will recognize this as " the canonical book of political scripture"; and it instructs us that, when the American colonies redeemed themselves from British bondage, and became so many *independent nations*, they proposed to form a NATIONAL UNION (not a *Federal* Union, sir, but a NATIONAL UNION). Those who were in favor of a union of the states in this form became known by the name of Federalists; those who wanted no union of the states, or disliked the proposed form of union, became known by the name of Anti-Federalists. By means which need not be enumerated, the Anti-Federalists became (after the expiration of twelve years) our national rulers, and for a period of sixteen years, until the close of Mr. Madison's administration in 1817, continued to exercise the exclusive direction of our public affairs. Here, sir, is the true history of the origin, rise, and progress of the party of National Republicans, who date back to the very origin of the government, and who then, as now, chose to consider the Constitution as having created not a Federal but a National Union; who regarded " consolidation " as no evil, and who doubtless consider it "a consummation to be wished" to build up a great " central government," " one and indivisible." Sir, there have existed, in every age and every country, two distinct orders of men—the *lovers of freedom* and the devoted *advocates of power*.

The same great leading principles, modified only by the peculiarities of manners, habits, and institutions, divided parties in the ancient republics, animated the Whigs and

Tories of Great Britain, distinguished in our own times the Liberals and Ultras of France, and may be traced even in the bloody struggles of unhappy Spain. Sir, when the gallant Riego, who devoted himself and all that he possessed to the liberties of his country, was dragged to the scaffold, followed by the tears and lamentations of every lover of freedom throughout the world, he perished amid the deafening cries of "Long live the absolute king!" The people whom I represent, Mr. President, are the descendants of those who brought with them to this country, as the most precious of their possessions, "an ardent love of liberty"; and while that shall be preserved, they will always be found manfully struggling against the *consolidation of the government* AS THE WORST OF EVILS.

Who, then, Mr. President, are the true friends of the Union? Those who would confine the Federal government strictly within the limits prescribed by the Constitution; who would preserve to the states and the people all powers not expressly delegated; who would make this a Federal and not a National Union, and who, administering the government in a spirit of equal justice, would make it a blessing, and not a curse. And who are its enemies? Those who are in favor of consolidation; who are constantly stealing power from the states, and adding strength to the Federal government; who, assuming an unwarrantable jurisdiction over the states and the people, undertake to regulate the whole industry and capital of the country. But, sir, of all descriptions of men, I consider those as the worst enemies of the Union who sacrifice the equal rights which belong to every member of the confederacy to combinations of interested majorities for personal or political objects. But the gentleman apprehends no evil from the dependence of the states on the Federal government; he can see no danger of corruption from the influence of money or patronage. Sir, I know that it is supposed to be a wise saying that "patronage is a source of weakness"; and in support of that maxim it has been said that "every ten appointments make a hundred enemies." But I am rather inclined to think, with the eloquent and sagacious orator now reposing on his laurels on the banks of the Roanoke, that "the power of conferring favors creates a crowd of dependents"; he gave a forcible illustration of the truth of the remark, when he told us of the effect of holding up the savory morsel to the eager eyes of the hungry hounds gathered around his door. It mattered not whether the gift was bestowed on "Towzer" or "Sweet-lips," "Tray," "Blanche," or Sweetheart"; while held in suspense, they were all governed by a nod, and when the morsel was bestowed, the expectation of the favors of to-morrow kept up the subjection of to-day.

The senator from Massachusetts, in denouncing what he is pleased to call the Carolina doctrine, has attempted to throw ridicule upon the idea that a state has any constitu-tional remedy by the exercise of its sovereign authority, against "a gross, palpable, and deliberate violation of the Constitution." He calls it "an idle" or "a ridiculous notion," or something to that effect, and added, that it would make the Union a "mere rope of sand." Now, sir, as the gentleman has not condescended to enter into any examination of the question and has been satisfied with throwing the weight of his authority into the scale, I do not deem it necessary to do more than to throw into the opposite scale the authority on which South Carolina relies; and there, for the present, I am perfectly willing to leave the controversy. The South Carolina doctrine, that is to say, the doctrine contained in an exposition reported by a com-mittee of the Legislature in December, 1828, and published by their authority, is the good old Republican doctrine of '98—the doctrine of the celebrated "Virginia Resolutions" of that year, and of "Madison's Report" of '99. It will be recollected that the legislature of Virginia, in December, '98, took into consideration the alien and sedition laws, then considered by all Republicans as a gross violation of the Constitution of the United States, and on that day passed, among others, the following resolution:—

"The General Assembly doth explicitly and peremptorily declare that it views the powers of the Federal government, as resulting from the compact to which the states are parties, as limited by the plain sense and intention of the instrument constituting that compact, as no further valid than they are authorized by the grants enumerated in that compact;

and that in case of a deliberate, palpable, and dangerous exercise of other powers not granted by the said compact, the states who are the parties thereto have the right, and are in duty bound, to interpose for arresting the progress of the evil, and for maintaining within their respective limits the authorities, rights, and liberties appertaining to them."

In addition to the above resolution, the General Assembly of Virginia "appealed to the other states, in the confidence that they would concur with that commonwealth, that the acts aforesaid (the alien and sedition laws) are unconstitutional, and that the necessary and proper measures would be taken by each for cooperating with Virginia in maintaining unimpaired the authorities, rights, and liberties reserved to the states respectively, or to the people."

But, sir, our authorities do not stop here. The state of Kentucky responded to Virginia, and on the tenth of November, 1798, adopted those celebrated resolutions, well known to have been penned by the author of the Declaration of American Independence. In those resolutions, the legislature of Kentucky declare "that the government created by this compact was not made the exclusive or final judge of the extent of the power delegated to itself, since that would have made its discretion, and not the Constitution, the measure of its powers; but that, as in all other cases of compact among parties having no common judge, each party has an equal right to judge for itself as well of infractions as of the mode and measure of redress."

Sir, at that day the whole country was divided on this very question. It formed the line of demarcation between the Federal and Republican parties; and the great political revolution which then took place turned upon the very questions involved in these resolutions. That question was decided by the people, and by that decision the Constitution was, in the emphatic language of Mr. Jefferson, "saved at its last gasp." I should suppose, sir, it would require more self-respect than any gentleman here would be willing to assume, to treat lightly doctrines derived from such high sources. Resting on authority like this, I will ask, gentlemen, whether South Carolina has not manifested a high regard for the Union, when under a tyranny ten times more grievous than the alien and sedition laws she has hitherto gone no further than to petition, remonstrate, and to solemnly protest against a series of measures which she believes to be wholly unconstitutional and utterly destructive of her interests.   Sir, South Carolina has not gone one step further than Mr. Jefferson himself was disposed to go, in relation to the present subject of our present complaints—not a step further than the statesmen from New England were disposed to go under similar circumstances; no further than the senator from Massachusetts himself once considered as within "the limits of a constitutional opposition." The doctrine that it is the right of a state to judge of the violations of the Constitution on the part of the Federal government, and to protect her citizens from the operations of unconstitutional laws, was held by the enlightened citizens of Boson, who assembled in Faneuil Hall on the twenty-fifth of January, 1809. They state, in that celebrated memorial, that "they looked only to the state legislature, which was competent to devise relief against the unconstitutional acts of the general government. That your power (say they) is adequate to that object, is evident from the organization of the confederacy."

Thus it will be seen, Mr. President, that the South Carolina doctrine is the Republican doctrine of '98—that it was promulgated by the fathers of the faith—that it was maintained by Virginia and Kentucky in the worst of times—that it constituted the very pivot on which the political revolution of that day turned—that it embraces the very principles, the triumph of which, at that time, saved the Constitution at its last gasp, and which New England statesmen were not unwilling to adopt when they believed themselves to be the victims of unconstitutional legislation. Sir, as to the doctrine that the Federal government is the exclusive judge of the extent as well as the limitations of its power, it seems to me to be utterly subversive of the sovereignty and independence of the states. It makes but little difference, in my estimation, whether Congress or the Supreme Court are invested with this power. If the Federal government, in all or any of its departments, is to prescribe the limits of its own authority, and the states are bound to submit to the decision, and are not to be allowed to examine and decide for themselves when the barriers of the Constitution shall be overleaped, this is practically " a government without limitation of powers." The states are at once reduced to mere petty corporations, and the people are entirely at your mercy. I have but one word more to add. In all the efforts that have been made by South Carolina to resist the unconstitutional laws which Congress has extended over her, she has kept steadily in view the preservation of the Union, by the only means by which she believes it can be long preserved— a firm, manly, and steady resistance against usurpation. The measures of the Federal government have, it is true, prostrated her interests, and will soon involve the whole South in irretrievable ruin. But even this evil, great as it is, is not the chief ground of our complaints. It is the principle involved in the contest—a principle which, substituting the discretion of Congress for the limitations of the Constitution, brings the states and the people to the feet of the Federal government, and leaves them nothing they can call their own. Sir, if the measures of the Federal government were less oppressive, we should still strive against this usurpation. The South is acting on a principle she has always held sacred—resistance to unauthorized taxation. These, sir, are the principles which induced the immortal Hampden to resist the payment of a tax of twenty shillings. Would twenty shillings have ruined his fortune? No! but the payment of half of twenty shillings, on the principle on which it was demanded, would have made him a slave. Sir, if acting on these high motives—if animated by that ardent love of liberty which has always been the most prominent trait in the Southern character, we would be hurried beyond the bounds of a cold and calculating prudence; who is there, with one noble and generous sentiment in his bosom, who would not be disposed, in the language of Burke, to exclaim, " You must pardon something to the spirit of liberty"?

PATRICK HENRY

TO THE CONVENTION OF DELEGATES

[Patrick Henry, the distinguished orator of the colonial South, was born in Studley, Va., in 1736. His father early established him in the business of a country store, but he failed after a short time. He married at eighteen, and after several commercial failures began to study law, and eventually took up practice at Hanover. A brilliant speech of his attracted notice, and secured his election later to the Virginia House of Burgesses. Here he seized the occasion to introduce the first resolution relative to the British imposition of stamp duties and thus initiated the American Revolution. He was one of the first to see the inevitable necessity of armed resistance to Great Britain, and to advocate war preparations. He was successively governor of his state for three years, and member of the House of Burgesses, where he made his presence chiefly felt in his opposition to the new Federal Constitution. He declined the offer of Washington of appointments as secretary of state and of chief justice of the United States, but would have acceded to Washington's appeal to reënter the state legislature had not death, which came to him June 6, 1799, put an end to his activities. His speech before the convention of delegates, the most famous of all his orations, was made at Richmond, Va., in 1775.]

MR. PRESIDENT: No man thinks more highly than I do of the patriotism, as well as abilities, of the very worthy gentlemen who have just addressed the House. But different men often see the same subject in different lights; and, therefore, I hope that it will not be thought disrespectful to those gentlemen, if, entertaining as I do, opinions of a character very opposite to theirs, I shall speak forth my sentiments freely and without reserve. This is no time for ceremony. The question before the House is one of awful moment to this country. For my own part I consider it as nothing less than a question of freedom or slavery; and in proportion to the magnitude of the subject ought to be the freedom of the debate. It is only in this way that we can hope to arrive at truth, and fulfill the great responsibility which we hold to God and our country. Should I keep back my opinions at such a time, through fear of giving offense, I should consider myself as guilty of treason toward my country, and of an act of disloyalty toward the majesty of heaven, which I revere above all earthly kings.

Mr. President, it is natural to man to indulge in the illusions of hope. We are apt to shut our eyes against a painful truth, and listen to the song of that siren, till she transforms us into beasts. Is this the part of wise men, engaged in a great and arduous struggle for liberty? Are we disposed to be of the number of those who, having eyes, see not, and having ears, hear not, the things which so nearly concern their temporal salvation? For my part, whatever anguish of spirit it may cost, I am willing to know the whole truth; to know the worst and to provide for it.

I have but one lamp by which my feet are guided; and that is the lamp of experience. I know of no way of judging of the future but by the past. And judging by the past, I wish to know what there has been in the conduct of the British ministry for the last ten years to justify those hopes with which gentlemen have been pleased to solace themselves and the House? Is it that insidious smile with which our petition has been lately received? Trust it not, sir; it will prove a snare to your feet. Suffer not yourselves to be betrayed with a kiss. Ask yourselves how this gracious reception of our petition comports with these warlike preparations which cover our waters and darken our land. Are fleets and armies necessary to a work of love and reconciliation? Have we shown ourselves so unwilling to be reconciled, that force must be called in to win back our love? Let us not deceive ourselves, sir. These are the implements of war and subjugation; the last arguments to which kings resort. I ask gentlemen, sir, what means this martial array, if its purpose be not to force us to submission? Can gentlemen assign any other possible motives for it? Has Great Britain any enemy, in this quarter of the world, to call for all this accumulation of navies and armies? No, sir, she has none. They are meant for us; they can be meant for no other. They are sent over to bind and rivet upon us those chains which the

British ministry have been so long forging. And what have
we to oppose to them? Shall we try argument? Sir, we
have been trying that for the last ten years. Have we anything new to offer on the subject? Nothing. We have held
the subject up in every light of which it is capable; but it
has been all in vain. Shall we resort to entreaty and humble
supplication? What terms shall we find which have not been
already exhausted? Let us not, I beseech you, sir, deceive
ourselves longer. Sir, we have done everything that could
be done to avert the storm which is now coming on. We
have petitioned; we have remonstrated; we have suppli-
cated; we have prostrated ourselves before the throne, and
have implored its interposition to arrest the tyrannical hands
of the ministry and parliament. Our petitions have been
slighted; our remonstrances have produced additional violence and insult; our supplications have been disregarded;
and we have been spurned, with contempt, from the foot of
the throne. In vain, after these things, may we indulge the
fond hope of peace and reconciliation. There is no longer
any room for hope. If we wish to be free—if we mean to
preserve inviolate those inestimable privileges for which we
have been so long contending—if we mean not basely to
abandon the noble struggle in which we have been so long
engaged, and which we have pledged ourselves never to
abandon until the glorious object of our contest shall be obtained, we must fight! I repeat it, sir, we must fight! An
appeal to arms and to the God of Hosts is all that is left us!
They tell us, sir, that we are weak; unable to cope with
so formidable an adversary. But when shall we be stronger?
Will it be the next week, or the next year? Will it be when
we are totally disarmed, and when a British guard shall be
stationed in every house? Shall we gather strength by irres-
olution and inaction? Shall we acquire the means of
effectual resistance by lying supinely on our backs, and hug-
ging the delusive phantom of hope, until our enemies shall
have bound us hand and foot? Sir, we are not weak, if we
make a proper use of the means which the God of nature hath
placed in our power. Three millions of people, armed in the
holy cause of liberty, and in such a country as that which we
possess, are invincible by any force which our enemy can

send against us. Besides, sir, we shall not fight our battles alone. There is a just God who presides over the destinies of nations; and who will raise up friends to fight our battles for us. The battle, sir, is not to the strong alone; it is to the vigilant, the active, the brave. Besides, sir, we have no election. If we were base enough to desire it, it is now too late to retire from the contest. There is no retreat but in submission and slavery! Our chains are forged! Their clanking may be heard on the plains of Boston! The war is inevitable—and let it come! I repeat it, sir, let it come!

It is in vain, sir, to extenuate the matter. Gentlemen may cry peace, peace—but there is no peace. The war is actually begun! The next gale that sweeps from the North will bring to our ears the clash of resounding arms! Our brethren are already in the field! Why stand we here idle? What is it that gentlemen wish? What would they have? Is life so dear, or peace so sweet, as to be purchased at the price of chains and slavery? Forbid it, Almighty God! I know not what course others may take; but as for me, give me liberty, or give me death!

DAVID BENNETT HILL

FOR BIMETALISM

[David Bennett Hill, an American political leader, was born in New York state, in 1843. He early took up the study of the law and was admitted to the bar as soon as he became of age. Having made his home in Elmira, in New York state, he plunged into the party politics of the place as a Democrat, and in a few years was elected to the legislature. He presided over the Democratic state conventions of 1877 and 1881, served in his home town as alderman and mayor, and in 1882 was made lieutenant-governor of New York state. When Grover Cleveland resigned the governorship to become President, David B. Hill became chief executive of the Empire State, a post to which he was twice elected by the people. When he relinquished the gubernatorial office he was chosen to the United States Senate, where he served six years (1891–97). At a subsequent period he was defeated for the governorship of New York. In 1896 he led those who refrained from balloting in the Democratic national convention at Chicago. As a speaker David Bennett Hill is incisive and eloquent, and always sure of an attentive hearing. The following speech, urging the adoption of bimetalism in the United States, was made in the Senate in February, 1893.]

MY own personal conviction is clear that with adequate preparation, revised laws, and competent administration and friendly administration, independent free bimetallic coinage would be within the power of the United States to establish and maintain; and for my own part I should far prefer that solution, with no entangling and foreign alliances or agreements, to any international arrangement whatsoever.

We do not half realize the overwhelming power of the United States. To have survived the finance of the last thirty years is proof of our stupendous resources and our independent power. Merely to have lived through two and a half years of the Sherman silver-purchase and treasury-note issue law without an actual smash; just to have escaped without our farmers and planters bleeding to death by the postponement of free bimetallic coinage is proof enough what adequate preparation, revised laws, and competent administration might have achieved for us and for all the world in that behalf.

I regret this delay profoundly, but we cannot shut our eyes to facts.

Would that the Columbian anniversary might have been celebrated by that world-wide demonstration of our independent power.

To those who can perceive what Mr. Gladstone has called the unseen and higher objects of human endeavor, even the vast assemblages and the multifarious collections of the Chicago Fair would in comparison have appeared like a children's crowded garden and baby playhouses filled with toys.

Until recently I cherished a hope of that inspiring exhibition of our unseen power, and then wrote these words:—

"Our great Republic halts upon the threshold of her noble destiny, distrusts her capacity to compete in her own markets or in foreign markets for primacy in the commerce of the world, and tightens the fetters of her tariff; misdoubts her power to reunite the two uncoupled international currencies of the world in the rated stable parity, and piles up new loads of disparaged unexportable silver. Surely it behooves the foremost nation of the world to shake off this bondage of fears and put forth her peaceable invincible strength."

But that hope is at present a vain hope. The reduction of net gold in the treasury by a hundred million dollars during the last four years from $218,000,000 in 1888 to the bare $100,000,000 gold reserve for the $346,000,000 greenbacks and a small working treasury department balance; the addition of $125,000,000 to our paper legal-tender debt since July, 1890, concurrently with the like reduction of our gold basis; the absence of a single dollar in gold to uphold, if it were widely questioned and rudely tested, the local legal parity of 416,412,835 silver dollars coined since March 1, 1878, with the gold unit of value established by the law of 1873, constitutes a financial record, improvident, incapable, and beyond all words disgraceful to any civilized nation—

how much more to this mighty people able to be rich and powerful beyond compare!

Coming at the tail of thirty years of like detestable finance, it excludes the present possibility of the United States alone undertaking independently to establish and maintain a free bimetallic coinage, except at the expense of some increase of gold bonded debt, which, instead of insuring our future prosperity by the solid inauguration of free bimetallic coinage, is now threatened as another costly sacrifice, to stave off the cumulative perils of the Sherman law.

Moreover, to free bimetallic coinage by international agreement, we are now shut out by the action of both political parties in nominating two candidates, and by the election of one, who had previously avowed their approval of free bimetallic coinage, subject to the condition of foreign cooperation.

I consider that the people of the United States are as much bound by their own act now to the prior effort for obtaining foreign cooperation, as they are bound by the joint resolution of the two parties together to press forward to the common goal.

The sole obstacle to foreign cooperation is Great Britain.

Our delegates to three monetary conferences, and our special commissioner to the three great powers in 1885, all have brought back concurrent testimony that France and Germany regard the cooperation of Great Britain as *sine qua non* to their cooperation in free bimetallic coinage, and that Great Britain hitherto has seen and as yet sees no reason to change her policy.

It is therefore obvious that the occasion for monetary conferences with European powers is past, and that the time for action suited to influence Great Britain has arrived.

Conferences have sufficiently published the bimetallic theory which has conquered the assent of the few great monetary experts of all nations, and which is unpopular in Great Britain, because for three or four generations free silver coinage has been discontinued in London, whereas it is popular and approved in the United States from its easy and successful working in practice during three-fourths of the whole of the life of our nation.

To Englishmen who say that a free bimetallic coinage law cannot fix the rated parity of silver and gold, we have answered: For eighty years it did. To Englishmen who say that silver mines are more prolific now, and say the adopted parity could not be kept, we have replied: The total bimetallic money measure is all silver plus all gold, joined in a rated parity; is inappreciably enlarged by the small annual increment from both metals; is indifferent to the proportion arriving from either output; and received a greater increment for years from the gold of California and Australia, which was merged in the bimetallic money mass without disturbance of the parity and with boundless advantage to mankind; so that any possible increase of the silver output is wholly beneficial —at first to miners, but vastly more to the producers of commodities; is equally sure of merger in the money mass, and if its present dislocation were ended by the renewal of free bimetallic coinage whereby the greater gold increment was received without disturbance of the party (because the gold monometalists of to-day, who were silver monometalists then, were prevented from boycotting gold) it would end nineteen years of commercial depression and monetary disorder, and in like manner renew the prosperity and arouse the enterprise of the world. It is therefore not a military invasion and a burning of her capital that should now be prepared for Great Britain by the United States, by ceasing from conference and taking action to constrain her cooperation in free bimetallic coinage. On the contrary, it is the invasion of Great Britain and Europe with a message of peace and good will.

By means of free bimetallic coinage the United States were able to confer upon all nations the boundless benefits of the gold of California. By means of free bimetallic coinage we shall be able to confer upon all nations in the same manner the unbounded benefits of the silver and gold of Colorado, Nevada, Wyoming, Idaho, New Mexico, and Arizona.

The time for conference, I say, is past. The time for independent action is come, unless the senators from the money-metal states propose not only to abstain, as they must, from independent free bimetallic coinage, but also to abstain, as they need not, from such independent action by the United States as will entail free bimetallic coinage by international cooperation.

Repeal of the Sherman law is the only action, in my opinion, needed to test and fulfill the endeavor to reach free bimetallic coinage by the route of international agreement. That is the point upon which all I have said or shall say converges.

We shall not have endeavored to establish cooperative international free bimetallic coinage until we have stopped treasury silver purchases.

We shall not have put forth one arm of our power until we have repealed the Sherman law unconditionally. It is the actual influence and probable effect in Great Britain of our unrepeal of the Sherman silver-purchase law that I am now to ask the Senate to consider.

From the day of the adoption of the French rates of free bimetallic coinage, making fifteen and a half weights of silver and one weight of gold—when coined—legal tender for payment of an identical sum—from that date—1785—down to the cessation of free bimetallic coinage in the last mint then open to it—September 6, 1873—the gold in British sovereigns and fifteen and a half times its weight of silver in Indian rupees were everywhere equally acceptable in payments. Never during that period was there one instant of these nineteen-year-long convulsions of disparity between silver and gold, not even amid the shock of tumbling thrones and contending empires.

Rippling fluctuations in the bimetallic parity, few and slight, wherever they occurred, were to be explained in the differing contemporaneous values of identical weights of pure gold of the two sides of the Atlantic to-day. Free coinage does not prevent these. Free bimetallic coinage had no concern to prevent these. They have all been tracked, tabulated, and explained by the masters of foreign exchange.

The gold in our eagle is one day worth more in London than in New York by some small percentage. It is exported. The gold in the sovereign is one day worth more in New York than in London. It is imported. But there is a fixed limit to these mere ripples of fluctuation. It is the limit of the cost of transfer, freight, insurance, brokerage. The variations in the diverse value of the same monometallic coins, though identical in weight and fineness, on the two sides of the Atlantic, or between any two foreign markets, are always tethered by the cost of transfer hither and thither.

Precisely the same ripples and fluctuations occurred to silver and gold during their free bimetallic coinage, and just so were they tethered, no matter how complicated in the commercial exchanges between monometallic nations or between these and bimetallic nations.

Such is the record in Hamburg, London, Paris, with every flutter in quotations fully accounted for.

In 1816 Great Britain stopped the free coinage of silver in London while continuing there the free coinage of gold. But the value of the gold sovereign and silver rupee underwent no new variation. At the cost of transfer, sometimes high, if collection and transfer were difficult, sometimes low, but always tethered, silver had often to be got for foreign remittance by the British merchant. But the free bimetallic coinage of France maintained the gold of the sovereign and the silver of the rupee in the same fixed parity as that in which her own franc of gold and franc of silver were maintained.

The silver in the rupees that were equivalent to the gold in the sovereign always weighed fifteen and a half times as much and were precisely likewise tethered. This long history of the stable parity of gold and silver due to free bimetallic coinage in France British merchants ascribed at last to the British constitution, British commerce, the nature of things, relative intrinsic value, cost of production, supply and demand.

When the real cause, free bimetallic coinage, ceased in 1873, and thereupon rippling exchange fluctuations were swallowed up in the violent convulsions of two dislocated, disjointed, monometalisms, the British merchant and banker continued to apply their misapprehensions of the cause of the old order of things to the facts in the new order.

Just as now, they imagine Americans want something else from free bimetallic coinage than equivalence of silver dollar and gold dollar, of silver franc and gold franc, equivalence of ten rupees or so and one gold sovereign; so they then believe the stable parity of silver in the rupee and gold in the sovereign from 1816 to 1873 (as recorded in the rippling fluctuations of the Indian exchange), and which parity was identical with the parity of the silver franc and the gold franc, to be due to something else than the sole cause of that parity, the free bimetallic coinage of France.

I fear that our silver purchases only confirmed their illusions, only made them hug tighter their sterling fetich. Insular, they mistook their entire dependence on French coinage legislation for independence of all the world. Provincial, whilst yet conducting the greatest single port of the world's commerce, they clung to the concomitant of great prosperity as if the concomitant had been its cause.

But perhaps it is not quite becoming for us to cast reproaches. I have heard it contended that our protective tariffs which have been the concomitant of our prosperity were its cause.

It is enough to say that Englishmen at that time perfectly justified the recent description of them by Mr. Gladstone saying that

" . . . no race stands in greater need of discipline in every form, and among other forms, than that which is administered by criticism vigorously directed to canvassing their character and claims."

Certainly no person of that insular and hidebound race had the sense to appreciate the great discernment of Mr. Disraeli when in the very year of the cessation of free bimetallic coinage he publicly said:—

" Our gold standard is not the cause but the consequence of our prosperity. It is quite evident that we must now prepare ourselves for great convulsions in the money market, not occasioned by speculation or any of the old causes which have been alleged, but by a new cause with which we are not sufficiently acquainted."

After nearly twenty years of needless suffering, it turns out the world moves a little. · Public opinion advances slowly in Great Britain as here. Increasing numbers of British statesmen, all Ireland, the leaders among the farming classes in England, Scotland, and Wales, the manufacturers and merchants of Lancashire, all who buy or sell between England and India, and all Indian civil servants, are leavening the lump of English opinion.

Out of the revenue collected from the people of India in silver, the Indian government has to make very heavy annual payments in London, fixed in gold, the burden and amount increasing in an almost geometrical progression therefore with every increase of their parity.

The Indian exchanges of course follow with exactly equal step the distending or the diminishing divergencies of gold and silver.

When with the rising hope that the United States would independently restore free bimetallic coinage, this divergence of gold and silver has diminished, the approach of the rupee and the sovereign to the rate of their old parity have consoled so many sufferers in Great Britain, that they have ceased to clamor for permanent and effectual relief that can only be afforded by the cause of that fixed parity, free bimetallic coinage.

When with the falling hope of its renewal by the United States, the divergence of gold and silver has increased, and the rupee and the sovereign have parted wider and wider from the rate of their old parity, then the sufferers have made themselves heard again, and have stirred up the mass of their fellow citizens to attention and sympathy.

The cause of free bimetallic coinage has made strides in Great Britain just in proportion as silver has parted farther from its former mint ratio with gold. The silver incomes have contracted, and the annual gold debt of India to England has been a heavier burden to the taxpayers of Hindostan, exacting larger sums in their only money, silver, while silver was diverging farther from gold. The evidence is uniform and irresistible that the limit of tolerable taxation in India, the limit of endurable suffering in Great Britain on the part of those afflicted by the dislocation of the gold money and the silver money of the British Empire, is already reached.

Repeal of the Sherman law will certainly abandon Great Britain to the untempered shocks of the two dislocated monometalisms and their utter lack of legal correlation. In that event the instruction will appear and be plain, which our silver purchases have so long concealed, that the rupee sovereign dislocation is kindred, common, and concurrent with our silver dollar and gold dollar dislocation, with the dislocation of the silver money and the gold money of all nations.

I have now only to make clear why repeal of the Sherman law, why independent action by the United States, abandoning at last the two dislocated free coinages to the unmitigated shocks of an utter absence of legal relation, will arrive to the address of Great Britain with any especial and particular force. It is certain that the present monetary disorder will not thereby be increased in Germany, France, or any other European nation, nor (leaving aside the silver mines) in the United States.

How is Great Britain especially exposed, how is she exposed as no other nation of the world is exposed, to the consequences of repeal of the silver-purchase law?

Here is the fact, well known to all the Senate, but upon which our reflection should now most deeply dwell.

Many mints, as I have said, are now open to the free coinage of silver. Many mints are open for the free coinage of gold. But in no other one kingdom, in no other one state, in no other one empire, only in the British empire, do there now coexist the two separate free coinages—the free coinage of silver as at Calcutta into full legal tender money and the free coinage of gold as at London into full legal tender money. Neither there nor elsewhere are the two free coinages coupled in a free bimetallic coinage. But there and there alone exists, in one empire, the free coinage of two metallic monetary units, the gold sovereign and the silver rupee, actually unrelated and without legal parity fixed by law.

The lost parity of gold and silver within and between all nations is the universal monetary disorder. It is international everywhere. In the British Empire, with its two unrelated free coinages, the disorder is worse; it is intestinal.

Some action by Great Britain, if we repeal the Sherman law, at once becomes unavoidable. Other European nations can take their time. Not so Great Britain.

If the Sherman silver law is repealed the United States

treasury will have no new difficulty. It will be relieved of its greatest danger, the danger of a run on its gold. The silver already coined will be kept in its merely local and national parity (412.5 troy grains of silver equaling 25.8 troy grains of gold) just as easily when the white metal is worth no more in the crucible than thirty-three cents as now when it is worth sixty-four cents. It will not be melted; it will merely remain, as now, impossible for a foreign remittance. It will remain for the little longer so many metallic assignats.

But that which we can endure, and which France and Germany can endure, Great Britain could not endure, for the reason that she alone is giving free coinage in one empire to two metallic monetary units not related by law.

Her condition will at once become intolerable because of the immediate wider and wider disparity and the convulsive disparity of Indian silver money and British gold money.

Her intolerable condition will also admit of instant relief and complete relief, but in no way under heaven save by the resumption of free bimetallic coinage.

The choice of Great Britain will be between two courses, one of instant complete relief, the other of delay and disaster, increasing and remediable finally in just one way.   For gold money will not cease to be the principal money basis of the colossal superstructure of private currencies in Great Britain; and silver will not cease to be the chief currency of that vast Indian possession, comprising more than one-seventh of the population of the globe.

(1.)   Great Britain can invite the United States to consider the cooperative resumption of free bimetallic coinage. Stable parity of gold in the sovereign and silver in the rupee, of the gold franc and the silver franc, of the silver dollar and the gold dollar will be the result.

(2.)   Great Britain can stop the free coinage of silver in Calcutta with recognized peril to her Indian Empire.   For such is the warning of more than one of her viceroys.

Face to face with the unavoidable choice, in my belief, Great Britain will choose promptly and choose wisely.

Until, by repeal of that Sherman law, we bring Great Britain face to face with the unavoidable choice, choosing can be shirked.

I have detained the Senate far too long, but I had no wish to deal with anything less than the whole theme in its chief bearings; and I hope I have been terse, since I could not be brief.

One word more. At present there is no other route to free bimetallic coinage than this international route. Inaction for long will be very costly to our silver producers and will close many mines.

But I would rather proclaim aloud than hide the fact that the silver producers by repeal of the Sherman law must prepare to endure for a season diminished returns for their output.

That price must be paid, I fear, to explode the false idea of our own and foreign gold monometalists, that our sincere desire for a great reform is a mere job of American silver miners.

That price must be paid, I fear, to shatter the foreign obstacle in the path not now closed toward free bimetallic coinage, namely, the international path.

That price must be paid, I fear, to bring home to British business and bosoms that there is no escape from her intestinal disorder except by restoring what France alone long gave to all nations—free bimetallic coinage—one money of two metals, one parity, and international monetary peace.

That price must be paid, I fear, to allay and remove the discontent of our farming and planting fellow citizens. I have explained its cause. It is the obscure but causing cause of the Farmers' Alliance and the Populist party. Two and a half years ago, when the act was passed by the Senate, it met with the opposition of every vote on this side of the chamber. If the question had been presented the next day whether the law should be repealed, there can be no question that all the senators upon this side of the chamber would have voted for the repeal. I think nothing has taken place from that day to this to furnish a reason why all of us on this side of the chamber at least may vote in favor of a repeal of the act, which it was then thought should not be placed upon the statute book.

Since that time the supreme council of our great Democratic party has met, and one of the first planks in the plat-

form is that the Democratic party stands pledged to the repeal
of the Sherman law. I think the party should live up to its
pledge. I know there will be some revulsion, I know there
will be some discontent, I know that the silver miners' interest will be disturbed; but, as I said, the price must be paid,
I fear, to wreck forever the efforts of any rapacious gold
monometalists who would fain double the debts of our people by discarding half the money measure, on the pretense
that there is probably too much silver under ground and that
the only quite universal money metal is just the one to get
rid of.

The price must be paid, I fear, since the money metals
are farther diverged from their old parity to-day than ever
they were before the silver senators consented to put their
virgin metal into unholy alliance with the rag-money tramp,
so tarnishing her good name.

If the senators from the money-metal states at the present
session of Congress, with sacrificing and disinterested thought
for the general welfare of the whole people of the United
States, shall unite to repeal at once the Sherman law, they
will compel persistence by both parties in behalf of free bimetallic coinage and its perfect parity of the silver and gold
dollar, they will surely reestablish the people's right, conclude with the people's favor, and survive in their remembrance.

GEORGE FRISBIE HOAR

SUBJUGATION OF THE PHILIPPINES INIQUITOUS

[George Frisbie Hoar, an American statesman whose eloquence has been and is a potent moral force in our national life, was born in Massachusetts in 1826. He came of old New England stock, graduated at Harvard, began to practice law, and was elected to Congress. He held his seat in the House of Representatives for four terms, when (in 1877) he was elected to the United States Senate and has been continuously reëlected ever since. As a public man Senator Hoar has stood consistently for true Americanism as interpreted in the light of the New England conscience—using this last term in its high sense. The government of the United States, according to him, is as much excluded from some domains as it is supreme in others. It is his opinion that any attempt of the national government to play a part alien to its nature or to the far-seeing design of the constitutional fathers, is not only a menace to American liberties but threatens the existence of the government. He has steadily opposed the expansion of the territory of the United States, including the Philippines and Hawaii, and the following speech gives his reasons with clearness and force. It was delivered in the Senate in May, 1902.]

MR. PRESIDENT: I have something to say upon the pending bill. I will say it as briefly and as compactly as I may. We have to deal with a territory ten thousand miles away, twelve hundred miles in extent, containing ten million people. A majority of the Senate think that people are under the American flag and lawfully subject to our authority. We are not at war with them or with anybody. The country is in a condition of profound peace as well as of unexampled prosperity. The world is in profound peace, except in one quarter, in South Africa, where a handful of republicans are fighting for their independence, and have been doing better fighting than has been done on the face of the earth since Thermopylæ, or certainly since Bannockburn.

Yet the Filipinos have a right to call it war. They claim to be a people and to be fighting for their rights as a people. The senator from Ohio [Mr. Foraker] admits that there is a people there, although he says they are not one people, but there are several. But we cannot be at war under the Constitution without an act of Congress.

We are not at war. We made peace with Spain on the fourteenth day of February, 1899. Congress has never declared war with the people of the Philippine Islands. The President has never asserted nor usurped the power to do it. We are only doing on a large scale exactly what we have done at home within a few years past, where the military forces of the United States have been called out to suppress a riot or a tumult or a lawless assembly, too strong for the local authorities. You have the same right to administer the water torture, or to hang men by the thumbs, to extort confession, in one case as in the other. You have the same right to do it in Cleveland or Pittsburg or at Colorado Springs as you have to do it within the Philippine Islands. I have the same right as an American citizen or an American senator to discuss the conduct of any military officer in the Philippine Islands that I have to discuss the conduct of a marshal or a constable or a captain in Pittsburg or in Cleveland if there were a labor riot there.

That duty I mean to perform to the best of my ability, fearlessly as becomes an American citizen, and honestly as becomes an American senator.

But I have an anterior duty and an anterior right to talk about the action of the American Senate, both in the past and in the present, for which, as no man will deny, I have my full share of personal responsibility.

The senator from Ohio, in his very brilliant and forcible speech, which I heard with delight and instruction, said that we were bound to restore order in the Philippine Islands, and we cannot leave them till that should be done. He said we were bound to keep the faith we pledged to Spain in the treaty, and that we were bound, before we left, to see that secured. He said we were bound, especially, to look out for the safety of the Filipinos who had been our friends, and that we could not, in honor, depart until that should be made secure.

All that, Mr. President, is true. So far as I know, no man has doubted it. But these things are not what we are fighting for; not one of them. There never was a time when, if we had declared that we only were there to keep faith with Spain, and that we only were there to restore order, that we were only there to see that no friend of ours should suffer at the hands of any enemy of ours, that the war would not have ended in that moment.

You are fighting for sovereignty. You are fighting for the principle of eternal dominion over that people, and that is the only question in issue in the conflict. We said in the case of Cuba that she had a right to be free and independent. We affirmed in the Teller resolution, I think without a negative voice, that we would not invade that right and would not meddle with her territory or anything that belonged to her. That declaration was a declaration of peace as well as of righteousness; and we made the treaty, so far as concerned Cuba, and conducted the war and have conducted ourselves ever since on that theory—that we had no right to interfere with her independence; that we had no right to her territory or to anything that was Cuba's. So we only demanded in the treaty that Spain should hereafter let her alone. If you had done to Cuba as you have done to the Philippine Islands, who had exactly the same right, you would be at this moment, in Cuba, just where Spain was when she excited the indignation of the civilized world and we compelled her to let go. And if you had done in the Philippines as you did in Cuba, you would be to-day or would soon be in those islands as you are in Cuba.

But you made a totally different declaration about the Philippine Islands. You undertook in the treaty to acquire sovereignty over her for yourself, which that people denied. You declared not only in the treaty, but in many public utterances in this Chamber and elsewhere, that you had a right to buy sovereignty with money, or to treat it as the spoils of war or the booty of battle. The moment you made that declaration, the Filipino people gave you notice that they treated it as a declaration of war. So your generals reported, and so Aguinaldo expressly declared. The President sent out an order to take forcible possession, by military power, of those islands. General Otis tried to suppress it, but it leaked out at Iloilo through General Miller. General Otis tried to suppress it and substitute that they should have all the rights of the most favored provinces. He stated that he did that because he knew the proclamation would bring on war. And the next day Aguinaldo covered the walls of Manila with a proclamation stating what President McKinley had done, and saying that if that were persisted in he and his people would fight, and General MacArthur testified that Aguinaldo represented the entire people. So you deliberately made up the issue for a fight for dominion on one side and a fight for liberty on the other.

Then when you had ratified the treaty you voted down the resolution in the Senate, known as the Bacon resolution, declaring the right of that people to independence, and you passed the McEnery resolution, which declared that you meant to dispose of those islands as should be for the interest of the United States. That was the origin of the war, if it be war. That is what the war is all about, if it be war; and it is idle for my brilliant and ingenious friend from Ohio to undertake to divert this issue to a contest on our part to enable us to keep faith with our friends among the Filipinos, or to restore order there, or to carry out the provisions of the treaty with Spain.

When we ratified the treaty of Paris we committed ourselves to one experiment in Cuba and another in the Philippine Islands. We had said already that Cuba of right ought to be free and independent. So when in the treaty Spain abandoned her sovereignty the title of Cuba became at once complete. We were only to stay there to keep order until we could hand over Cuba to a government her people had chosen and established.

By the same treaty we bought the Philippine Islands for twenty million dollars and declared and agreed that Congress shall dispose of them. So, according to those who held that treaty valid, it became the duty of the President to reduce them to submission, and of Congress to govern them.

Here the two doctrines are brought into sharp antagonism.

In Cuba, of right, just government, according to you, must rest on the consent of the governed. Her people are to "institute a new government, laying its foundation on such principles and organizing its powers in such form as to them shall seem most likely to effect their safety and happiness."

In the Philippine Islands a government is to be instituted by a power ten thousand miles away, to be in the beginning a despotism, established by military power.

It is to be a despotism where there is treason without an overt act, and elections, if they have them, without political debate, and schools where they cannot teach liberty. It is to be established by military power, and to be such, to use the language of the McEnery resolution, such as shall seem "for the interest of the United States."

You have given both doctrines a three-years' trial. Three years is sometimes a very long time and sometimes a very short time in human affairs. I believe the whole life of the Saviour, after he first made his divine mission known, lasted but three years. Three years has wrought a mighty change in Cuba, and it has wrought a mighty change in the Philippine Islands. We have had plenty of time to try both experiments.

Now, what has each cost you, and what has each profited you?

In stating this account of profit and loss I hardly know which to take up first, principles and honor or material interests—I should have known very well which to have taken up first down to three years ago—what you call the sentimental, the ideal, the historical on the right side of the column; the cost or the profit in honor or shame and in character and in principle and moral influence, in true national glory; or the practical side, the cost in money and gain, in life and health, in wasted labor, in diminished national strength, or in prospects of trade and money getting.

Gentlemen talk about sentimentalities, about idealism. They like practical statesmanship better. But, Mr. President, this whole debate for the last four years has been a debate between two kinds of sentimentality. There has been practical statesmanship in plenty on both sides. Your side have carried their sentimentalities and ideals out in your practical statesmanship. The other side have tried and begged to be allowed to carry theirs out in practical statesmanship also. On one side have been these sentimentalities. They were the ideals of the fathers of the revolutionary time, and from their day down till the day of Abraham Lincoln and Charles Summer was over. The sentimentalities were that all men in political right were created equal; that governments derive their just powers from the consent of the governed, and are instituted to secure that equality; that every people—not every scattering neighborhood or settlement without organic life, not every portion of a people who may be temporarily discontented, but the political being that we call a people—has the right to institute a government for itself and to lay its foundation on such principles and organize its powers in such form as to it and not to any other people shall seem most likely to effect its safety and happiness. Now, a good deal of practical statesmanship has followed from these ideals and sentimentalities. They have built forty-five states on firm foundations. They have covered South America with republics. They have kept despotism out of the Western Hemisphere. They have made the United States the freest, strongest, richest of the nations of the world. They have made the word "republic" a name to conjure by the round world over. By their virtue the American flag—beautiful as a flower to those who love it; terrible as a meteor to those who hate it—floats everywhere over peaceful seas, and is welcomed everywhere in friendly ports as the emblem of peaceful supremacy and sovereignty in the commerce of the world.

Has there been any practical statesmanship in our dealing with Cuba? You had precisely the same problem in the East and in the West. You knew all about conditions in Cuba. There has been no lack of counselors to whisper in the ear of the President and Senate and House the dishonorable counsel that we should hold on to Cuba, without regard to our pledges or our principles, and that the resolution of the Senator from Colorado [Mr. Teller] was a great mistake. "Ye shall not surely die," said the serpent—

> "Squat like a toad, close at the ear of Eve."

I do not know how other men may feel, but I think that the statesmen who have had something to do with bringing Cuba into the family of nations, when they look back on their career, that my friends who sit around me, when each comes to look back upon a career of honorable and brilliant public service, will count the share they had in that as among the brightest, the greenest, and the freshest laurels in their crown.

You also, my imperialistic friends, have had your ideals and your sentimentalities. One is that the flag shall never be hauled down where it has once floated. Another is that you will not talk or reason with a people with arms in their hands. Another is that sovereignty over an unwilling people may be bought with gold. And another is that sovereignty may be got by force of arms, as the booty of battle or the spoils of victory.

What has been the practical statesmanship which comes from your ideals and your sentimentalities? You have wasted six hundred millions of treasure. You have sacrificed nearly ten thousand American lives—the flower of our youth. You have devastated provinces. You have slain uncounted thousands of the people you desire to benefit. You have established reconcentration camps. Your generals are coming home from their harvest, bringing their sheaves with them, in the shape of other thousands of sick and wounded and insane to drag out miserable lives, wrecked in body and mind. You make the American flag in the eyes of a numerous people the emblem of sacrilege in Christian churches, and of the burning of human dwellings, and of the horror of the water torture. Your practical statesmanship, which disdains to take George Washington and Abraham Lincoln or the soldiers of the Revolution or of the Civil War as models, has looked in some cases to Spain for your example. I believe—nay, I know—that in general our officers and soldiers are humane. But in some cases they have carried on your warfare with a mixture of American ingenuity and Castilian cruelty.

Your practical statesmanship has succeeded in converting a people who three years ago were ready to kiss the hem of the garment of the American and to welcome him as a liberator, who thronged after your men when they landed on those islands with benediction and gratitude, into sullen and irreconcilable enemies, possessed of a hatred which centuries cannot eradicate.

The practical statesmanship of the Declaration of Independence and the Golden Rule would have cost nothing but a few kind words. They would have bought for you the great title of liberator and benefactor, which your fathers won for your country in the South American Republics and in Japan and which you have won in Cuba. They would have bought for you the undying gratitude of a great and free people and the undying glory which belongs to the name of liberator. That people would have felt for you as Japan felt for you when she declared last summer that she owed everything to the United States of America.

What have your ideals cost you, and what have they bought for you?

1.   For the Philippine Islands you have had to repeal the Declaration of Independence.

For Cuba you have had to re-affirm it and give it new luster.

2.   For the Philippine Islands you have had to convert the Monroe doctrine into a doctrine of mere selfishness.

For Cuba you have acted on it and vindicated it.

3.   In Cuba you have got the eternal gratitude of a free people.

In the Philippine Islands you have got the hatred and sullen submission of a subjugated people.

4.   From Cuba you have brought home nothing but glory.

From the Philippines you have brought home nothing of glory.

5.   In Cuba no man thinks of counting the cost. The few soldiers who came home from Cuba wounded or sick carry about their wounds and their pale faces as if they were medals of honor. What soldier glories in a wound or an empty sleeve which he got in the Philippines?

6. The conflict in the Philippines has cost you six hundred million dollars, thousands of American soldiers—the flower of your youth—the health and sanity of thousands more, and hundreds of thousands of Filipinos slain.

Another price we have paid as the result of your practical statesmanship. We have sold out the right, the old American right, to speak out the sympathy which is in our hearts for people who are desolate and oppressed everywhere on the face of the earth.

Let me take two examples out of a thousand with which to contrast the natural result of the doctrine of your fathers with yours.

I do not think there ever was a more delightful occurrence in the history of Massachusetts since the Puritans or the Pilgrims landed there, than the visit to Harvard two years ago of the Cuban teachers to the Harvard summer school. The old university put on her best apparel for the occasion. The guests were manly boys and fair girls, making you think of Tennyson's sweet girl graduates, who came to sit at the feet of old Harvard to learn something which they could teach to their pupils, and to carry back to their country and teach their own children undying gratitude to the great Republic. It was one of the most delightful lessons in all history of the gratitude of a people to its liberator, and of the affection of the liberator-Republic to the people it had delivered. Was there ever a more fitting subject for poetry or for art than the venerable President Eliot, surrounded with his staff of learned teachers and famous scholars, the foremost men in the Republic of letters and science, as he welcomed them, these young men and women, to the delights of learning and the blessings of liberty?

Contrast this scene with another. It is all you have to show, that you have brought back, so far, from the Philippine Islands. You have no grateful youth coming to sit at your feet. You do not dare to bring here even a friendly Filipino to tell you, with unfettered lips, what his people think of you, or what they want of you. I read the other day in a Nebraska paper a terrible story of the passage through Omaha of a carload of maniacs from the Philippine Islands.

The story, I believe, has been read in the Senate. I telegraphed to Omaha to the editor of a paper, of high reputation—I believe a zealous supporter of the policy of Imperialism—to learn if the story was authentic. I am told in reply, and I am glad to know it, that the picture is sensational and exaggerated, but the substantial fact is confirmed that that load of young soldiers passed through that city lately, as other like cargoes have passed through before, maniacs and broken in mental health as the result of service in the Philippine Islands.

It is no answer to tell me that such horrors exist everywhere; that there are other maniacs at St. Elizabeth, and that every state asylum is full of them. Those unhappy beings have been visited, without any man's fault, by the mysterious Providence of God, or if their affliction comes from any man's fault it is our duty to make it known and to hold the party guilty responsible. It is a terrible picture that I have drawn. It is a picture of men suffering from the inevitable result which every reasonable man must have anticipated of the decisions made in this Chamber when we elected to make war for the principle of despotism instead of a policy of peace, in accordance with the principles of the Declaration of Independence.

Mr. President, every one of these maniacs, every one of the many like freights of horror that comes back to us from the Philippine Islands, every dead soldier, every wounded or wrecked soldier was once an American boy, the delight of some American home, fairer and nobler in his young promise, as we like to think, than any other the round world over. Ah! Mr. President, it was not twenty million dollars that we paid as the price of sovereignty. It was the souls of these boys of ours that entered into the cost. When you determined by one vote to ratify the Spanish treaty; when you determined by one vote to defeat the Bacon resolution; when you declared, in the McEnery resolution, that we would dispose of that people as might be for the interest of the United States; when the senator from Wisconsin said we would not talk to a people who had arms in their hands, although they begged that there should be no war, and that we would at least hear them; when some of you went about the country declaring that the flag never should be hauled down where it once floated, you did not know, because in your excitement and haste your intellectual vision was dazzled with empire, you did not know that this was to come. But you might have known it. A little reflection and a little reason would have told you. I wonder if the Republican editor who made that known was attacking the American army. I wonder if those of us who do not like that are the friends or the enemies of the American soldier.

I cannot understand how any man, certainly how any intelligent student of history, could have failed to foretell exactly what has happened when we agreed to the Spanish treaty. Everything that has happened since has been the natural, inevitable, inexorable result of the policy you then declared.

If you knew anything of human nature you knew that the great doctrine that just government depends on the consent of the governed, as applied to the relation of one people to another, has its foundation in the nature of man itself. No people will submit, if it can be helped, to the rule of any other people. You must have known perfectly well, if you had stopped to consider, that so far as the Philippine people were like us they would do exactly what we did and would do again in a like case. So far as they were civilized they would resist you with all the power of civilized war. So far as they were savage they would resist you by all the methods of savage warfare.

You never could eradicate from the hearts of that people by force the love of liberty which God put there.

> "For He that worketh high and wise,
>   Nor pauseth in His plan,
> Will take the sun out of the skies
>   Ere freedom out of man."

This war, if you call it war, has gone on for three years. It will go on in some form for three hundred years, unless this policy be abandoned. You will undoubtedly have times of peace and quiet, or pretended submission. You will buy men with titles, or office, or salaries. You will intimidate cowards. You will get pretended and fawning submission. The land will smile and smile and seem at peace. But the volcano will be there.   The lava will break out again.   You can never settle this thing until you settle it right.

I think my friends of the majority, whatever else they may claim—and they can rightly claim a great deal that is good and creditable for themselves—will not claim to be prophets.   They used to prophesy a good deal two years ago.   We had great prophets and minor prophets.   All predicted peace and submission, and a flag followed by trade, with wealth flowing over this land from the Far East, and the American people standing in the Philippine Islands looking over with eager gaze toward China.   Where are now your prophets which prophesied unto you?   I fear that we must make the answer that was made to the children of Israel: "They prophesied falsely, and the prophets have become wind, and the word is not in them."

I believe the American army, officers and soldiers, to be made up of as brave and humane men, in general, as ever lived. They have done what has always been done, and until human nature shall change, always will be done in all like conditions.   The chief guilt is on the heads of those who created the conditions.

One thing, however, I am bound to say in all frankness. I do not know but my statement may be challenged.   But I am sure that nearly every well-informed man who will hear it or read it will know that it is true.   That is, that you will never get officers or soldiers in the standing army, as a rule, to give testimony which they think will be disagreeable to their superiors or to the war department.

Was it ever heard before that a civilized, humane, and Christian nation made war upon a people and refused to tell them what they wanted of them?   You refuse to tell these people this year or next year or perhaps for twenty years whether you mean in the end to deprive them of their independence or no.   You say you want them to submit.   To submit to what?   To mere military force?   But for what purpose or what end is that military force to be exerted? You decline to tell them.   Not only you decline to say what you want of them, except bare and abject surrender, but you will not even let them tell you what they ask of you.

The evidence is that some of them favor their admission

as an American state, and others favor a government of their own under your protection. Others would like to come in as a territory under our Constitution. But is there any evidence that one human being there is ready to submit to your government without any rights under our Constitution, or without any prospect of coming in as an American state? Or is there any evidence that any single American citizen, in the Senate or out of it, is willing that we should do anything that a single Filipino is ready to consent to?

I have no doubt they will take the oath of allegiance. Undoubtedly they will go through the form of submission. Undoubtedly you have force enough to make the whole region a howling wilderness if you think fit. Undoubtedly you can put up a form of government in which they will seem to take some share, and they will take your offices and your salaries. But when you come to getting anything which is not merely temporary; when you come to announce anything in principle, such as those on which governments are founded, you have not any evidence of any considerable number of people there ready to submit to your will unless they are compelled by sheer brutal force.

I suppose, Mr. President, that those of us who are of English descent like to think that the race from which we come will compare favorably with most others in the matter of humanity. Yet history is full of the terrible cruelties committed by Englishmen when men of other races refused to submit to their authority. I think my friends who seek to extenuate this water torture, or to apologize for it, may perhaps like to look at the precedent of the dealings with the Irish rebels in 1799.

In " Howell's State Trials " there will be found the proceedings in a suit by Mr. Wright against James Judkin Fitzgerald, a sheriff, who ordered a citizen to be flogged for the purpose of extorting information. I believe fifty lashes were administered and then fifty more by Fitzgerald, and in many other cases the same course was taken. It was wholly to extract information, as this water torture has been to get information. Fitzgerald, the sheriff, told his own story. He pointed out the necessity of his system of terror. He said he got one man he had flogged to confess that the plaintiff was a secretary of the United Irishmen, and this information he could not get from him before; that Mr. Wright himself had offered to confess, but his memory had been so impaired by the flogging that he could not command the faculty of recollection. Notwithstanding, he had by the terror of his name and the severity of his flogging succeeded most astonishingly, particularly in one instance, where, by the flogging of one man, he and thirty-six others acknowledged themselves United Irishmen.

Now, that was abundantly proved; and the sheriff who had tortured and flogged these men who were only fighting that Ireland should not be ruled without the consent of the governed had the effrontery to ask for an act of indemnity from the House of Commons against the damages which had been recovered against him, and that claim found plenty of advocates. The ministry undertook to extenuate the action of this monster by citing the cruelties which the Irish people had inflicted in their turn, and by saying that very material discoveries were made relative to concealed arms as the result of these tortures. The defenders of the administration said the most essential service had been rendered to the state and to the country by Mr. Fitzgerald. The attorney-general trusted the House would cheerfully accede to the prayer of the petition. Mr. Wright, the man who had been tortured, was a man of excellent character and education, and a teacher of the French language. As soon as he knew there were charges against him he went to the house of the defendant to give himself up and demand a trial. I will not take the time of the Senate to read the debates. The argument for the government would do very well for some of the arguments we have heard here, and the arguments we have heard here would have done very well there. The House passed a general bill to indemnify all sheriffs and magistrates who had acted for the suppression of the rebellion in a way not warranted by law, and to secure them against actions at law for so doing. The sole question at stake was the right of torture to extort information. The bill passed the House, and afterwards Fitzgerald got a considerable pension, and was created a baronet of the United Kingdom.

Now, I agree that this precedent, so far as it may be held

to have set an example for what has been done in the Philippine Islands, may be cited against me. I cite it only to show that such things are inevitable when you undertake by brute force to reduce to subjection an unwilling people, and that, therefore, when you enter upon that undertaking you yourselves take the responsibility for everything that follows.

Mr. President, it is said that these horrors which never would have come to the public knowledge had not the Senate ordered this investigation, were unknown to our authorities at home. I hope and believe they were unknown to the war department. I know they were unknown to President Roosevelt, and I know they were unknown to President McKinley. But I cannot think—perhaps I am skeptical—that the recent declaration of that honorable gentleman, the secretary of war, made on a memorable occasion, that the war on our part has been conducted with unexampled humanity, will be accepted by his countrymen.

We used to talk, some of us, about the horrors of Andersonville, and other things that were done during the Civil War. We hope, all of us, never to hear them mentioned again. But is there anything in them worse than that which an officer of high rank in the army, vouched for by a senator on this floor, from personal knowledge, as a man of the highest honor and veracity, writes about the evils of these reconcentrado camps in the Philippine Islands? Now all this cost, all these young men gone to their graves, all these wrecked lives, all this national dishonor, the repeal of the Declaration of Independence, the overthrow of the principle on which the Monroe doctrine was placed by its author, the devastation of provinces, the shooting of captives, the torture of prisoners and of unarmed and peaceful citizens, the hanging men up by the thumbs, the carloads of maniac soldiers that you bring home, are all because you would not tell and will not tell now whether you mean in the future to stand on the principles which you and your fathers always declared in the past.

The senator from Ohio says it is not wise to declare what we will do at some future time. Mr. President, we do not ask you to declare what you will do at some future time. We ask you to declare an eternal principle good at the present time and good at all times. We ask you to reaffirm it, because the men most clamorous in support of what you are doing deny it. That principle, if you act upon it, prevents you from crushing out a weak nation, because of your fancied interest now or hereafter. It prevents you from undertaking to judge what institutions are fit for other nations on the poor plea that you are the strongest. We are asking you at least to go no further than to declare what you would not do now or hereafter, and the reason for declaring it is that half of you declare you will hold this people in subjection and the other half on this matter are dumb. You declared what you would not do at some future time when you all voted that you would not take Cuba against the will of her people, did you not? We ask you to declare not at what moment you will get out of the Philippine Islands, but only on what eternal principle you will act, in them or out of them. Such declarations are made in all history. They are made in every important treaty between nations.

The Constitution of the United States is itself but a declaration of what this country will do and what it will not do in all future times. The Declaration of Independence, if it had the practical meaning it has had for a hundred years, is a declaration of what this country would do through all future times. The Monroe doctrine, to which sixteen republics south of us owe their life and their safety, was a declaration to mankind of what we would do in all future time. Among all the shallow pretenses of imperialism this statement that we will not say what we will do in the future is the most shallow of all. Was there ever such a flimsy pretext flaunted in the face of the American people as that of gentlemen who say: If any other nation on the face of the earth or all other nations together attempt to overthrow the independence of any people to the south of us in this hemisphere, we will fight and prevent them, and at the same time think it dishonorable to declare whether we will ever overthrow the independence of a weaker nation in another hemisphere.

If we take your view of it we have crushed out the only republic in Asia and put it under our heel and we are now at war with the only Christian people in the East. Even, as I said, the senator from Ohio admits they are a people, he

only says there are several peoples and not one, as if the
doctrine that one people has no right to buy sovereignty over
another, or to rule another against its will, did not apply in
the plural number.   You cannot crush out an unwilling people, or buy sovereignty over them, or treat them as spoils of
conquest, or booty of battle in the singular, or at retail, but
you have a perfect right to do it by wholesale.   Suppose
there are several peoples in the Philippines.   They have population enough to make a hundred and twelve states of the
size of Rhode Island or Delaware when they adopted the
Constitution.

I suppose, according to this modern doctrine, that if, when
the Holy Alliance threatened to reduce the colonies which
had thrown off the yoke of Spain in South America, not a
whit more completely than the Philippine people had thrown
off the yoke of Spain in Asia, if they had undertaken to subdue them all at once, John Quincy Adams and James Monroe
would have held their peace and would at least have said it
was not wise to say what we would do in the future.   If we
had the right to protect nascent republics from the tyranny
of other people and to declare that we would do it in
the future, and if need be would encounter the whole
continent of Europe single-handed in that case, is it any
less fitting to avow that we will protect such peoples from
ourselves?   How is it that these gentlemen who will not
tell you what they will do in the future in regard to the
Philippine Islands were so eager and greedy to tell you what
they would do and what they would not do in the case of
Cuba when we first declared war on Spain?   You can make
no distinction between these two cases except by having a
motive, which I do not for one moment impute, that when
you made war upon Spain you were afraid of Europe if you
did not make the declaration.

These people are given to us as children, to lead them
out of their childhood into manhood.   They were docile and
affectionate in the beginning.   But they needed your kindness
and justice, and a respect in them for the rights we claimed for
ourselves, and the rights we had declared always were inherent
in all mankind.   You preferred force to kindness, and power
to justice, and war to peace, and pride to generosity.

You said you would not treat with a man with arms in his hands. You have come, instead, to torture him when he was unarmed and defenseless. Yet you said you would make his conduct the measure of your own; that if he lied to you, you would lie to him; that if he were cruel to you, you would be cruel to him; that if he were a savage, you would be a savage also. You held an attitude toward him which you hold to no strong or to no civilized power. You decorate an officer for the capture of Aguinaldo by treachery, and the next week ratify The Hague convention and denounce such action, and classify it with poisoning and breaking of faith.

You tell us, Mr. President, that the Philippine people have practiced some cruelties themselves. The investigation has not yet gone far enough to enable you to tell which side began these atrocities. One case which one of the members of the majority of the committee told the Senate the other day was well established by proving that it occurred long before April, 1901, and was so published, far and wide, in the press of this country at that time. I do not learn that there was any attempt to investigate it, either by the war department or by Congress, until the beginning of the present session of Congress. But suppose they did begin it. Such things are quite likely to occur when weakness is fighting for its rights against strength. Is their conduct any excuse for ours? The Philippine people is but a baby in the hands of our Republic. The young athlete, the giant, the Hercules, the Titan, forces a fight upon a boy ten years old and then blames the little fellow because he hits below the belt.

I see that my enthusiastic friend from North Carolina seeks to break the force of these revelations by saying that they are only what some Americans are wont to do at home. It is benevolent assimilation over again. It is just what the junior senator from Indiana predicted. He thought we should conduct affairs in the Philippine Islands so admirably that we should pattern our domestic administration on that model. But did I understand that the senator from North Carolina proposes, if his charge against the Democrats there is true, to make North Carolina a howling wilderness, or to

burn populous towns of ten thousand people, to get the
people of North Carolina into reconcentration camps, and to
slay every male child over ten years old?   I know nothing
about the truth of the senator's charges.   They have never
been investigated by the Senate so far.   We had some painful
investigations years ago by committees in this body and of
the other House, notably one of which the senior senator
from Colorado was chairman.   But I never heard that you
undertook to apply to Americans the methods which, if not
justified, at least are sought to be extenuated, in the Philippine Islands.

Mr. President, if the stories which come to me in private
from officers of the army and from the kindred and friends
of soldiers are to be trusted; if the evidence which seems to
be just beginning before the Senate committee can be trusted,
there is nothing in the conduct of Spain in Cuba worse than
the conduct of Americans in the Philippine Islands.   If this
evidence be true, and nobody is as yet ready to deny it, and
Spain were strong enough, she would have the right
to-morrow to wrest the Philippine Islands from our grasp on
grounds as good, if not better, than those which justified us
when we made war upon her.   The United States is a strong
and powerful country—the strongest and most powerful on
earth, as we love to think.   But it is the first time in the
history of this people for nearly three hundred years when
we had to appeal to strength and not to the righteousness of
our cause to maintain our position in a great debate of justice
and liberty.

Gentlemen tell us that that the Filipinos are savages, that
they have inflicted torture, that they have dishonored our
dead and outraged the living.   That very likely may be true.
Spain said the same thing of the Cubans.   We have made
the same charges against our own countrymen in the disturbed days after the war.   The reports of committees and
the evidence in the documents in our library are full of them.
But who ever heard before of an American gentleman, or an
American, who took as a rule for his own conduct the conduct of his antagonist, or who claimed that the Republic
should act as savages because she had savages to deal with?
I had supposed, Mr. President, that the question, whether a

gentleman shall lie or murder or torture, depended on his
sense of his own character, and not on his opinion of his
victim. Of all the miserable sophistical shifts which have
attended this wretched business from the beginning, there is
none more miserable than this.

You knew—men are held to know what they ought to
know in morals and in the conduct of states—and you knew
that this people would resist you, you knew you were to
have a war; you knew that if they were civilized, so far as
they were civilized and like you, the war would be conducted
after the fashion of civilized warfare, and that so far as they
were savage the war would be conducted on their part after
the fashion of savage warfare; and you knew also that if
they resisted and held out, their soldiers would be tempted
to do what they have done, and would yield to that temptation.

And I tell you, Mr. President, that if you do not disregard the lessons of human nature thus far, and do not retrace
your steps and set an example of another conduct, you will
have and those who follow you will have a like experience
hereafter. You may pacify this country on the surface; you
may make it a solitude, and call it peace; you may burn
towns; you may exterminate populations; you may kill the
children or the boys over ten, as Herod slew the firstborn of
the Israelites. But the volcano will be there. You will not
settle this thing in a generation or in a century or in ten
centuries, until it is settled right. It never will be settled
right until you look for your counselors to George Washington and Thomas Jefferson and John Quincy Adams and Abraham Lincoln, and not to the reports of the war department.

There is much more I should like to say, but I have
spoken too long already. I have listened to what many gentlemen have said—gentlemen whom I love and honor—with
profound sorrow. They do over again in the Senate what
Burke complained of to the House of Commons:—

" In order to prove that the Americans have no right to their liberties
we are every day endeavoring to subvert the maxims which preserve the
whole spirit of our own. To prove that the Americans ought not to be
free we are obliged to depreciate the value of freedom itself; and we
never seem to gain a paltry advantage over them in debate without at-

tacking some of those principles or deriding some of those feelings for which our ancestors have shed their blood."

I wish to cite another weighty maxim from Burke:—

"America, gentlemen say, is a noble object—it is an object well worth fighting for.   Certainly it is, if fighting a people be the best way of gaining them.   Gentlemen in this respect will be led to their choice of means by their complexions and their habits.   Those who understand the military art will of course have some predilection for it.   Those who wield the thunder of the state may have more confidence in the efficacy of arms.   But I confess, possibly for the want of this knowledge, my opinion is much more in favor of prudent management than of force— considering force not as an odious, but a feeble instrument, for preserving a people so numerous, so active, so growing, so spirited as this, in a profitable connection with us."

" There is nothing—"

says Gibbon, the historian of " The Decline and Fall of the Roman Empire "—

" more adverse to nature and reason than to hold in obedience remote countries and foreign nations in opposition to their inclination and interest.   A torrent of barbarians may pass over the earth, but an extensive empire must be supported by a refined system of policy and oppression ; in the center, an absolute power, prompt in action and rich in resources ; a swift and easy communication with the extreme parts ; fortifications to check the first effort of rebellion ; a regular administration to protect and punish ; and a well-disciplined army to inspire fear, without provoking discontent and despair."

Lord Elgin, governor-general of India and formerly governor-general of Canada, well known and highly esteemed in the United States, declared as the result of his experience in the East: " It is a terrible business, however —this living among inferior races.   I have seldom from man or woman since I came to the East heard a sentence which was reconcilable with the hypothesis that Christianity had ever come into the world.   Detestation, contempt, ferocity, vengeance, whether Chinamen or Indians be the object.   One moves among them with perfect indifference, treating them not as dogs, because in that case one would whistle to them and pat them, but as machines with which one can have no communion or sympathy.   When the passions of fear and hatred are ingrafted on this indifference, the result is frightful—an absolute callousness as to the sufferings of the objects of those passions, which must be witnessed to be understood and believed."

The glowing narrative of Macaulay, the eloquence of Burke and Sheridan, have made the crimes committed in India under the rule of Warren Hastings familiar to mankind. Yet I believe the verdict of history has acquitted Hastings, as the tribunal that tried him acquitted him.   He was dismissed, exculpated, from the bar of the House of Lords, and decorated.   He was sworn of the Privy Council and received at court.   A large purse was made up for him by the East India Company.   Yet no man doubts the truth of Burke's terrible indictment.   He was acquitted because England, and not he, was the criminal.   When England undertook to assert her rule in India what followed was the inevitable consequence of the decision.

Lord Erskine, the foremost advocate who ever spoke the English tongue on English soil, placed with unerring sagacity the defense of Hastings on this ground alone.   He admitted that Hastings, in ruling India, " may, and must, have offended against the laws of God and nature."   " If he was the faithful viceroy of an empire wrested in blood from the people to whom God and nature had given it, he may and must have preserved that unjust dominion over timorous and abject nations by a terrifying superiority."   " A government having no root in consent or affection, no foundation in similarity of interests, nor support from any one principle which cements men in society together could only be upheld by alternate stratagem and force."   Erskine adds: "To be governed at all, they must be governed with a rod of iron; and our empire in the East would long since have been lost to Great Britain if civil skill and military prowess had not united their efforts to support an authority which Heaven never gave— by means which it never can sanction."

Mr. President, this is the eternal law of human nature. You may struggle against it, you may try to escape it, you may persuade yourself that your intentions are benevolent, that your yoke will be easy and your burden will be light, but it will assert itself again and again. Government without the consent of the governed—an authority which Heaven never gave—can only be supported by means which Heaven never can sanction.

The American people have got this one question to answer. They may answer it now; they can take ten years, or twenty years, or a generation, or a century to think of it. But it will not down. They must answer it in the end: Can you lawfully buy with money, or get by brute force of arms, the right to hold in subjugation an unwilling people, and to impose on them such constitution as you, and not they, think best for them?

We have answered this question a good many times in the past. The fathers answered it in 1776, and founded the Republic upon their answer, which has been the cornerstone. John Quincy Adams and James Monroe answered it again in the Monroe doctrine, which John Quincy Adams declared was only the doctrine of the consent of the governed. The Republican party answered it when it took possession of the forces of government at the beginning of the most brilliant period in all legislative history. Abraham Lincoln answered it when, on that fatal journey to Washington in 1861, he announced that the doctrine of the consent of the governed was the cardinal doctrine of his political creed, and declared, with prophetic vision, that he was ready to be assassinated for it if need be. You answered it again yourselves when you said that Cuba, who had no more title than the people of the Philippine Islands had to their independence, of right ought to be free and independent.

The question will be answered again hereafter. It will be answered soberly and deliberately and quietly as the American people are wont to answer great questions of duty. It will be answered, not in any turbulent assembly, amid shouting and clapping of hands and stamping of feet, where men do their thinking with their heels and not with their brains. It will be answered in the churches and in the schools and in the colleges; and it will be answered in fifteen million American homes, and it will be answered as it has always been answered. It will be answered right.

A famous orator once imagined the nations of the world

uniting to erect a column to Jurisprudence in some stately capital. Each country was to bring the name of its great jurist to be inscribed on the side of the column, with a sentence stating what he and his country through him had done toward establishing the reign of law in justice for the benefit of mankind.

Rome said, " Here is Numa, who received the science of law from the nymph Egeria in the cavern and taught its message to his countrymen. Here is Justinian, who first reduced law to a code, made its precepts plain, so that all mankind could read it, and laid down the rules which should govern the dealing of man with man in every transaction of life."

France said, " Here is D'Aguesseau, the great chancellor, to whose judgment seat pilgrims from afar were wont to repair to do him reverence."

England said: " Here is Erskine, who made it safe for men to print the truth, no matter what tyrant might dislike to read it."

Virginia said: " Here is Marshall, who breathed the vital principle into the Constitution, infused into it, instead of the letter that killeth, the spirit that maketh alive, and enabled it to keep state and nation each in its appointed bounds, as the stars abide in their courses."

I have sometimes fancied that we might erect here in the capital of the country a column to American Liberty which alone might rival in height the beautiful and simple shaft which we have erected to the fame of the Father of the Country. I can fancy each generation bringing its inscription, which should recite its own contribution to the great structure of which the column should be but the symbol.

The generation of the Puritan and the Pilgrim and the Huguenot claims the place of honor at the base. "I brought the torch of Freedom across the sea. I cleared the forest. I subdued the savage and the wild beast. I laid in Christian liberty and law the foundations of empire."

The next generation says: "What my fathers founded I builded. I left the seashore to penetrate the wilderness. I planted schools and colleges and courts and churches."

Then comes the generation of the great colonial day: "I

stood by the side of England on many a hard-fought field.
I helped humble the power of France. I saw the lilies go
down before the lion at Louisburg and Quebec. I carried
the cross of St. George in triumph in Martinique and the
Havana. I knew the stormy pathways of the ocean. I followed the whale from the Arctic to the Antarctic seas, among
tumbling mountains of ice and under equinoctial heat, as the
great English orator said, 'No sea not vexed by my fisheries;
no climate not witness to my toils.'"

Then comes the generation of the revolutionary time:
"I encountered the power of England. I declared and won
the independence of my country. I placed that declaration
on the eternal principles of justice and righteousness which
all mankind have read, and on which all mankind will one
day stand. I affirmed the dignity of human nature and the
right of the people to govern themselves. I devised the
securities against popular haste and delusion which made
that right secure. I created the supreme court and the
Senate. For the first time in history I made the right of the
people to govern themselves safe, and established institutions
for that end which will endure forever."

The next generation says: "I encountered England
again. I vindicated the right of an American ship to sail
the seas the wide world over without molestation. I made
the American sailor as safe at the ends of the earth as my
fathers had made the American farmer safe in his home. I
proclaimed the Monroe doctrine in the face of the Holy
Alliance, under which sixteen republics have joined the
family of nations. I filled the Western Hemisphere with
republics from the Lakes to Cape Horn, each controlling its
own destiny in safety and in honor."

Then comes the next generation: "I did the mighty
deeds which in your younger years you saw and which your
fathers told. I saved the Union. I put down the rebellion.
I freed the slave. I made of every slave a freeman, and of
every freeman a citizen, and of every citizen a voter."

Then comes another who did the great work in peace, in
which so many of you had an honorable share: "I kept the
faith. I paid the debt. I brought in conciliation and peace
instead of war. I secured in the practice of nations the great

doctrine of expatriation. I devised the homestead system. I covered the prairie and the plain with happy homes and with mighty states. I crossed the continent and joined together the seas with my great railroads. I declared the manufacturing independence of America, as my fathers affirmed its political independence. I built up our vast domestic commerce. I made my country the richest, freest, strongest, happiest people on the face of the earth."

And now what have we to say? What have we to say? Are we to have a place in that honorable company? Must we engrave on that column: "We repealed the Declaration of Independence. We changed the Monroe doctrine from a doctrine of eternal righteousness and justice, resting on the consent of the governed, to a doctrine of brutal selfishness, looking only to our own advantage. We crushed the only republic in Asia. We made war on the only Christian people in the East. We converted a war of glory to a war of shame. We vulgarized the American flag. We introduced perfidy into the practice of war. We inflicted torture on unarmed men to extort confession. We put children to death. We established reconcentrado camps. We devastated provinces. We baffled the aspirations of a people for liberty."

No, Mr. President. Never! Never! Other and better counsels will yet prevail. The hours are long in the life of a great people. The irrevocable step is not yet taken.

Let us at least have this to say: "We, too, have kept the faith of the fathers. We took Cuba by the hand. We delivered her from her age-long bondage. We welcomed her to the family of nations. We set mankind an example never beheld before of moderation in victory. We led hesitating and halting Europe to the deliverance of their beleaguered ambassadors in China. We marched through a hostile country—a country cruel and barbarous—without anger or revenge. We returned benefit for injury, and pity for cruelty. We made the name of America beloved in the East as in the West. We kept faith with the Philippine people. We kept faith with our own history. We kept our national honor unsullied. The flag which we received without a rent we handed down without a stain." [Applause on the floor and in the galleries.]

WILLIAM STEELE HOLMAN

ECONOMY IN PUBLIC EXPENDITURES

[William Steele Holman was born in Indiana in 1822. He was educated at the common schools and Franklin College, Indiana, and began active life by school-teaching. He then studied law, and was admitted to the bar at twenty-one. He was appointed a judge of probate the same year. From 1847 to 1849 he was district attorney, and entered the state legislature in 1851. After serving four years as judge of the Court of Common Pleas, he practiced law for two years, then entered Congress in 1858, as a Democrat, where, from the Thirty-sixth to the Fifty-third Congress, he sat almost continuously, his country having claimed over thirty years' service of him when he died in 1897. Though he could scarcely be accounted an orator, Mr. Holman may be said to have had much parliamentary and executive ability, and from his watchfulness over public expenditures he was termed "the great objector," and "the Watch-Dog of the Treasury." The following characteristic speech on his favorite subject was delivered in the House of Representatives in 1895.]

THE census of 1890 shows the astounding fact that, while the circulating medium of our country was only a little over $1,600,000,000, the tax collected by the Federal, state, and local governments amounted to $1,040,473,013. So instead of ours being, as was the boast of our fathers, less burdened by government than the people of any other nation, we are now in the front ranks. With silver demonetized, a remorseless reduction of the circulating medium, and ever-increasing taxation, how can the country prosper?

Gentlemen, if the Democratic party is to be a controlling force in the affairs of our government in the future, you must retrace your steps. If that great party which established the policy over which our republican system rests will compel the old-time economy in government, restore the coinage of money as established by our fathers, and cut loose from

Great Britain in financial affairs, the future prosperity of our people will be assured.

No one can explain the present condition of our industries, the extraordinary reduction of prices of labor and of lands and of all the products of industry, especially products of lands, except as a necessary result of the movement which began in 1872 to reduce the volume of money in Europe and America, a measure consummated as to our country by the act which demonetized the silver dollar in 1873, and excessive taxation, Federal, state, and local.

I am in favor of the free coinage of silver for the same reason that I have always opposed banks of issue. Under our system of government—equal rights to all men, all money should be a legal tender, and issued by the Federal government—why should the laboring man receive the wages of a day and find the paper he received worthless the next morning? Why should money be issued that is not for all purposes a legal tender?

Under our Federal system, as now expressed by the decision of the Supreme Court of the United States, legal-tender notes issued by the United States are a legal tender for all debts public and private. And why not? This final decision will never be reversed. Why should it be reversed?

We have now in circulation of these United States notes (greenbacks) $346,681,016 and $150,705,157 issued under the Act of 1890; in all $497,386,173, all legal-tender money drawing no interest. Why should this vast sum be withdrawn from circulation? The national banks!

On the basis of 15 to 1, 15½ to 1 in Europe, and on the basis of 16 to 1, the American ratio of gold and silver, the two metals have been comparatively stable, and have formed a reliable and satisfactory basis for the final money of redemption both in Europe and in America. Although England as far back as 1816 saw an advantage on account of the indebtedness of Continental Europe to her in adopting an exclusive gold standard, yet all the nations of Continental Europe, until the close of the Franco-German war, found the use of both gold and silver equally necessary to their prosperity.

Since 1872 it is obvious a movement has been on foot to

reduce the volume of money to correspond substantially with
the basis of the currency of England, based on a single standard—gold alone—recognizing silver only as a subsidiary
coin.

Germany on account of the enormous fines she levied on
France at the conclusion of the Franco-German war saw the
advantage of adopting a single standard.

Sweden, Denmark, Norway, Italy, Austria-Hungary, and
even Belgium have been influenced by the British policy.
As the wealth of the world has increased, the capitalists of
all the nations have seen that to the capitalized wealth of the
world, a single standard was enormously beneficial, as it necessarily increased the value of money, and capital of late
years has controlled the financial policy of the world.

In 1873 a movement in harmony with the policy of England and Germany became obviously beneficial to the capitalists of the United States, hence the covert legislative procedure by which the silver dollar was eliminated from our
monetary system. No one pretends now that there was an
intelligent legislative purpose in 1872 and 1873 to abandon
the coinage of the silver dollar on the old basis of 16 of
silver to 1 of gold, and it is clear that the Act of 1873, by
which the silver dollar was eliminated from our monetary
system, was not an act of open and honest legislation. It
can be only claimed that in consequence of the suspension
of specie payments at that time the subject did not receive
serious attention in either House of Congress.

It is well known that the bill which demonetized the
silver dollar passed the House of Representatives without
having been read in the House, although the reading of the
bill was called for; but the bill, upon a suspension of the
rules, passed that House without being read.

It has been claimed repeatedly in both Houses that no
large number of silver dollars had been coined in our mints.
This is misleading, for the Mexican dollar and the Spanish
milled dollar were, up to 1837, and, I think, to a much later
day, in large circulation in the United States, and recognized
in our monetary system as legal-tender money.

Why should we retire the greenback money and the
United States notes issued under the Act of 1890—legal-

tender money? For whose benefit is this to be done? Certainly not for the benefit of the people.

The demand of the bankers is that we should have honest money, that the issue of paper money is a business that belongs to banks. With the fact established that the issue of paper money is within the province of Congress, and may be made a legal tender, how can it be said that money issued by banks, not a legal tender, is a more honest money than notes issued by the United States—issued upon the faith of the whole people of the United States, and a full legal tender for the payment of all debts, public and private? But on what basis rests the pretension that banks alone should have the right to issue paper money? Does not the government alone possess the power to issue gold and silver money and to give paper money a legal-tender power and value?

Of course the issuing of paper money, ultimately redeemable in coin, either gold or silver, or both, is very profitable, but why should a few gentlemen of ample fortunes have the monopoly of this as against the whole people of the United States? Why should the legal-tender notes now in circulation be retired for the benefit of the bankers? As legal-tender notes the benefit of this money inures to the whole people, as the issue of national banks to a few bankers! Of course, all paper money ought, in the interest of stability, to be redeemable in coin.

It is said that if paper money is issued by national banks it will have elasticity. Some of the accomplished financiers demand an elastic currency, others demand a stable currency. The management of these accomplished financiers during the last one hundred years in this country shows very conclusively that banks are carried on for the benefit of bankers—not for the general welfare; that an elastic currency, so called, can be readily employed to promote the fortunes of the few by contraction and expansion, to the impoverishment of the people.

For years the friends of the national bank system have spoken of the greenbacks as a dishonest money, and more recently of the silver dollar as a disgrace and dishonor to our country on account of the depreciation of the commercial value of silver. The audacity and selfishness of all

this must be manifest to all men. I do not know that in all
the history of monetary affairs a more thoroughly honest
paper money has ever been issued than the greenback
dollar. It is in our country, for all purposes, exactly equal
to a gold or silver dollar. Its existence and circulation
inures to the benefit of the whole people. In any view it is
a loan made by the people to themselves, without interest,
and yet for all purposes in our own country absolute money.

If you retire the $497,386,173, for all purposes real
money, you do it for the benefit of the national bankers,
they furnish the money, based upon exactly the same
security—the credit of the United States—the whole people
having the benefit of the one currency without interest, a
few bankers holding bonds, the profits and benefits of the
other. This is all there is in it.

It is said, however, that under the redemption act of
1875, under which $100,000,000 was placed in the Treasury
to redeem greenback money, you are bound to keep up that
fund, and that whenever the skillful financier can use the
greenback under that law to enable him to withdraw gold
from the Treasury for sale in Europe or India, you can use
and reuse and reuse greenbacks for that purpose. In other
words, you borrow gold from the English banks, and a few
days later the Rothschilds, through their agent in New
York, gather up greenbacks and present them at the Treasury for redemption in gold.

Nothing in the whole history of the financial world has
tended so completely to make the people subservient to
capital, enriching the few and impoverishing the many.
And who is responsible for that Act of 1875?

Did any government in the history of mankind so completely place its treasury at the mercy of Shylocks?

And yet all men know that there is no excuse for this,
except sheer favoritism of capital. We pay the current
expenses of the government in greenbacks, silver, gold, as
is the most convenient, but if the broker comes with his
greenbacks for gold to be shipped to the Rothschilds, in
Europe, we reduce the gold reserve without hesitation, and
issue interest bearing bonds to get the gold back!

There are outstanding some gold certificates issued for

gold deposits amounting to comparatively little. Of course these certificates must be paid in gold, but the amount is unimportant. There is not a word in all the statutes that commits the government to the payment of any other securities in gold coin.

Our public debt was created on a paper-money basis. The five-twenties which constituted the great body of our public debt were payable, the interest in coin and the principle in lawful money. By the Act of 1869 the interest and principle were made payable in coin. No act of Congress has ever gone beyond this.

Congress has never provided for the payment of any portion of our liabilities in gold except our gold certificates. "Coin" is the word uniformly used in the statutes. It is the word used in the Act of 1875, as well as the Act of 1869. It was Secretary McCulloch, of the Treasury, who suggested the idea that the government should pay on the gold basis; and, with a subserviency to capital never before known in the history of the world, that suggestion has been followed to the present time by government officials.

With the present policy accepted (not supported by law) you may issue bonds and increase the taxation of the people by buying gold from the Rothschilds, and you will still continually suffer the dishonor of increasing the public debt in time of profound peace! Will the American people acquiesce in this?

The remedy for all this is very simple. Adopt the policy of such a government as France—a government that has always maintained, under all conditions, its credit and its honor. If a demand is made, as the House has been informed, for a small amount of gold, it will readily be paid. If the amount is large, the authorities will determine for themselves whether the payment should be made in gold or silver, and of course France is never dishonored by her agents knocking at the bank of the Rothschilds for gold. On the contrary, England, with a gold standard, has within three years been asking France, a bimetallic country, to help her out in her trouble with the Argentine Republic.

Our people are mortified and astonished at the issuing of bonds and the increase of our public debt. The sensibilities of the people of our country have never been so profoundly aroused on a financial question as on this. The general feeling is that reasonable economy and the payment of our debts on an honest basis would have prevented this discredit to our nation, this dishonor to our people. Were we in honor bound to pay in gold? Did not Congress expressly declare in the Forty-fifth Congress that our debts were simply payable in coin?

On January 12, 1874, the condition of affairs in our country was not dissimilar to what it is now, and the following proceedings occurred in Congress:—

" THE SPEAKER.—' There comes over from a previous Monday's proceedings a motion by the gentleman from Pennsylvania [Mr. Kelley] to suspend the rules and agree to the resolution which the clerk will report in full.'

" The clerk read as follows :—

" ' Resolved, That it is the sense of this House that the taxes which now burden the people should not be increased, but that the extraordinary means, if any be required, for the support of the government during the temporary paralysis in the industries of the country now prevailing should be met by a temporary loan or loans bearing a low rate of interest in currency and redeemable in United States notes.'

" MR. GARFIELD.—' Will the gentleman from Pennsylvania allow me to make a suggestion? He must know that everybody recognizes the great importance of the subject which is brought up by his resolution, and I am sure that no one would be readier than he to debate this question and show the reasons for his opinions on this as well as on all other political topics. Therefore I hope he will allow a debate on the very important issues involved in his resolution. I appeal to the gentleman from Pennsylvania to consent to this.'

" Mr. Kelley declined agreeing to delay, and on a yea-and-nay vote the resolution failed to receive a two-thirds vote. Immediately after the following proceedings occurred.

" MR. HOLMAN.—' I ask for action at this time upon the resolution which I send to the clerk's desk and desire to have read, and I move that the rules be suspended and the resolution be passed.'

" The clerk read as follows :—

" ' Resolved, That in the judgment of this House there is no necessity for increased taxation or an increase of the public debt by a further loan if there shall be severe economy in the public expenditures; and in view of the condition of the national finances, this House will reduce the appropriations and public expenditures to the lowest point consistent with a proper administration of public affairs.' "

This resolution was adopted by a yea-and-nay vote—yeas 221, nays 3.

" The clerk read MR. HAWLEY'S resolution as follows:—

" ' *Resolved*, That in the opinion of this House the expenditures of the nation can and should be so reduced and regulated that they can be met by the existing taxes ; and in no event should there be an increase of either interest-bearing or non-interest-bearing obligations of the government.' "

The question was taken; and (two-thirds voting in favor thereof) the rules were suspended and the resolution was adopted.

It is not necessary for me to say that after this emphatic action of the House no increase of the public debt was permitted or bonds issued temporary or otherwise. During that Congress—the Forty-third—in view of the then condition of our financial affairs, a heavy reduction was made in the expenses of the government. In the next Congress—the Forty-fourth, the House being Democratic—the reduction made under the appropriations of the preceding Congress was over $58,000,000, and no public interest suffered.

The whole country can see that the trouble is over the increased expenditures of the government and the gradual reduction of the volume of our money by the adoption of the gold standard. There would not be the slightest embarrassment in the affairs of our government and but little in the commercial affairs of our country if there was reasonable frugality in the conduct of our affairs, and if the government paid its debts, as an honest man would, with lawful money under its control.

We have treated our public creditors with a magnanimity unexampled in modern history. Our public securities were acquired on a paper basis. Our public creditors afterwards secured the law of 1869 to pay in coin, and now the holders demand gold !

I wish to repeat that the favoritism shown by this government to its public creditors and holders of its securities has no precedent in history.

Democrats, if you hope to secure again the confidence of the Democratic masses of our people, you must retrace your steps and go back to the teachings of the men who laid the foundation of the government.

Gentlemen, you cannot maintain the confidence of our people while you increase year after year an already over-grown navy and maintain an army beyond the necessity of the government, with ever-increasing expenditures, in great and splendid establishments everywhere, making ours the most extravagant government in the world in proportion to population and wealth.

If the Democratic party will go back to the teachings of its founder, it will renew its youth. Jefferson demanded a government that should not take " from the mouth of labor the bread it had earned." Jackson expressed the same great thought in the following words :—

"   .   .   .   to persuade my countrymen, so far as I may, that it is not in a splendid government, supported by powerful monopolies and aris-tocratical establishments, that they will find happiness or their liberties protection, but in a plain system, void of pomp—protecting all and grant-ing favors to none—dispensing its blessings like the dews of Heaven, unseen and unfelt, save in the freshness and beauty they contribute to produce.   It is such a government that the genius of our people requires ; such a one only under which our states may remain for ages to come united, prosperous, and free."

Democrats, whenever you assure the people of our country that you will go back to the teachings of the fathers, and administer the affairs of our government frugally and only for the general welfare, as a republican government ought to be administered, and must be if free institutions are to be maintained, you may confidently hope that the people will restore the Democratic party to power.   Not till then.

JOHN JAMES INGALLS

ON THE POLITICAL SITUATION

[John James Ingalls, an American statesman and senator, famous for his caustic eloquence, was born in Massachusetts in 1833. He graduated at Williams College, in his native state, in 1855, and adopted the profession of the law. Settling in Kansas while yet a young man, his abilities made him one of the prominent political figures when the territory finally assumed the responsibilities of statehood. In 1873 he was elected as a Republican United States senator from Kansas, and was reëlected in 1879 and 1885. In 1887 he was made president *pro tem.* of the senate, but four years later he lost his seat in the upper house of Congress in consequence of the growth of the Farmers' Alliance movement in Kansas and the reaction in that state against the Republican party. He thereupon became a lecturer and writer and resumed the practice of law. He died in 1900. The following speech was made in the senate in 1891.]

THE Anglo-Saxon, Mr. President, is not by nature or instinct an anarchist, a socialist, a nihilist, or a communist. He does not desire the repudiation of debts, public or private, and he does not favor the forcible redistribution of property. He came to this continent, as he has gone everywhere else on the face of the earth, with a purpose. The forty thousand English colonists who came to this country between 1620 and 1650 formed the most significant, the most formidable migration that has ever occurred upon this globe since time began. They brought with them social and political ideas, novel in their application, of inconceivable energy and power, the home, the family, the state, individualism, the right of personal effort, freedom of conscience, an indomitable love of liberty and justice, a genius for self-government, an unrivalled capacity for conquest, but preferring charters to the sword, and they have been inexorable and relentless in the accomplishment of their designs. They were fatigued with caste and privilege and prerogative. They were tired of monarchs, and so, upon the bleak and inhospitable shores of New England, they decreed the sovereignty of the people, and there they builded " a church without a bishop and a state without a king."

The result of that experiment, Mr. President, has been ostensibly successful. Under the operation of those great forces, after two hundred and seventy years, this country exhibits a peaceful triumph over many subdued nationalities, through a government automatic in its functions and sustained by no power but the invisible majesty of law. With swift and constant communication by lines of steam transportation by land and lake and sea, with telegraphs extending their nervous reticulations from state to state, the remotest members of this gigantic republic are animated by a vitality as vigorous as that which throbs at its mighty heart, and it is through the quickened intelligence that has been communicated by those ideas that these conditions, which have been fatal to other nations, have become the pillars of our strength and the bulwarks of our safety.

By these and other emancipating devices of society the laborer and the artisan acquire the means of study and recreation. They provide their children with better opportunities than they possessed. Emerging from the obscure degradation to which they have been consigned by monarchies, they have assumed the leadership in politics and society. The governed have become the governors; the subjects have become the kings. They have formed states; they have invented political systems; they have made laws; they have established literatures; and it is not true, Mr. President, in one sense, that during this extraordinary period the rich have grown richer and the poor have grown poorer. There has never been a time, since the angel stood with the flaming sword before the gates of Eden, when the dollar of invested capital paid as low a return in interest as it does to-day; nor has there been an hour when the dollar that is earned by the laboring man would buy so much of everything that is essential for the welfare of himself and his family as it will to-day.

We have become, Mr. President, the wealthiest nation upon the face of this earth, and the greater part of these enormous accumulations has been piled up during the past fifty years. From 1860 to 1880, notwithstanding the losses incurred by the most destructive war of modern times, the emancipation of four billions of slave property, the expenses of feeding the best fed, of clothing the best clothed, and of sheltering the best-sheltered people in the world, notwithstanding all the losses by fire and flood during that period of twenty years, the wealth of the country increased at the rate of $250,000 for every hour. Every time that the clock ticked above the portal of this chamber the aggregated, accumulated permanent wealth of this country increased more than $70.

Mr. President, is it any wonder that this condition of things can exist without exciting profound apprehension? I heard, or saw rather, for I did not hear it—I saw in the morning papers that, in his speech yesterday, the senator from Ohio [Mr. Sherman] devoted a considerable part of his remarks to the defense of millionaires; that he declared that they were the froth upon the beer of our political system. [Mr. Sherman: I said speculators.]

Speculators. They are very nearly the same, for the millionaires of this country, Mr. President, are not the producers and the laborers. They are arrayed like Solomon in all his glory, but "they toil not, neither do they spin"—yes, they do spin. This class, Mr. President, I am glad to say, is not confined to this country alone. These gigantic accumulations have not been the result of industry and economy. There would be no protest against them if they were. There is an anecdote floating around the papers—speaking about beer—that some gentleman said to the keeper of a saloon that he would give him a recipe for selling more beer, and when he inquired what it was, he said, "Sell less froth." If the millionaires and speculators of this country are the froth upon the beer of our system, the time has come when we should sell more beer by selling less froth.

A table has been compiled for the purpose of showing how wealth in this country is distributed, and it is full of the most startling admonition. It has appeared in the magazines; it has been commented upon in this chamber; it has been the theme of editorial discussion. It appears from this compendium that there are in the United States two hundred persons who have an aggregate of more than $20,000,000 each; and there has been one man—the Midas of the century—at whose touch everything seemed to turn to gold, who acquired within less than the lifetime of a single individual, out of the aggregate of the national wealth that was earned by the labor of all applied to the common bounty of nature, an aggregate that exceeded the assessed valuation of four of the smallest states in this Union. [Mr. Hoar: And more than the whole country had when the Constitution was formed.]

Yes, and, as the senator from Massachusetts well observes —and I thank him for the suggestion—much more, many times more than the entire wealth of the country when it was established and founded. Four hundred persons possess $10,000,000 each, 1,000 persons $5,000,000 each, 2,000 persons $2,500,000 each, 6,000 persons $1,000,000 each, and 15,000 persons $500,000 each, making a total of 31,100 people who possess $36,250,000,000.

Mr. President, it is the most appalling statement that ever fell upon mortal ears. It is, so far as the results of democracy as a social and political experiment are concerned, the most terrible commentary that ever was recorded in the book of time: and Nero fiddles while Rome burns. It is thrown off with a laugh and a sneer as the " froth upon the beer " of our political and social system. As I said, the assessed valuation recorded in the great national ledger standing to our credit is about $65,000,000,000.

Our population is 62,500,000, and by some means, some device, some machination, some incantation, honest or otherwise, some process that cannot be defined, less than a two-thousandth part of our population have obtained possession, and have kept out of the penitentiary in spite of the means they have adopted to acquire it, of more than one-half of the entire accumulated wealth of the country.

That is not the worst, Mr. President. It has been chiefly acquired by men who have contributed little to the material welfare of the country, and by processes that I do not care in appropriate terms to describe; by the wrecking of the fortunes of innocent men, women, and children; by jugglery, by bookkeeping, by financiering, by what the senator from

Ohio calls " speculation "—and this process is going on with frightful and constantly accelerating rapidity.

The entire industry of this country is passing under the control of organized and confederated capital. More than fifty of the necessaries of life to-day, without which the cabin of the farmer and the miner cannot be lighted, or his children fed or clothed, have passed absolutely under the control of syndicates and trusts and corporations composed of speculators, and, by means of these combinations and confederations, competition is destroyed, small dealings are rendered impossible ; competence can no longer be acquired, for it is superfluous and unnecessary to say that if, under a system where the accumulations distributed per capita would be less than a thousand dollars, 31,000 obtained possession of more than half of the accumulated wealth of the country, it is impossible that others should have a competence or an independence.

So it happens, Mr. President, that our society is becoming rapidly stratified—almost hopelessly stratified—into the condition of superfluously rich and helplessly poor. We are accustomed to speak of this as " the land of the free and the home of the brave." It will soon be the home of the rich and the land of the slave.

Mr. President, this is a serious problem. It may well engage the attention of the representatives of the States and of the American people. I have no sympathy with that school of political economists which teaches that there is an irreconcilable conflict between labor and capital, and which demands indiscriminate, hostile, and repressive legislation against men because they are rich, and corporations because they are strong. Labor and capital should not be antagonists, but allies rather. They should not be opponents and enemies, but colleagues and auxiliaries whose cooperating rivalry is essential to national prosperity. But I cannot forbear to affirm that a political system under which such despotic power can be wrested from the people and vested in a few is a democracy only in name.

A financial system under which more than half of the enormous wealth of the country, derived from the bounty of nature and the labor of all, is owned by a little more than thirty thousand people, while one million American citizens able and willing to toil are homeless tramps, starving for bread, requires readjustment.

A social system which offers to tender, virtuous, and dependent women the alternative between prostitution and suicide as an escape from beggary is organized crime for which some day unrelenting justice will demand atonement and expiation.

Mr. President, it may be cause, it may be coincidence, it may be effect, it may be " post hoc " or it may be " propter hoc," but it is historically true that this great blight that has fallen upon our industries, this paralysis that has overtaken our financial system, coincided in point of time with the diminution of the circulating medium of the country. The public debt was declared to be payable in coin, and then the money power of silver was destroyed. The value of property diminished in proportion, wages fell, and the value of everything was depreciated except debts and gold. The mortgage, the bond, the coupon, and the tax have retained immortal youth and vigor. They have not depreciated. The debt remains, but the capacity to pay has been destroyed. The accumulation of years disappears under the hammer of the sheriff, and the debtor is homeless, while the creditor obtains the security for his debt for a fraction of what it was actually worth when the debt was contracted.

There is, Mr. President, a deep-seated conviction among the people, which I fully share, that the demonetization of silver in 1873 was one element of a great conspiracy to deliver the fiscal system of this country over to those by whom it has, in my opinion, finally been captured. I see no proof of the assertion that the Demonetization Act of 1873 was fraudulently or corruptly procured, but from the statements that have been made it is impossible to avoid the conviction that it was part of a deliberate plan and conspiracy formed by those who have been called speculators to still further increase the value of the standard by which their accumulations were to be measured. The attention of the people was not called to the subject. It is one of the anomalies and phenomena of legislation.

Mr. President, there is not a state west of the Alleghany

Mountains and south of the Potomac and Ohio rivers that is not in favor of the free coinage of silver. There is not a state in which, if that proposition were to be submitted to a popular vote, it would not be adopted by an overwhelming majority. I do not mean by that inclusion to say that in those states east of the Alleghanies and north of the Ohio and Potomac rivers there is any hostility or indisposition to receive the benefits that would result from the remonetization of silver. On the contrary, in the great commonwealths that lie to the northeast upon the Atlantic seaboard, New York, Pennsylvania, and the manufacturing and commercial states, I am inclined to believe from the tone of the press, from the declarations of many assemblies, that if the proposition were to be submitted there it would also receive a majority of the votes.

Mr. President, it is to that region, with that population, and with such a future, that the political power of this country has at last been transferred, and they are now unanimously demanding the free coinage of silver. It is for that reason that I shall cordially support the amendment proposed by the senator from Nevada. In doing so I not only follow the dictates of my own judgment, but I carry out the wishes of a great majority of my constituents, irrespective of party or of political affiliation. I have been for the free coinage of silver from the outset, and I am free to say that after having observed the operations of the Act of 1878 I am more than ever convinced of the wisdom of that legislation and the futility of the accusations by which it was assailed.

The people of the country that I represent have lost their reverence for gold. They have no longer any superstition about coin. Notwithstanding the declarations of the monometallists, notwithstanding the assaults that have been made by those who are in favor of still further increasing the value of the standard by which their possessions are measured, they know that money is neither wealth, nor capital, nor value, and that it is merely the creation of the law by which all these are estimated and measured.

We speak, sir, about the volume of money, and about its relation to the wealth and capital of the country. Let me ask you, sir, for a moment, what would occur if the circulating medium were to be destroyed? Suppose that the gold and silver were to be withdrawn suddenly from circulation and melted up into bars and ingots and buried in the earth from which they were taken. Suppose that all the paper money, silver certificates, gold coins, national bank-notes, treasury-notes, were stacked in one mass at the end of the treasury building and the torch applied to them, and they were to be destroyed by fire, and their ashes scattered, like the ashes of Wickliffe, upon the Potomac, to be spread abroad, wide as its waters be.

What would be the effect? Would not this country be worth exactly as much as it is to-day?' Would there not be just as many acres of land, as many houses, as many farms, as many days of labor, as much improved and unimproved merchandise, and as much property as there is to-day? The result would be that commerce would languish, the sails of the ships would be furled in the harbors, the great trains would cease to run to and fro on their errands, trade would be reduced to barter, and the people finding their energies languishing, civilization itself would droop, and we should be reduced to the condition of the nomadic wanderers upon the primeval plains.

Suppose, on the other hand, that instead of being destroyed, all the money in this country were to be put in the possession of a single man—gold, and paper, and silver— and he were to be moored in mid-Atlantic upon a raft with his great hoard, or to be stationed in the middle of Sahara's desert without food to nourish, or shelter to cover, or the means of transportation to get away. Who would be the richest man, the possessor of the gigantic treasure or the humblest settler upon the plains of the West, with a dugout to shelter him, and with corn-meal and water enough for his daily bread?

Mr. President, money is the creation of law, and the American people have learned that lesson, and they are indifferent to the assaults, they are indifferent to the arguments, they are indifferent to the aspersions which are cast upon them for demanding that the law of the United States shall place the image and superscription of Cæsar upon silver enough and gold enough and paper enough to enable them to transact without embarrassment, without hindrance, without delay, and without impoverishment their daily business affairs, and that shall give them a measure of values that will not make their earnings and their belongings the sport and the prey of speculators.

Mr. President, this contest can have but one issue. The experiment that has begun will not fail. It is useless to deny that many irregularities have been tolerated here; that many crimes have been committed in the sacred name of liberty; that our public affairs have been scandalous episodes to which every patriotic heart reverts with distress; that there have been envy and jealousy in high places; that there have been treacherous and lying platforms; that there have been shallow compromises and degrading concessions to popular errors; but, amid all these disturbances, amid all these contests, amid all these inexplicable aberrations, the path of the nation has been steadily onward.

At the beginning of our second century we have entered upon a new social and political movement whose results cannot be predicted, but which are certain to be infinitely momentous. That the progress will be upward I have no doubt. Through the long and desolate tract of history, through the seemingly aimless struggles, the random gropings of humanity, the turbulent chaos of wrong, injustice, crime, doubt, want, and wretchedness, the dungeon and the block, the inquisition and the stake, the trepidations of the oppressed, the bloody exultations and triumph of tyrants—

> " The uplifted ax, the agonizing wheel,
> Luke's iron crown and Damien's bed of steel "—

the tendency has been toward the light. Out of every conflict some man or sect or nation has emerged with higher privileges, greater opportunities, purer religion, broader liberty, and greater capacity for happiness; and out of this conflict in which we are now engaged I am confident finally will come liberty, justice, equality; the continental unity of the American republic, the social fraternity and the industrial independence of the American people.

ROBERT G. INGERSOLL

"THE VISION OF WAR"

[Robert Green Ingersoll, lawyer, politician, and orator, was born in
Dresden, N.Y., August 11, 1833. Removing with his family to Illinois
in 1845, he went through the common schools, studied law, and was admitted to the bar. His first political alliance was with the Democratic
party, and by them he was nominated for Congress in 1860. He was not
elected. In 1862 he organized the Eleventh Illinois Cavalry, and went
into service as its colonel. In 1864 he became a Republican in politics,
and two years later was appointed Attorney-General of Illinois. Being
sent as a delegate to the National Republican Convention in 1876, he
flashed upon the country as an orator of unusual power, enlarging a hitherto local reputation into one of national dimensions. His speech in
nominating James G. Blaine for President was the means of his achieving
fame. The nomination and election went to Rutherford B. Hayes, who in
the following year offered to Mr. Ingersoll the ministership to Germany,
which was not accepted. Thereafter he practiced law in Washington
and New York, and devoted much time to delivering lectures antago-
nistic to religion. He died at Dobbs Ferry, N. Y., July 21, 1899. "The
Vision of War" forms part of a speech delivered at Indianapolis to the
veteran soldiers in 1876. The "Reunion Address" was made at Elm-
wood, Ill., in 1875. The speech entitled "Blaine—the Plumed Knight"
was made in the Republican National Convention, held in Cincinnati,
June 15, 1876. Mr. Blaine was often alluded to thereafter as "the
plumed knight."]

THE past rises before me like a dream. Again we are
in the great struggle for national life. We hear the
sounds of preparation; the music of boisterous drums; the
silver voices of heroic bugles. We see thousands of assemblages, and hear the appeals of orators. We see the pale
cheeks of women, and the flushed faces of men; and in those
assemblages we see all the dead whose dust we have covered
with flowers. We lose sight of them no more. We are with
them when they enlist in the great army of freedom. We

see them part with those they love. Some are walking for the last time in quiet, woody places with the maidens they adore. We hear the whisperings and the sweet vows of eternal love as they lingeringly part forever. Others are bending over cradles, kissing babes that are asleep. Some are receiving the blessings of old men. Some are parting with mothers who hold them and press them to their hearts again and again and say nothing. Kisses and tears, tears and kisses — divine mingling of agony and love! And some are talking with wives, and endeavoring with brave words, spoken in the old tones, to drive from their hearts the awful fear. We see them part. We see the wife standing in the door with the babe in her arms—standing in the sunlight, sobbing. At the turn in the road a hand waves—she answers by holding high in her loving arms the child. He is gone, and forever!

We see them all as they march proudly away under the flaunting flags, keeping time to the grand, wild music of war,— marching down the streets of the great cities, through the towns and across the prairies, down to the fields of glory, to do and to die for the eternal right.

We go with them, one and all. We are by their side on all the gory fields, in all the hospitals of pain, on all the weary marches. We stand guard with them in the wild storm and under the quiet stars. We are with them in ravines running with blood, in the furrows of old fields. We are with them between contending hosts, unable to move, wild with thirst, the life ebbing slowly away among the withered leaves. We see them pierced by balls and torn with shells, in the trenches, by forts, and in the whirlwind of the charge, where men become iron, with nerves of steel.

We are with them in the prisons of hatred and famine; but human speech can never tell what they endured.

We are at home when the news comes that they are dead. We see the maiden in the shadow of her first sorrow. We see the silvered head of the old man bowed with the last grief.

The past rises before us and we see four millions of human beings governed by the lash; we see them bound hand and foot; we hear the strokes of cruel whips; we see the hounds tracking women through tangled swamps. We see babes sold from the breasts of mothers. Cruelty unspeakable! Outrage infinite!

Four million bodies in chains! four million souls in fetters! All the sacred relations of wife, mother, father, and child trampled beneath the brutal feet of might. And all this was done under our own beautiful banner of the free.

The past rises before us. We hear the roar and shriek of the bursting shell. The broken fetters fall. These heroes died. We look. Instead of slaves, we see men and women and children. The wand of progress touches the auction block, the slave pen, the whipping post, and we see homes and firesides and schoolhouses and books, and where all was want and crime and cruelty and fear, we see the faces of the free.

These heroes are dead. They died for liberty, they died for us. They are at rest! They sleep in the land they made free, under the flag they rendered stainless, under the solemn pines, the sad hemlocks, the tearful willows, and the embracing vines. They sleep beneath the shadows of the clouds, careless alike of sunshine or of storm, each in the windowless Palace of Rest. Earth may run red with other wars; they are at peace. In the midst of battle, in the roar of conflict, they found the serenity of death. I have one sentiment for soldiers living and dead: Cheers for the living, tears for the dead.

A vision of the future rises:

I see our country filled with happy homes, with firesides of content—the foremost of all the earth.

I see a world where thrones have crumbled and kings are dust. The aristocracy of idleness has perished from the earth.

I see a world without a slave. Man at last is free. Nature's forces have by science been enslaved. Lightning and light, wind and wave, frost and flame, and all the secret, subtle powers of earth and air are the tireless toilers for the human race.

I see a world at peace, adorned with every form of art, with music's myriad voices thrilled, while lips are rich with words of love and truth; a world in which no exile sighs, no prisoner mourns; a world on which the gibbet's shadow does not fall; a world where labor reaps its full reward, where work and worth go hand in hand, where the poor girl trying to win bread with the needle—the needle that has been called "the asp for the breast of the poor"—is not driven to the desperate choice of crime or death, of suicide or shame.

I see a world without the beggar's outstretched palm, the miser's heartless, stony stare, the piteous wail of want, the livid lips of lies, the cruel eyes of scorn.

I see a race without disease of flesh or brain,—shapely and fair,—the married harmony of form and function,—and, as I look, life lengthens, joy deepens, love canopies the earth; and over all, in the great dome, shines the eternal star of human hope.

REUNION ADDRESS

This country, according to my idea, is the one success of the world. Men here have more to eat, more to wear, better houses, and, on an average, a better education than those of any other nation now living, or any that has passed away.

Was the country worth saving?

See what we have done in this country since 1860. We were not much of a people then, to be honor bright about it. We were carrying, in the great race of national life, the weight of slavery, and it poisoned us; it paralyzed our best energies; it took from our politics the best minds; it kept from the bench the greatest brains.

But what have we done since 1860, since we really became a free people, since we came to our senses, since we have been willing to allow a man to express his honest thoughts on every subject?

Do you know how much good we did? The war brought men together from every part of the country and gave them an opportunity to compare their foolishness. It gave them an opportunity to throw away their prejudices, to find that a man who differed with them on every subject might be the very best of fellows. That is what the war did.

I sometimes have thought it did men good to make the

trip to California in 1849. As they went over the plains they dropped their prejudices on the way. I think they did, and that's what killed the grass.

From 1860 to 1880, in spite of the waste of war, in spite of all the property destroyed by flame, in spite of all the waste, our profits were one billion three hundred and seventy-four million dollars. Think of it! From 1860 to 1880! That is a vast sum.

From 1880 to 1890 our profits were two billion one hundred and thirty-nine million dollars.

Men may talk against wealth as much as they please; they may talk about money being the root of all evil, but there is little real happiness in this world without some of it. It is very handy when staying at home and it is almost indispensable when you travel abroad. Money is a good thing. It makes others happy; it makes happy those whom you love, and if a man can get a little together, when the night of death drops the curtain upon him, he is satisfied that he has left a little to keep the wolf from the door of those who, in life, were dear to him. Yes, money is a good thing, especially since special providence has gone out of business.

I can see to-day something beyond the wildest dream of any patriot who lived fifty years ago. The United States to-day is the richest nation on the face of the earth. The old nations of the world, Egypt, India, Greece, Rome, every one of them, when compared with this great Republic, must be regarded as paupers.

How much do you suppose this nation is worth to-day? I am talking about land and cattle, products, manufactured articles, and railways. Over seventy thousand million dollars. Just think of it!

Take a thousand dollars and then take nine hundred and ninety-nine thousand; so you will have one thousand piles of one thousand each. That makes only a million, and yet the United States to-day is worth seventy thousand million. This is thirty-five per cent. more than Great Britain is worth.

We are a great nation. We have got the land. This land was being made for many millions of years. Its soil was being made by the great lakes and rivers, and being brought down from the mountains for countless ages.

This continent was standing like a vast pan of milk, with the cream rising for millions of years, and we were the chaps that got there when the skimming began.

We are rich and we ought to be rich. It is our own fault if we are not. In every department of human endeavor, along every path and highway, the progress of the Republic has been marvelous, beyond the power of language to express.

Let me show you: In 1860 the horse-power of all the engines, the locomotives, and steamboats that traversed the lakes and rivers, the entire power was three million five hundred thousand. In 1890 the horse-power of engines and locomotives and steamboats was over seventeen million.

Think of that and what it means! Think of the forces at work for the benefit of the United States, the machines doing the work of thousands and millions of men!

And remember that every engine that puffs is puffing for you; every road that runs is running for you. I want you to know that the average man and woman in the United States to-day has more of the conveniences of life than kings and queens had one hundred years ago.

Yes, we are getting along.

In 1860 we used one billion eight hundred million dollars' worth of products, of things manufactured and grown, and we sent to other countries two hundred and fifty million dollars' worth.

In 1893 we used three billion eighty-nine million dollars' worth, and we sent to other countries six hundred and fifty-four million dollars' worth.

You see these vast sums are almost inconceivable. There is not a man to-day with brains large enough to understand these figures, to understand how many cars this money put upon the tracks, how much coal was devoured by the locomotives, how many men plowed and worked in the fields, how many sails were given to the wind, how many ships crossed the sea.

I tell you there is no man able to think of the ships that were built, the cars that were made, the mines that were opened, the trees that were felled—no man has imagination enough to grasp the meaning of it all. No man has any conception of the sea till he crosses it. I knew nothing of how broad this country is until I went over it in a slow train.

Since 1860 the productive power of the United States has more than trebled.

I like to talk about these things because they mean good houses, carpets on the floors, pictures on the walls, some books on the shelves. They mean children going to school with their stomachs full of good food; prosperous men and proud mothers.

All my life I have taken a much deeper interest in what men produce than in what nature does. I would rather see the prairies, with the oats and the wheat and the waving corn, and the schoolhouse, and hear the thrush sing amid the happy homes of prosperous men and women—I would rather see these things than any range of mountains in the world. Take it as you will, a mountain is of no great value.

In 1860 our land was worth four billion five hundred million dollars; in 1890 it was worth fourteen billion dollars.

In 1860 all the railroads in the United States were worth four hundred million dollars; now they are worth a little less than ten thousand million dollars.

I want you to understand what these figures mean.

For thirty years we spent, on an average, one million dollars a day in building railroads. I want you to think what that means. All that money had to be dug out of the ground. It had to be made by raising something or manufacturing something. We did not get it by writing essays on finance or discussing the silver question. It had to be made with the ax, the plow, the reaper, the mower—in every form of industry—all to produce these splendid results.

We have railroads enough now to make seven tracks around the great globe, and enough left for side tracks. That is what we have done here, in what the European nations are pleased to call the "new world."

I am telling you these things because you may not know them, and I did not know them myself until a few days ago. I am anxious to give away information, for it is only by giving it away that you can keep it. When you have told it, you remember it. It is with information as it is with liberty, the **only way to be dead sure of it is to give it to other people.**

In 1860 the houses in the United States, the cabins on the frontier, the buildings in the cities, were worth six thousand million dollars. Now they are worth over twenty-two thousand million dollars. To talk about figures like these is enough to make a man dizzy.

In 1860 our animals of all kinds, including the Illinois deer—commonly called swine—the oxen and horses, and all others, were worth about one thousand million dollars; now they are worth about four thousand million dollars.

Are we not getting rich? Our national debt to-day is nothing. It is like a man who owes a cent and has a dollar.

Since 1860 we have been industrious. We have created two million five hundred thousand new farms. Since 1860 we have done a good deal of plowing; there have been a good many tired legs. I have been that way myself. Since 1860 we have put in cultivation two hundred million acres of land. Illinois, the best state in the Union, has thirty-five million acres of land, and yet, since 1860 we have put in cultivation enough land to make six states of the size of Illinois. That will give you some idea of the quantity of work we have done. I will admit I have not done much of it myself, but I am proud of it.

In 1860 we had four million five hundred and sixty-five thousand farmers in this country, whose land and implements were worth over sixteen thousand million dollars. The farmers of this country, on an average, are worth five thousand dollars, and the peasants of the Old World, who cultivate the soil, are not worth, on an average, ten dollars beyond the wants of the moment. The farmers of our country produce, on an average, about one million four hundred thousand dollars' worth of stuff a day.

What else? Have we in other directions kept pace with our physical development? Have we developed the mind? Have we endeavored to develop the brain? Have we endeavored to civilize the heart? I think we have.

We spend more for schools per head than any nation in the world. And the common school is the breath of life.

Great Britain spends one dollar and thirty cents per head on the common schools; France spends eighty cents; Austria, thirty cents; Germany, fifty cents; Italy, twenty-five cents; and the United States over two dollars and fifty cents.

I tell you, the schoolhouse is the fortress of liberty. Every schoolhouse is an arsenal filled with weapons and ammunition to destroy the monsters of ignorance and fear.

As I have said ten thousand times, the schoolhouse is my cathedral. The teacher is my preacher.

Eighty-seven per cent. of all the people of the United States, over ten years of age, can read and write. There is no parallel for this in the history of the wide world.

Over forty-two millions of educated citizens, to whom are opened all the treasures of literature!

Forty-two millions of people, able to read and write! I say, there is no parallel for this. The nations of antiquity were very ignorant when compared with this great Republic of ours. There is no other nation in the world that can show a record like ours. We ought to be proud of it. We ought to build more schools, and build them better. Our teachers ought to be paid more, and everything ought to be taught in the public school that is worth knowing.

I believe that the children of the Republic, no matter whether their fathers are rich or poor, ought to be allowed to drink at the fountain of education, and it does not cost more to teach everything in the free schools than it does teaching reading and writing and ciphering.

Have we kept up in other ways? The post-office tells a wonderful story. In Switzerland, going through the post-office in each year, are letters, etc., in the proportion of seventy-four to each inhabitant. In England the number is sixty; in Germany, fifty-three; in France, thirty-nine; in Austria, twenty-four; in Italy, sixteen; and in the United States, our own home, one hundred and ten. Think of it. In Italy only twenty-five cents paid per head for the support of public schools and only sixteen letters.

There is another thing. A great deal has been said, from time to time, about the workingman. I have as much sympathy with the workingman as anybody on the earth—who does not work? There has always been a desire in this world to let somebody else do the work, nearly everybody having the modesty to stand back whenever there is anything

to be done. In savage countries they make the women do
the work, so that the weak people have always the bulk of
the burdens. In civilized communities the poor are the
ones, of course, that work, and probably they are never fully
paid. It is pretty hard for a manufacturer to tell how much
he can pay until he sells the stuff which he manufactures.
Not every man who manufactures is rich. I know plenty of
poor corporations; I know tramp railroads that have not a
dollar. And you will find some of them as anarchistic as
you will find their men. What a man can pay, depends
upon how much he can get for what he has produced. What
the farmer can pay his help depends upon the price he
receives for his stock, his corn, and his wheat.

But wages in this country are getting better day by
day. We are getting a little nearer to being civilized day
by day; and when I want to make up my mind on a subject I try to get a broad view of it, and not decide it on one
case.

In 1860 the average wages of the workingman were, per
year, two hundred and eighty-nine dollars. In 1890 the
average was four hundred and eighty-five. Thus the average
has almost doubled in thirty years. The necessaries of life
are far cheaper than they were in 1860. Now, to my mind,
that is a hopeful sign. And when I am asked how can the
dispute between employer and employé be settled, I answer,
it will be settled when both parties become civilized.

It takes a long time to educate a man up to the point
where he does not want something for nothing. Yet, when
a man is civilized, he does not. He wants for a thing just
what it is worth; he wants to give labor its legitimate
reward; and when he has something to sell he never wants
more than it is worth. I do not claim to be civilized myself;
but all these questions will be settled by civilization.

We have one-seventh of the good land of this world. I
often hear people say that we have too many folks here:
that we ought to stop immigration; that we have no more
room. The people who say this know nothing of their country. They are ignorant of their native land. I tell you that
the valley of the Mississippi and the valleys of its tributaries
can support a population of five hundred millions of men,

women, and children. Don't talk of our being overpopulated; we have only just started.

Here, in this land of ours, five hundred million men and women and children can be supported and educated without trouble. We can afford to double two or three times more. But what have we got to do? We have got to educate them when they come. That is to say, we have got to educate their children, and in a few generations we shall have them splendid American citizens, proud of the Republic.

We have no more patriotic men under the flag than the men who came from other lands, the hundreds and thousands of those who fought to preserve this country. And I think just as much of them as I would if they had been born on American soil. What matters where a man was born? It is what is inside of him you have to look at—what kind of heart he has, and what kind of head. I do not care where he was born; I simply ask, Is he a man? Is he willing to give to others what he claims for himself? That is the supreme test.

Now, I have a hobby. I do not suppose any of you have heard of it. I think the greatest thing for a country is for all of its citizens to have a home. I think that it is around the fireside of home that the virtues grow, including patriotism. We want homes.

Until a few years ago it was the custom to put men in prison for debt. The authorities threw a man into jail when he owed something which he could not pay, and by throwing him into jail they deprived him of an opportunity to earn what would pay it. After a little time they got sense enough to know that they could not collect a debt in this way, and that it was better to give him his freedom and allow him to earn something if he could. Therefore imprisonment for debt was done away with.

When I look about me to-day, when I think of the advance of my country, then I think of the work that has been done.

Think of the millions who crossed the mysterious sea, of the thousands and thousands of ships with their brave prows toward the West.

Think of the little settlements on the shores of the ocean, on the banks of rivers, on the edges of forests.

Think of the countless conflicts with savages—of the midnight attacks—of the cabin floors wet with the blood of dead fathers, mothers, and babes.

Think of the winters of want, of the days of toil, of the nights of fear, of the hunger and hope.

Think of the courage, the sufferings, and hardships.

Think of the homesickness, the disease, and death.

Think of the labor; of the millions and millions of trees that were felled, while the aisles of the great forests were filled with the echoes of the ax; of the many millions of miles of furrows turned by the plow; of the millions of miles of fences.built; of the countless logs changed to lumber by the saw; of the millions of huts, cabins, and houses.

Think of the work. Listen, and you will hear the hum of wheels, the wheels with which our mothers spun the flax and wool. Listen, and you will hear the looms and flying shuttles with which they wove the cloth.

Think of the thousands still pressing toward the West, of the roads they made, of the bridges they built; of the homes, where the sunlight fell, where the bees hummed, the birds sang, and the children laughed; of the little towns with mill and shop, with inn and schoolhouse; of the old stages, of the crack of the whips and the drivers' horns; of the canals they dug.

Think of the many thousands still passing toward the West, passing over the Alleghanies to the shores of the Ohio and the great lakes—still onward to the Mississippi, the Missouri.

See the endless processions of covered wagons drawn by horses, by oxen—men and boys and girls on foot, mothers and babes inside. See the glimmering camp-fires at night. See the thousands up with the sun and away, leaving the perfume of coffee on the morning air, and sometimes leaving the new-made grave of wife or child. Listen, and you will hear the cry of " Gold! " and you will see many thousands crossing the great plains, climbing the mountains, and pressing on to the Pacific.

Think of the toil, the courage it has taken to possess this land!

Think of the ore that was dug, the furnaces that lit the

nights with flame; of the factories and mills by the rushing streams.

Think of the inventions that went hand in hand with the work; of the flails that were changed into threshers; of the sickles that became cradles, and the cradles that were changed to reapers and headers; of the wooden plows that became iron and steel; of the spinning-wheel that became the jenny, and the old looms transformed to machines that almost think; of the steamboats that traversed the rivers, making the towns that were far apart neighbors and friends; of the stages that became cars; of the horses changed to locomotives with breath of flame, and the roads of dust and mud to highways of steel; of the rivers spanned and the mountains tunneled.

Think of the inventions, the improvements that changed the hut to the cabin, the cabin to the house, the house to the palace, the earthen floors and bare walls to carpets and pictures; that changed famine to feast, toil to happy labor, and poverty to wealth.

Think of the cost.

Think of the separation of families; of boys and girls leaving the old home, taking with them the blessings and kisses of fathers and mothers. Think of the homesickness, of the tears shed by the mothers left by the daughters gone. Think of the millions of brave men, deformed by labor, now sleeping in their honored graves.

Think of all that has been wrought, endured, and accomplished for our good, and let us remember with gratitude, with love and tears, the brave men, the patient, loving women who subdued this land for us.

Then think of the heroes who served this country; who gave us this glorious present and hope of a still more glorious future; think of the men who really made us free, who secured the blessings of liberty, not only to us, but to billions yet unborn.

This country will be covered with happy homes and free men and free women.

To-day we remember the heroic dead, those whose blood reddens the paths and highways of honor; those who died upon the field, in the charge, in prison pens, or in famine's clutch; those who gave their lives that liberty should not perish from the earth. And to-day we remember the great leaders who have passed to the realm of silence, to the land of shadow. Thomas, the rock of Chickamauga, self-poised, firm, brave, faithful; Sherman, the reckless, the daring, the prudent, and the victorious; Sheridan, a soldier fit to have stood by Julius Cæsar, and to have uttered the words of command; and Grant, the silent, the invincible, the unconquered; and rising above them all, Lincoln, the wise, the patient, the merciful, the grandest figure in the Western world. We remember them all to-day, and hundreds of thousands who are not mentioned, but who are equally worthy, hundreds of thousands of privates deserving of equal honor with the plumed leaders of the host.

And what shall I say to you, survivors of the death-filled days? To you, my comrades, to you whom I have known in the great days, in the time when the heart beat fast and the blood flowed strong, in the days of high hope—what shall I say? All that I can say is that my heart goes out to you, one and all. To you who bared your bosoms to the storms of war; to you who left loved ones to die, if need be, for the sacred cause. May you live long in the land you helped to save; may the winter of your age be as green as spring, as full of blossoms as summer, as generous as autumn; and may you, surrounded by plenty, with your wives at your sides and your grandchildren on your knees, live long. And when at last the fires of life burn low; when you enter the deepening dusk of the last of many, many happy days; when your brave hearts beat weak and slow, may the memory of your splendid deeds—deeds that freed your fellow-men; deeds that kept your country on the map of the world; deeds that kept the flag of the Republic in the air—may the memory of these deeds fill your souls with peace and perfect joy. Let it console you to know that you are not to be forgotten. Centuries hence your story will be told in art and song, and upon your honored graves flowers will be lovingly laid by millions of men and women now unborn.

Again expressing the joy that I feel in having met you, and again saying farewell to one and all, and wishing you all the blessings of life, I bid you good-by.

BLAINE—"THE PLUMED KNIGHT"

Massachusetts may be satisfied with the loyalty of Benjamin H. Bristow; so am I; but if any man nominated by this convention cannot carry the state of Massachusetts, I am not satisfied with the loyalty of that state. If the nominee of this convention cannot carry the grand old Commonwealth of Massachusetts by seventy-five thousand majority, I would advise them to sell out Faneuil Hall as a Democratic headquarters. I would advise them to take from Bunker Hill that old monument of glory.

The Republicans of the United States demand as their leader in the great contest of 1876 a man of intelligence, a man of integrity, a man of well-known and approved political opinions. They demand a statesman; they demand a reformer after, as well as before, the election. They demand a politician in the highest, broadest, and best sense—a man of superb moral courage. They demand a man acquainted with public affairs—with the wants of the people—with not only the requirements of the hour, but with the demands of the future. They demand a man broad enough to comprehend the relations of this government to the other nations of the earth. They demand a man well versed in the powers, duties, and prerogatives of each and every department of this government. They demand a man who will sacredly preserve the financial honor of the United States—one who knows enough to know that the national debt must be paid through the prosperity of this people; one who knows enough to know that all the financial theories in the world cannot redeem a single dollar; one who knows enough to know that all the money must be made, not by law, but by labor; one who knows enough to know that the people of the United States have the industry to make the money and the honor to pay it over just as fast as they make it.

The Republicans of the United States demand a man who knows that prosperity and resumption, when they come, must come together; that when they come they will come hand in hand through the golden harvest fields; hand in hand by the whirling spindles and turning wheels; hand in hand past the open furnace doors; hand in hand by the flaming forges; hand in hand by the chimneys filled with eager fire—greeted and grasped by the countless sons of toil.

This money has to be dug out of the earth. You cannot make it by passing resolutions in a political convention.

The Republicans of the United States want a man who knows that this government should protect every citizen at home and abroad; who knows that any government that will not defend its defenders and protect its protectors is a disgrace to the map of the world. They demand a man who believes in the eternal separation and divorcement of church and school. They demand a man whose political reputation is spotless as a star; but they do not demand that their candidate shall have a certificate of moral character signed by a Confederate Congress. The man who has in full, heaped and rounded measure, all these splendid qualifications is the present grand and gallant leader of the Republican party—James G. Blaine.

Our country, crowned with the vast and marvelous achievements of its first century, asks for a man worthy of the past and prophetic of her future; asks for a man who has the audacity of genius; asks for a man who is the grandest combination of heart, conscience, and brain beneath her flag. Such a man is James G. Blaine.

For the Republican host, led by this intrepid man, there can be no defeat.

This is a grand year; a year filled with the recollections of the Revolution, filled with proud and tender memories of the past, with the sacred legends of liberty; a year in which the sons of freedom will drink from the fountains of enthusiasm; a year in which the people call for a man who has preserved in Congress what our soldiers won upon the field; a year in which we call for the man who has torn from the throat of treason the tongue of slander—for the man who has snatched the mask of Democracy from the hideous face of Rebellion—for the man who, like an intellectual athlete, has stood in the arena of debate and challenged all comers, and who, up to the present moment, is a total stranger to defeat.

Like an armed warrior, like a plumed knight, James G. Blaine marched down the halls of the American Congress and threw his shining lance full and fair against the brazen foreheads of the defamers of his country and the maligners of his honor. For the Republicans to desert this gallant leader now is as though an army should desert their general upon the field of battle.

James G. Blaine is now, and has been for years, the bearer of the sacred standard of the Republican party. I call it sacred, because no human being can stand beneath its folds without becoming and without remaining free.

Gentlemen of the convention, in the name of the great Republic, the only republic that ever existed upon this earth; in the name of all her defenders and of all her supporters; in the name of all her soldiers living; in the name of all her soldiers dead upon the field of battle; and in the name of those who perished in the skeleton clutch of famine at Andersonville and Libby, whose sufferings he so vividly remembers, Illinois—Illinois nominates for the next President of this country that prince of parliamentarians, that leader of leaders, James G. Blaine.

THOMAS JEFFERSON

INAUGURAL ADDRESS OF 1801

[Thomas Jefferson, third President of the United States, was born at Shadwell, Va., April 13, 1743. He graduated from William and Mary College in 1762. Turning next to the study of law, he completed his course and began practice in 1767. From the Virginia House of Burgesses he passed in June, 1775, to the Colonial Congress, where he put into formal expression the Declaration of Independence. He followed Patrick Henry as governor of Virginia, but reentered Congress in 1783, and in the following year went on a diplomatic mission to Europe, succeeding Franklin as minister to France. He returned to America, and became Washington's secretary of state in 1790; but retired in 1793. From this time he assumed the virtual leadership of a new political party that opposed the Federal plans of strong centralization. While its power grew it was hardly sufficient to have elected Jefferson Vice-President in 1797 had not that end been assisted by disaffection in the Federal party. In 1800 Jefferson was elected President. His administration, which covered two terms, was notable for several important events. Chief among those of his first term was the purchase of Louisiana from the French. His second term marked the beginning of hostilities with England that culminated in the War of 1812. He retired from public life in 1809, and died at Monticello, July 4, 1826. The first inaugural address was made in Washington in 1801 ; of the addresses to the Indians, the first was made in 1806, and the second and third in 1808 and 1809.]

CALLED upon to undertake the duties of the first executive office of our country, I avail myself of the presence of that portion of my fellow citizens which is here assembled to express my grateful thanks for the favor with which they have been pleased to look toward me, to declare a sincere consciousness that the task is above my talents, and that I approach it with those anxious and awful presentiments which the greatness of the charge and the weakness of my powers so justly inspire. A rising nation, spread over a wide and fruitful land, traversing all the seas with the rich

productions of their industry, engaged in commerce with
nations who feel power and forget right, advancing rapidly
to destinies beyond the reach of mortal eye; when I contemplate these transcendent objects and see the honor, the
happiness, and the hopes of this beloved country committed
to the issue and the auspices of this day, I shrink from the
contemplation, and humble myself before the magnitude of
the undertaking.   Utterly, indeed, should I despair, did not
the presence of many whom I here see remind me that,
in the other high authorities provided by our Constitution,
I shall find resources of wisdom, of virtue, and of zeal, on
which to rely under all difficulties.   To you, then, gentlemen, who are charged with the sovereign functions of legislation, and to those associated with you, I look with encouragement for that guidance and support which may enable us
to steer with safety the vessel in which we are all embarked,
amid the conflicting elements of a troubled world.

During the contest of opinion through which we have
passed, the animation of discussion and of exertions has
sometimes worn an aspect which might impose on strangers
unused to think freely, and to speak and to write what they
think; but this being now decided by the voice of the nation,
announced according to the rules of the Constitution, all will
of course arrange themselves under the will of the law, and
unite in common efforts for the common good.   All, too,
will bear in mind this sacred principle, that, though the will
of the majority is in all cases to prevail, that will, to be rightful, must be reasonable; that the minority possess their
equal rights, which equal law must protect, and to violate
would be oppression.   Let us, then, fellow citizens, unite
with one heart and one mind, let us restore to social intercourse that harmony and affection, without which liberty,
and even life itself, are but dreary things.   And let us reflect
that, having banished from our land that religious intolerance
under which mankind so long bled and suffered, we have yet
gained little if we countenance a political intolerance as despotic, as wicked, and capable of as bitter and bloody perse-
cutions.   During the throes and convulsions of the ancient
world, during the agonizing spasms of infuriated man, seeking through blood and slaughter his long-lost liberty, it was

not wonderful that the agitation of the billows should reach even this distant and peaceful shore; that this should be more felt and feared by some, and less by others; that this should divide opinions as to measures of safety; but every difference of opinion is not a difference of principle. We have called by different names brethren of the same principle. We are all Republicans; we are all Federalists. If there be any among us who would wish to dissolve this Union, or to change its republican form, let them stand undisturbed as monuments of the safety with which error of opinion may be tolerated, where reason is left free to combat it. I know, indeed, that some honest men fear that a republican government cannot be strong; that this government is not strong enough. But would the honest patriot, in the full tide of successful experiment, abandon a government which has so far kept us free and firm, on the theoretic and visionary fear that this government, the world's best hope, may, by possibility, want energy to preserve itself? I trust not. I believe this, on the contrary, the strongest government on earth. I believe it the only one where every man, at the call of the laws, would fly to the standard of the law, and would meet invasions of the public order as his own personal concern. Sometimes it is said that man cannot be trusted with the government of himself. Can he then be trusted with the government of others? or have we found angels in the forms of kings to govern him? Let history answer this question.

Let us, then, with courage and confidence, pursue our own federal and republican principles, our attachment to our Union and representative government. Kindly separated by nature and a wide ocean from the exterminating havoc of one-quarter of the globe; too high-minded to endure the degradations of the others; possessing a chosen country, with room enough for our descendants to the thousandth and thousandth generation; entertaining a due sense of our equal right to the use of our own faculties, to the acquisitions of our industry, to honor and confidence from our fellow citizens, resulting not from birth, but from our actions and their sense of them; enlightened by a benign religion, professed, indeed, and practiced in various forms, yet all of them including honesty, truth, temperance, gratitude, and the love of man, acknowledging and adoring an overruling Providence, which, by all its dispensations, proves that it delights in the happiness of man here, and his greater happiness hereafter; with all these blessings, what more is necessary to make us a happy and prosperous people? Still one thing more, fellow citizens—a wise and frugal government, which shall restrain men from injuring one another, shall leave them otherwise free to regulate their own pursuits of industry and improvement, and shall not take from the mouth of labor the bread it has earned. This is the sum of good government, and this is necessary to close the circle of our felicities.

About to enter, fellow-citizens, on the exercise of duties which comprehend everything dear and valuable to you, it is proper that you should understand what I deem the essential principles of our government, and consequently those which ought to shape its administration. I will compress them within the narrowest compass they will bear, stating the general principles, but not all its limitations. Equal and exact justice to all men, of whatever state or persuasion, religious or political; peace, commerce, and honest friendship with all nations, entangling alliances with none; the support of the state governments in all their rights, as the most competent administrations for our domestic concerns, and the surest bulwarks against anti-republican tendencies; the preservation of the general government in its whole constitutional vigor, as the sheet anchor of our peace at home and safety abroad; a jealous care of the right of election by the people; a mild and safe corrective of abuses, which are lopped by the sword of revolution, where peaceable remedies are unprovided; absolute acquiescence in the decisions of the majority, the vital principle of republics, from which is no appeal but to force, the vital principle and immediate parent of despotism; a well-disciplined militia, our best reliance in peace, and for the first moments of war, till regulars may relieve them; the supremacy of the civil over the military authority; economy in the public expense, that labor may be lightly burdened; the honest payment of our debts, and sacred preservation of the public faith; encouragement of agriculture, and of commerce as its handmaid; the diffusion of information, and arraignment of all abuses at the bar of public reason; freedom of religion; freedom of the press; and freedom of person, under the protection of the habeas corpus; and trial by juries, impartially selected. These principles form the bright constellation which has gone before us, and guided our steps through an age of revolution and reformation. The wisdom of our sages and blood of our heroes have been devoted to their attainment; they should be the creed of our political faith; the text of civil instruction; the touchstone by which to try the services of those we trust; and should we wander from them, in moments of error or alarm, let us hasten to retrace our steps, and to regain the road which alone leads to peace, liberty, and safety.

I repair, then, fellow citizens, to the post you have assigned me. With experience enough in subordinate offices to have seen the difficulties of this, the greatest of all, I have learned to expect that it will rarely fall to the lot of imperfect man to retire from this station with the reputation and the favor which bring him into it. Without pretensions to that high confidence you reposed in our first and great revolutionary character, whose preeminent services had entitled him to the first place in his country's love, and destined for him the fairest page in the volume of faithful history, I ask so much confidence only as may give firmness and effect to the legal administration of your affairs. I shall often go wrong through defect of judgment. When right, I shall often be thought wrong by those whose positions will not command a view of the whole ground. I ask your indulgence for my own errors, which will never be intentional; and your support against the errors of others, who may condemn what they would not, if seen in all its parts. The approbation implied by your suffrage is a consolation to me for the past; and my future solicitude will be to retain the good opinion of those who have bestowed it in advance, to conciliate that of others by doing them all the good in my power, and to be instrumental in the happiness and freedom of all.

Relying, then, on the patronage of your good will, I advance with obedience to the work, ready to retire from it whenever you become sensible how much better choices it is in your power to make. And may that infinite Power, which rules the destinies of the universe, lead our councils to what is best, and give them a favorable issue for your peace and prosperity!

TO THE WOLF AND PEOPLE OF THE MANDAN NATION

My Children,—the Wolf and people of the Mandan nation: I take you by the hand of friendship and give you a hearty welcome to the seat of the Government of the United States. The journey which you have taken to visit your fathers on this side of our island is a long one, and your having undertaken it is a proof that you desired to become acquainted with us. I thank the Great Spirit that he has protected you through the journey, and brought you safely to the residence of your friends, and I hope he will have you constantly in his safe keeping, and restore you in good health to your nations and families.

My friends and children, we are descended from the old nations which live beyond the great water, but we and our forefathers have been so long here that we seem, like you, to have grown out of this land. We consider ourselves no longer of the old nations beyond the great water, but as united in one family with our red brethren here. The French, the English, the Spaniard have now agreed with us to retire from all the country which you and we hold between Canada and Mexico, and never more to return to it. And remember the words I now speak to you, my children: they are never to return again. We are now your fathers; and you shall not lose by the change. As soon as Spain had agreed to withdraw from all the waters of the Missouri and Mississippi, I felt the desire of becoming acquainted with all my red children beyond the Mississippi, and of uniting them with us, as we have those on this side of that river, in the bonds of peace and friendship. I wished to learn what we could do to benefit them by furnishing them the necessaries they want, in exchange for their furs and peltries. I therefore sent our beloved man, Captain Lewis, one of my own

THOMAS JEFFERSON

Photogravure after a painting by Gilbert Stuart

Copyright 1897, by A.W. Elson & Co., Boston

family, to go up the Mississippi River to get acquainted with all the Indian nations in its neighborhood, to take them by the hand, deliver my talks to them, and to inform us in what way we could be useful to them.   Your nation received him kindly, you have taken him by the hand and been friendly to him.   My children, I thank you for the services you rendered him, and for your attention to his words.   He will now tell us where we should establish trading houses to be convenient to you all, and what we must send to them.

My friends and children, I have now an important advice to give you.   I have already told you that you and all the red men are my children, and I wish you to live in peace and friendship with one another, as brethren of the same family ought to do.   How much better is it for neighbors to help than to hurt one another! how much happier must it make them!   If you will cease to make war on one another, if you live in friendship with all mankind, you can employ all your time in providing food and clothing for yourselves and your families.   Your men will not be destroyed in war, and your women and children will lie down to sleep in their cabins without fear of being surprised by their enemies, and killed or carried away.   Your numbers will be increased instead of diminishing, and you will live in plenty and in quiet.   My children, I have given this advice to all your red brethren on this side of the Mississippi.   They are following it, they are increasing in their numbers, are learning to clothe and provide for their families as we do.   Remember, then, my advice, my children, carry it home to your people, and tell them that from the day that they have become all of the same family, from the day that we became father to them all, we wish, as a true father should do, that we may all live together as one household, and that before they strike one another they should go to their father and let him endeavor to make up the quarrel.

My children, you are come from the other side of our great island, from where the sun sets, to see your new friends at the sun rising.   You have now arrived where the waters are constantly rising and falling every day, but you are still distant from the sea.   I very much desire that you should not stop here but go and see your brethren as far as the edge of the great water. I am persuaded you have so far seen that every man by the way has received you as his brothers, and has been ready to do you all the kindness in his power. You will see the same thing quite to the sea-shore; and I wish you, therefore, to go and visit our great cities in that quarter, and see how many friends and brothers you have here. You will then have travelled a long line from west to east, and if you had time to go from north to south, from Canada to Florida, you would find it as long in that direction, and all the people as sincerely your friends. I wish you, my children, to see all you can, and to tell your people all you see; because I am sure the more they know of us, the more they will be our hearty friends. I invite you, therefore, to pay a visit to Baltimore, Philadelphia, New York, and the cities still beyond that, if you are willing to go further. We will provide carriages to convey you, and a person to go with you to see that you want for nothing. By the time you come back the snows will be melted on the mountains, the ice in the rivers broken up, and you will be wishing to set out on your return home.

My children, I have long desired to see you; I have now opened my heart to you; let my words sink into your hearts and never be forgotten. If ever lying people or bad spirits should raise up a cloud between us, call to mind what I have said, and what you have seen yourselves. Be sure there are some lying spirits between us; let us come together as friends and explain to each other what is misrepresented or misunderstood, then the clouds will fly away like morning fog, and the sun of friendship appear and shine forever bright and clear between us.

My children, it may happen that while you are here, occasion may arise to talk about many things which I do not now particularly mention. The secretary of war will always be ready to talk with you, and you are to consider whatever he says as said by myself. He will also take care of you and see that you are furnished with all comforts here.

TO BEAVER, THE HEAD-WARRIOR OF THE DELAWARES

My Son, I am glad to see you here to take you by the hand. I am the friend of your nation and sincerely wish them well. I shall now speak to them as their friend, and advise them for their good.

I have read your speech to the secretary of war, and considered it maturely. You therein say that after the conclusion of the treaty of Greenville, the Wapanakies and other tribes of Indians mutually agreed to maintain peace among themselves and with the United States. This, my son, was wise, and I entirely approve of it. And I equally commend you for what you further say, that yours and the other tribes have constantly maintained the articles of peace with us, and have ceased to listen to bad advice. I hope, my son, that you will continue in this good line of conduct, and I assure you the United States will forever religiously observe the treaty on their part, not only because they have agreed to it, but because they esteem you; they wish you well, and would endeavor to promote your welfare, even if there were no treaty; and rejoicing that you have ceased to listen to bad advice they hope you will listen to that which is good.

My son, you say that the Osage nation has refused to be at peace with your nation or any others; that they have refused the offers of peace, and extended their aggressions to all people. This is all new to me. I never heard of an Osage coming to war on this side of the Mississippi. Have they attacked your towns, killed your people, or destroyed your game? Tell me in what year they did this? or what is the aggression they have committed on you and the other tribes this side the Mississippi? But if they have defended themselves and their country, when your tribes have gone over to destroy them, they have only done what brave men ought to do, and what just men ought never to have forced them to do. Your having committed one wrong on them gives you no right to commit a second; and be assured, my son, that the Almighty Spirit which is above will not look down with indifference on your going to war against his children on the other side of the Mississippi, who have never come to attack you. He is their father as well as your father, and he did not make the Osages to be destroyed by you. I tell you that if you make war unjustly on the Osages he will punish your nation for it. He will send upon your nation famine, sickness, or the tomahawk of a stronger nation, who will cut you off from the land. Consider this thing well, then, before it is too late, and before you strike. His hand is uplifted over your heads, and his stroke will follow yours. My son, I tell you these things because I wish your nation well. I wish them to become a peaceable, prosperous, and happy nation; and if this war against the Osages concerned yourselves alone, I would confine myself to giving you advice, and leave it to yourselves to profit by it. But this war deeply concerns the United States. Between you and the Osages is a country of many hundred miles extent belonging to the United States. Between you also is the Mississippi, the river of peace. On this river are floating the boats, the people, and all the produce of the western States of the Union. This commerce must not be exposed to the alarm of war parties crossing the river, nor must a path of blood be made across our country. What we say to you, my son, we say also to the Osages. We tell them that armed bands of warriors, entering on the lands or waters of the United States without our consent, are the enemies of the United States. If, therefore, considerations of your own welfare are not sufficient to restrain you from this unauthorized war, let me warn you on the part of the United States to respect their rights, not to violate their territory.

You request, my son, to be informed of our warfares, that you may be enabled to inform your nation on your return. We are yet at peace, and shall continue so, if the injustice of the other nations will permit us. The war beyond the water is universal. We wish to keep it out of our island. But should we go to war, we wish our red children to take no part in it. We are able to fight our own battles, and we know that our red children cannot afford to spill their blood in our quarrels. Therefore, we do not ask it, but wish them to remain home in quiet, taking care of themselves and their families.

You complain that the white people in your neighborhood have stolen a number of your horses. My son, the secretary of war will take measures for inquiring into the truth of this, and if it so appears, justice shall be done you.

The two swords which you ask shall be given to you; and we shall be happy to give you every other proof that we esteem you personally, my son, and shall always be ready to do anything which may advance your comfort and happiness. I hope you will deliver to your nation the words I have spoken to you, and assure them that in everything which can promote their welfare and prosperity they shall ever find me their true and faithful friend and father, that I hold them fast by the hand of friendship, which I hope they will not force me to let go.

SPEECH TO THE CHIEFS OF VARIOUS INDIAN TRIBES

My Children: This is the first time I have had the pleasure of seeing the distinguished men of our neighbors the Wyandots, Ottawas, and Chippewas at the seat of our government. I welcome you to it as well as the Powtewatamies and Shawanese, and thank the Great Spirit for having conducted you hither in safety and health. I take you and your people by the hand and salute you as my children; I consider all my red children as forming one family with the whites, born in the same land with them, and bound to live like brethren, in peace, friendship, and good neighborhood. In former times, my children, we were not our own masters, but were governed by the English. Then we were often at war with our neighbors. Ill blood was raised and kept up between us, and in the war in which we threw off the English government, many of the red people, mistaking their brothers and real friends, took sides with the English government against us; and it was not till many years after we made peace with the English that the treaty of Greenville closed our last wars with our Indian neighbors. From that time, my children, we have looked on you as a part of ourselves, and have cherished your prosperity as our own. We saw that these things were wasting away your numbers to nothing; that the intemperate use of ardent spirits produced poverty, trouble, and murders among you; your wars with another were lessening your numbers, and attachment to the hunter life, after game had nearly left you, produced famine, sickness, and deaths among you in the scarce season of every year. It has been our endeavor, therefore, like true fathers and brothers, to withhold strong liquors from you, to keep you in peace with one another, and to encourage and aid you in the culture of the earth, and in raising domestic animals, to take the place of the wild ones. This we have done, my children, because we are your friends, and wish you well. If we feared you, if we were your enemies, we should have furnished you plentifully with whiskey, let the men destroy one another in perpetual wars, and the women and children waste away for want of food, and remain insensible that they could raise it out of the earth. We have been told, my children, that some of you have been doubting whether we or the English were your truest friends. What do the English do for you? They furnish you with plenty of whiskey, to keep you in idleness, drunkenness, and poverty, and they are now exciting you to join them in war against us, if war should take place between them and us. But we tell you to stay at home in quiet, to take no part in quarrels which do not concern you. The English are now at war with all the world but us, and it is not yet known whether they will not force us also into it. They are strong on the water, but weak on the land. We live on the land and we fear them not. We are able to fight our own battles; therefore we do not ask you to spill your blood in our quarrels, much less do we wish to be forced to spill it with our own hands. You have travelled through our country from the lakes to the tide waters. You have seen our numbers in that direction, and were you to pass along the seashore you would find them much greater. You know the English numbers, their scattered forts and string of people, along the borders of the lakes and the St. Lawrence; how long do you think it will take us to sweep them out of the country? and when they are swept away, what is to become of those who join them in their war against us? My children, if you love the land in which you were born, if you wish to inhabit the earth which covers the bones of your fathers, take no part in the war between the English and us, if we should have war. Never will we do an unjust act towards you. On the contrary, we wish to befriend you in every possible way; but the tribe which shall begin an unprovoked war against us, we will extirpate from the earth, or drive to such a distance as that they shall never again be able to strike us. I tell you these things, my children, not to make you afraid. I know you are brave men and therefore cannot fear. But you are also wise men and prudent men. I say it, therefore, that in wisdom and prudence you may look forward. That you may go to the graves of your fathers and say, " Fathers, shall we abandon you? " That you may look in the faces of your wives and children and ask, " Shall we expose these our own flesh and blood to perish from want in a distant country and have our race and name extinguished from the face of the earth? " Think of these things, my children, as wise men, and as men loving their fathers, their wives, and children, and the name and memory of their nation. I repeat, that we will never do an unjust act toward you. On the contrary, we wish you to live in peace, to increase in numbers, to learn to labor as we do, and furnish food for your increasing numbers, when the game shall have left you. We wish to see you possessed of property, and protecting it by regular laws. In time, you will be as we are; you will become one people with us. Your blood will mix with ours, and will spread, with ours, over this great island. Hold fast, then, my children, the chain of friendship which binds us together, and join us in keeping it forever bright and unbroken.

I invite you to come here, my children, that you might hear, with your own ears, the words of your father; that you might see, with your own eyes, the sincere disposition of the United States toward you. In your journey to this place you have seen great numbers of your white brothers; you have been received by them as brothers, have been treated kindly and hospitably, and you have seen and can tell your people that their hearts are now sincerely with you. This is the first time I have ever addressed your chiefs, in person, at the seat of government,—it will also be the last. Sensible that I am become too old to watch over the extensive concerns of the seventeen states and their territories, I requested my fellow citizens to permit me to live with my family, and to choose another president for themselves, and father for you. They have done so; and in a short time I shall retire and resign into his hands the care of your and our concerns. Be assured, my children, that he will have the same friendly dispositions towards you which I have had, and that you will find in him a true and affectionate father. Indeed, this is now the disposition of all our people towards you; they look upon you as brethren, born in the same land and having the same interests. Tell your people, therefore, to entertain no uneasiness on account of this change, for there will be no change as to them. Deliver to them my adieus, and my prayers to the Great Spirit for their happiness. Tell them that during my administration I have held their hand fast in mine; and that I will put it into the hand of their new father, who will hold it as I have done.

LOUIS KOSSUTH

SPEECH IN FANEUIL HALL

[Louis Kossuth was born in Monok, Hungary, in 1802. He became a lawyer, founded a patriotic paper, and until the convocation of the Diet of 1847–8 was a rising Magyar agitator. A splendid speech delivered before the Diet in 1848, on the occasion of the revolution at Paris, revealed him as an orator, and began the agitation that established the Austro-Hungarian monarchy as we know it. In the subsequent struggle with Austria, Hungary was defeated, Kossuth was exiled, after undergoing imprisonment, and his subsequent attitude was merely one of protest, until the coronation of Francis Joseph as King of Hungary (1867). Even then, however, he refused to be reconciled to the established order and died in nominal exile at Turin in 1894. The centenary of Kossuth's birth was celebrated throughout Hungary with remarkable enthusiasm in September of the year 1902, his two sons participating in the church services at Budapest. In 1851–'52 he visited the United States, where he received an enthusiastic welcome. The following address, one of several that he made in this country, was delivered in Boston, in 1852.]

LADIES AND GENTLEMEN: Do me the justice to believe that I rise not with any pretension to eloquence, within the Cradle of American Liberty. If I were standing upon the ruins of the prytaneum and had to speak whence Demosthenes spoke, my tongue would refuse to obey, my words would die away upon my lips, and I would listen to the winds, fraught with the dreadful realization of his unheeded prophesies.

My tongue is fraught with a downtrodden nation's wrongs. The justice of my cause is my eloquence; but misfortune may approach the altar whence the flame arose which roused your fathers from degradation to independence. I claim my people's share in the benefit of the laws of nature and of nature's God. I will nothing add to the historical reputation of these walls; but I dare hope not to sully them by appealing to those maxims of truth, the promulgation of which made often tremble these walls, from the thundering cheers of freemen roused by the clarion sound of inspired oratory.

"Cradle of American Liberty!"—it is a great name; but there is something in it which saddens my heart. You should not say "American liberty." You should say "Liberty in America." Liberty should not be either American or European—it should be just "Liberty." God is God. He is neither America's God nor Europe's God; he is God. So should liberty be. "American liberty" has much the sound as if you would say "American privilege." And there is the rub. Look to history, and when your heart saddens at the fact that liberty never yet was lasting in any corner of the world and in any age, you will find the key of it in the gloomy truth that all who yet were free regarded liberty as their privilege instead of regarding it as a principle. The nature of every privilege is exclusiveness; that of a principle is communicative. Liberty is a principle —its community is its security—exclusiveness is its doom.

What is aristocracy? It is exclusive liberty; it is privilege; and aristocracy is doomed because it is contrary to the destiny and welfare of man. Aristocracy should vanish, not in the nations, but also from amongst the nations. So long as that is not done liberty will nowhere be lasting on earth. It is equally fatal to individuals as to nations to believe themselves beyond the reach of vicissitudes. To this proud reliance, and the isolation resulting therefrom, more victims have fallen than to oppression by immediate adversities. You have prodigiously grown by your freedom of seventy-five years; but what is seventy-five years to take for a charter of immortality? No, no! my humble tongue tells the records of eternal truth. A privilege never can be lasting. Liberty restricted to one nation never can be sure. You may say, "We are the prophets of God"; but you shall not say "God is only our God." The Jews have said so, and the pride of Jerusalem lies in the dust. Our Saviour taught all humanity to say "Our Father in heaven"; and his Jerusalem is lasting to the end of days.

"There is a community in man's destiny." That was the

greeting which I read on the arch of welcome on the Capitol
Hill of Massachusetts.   I pray to God the republic of
America would weigh the eternal truth of those words and
act accordingly.   Liberty in America would then be sure to
the end of time.   But if you say "American liberty," and
take that grammar for your policy, I dare say the time will
yet come when humanity will have to mourn over a new
proof of the ancient truth, that without community national
freedom is never sure.   You should change "American
liberty" into "Liberty"—then liberty would be forever sure
in America, and that which found a cradle in Faneuil Hall
never would find a coffin through all coming days.   I like
not the word "cradle" connected with the word "liberty"—it
has a scent of mortality.   But these are vain words, I know;
though in the life of nations the spirit of future be marching
in present events, visible to every reflecting mind, still those
who foretell them are charged with arrogantly claiming the
title of prophets, and prophecies are never believed.   However, the cradle of American liberty is not only famous from
the reputation of having been always the lists of the most
powerful eloquence; it is still more conspicuous for having
seen that eloquence attended by practical success.   To understand the mystery of this rare circumstance a man must see
the people of New England and especially the people of
Massachusetts.

In what I have seen of New England there are two things
the evidence of which strikes the observer at every step—prosperity and intelligence.   I have seen thousands assembled,
following the noble impulses of generous hearts; almost the
entire population of every city, of every town, of every village, where I passed, gathered around me, throwing the flowers of consolation in my thorny way.   I can say I have seen
the people here, and I have looked at it with a keen eye,
sharpened in the school of a toilsome life.   Well, I have seen
not a single man bearing the mark of that poverty upon himself which in old Europe strikes the eye sadly at every step.
I have seen no ragged poor; I have seen not a single house
bearing the appearance of desolated poverty.   The cheerful-
ness of a comfortable condition, the result of industry, spreads
over the land.   One sees at a glance that the people work

assiduously—not with the depressing thought just to get from day to day, by hard toil, through the cares of a miserable life, but they work with the cheerful consciousness of substantial happiness. And the second thing which I could not fail to remark is the stamp of intelligence impressed upon the very eyes and outward appearance of the people at large. I and my companions have seen that people in the factories, in the workshops, in their houses, and in the streets, and could not fail a thousand times to think " how intelligent that people looks." It is to such a people that the orators of Faneuil Hall had to speak, and therein is the mystery of their success. They were not wiser than the public spirit of their audience, but they were the eloquent interpreters of the people's enlightened instinct.

No man can force the harp of his own individuality into the people's heart; but every man may play upon the chords of his people's heart, who draws his inspiration from the people's instinct. Well, I thank God for having seen the public spirit of the people of Massachusetts bestowing its attention to the cause I plead and pronouncing its verdict. After the spontaneous manifestations of public opinion which I have met in Massachusetts, there can be not the slightest doubt that his excellency, the high-minded governor of Massachusetts, when he wrote his memorable address to the Legislature— the joint committee of the legislative assembly, after a careful and candid consideration of the subject, not only concurring in the views of the executive government, but elucidating them in a report the irrefutable logic and elevated statesmanship of which will forever endear the name of Hazewell to oppressed nations; and the Senate of Massachusetts adopting the resolutions proposed by the legislative committee, in respect to the question of national intervention—I say the spontaneous manifestation of public opinion leaves not the slightest doubt that all these executive and legislative proceedings not only met the full approbation of the people of Massachusetts, but were in fact nothing else but the solemn interpretation of that public opinion of the people of Massachusetts. A spontaneous outburst of popular sentiments tells often more in a single word than all the skill of elaborate eloquence could. I have met that word. " We worship not the man, but we worship the principle," shouted out a man in Worcester, amidst the thundering cheers of a countless multitude. It was a word like those words of flame spoken in Faneuil Hall out of which liberty in America was born. That word is a revelation that the spirit of eternal truth and of present exigencies moves through the people's heart. That word is teeming with the destinies of America.

Would to God that in the leading quarters small party considerations should never prevent the due appreciation of the people's instinctive sagacity! It is with joyful consolation and heartfelt gratitude I own that of that fear I am forever relieved in respect to Massachusetts. Once more I have met the revelation of the truth that the people of Massachusetts worship principles. I have met it on the front of your capitol, in those words raised to the consolation of the oppressed world, by the constitutional authorities of Massachusetts, to the high heaven, upon an arch of triumph,—"Remember that there is a community in mankind's destiny."

I cannot express the emotion I felt when, standing on the steps of your capitol, these words above my head, the people of Massachusetts tendered me its hand in the person of its chief magistrate. The emotion which thrilled through my heart was something like that Lazarus must have felt when the Saviour spoke to him, " Rise "; and when I looked up with a tender tear of heartfelt gratitude in my eyes, I saw the motto of Massachusetts all along the capitol, " We seek with the sword the mild quietness of liberty."

You have proved this motto not to be an empty word. The heroic truth of it is recorded in the annals of Faneuil Hall, it is recorded on Bunker Hill, recorded in the Declaration of Independence.

Having read that motto, coupled with the acknowledgment of the principle that there is a community in the destiny of all humanity, I know what answer I have to take to those millions who look with profound anxiety to America.

Gentlemen, the Mahometans say that the city of Bokhara receives not light from without, but is lustrous with its own light. I don't know much about Bokhara; but so much I know, that Boston is the sun whence radiated the light of re-

sistance against oppression. And from what it has been my
good fortune to experience in Boston I have full reason to
believe that the sun which shone forth with such a bright
luster in the days of oppression has not lost its luster by
freedom and prosperity. Boston is the metropolis of Massachusetts, and Massachusetts has given its vote. It has given
it after having, with the penetrating sagacity of its intelligence, looked attentively into the subject and fixed with calm
consideration its judgment thereabout. After having had
so much to speak, it was with infinite gratification I heard
myself addressed in Brookfield, Framingham, and several
other places, with these words, "We know your country's
history; we agree with your principles; we want no speech;
just let us hear your voice, and then go on; we trust and
wish you may have other things to do than speak."

Thus having neither to tell my country's tale, because it is
known, nor having to argue about principles, because they
are agreed with, I am in the happy condition of being able to
restrain myself to a few desultory remarks about the nature
of the difficulties I have to contend with in other quarters,
that the people of Massachusetts may see upon what ground
those stand who are following a direction contrary to the
distinctly pronounced opinion of Massachusetts in relation
to the cause I plead.

Give me leave to mention that, having had an opportunity
to converse with leading men of the great political parties,
which are on the eve of an animated contest for the presidency—would it had been possible for me to have come to
America either before that contest was engaged, or after it
will be decided! I came, unhappily, in a bad hour—I
availed myself of that opportunity to be informed about what
are considered to be the principal issues in case the one or
the other party carries the prize; and, indeed, having got
the information thereof, I could not forbear to exclaim, "But,
my God! all these questions together cannot outweigh the
all-overruling importance of foreign policy!" It is there, in
the question of foreign policy, that the heart of the next
future throbs. Security and danger, developing prosperity,
and its check, peace and war, tranquillity and embarrassment—yes, life and death will be weighed in the scale of

foreign policy! It is evident things are come to the point where they have been in ancient Rome, when old Cato never spoke privately or publicly about whatever topic without closing his speech with these words: "However, my opinion is that Carthage must be destroyed;" thus advertising his countrymen that there was one question outweighing in importance all other questions, from which public attention should never for a moment be withdrawn.

Such, in my opinion, is the condition of the world now. Carthage and Rome had no place on earth together. Republican America and all-overwhelming Russian absolutism cannot much longer subsist together on earth. Russia active—America passive—there is an immense danger in that fact; it is like the avalanche in the Alps which the noise of a bird's wing may move and thrust down with irresistible force, growing every moment. I cannot but believe it were highly time to do as old Cato did and finish every speech with these words: "However, the law of nations should be maintained and absolutism not permitted to become omnipotent."

I could not forbear to make these remarks; and the answer I got was, "That is all true, and all right, and will be attended to when the election is over; but, after all, the party must come into power, and you know there are so many considerations—men want to be managed, and even prejudices spared, and so forth."

And it is true, but it is sorrowful that it is true. That reminds me of what, in Schiller's "Maria Stuart," Mortimer says to Lord Leicester, the all-mighty favorite of Elizabeth: "O God, what little steps has such a great lord to go at this court!" There is the first obstacle I have to meet with. This consolation, at least, I have, that the chief difficulty I have to contend with is neither lasting nor an argument against the justice of my cause or against the righteousness of my principles. Just as the calumnies by which I am assailed can but harm my own self but cannot impair the justice of my country's cause or weaken the propriety of my principles—so that difficulty, being just a difficulty and no argument, cannot change the public opinion of the people, which always cares more about principles than about wire-pullings.

The second difficulty I have to contend with is rather curious. Many a man has told me that if I had only not fallen into the hands of the Abolitionists and Free-Soilers he would have supported me; and had I landed somewhere in the South, instead of New York, I would have met quite different things from that quarter; but being supported by the Free-Soilers, of course I must be opposed by the South. On the other side, I received a letter from which I beg leave to quote a few lines:—

" You are silent on the subject of slavery. Surrounded as you have been by slaveholders ever since you put your foot on English soil, if not during your whole voyage from Constantinople—and ever since you have been in this country surrounded by them, whose threats, promises, and flattery make the stoutest hearts succumb—your position has put me in mind of a scene described by the apostle of Jesus Christ, when the devil took him up into a high mountain."

Now, gentlemen, thus being charged from one side with being in the hands of Abolitionists and from the other side with being in the hands of the slaveholders, I indeed am at a loss what course to take, if these very contradictory charges were not giving me the satisfaction to feel that I stand just where it is my duty to stand, on a truly American ground.

I must beg leave to say a few words in that respect, the more because I could not escape vehement attacks for not committing myself even in that respect with whatever interior party question. I claim the right for my people to regulate its own domestic concerns. I claim this as a law of nations, common to all humanity; and because common to all I claim to see them protected by the United States, not only because they have the power to defend what despots dare offend, but also because it is the necessity of their position to be a power on earth, which they would not be if the law of nations can be changed and the general condition of the world altered without their vote. Now, that being my position and my cause, it would be the most absurd inconsistency if I would offend that principle which I claim and which I advocate.

And O my God, have I not enough sorrows and cares to bear on these poor shoulders? Is it not astonishing that the moral power of duties and the iron will of my heart sustain yet this shattered frame; that I am desired yet to take up additional cares? If the cause I plead be just, if it be worthy of your sympathy, and at the same time consistent with the impartial considerations of your own moral and material interests—which a patriot never should disregard, not even out of philanthropy—then why not weigh that cause with the scale of its own value and not with a foreign one? Have I not difficulties enough to contend with that I am desired to increase them yet with my own hands? Father Mathew goes on preaching temperance, and he may be opposed or supported on his own ground; but whoever imagined opposition to him because at the same time he takes not into his hands to preach fortitude or charity? And indeed to oppose or to abandon the cause I plead, only because I mix not with the agitation of an interior question, is a greater injustice yet, because to discuss the question of foreign policy I have a right. My nation is an object of that policy; we are interested in it; but to mix with interior party movements I have no right, not being a citizen of the United States.

The third difficulty which I meet, so far as I am told, is the opposition of the commercial interest. I have the agreeable duty to say that this opposition, or rather indifference, is only partial. I have met several testimonials of the most generous sympathy from gentlemen of commerce. But if, upon the whole, it should be really true that there is more coolness, or even opposition, in that quarter than in others, then I may say that there is an entire misapprehension of the true commercial interests in it. I could say that it would be strange to see commerce, and chiefly the commerce of a republic, indifferent to the spread of liberal institutions. That would be a sad experience, teeming with incalculable misfortunes, reserved to the nineteenth century. Until now history has recorded that " commerce has been the most powerful locomotive of principles and the most fruitful ally of civilization, intelligence, and of liberty." It was merchants whose names are shining with immortal luster from the most glorious pages of the golden books of Venice, Genoa, etc. Commerce, republican commerce, raised single cities to the position of mighty powers on earth and maintained them in that proud position for centuries; and surely it was neither indifference nor opposition to republican principles by which they have thus ennobled the history of commerce and of humanity. I know full well that since the treasures of commerce took their way into the coffers of despotism in the shape of eternal loans and capital began to speculate upon the oppression of nations, a great change has occurred in that respect.

But, thanks to God, the commerce of America is not engaged in that direction, hated by millions, cursed by humanity! Her commerce is still what it was in former times, the beneficent instrumentality of making mankind partake of all the fruits and comforts of the earth and of human industry. Here it is no paper speculation upon the changes of despotism; and therefore, if the commercial interests of republican America are considered with that foresighted sagacity without which there is no future and no security in them, I feel entirely sure that no particular interest can be more ambitious to see absolutism checked and freedom and democratic institutions developed in Europe than the commerce of republican America. It is no question of more or less profit; it is a question of life and death to it. Commerce is the heel of Achilles, the vulnerable point of America. Thither will, thither must be aimed the first blow of victorious absolutism; the instinct of self-preservation would lead absolutism to strike that blow if its hatred and indignation would not lead to it. Air is not more indispensable to life than freedom and constitutional government in Europe to the commerce of America.

Though many things which I have seen have upon calm reflection induced me to raise an humble word of warning against materialism, still I believe there was more patriotic solicitude than reality in the fact that Washington and John Adams, at the head of the war department, complained of a predominating materialism (they styled it avarice), which threatened the ruin of America. I believe that complaint would even to-day not be more founded than it was in the infant age of your republic; still, if there be any motive for that complaint of your purest and best patriots,—if the commerce of America would know, indeed, no better guiding star than only the momentary profit of a cargo just floating over the Atlantic,—I would be even then at a loss how else to account for the indifference of the commerce of America in the cause of European liberty than by assuming that it is believed the present degraded condition of Europe may endure, if only the popular agitations are deprived of material means to disturb that which is satirically called tranquillity.

But such a supposition would, indeed, be the most obnoxious, the most dangerous fallacy. As the old philosopher, being questioned how he could prove the existence of God, answered, "By opening the eyes"; just so, nothing is necessary but to open the eyes in order that men of the most ordinary common sense become aware of it, that the present condition of Europe is too unnatural, too contrary to the vital interests of the countless millions to endure even for a short time. A crisis is inevitable; no individual influence can check it; no indifference or opposition can prevent it. Even men like myself, concentrating the expectations and confidence of oppressed millions in themselves, have only just enough power, if provided with the requisite means, to keep the current in a sound direction, so that in its inevitable eruption it may not become dangerous to social order, which is indispensable to the security of person and property, without which especially no commerce has any future at all. And that being the unsophisticated condition of the world, and a crisis being inevitable, I indeed cannot imagine how those who desire nothing but peace and tranquillity can withhold their helping hands, that the inevitable crisis should not only be kept in a sound direction, but also carried down to a happy issue, capable to prevent the world from boiling continually like a volcano, and insuring a lasting peace and a lasting tranquillity, never possible so long as the great majority of nations are oppressed, but sure so soon as the nations are content—and content they can only be when they are free.

Indeed, if reasonable logic has not yet forsaken the world, it is the men of peace, it is the men of commerce, to the support of whom I have a right to look. Others may support my cause out of generosity—these must support me out of considerate interest; others may oppose me out of egotism—American commerce, in opposing me, would commit suicide.

Gentlemen, of such narrow nature are the considerations

which oppose my cause. Of equally narrow, inconsistent scope are all the rest, with the enumeration of which I will not abuse your kind indulgence. Compare with them the broad basis of lofty principles upon which the Commonwealth of Massachusetts took its stand in bestowing the important benefit of its support to my cause; and you cannot forbear to feel proudly that the spirit of old Massachusetts is still alive, entitled to claim that right in the councils of the united Republic which it had in the glorious days when, amidst dangers, wavering resolutions, and partial despondency, Massachusetts took boldly the lead to freedom and independence.

Those men of immortal memory, who within these very walls lighted with the heavenly spark of their inspiration the torch of freedom in America, avowed for their object the welfare of mankind; and when you raised the monument of Bunker Hill it was the genius of freedom thrilling through the heart of Massachusetts which made one of your distinguished orators say that the days of your ancient glory will continue to rain influence on the destinies of mankind to the end of time. It is upon this inspiration I rely, in the name of my down-trodden country—to-day the martyr of mankind, to-morrow the battlefield of its destiny.

Time draws nigh when either the influence of Americans must be felt throughout the world, or the position abandoned to which you rose with gigantic vitality out of the blood of your martyrs.

I have seen the genius of those glorious days spreading its fiery wings of inspiration over the people of Massachusetts. I feel the spirit of olden times moving through Faneuil Hall. Let me cut short my stammering words; let me leave your hearts alone with the inspiration of history; let me bear with me the heart-strengthening conviction that I have seen Boston still a radiating sun, as it was of yore, but risen so high on mankind's sky as to spread its warming rays of elevated patriotism far over the waves. American patriotism of to-day is philanthropy for the world.

Gentlemen, I trust in God, I trust in the destinies of humanity, and intrust the hopes of oppressed Europe to the consistent energy of Massachusetts.

ROBERT MARION LA FOLLETTE

WHICH SHALL RULE, MANHOOD OR MONEY?

[Robert Marion La Follette, the present Governor of Wisconsin, was born at Primrose, Wis., in 1855. His education was completed at the University of Wisconsin, where he graduated in 1879, and subsequently received the degree of LL.D. in 1901. Choosing the law as a profession, he was admitted to the bar in 1880, and quickly rose to distinction. He was made District Attorney of Dane County, and was elected as a Republican Member of Congress from his native state in 1887. He took a prominent part in framing the McKinley Bill. Mr. La Follette is a leader in the political life of his state, and as an orator combines energy and clearness with logical cogency. The following extracts are from a speech which was delivered at Milwaukee in the West Side Turner Hall on September 30, 1902, and suggests the speaker's power of reasoning in the discussion of subjects of great political importance.]

UNDER our form of government the citizen should determine all the issues, and you will exercise your right of suffrage in this election upon national and upon state questions as well. I would in no wise disparage the importance of national issues in this campaign. But within the limits of a single address I should be unwilling to attempt a thorough discussion of both. I should not feel, however, that I had discharged my duty as a Republican on this occasion if I passed by national issues in silence.

Though there may appear to be difference among Republicans on the tariff issue, it would seem to arise from misunderstanding rather than disagreement. From Hamilton to Clay, and from Clay to McKinley, the principle upon which a protective tariff rested for support has not changed. The true measure of a protective duty when Hamilton wrote his great report on manufactures in 1791 and the true measure of a protective duty to-day is the difference between the cost of production in this country and the competing country. A tariff that is either higher or lower than that should not be called a protective tariff. If it is higher, it is prohibitory ; if it is lower, it is not protective.

It is charged that the tariff is responsible for trusts. This charge is most strongly pressed by those who opposed protection before trusts were known. They ignore the fact that the organization of trusts and combinations began but a few years ago, and that they are fast gaining control of business everywhere. They are not confined to any country, or the offspring of any tariff policy. They rule the market in free-trade products in this country, and in whatever products they choose in free-trade countries. But the fact remains that the organization of combinations of capital great enough to master the production and fix the price of articles embraced within protective tariff schedules brings upon that system the popular disapproval which the public entertains toward trusts generally.

In these days of marvelous financial and commercial evolution, of colossal combinations of capital, such as the world has never before known, it is well to recall first principles. Every writer on protection, every tariff leader in Congress and before the country, placed free competition between protected industries as a necessary complement to a protective tariff.

When competition was free between the protected industries of the country, the fact that a duty was above the level necessary for protection to American labor was not so important, because competition could ever be depended upon to reduce the price for the consumer upon any protected product to the lowest point to which it could be produced in this country, and pay American wages to American labor. The natural law of competition was the same protection to the consumer that the tariff was to the producer.

But a new law, an artificial law, is supplanting the natural law of competition. By secret agreement the producers of like articles limit the number or quantity produced and fix prices. Combination is destroying competition.

I believe that the hour has come when tariff revision must stand close guard over tariff schedules. But this revision should be on the true protective principle of guarding American labor from free competition with cheaper foreign labor, and yet take the place of suppressed competition.

.   .   .   .

I believe that not only all Republicans, but all citizens, independent of political consideration, would concede that tariff revision cannot effectively grapple with—indeed, would be but a feeble, inadequate, and uncertain remedy for—the trust evils which confront us to-day. Their gigantic power, their mastery of the industrial world, cannot be exaggerated.

Anthracite coal was free from duty until 1897, when 67 cents per ton was levied on all 92 per cent. pure. The entire control of the coal fields was secured prior to that time, and the creation of this monster monopoly had no relation whatever to the duty. But glance at the situation, the problem it presents.

The second most important product of the earth is coal. The supply is severely limited. There is absolutely nothing to take its place for the purpose of fuel and power in the world. The entire wood supply would last but a very short time. The anthracite or hard coal of the United States lies in three different fields, covering in the aggregate not to exceed eight miles by sixty miles. Ninety-five per cent. of the entire coal fields is owned and controlled by eight railway companies. The lines of these eight railways furnish the sole available means for transportation of anthracite coal to market. In pursuit of a settled policy these railway companies have forced private owners to sell their coal mines and coal lands at half value, first, by increasing the freight rates, and second, by refusing to carry the coal for private owners at any price whenever such owners could not be brought to terms by the establishment of exorbitant transportation rates. Owning the coal and owning the railroads over which the coal is transported to market, they fixed the freight rates at an exorbitant figure in order to make consumers pay dividends on the over-capitalization of the railroads and coal mines. While rates for other and like products have fallen, anthracite coal rates have been advanced by the railways until they are nearly twice as great as those for cotton or wheat. They limit the supply in order to force a strong demand and high market price. As shown by sworn testimony upon trials and investigations, more than $200,000,000 in excess of a fair market price has been exacted from consumers.

This coal trust bears harder upon the unfortunate, helpless labor that mines the product at the wage level of a generation ago than upon the consumer, who in these days must purchase, hat in hand. Its attitude of indifference to the appeal of press and pulpit suggests utter contempt for public opinion. This is typical of the oppression which awaits the people of the country unless the *Federal Government is empowered to strip these combinations of their unlawful power.*

The plan developed and consummated in building up the anthracite coal trust is indicative of the power of the railroads in combination. As the magnitude of the question presented is understood, it becomes manifest that no power outside the supreme power of the land can control the situation. These great combinations of wealth, owning most of the material products of the earth, controlling what they do not own, and combining with the railways, forget, in their greedy strife for more, that all men are born free and equal and with certain inalienable rights. These trusts, clothed with corporate power, availing themselves of every advantage of the law, yet living and growing in greatness and power in violation of it, constitute a national and interstate problem that must be dealt with fearlessly and effectively.

We believe with the President, as recognized by him in daily speech, that these great monopolies constitute the foremost of national questions. We uphold his hands in his effort to curb these trusts by the enforcement of laws now upon the statute books. There is probably not an important trust in the United States which does not have the assistance of railroads in destroying its competitors in business. The limitation and control of these public-service corporations in their legitimate field, as common carriers, is an important element in the practical solution of the problem with which we have to deal.

Republicans will support the recommendations made in his message as to the interstate commerce law in which he says:

ROBERT M. LA FOLLETTE

Photogravure after a photograph from life

"The act should be amended. The railway is a public servant. Its rates should be just to and open to all shippers alike. The government should see to it that this is so, and should provide a speedy, inexpensive, and effective remedy to that end."

. . . . .

In accepting renomination for the office of governor at the hands of the Republican party, I said:

"The gravest danger menacing republican institutions to-day is the overbalancing control of city, state, and national legislatures by the wealth and power of public-service corporations."

I made this statement advisedly then. I repeat it now. Not in a spirit of hostility to any interest, but deeply impressed with its profound significance to republican institutions and its ultimate influence upon all citizens and all citizenship.

The idea is not new. It is not peculiar to Wisconsin.

The responsibility it brings cannot be shirked or pushed aside or postponed. The national government, every state government—particularly that of every rich and prosperous state—every city government—particularly that of every large city—has this problem to solve; not at some other time, but now.

Philadelphia giving away franchises, not supposedly, not guessed at, or estimated to be worth two and a half million dollars, but for which she had been offered two and a half million dollars; Milwaukee giving away her eight-million-dollar street-car franchise against the protest and indifferent to the public indignation of her citizens; Chicago discovering that she is robbed in tax payments by corporate owners of property of immense value through fraud and forgery on a gigantic scale; aldermen of St. Louis organized to boodle the city, with their criminal compact for secrecy that would chill the blood of common cutthroats—are all a part of the testimony that to-day's daily papers bring of the great proportions and grave seriousness of the problems which control of legislation by aggregate wealth and corporate power presents for solution to this day and generation.

. . . . . .

The question of primary elections is one of government

for the people and by the people. Under our system of government by political parties, two elements, equal in importance, are involved in the exercise of suffrage : one, the making of the ballot; the other, the casting of the ballot. The right to cast the ballot is regarded as sacred. The right to make the ballot is equally sacred. No man would be willing to delegate his power to vote the ballot at general elections. No man should be compelled to delegate his power to make his ballot. Boss Tweed said, "You may elect whichever candidates you please to office, if you will allow me to select the candidates." The boss can always afford to say, "You may vote any ticket you please so long as I make all the tickets." The character of the men nominated and the influences to which they owe their nomination determine the character of government.

The result and the only result sought by a primary election is to give to every man an equal voice in the selection of all candidates; to lodge in the people the absolute right to say who their candidates for office shall be; to root out forever the power of the political boss to control the selection of officials through the manipulation of caucuses and conventions. A primary election should provide the same safeguards for nominating candidates as for electing them. It should fix the day, name the hour, use the same polling places, have the same election officers, provide the Australian ballot, containing the names of all the candidates to be voted upon at the election. It should be an election, possessing all the legal sanctions of an election.

. . . .

It is needless to trace the evolution of the political machine, its combination with aggregate wealth and corporate power, making the interests of the citizen and the state subservient to their selfish ends. The names of the great bosses to-day are better known than the great statesmen. The tendency to monopolization of political control by a few men in each party, county, city, state, and community has operated, except in cases of profound interest, excitement, and tremendous effort, to disfranchise the great majority of citizens in so far as participating in the caucus and convention is concerned.

. . . .

How unworthy this attitude of aggregate wealth toward the state, toward individual taxpayers and private corporations! How mean the spirit! How unpatriotic this defiance of the plain, simple demands of justice! And they control and manipulate legislation and undermine representative government only that they may escape the payment of an equal and just share of the public tax.

Shame upon the American citizen whose spirit does not rise in indignation against such violation, not only of the common and statutory law, but of every principle upon which American government is founded and every line of the glorious history of our country. We have become a race of degenerates if we do not resent the arrogance of these corporations which owe the state a million dollars a year in taxes, and refuse to pay; these corporations which deny the ascertained facts, flippantly reject the finding of the tax commission they asked to have established at public expense, and whose recommendations they promised to accept; these corporations which, in defiance of law and morals, would control legislation through bribery and threats. These resisting public-service corporations must bear their just and equal share of the taxes, and not one dollar of it shall be taken from the pockets of shippers or the general public.

For it should still be remembered that there is ever lodged in the hands of the free and independent citizenship of this commonwealth the final power of self-preservation. Let it not be forgotten when it is proposed to "take it out of the people by increasing their rates" that there rests with the state itself, secured to it for all time by that great jurist, Chief Justice Ryan, and his associates upon the supreme bench, ample authority to fix railroad transportation at proper and reasonable rates, protecting all shippers and all citizens of Wisconsin.

.   .   .   .

The day that Chief Justice Ryan prophesied would come is here. The issue which he said would arise is pending.

"Which shall rule—wealth or man? Which shall lead—money or intellect? Who shall fill public stations—educated and patriotic free men, or the feudal serfs of corporate power?"

In this contest the Republican party of Wisconsin to-day stands undeniably, unequivocally, emphatically the organized instrument of the people of the state.

Though it failed to accomplish that which was promised two years ago, it has taken no backward step, yielded no principle, sounded no retreat; it better understands the nature of the conflict; it is better equipped to meet it, more determined in resolution to win a lasting victory and write its platform pledges into statutory law.

These plain truths will triumph. Unless I mistake the temper of Wisconsin citizenship, they will triumph now. Every man of every party who places patriotism above party will bring the support of his convictions, will bring all that is best in him, to this progressive movement for good government, which means so much, not alone to Wisconsin, but to all states struggling with the same forces, contending for the same principles. The good citizens of this state will unite to redeem representative government in this commonwealth and make Wisconsin a model state. The way is open and the power is in your hands. Demand of every candidate for the Senate and Assembly that he shall publicly declare how he will vote upon questions in which you are most deeply interested. If he talks about exercising his independent judgment on these issues, have him plainly understand that this is a representative government, and that he has no right to interpose his independent judgment or aught else against the known will of his constituents.

If the chosen representative does not represent the citizen, his voice is stifled; he is denied any part in government. If majority decision as determined by the law of the land is ignored and reversed, if the expressed will of the people is scorned and scorned again, then the popular government fails; then government of the people, by the people, and for the people is at an end. Its forms may be observed —you may have the mockery of " elections," and the farce of " representation "—but a government based upon the will of the people has perished from the earth.

LUCIUS QUINTUS CINCINNATUS LAMAR

ON NATIONAL AID TO EDUCATION

[Lucius Quintus Cincinnatus Lamar, an American statesman and jurist, noted for his eloquence of speech, was born in Georgia in 1825. He belonged to a leading Southern family, received a college education, became a lawyer, settled in Mississippi, and was sent to Congress from that State. When the Civil War came, he entered the Confederate army with the rank of colonel. He also went upon a mission to Europe in the interests of the Confederacy. After the reconstruction period he was again elected to Congress, and was also United States Senator from Mississippi. President Cleveland appointed him secretary of the interior, and, later, associate justice of the Supreme Court of the United States. He died in 1893. The following speech was made in the Senate, in committee of the whole, on March 28, 1884, considering the bill to aid the Southern States in the establishment and support of common schools.]

MR. PRESIDENT: I shall detain the Senate only a few moments—not with the expectation of adding anything new to the arguments that have been advanced on this subject, but simply to state my own reasons for the vote which I shall give. I have bestowed upon the constitutional question involved in this measure the study which its importance deserves. I shall not go over the ground already occupied by the senator from Florida (Mr. Jones), the senator from Arkansas (Mr. Garland), and the senator from Alabama (Mr. Pugh), nor will I recite the imposing authorities arrayed by the senator from Georgia (Mr. Brown). I have no doubt about the constitutional authority of Congress to pass this measure. Indeed, if we should reject it on the ground that it is unconstitutional for Congress to give aid to the states in the exercise of their exclusive jurisdiction over the education of their people, we would be reversing the settled policy of this government.

The refinements and subtleties about the distinction between the granting of land and an appropriation of money for educational purposes do not satisfy my mind. Even if such a distinction would hold, it does not apply to the constitutional question that is made. It is not the kind of aid granted, whether it be in land or in money, but the purpose for which it is granted—that is to be considered. It is the threatened intervention of the Federal Government in the educational affairs of a state to which the constitutional objection applies, and intervention is as menacing when it comes in the form of a land grant as when it comes in the shape of an appropriation. I do not regard it as a menace in either case.

Nor do the objections so forcibly presented by the senator from Missouri (Mr. Vest) strike my mind as sufficiently strong to justify a vote against this measure. The specification of the studies, the mere prescription that geography, reading, writing and arithmetic shall be taught in those schools, I do not think can be called a condition or dictation—they are words of description. It is simply saying that common-school education shall be taught, and it is another mode of expressing the very object of the bill as it has been reported. If, instead of the words, "reading, writing, arithmetic and geography," the words, "the usual common-school education," had been substituted, it seems to me that the same object would have been accomplished.

I, however, do not intend, I say, to repeat the argument which has been forcibly presented in support of the constitutionality of this measure. I do not see any entering wedge, as it is called, in this bill toward federal intervention in the jurisdiction of the state over the education of its children; and if there exists any such tendency in the public mind, in my opinion, the passage of this bill will arrest it.

Nor do I see any dangerous precedent in it. I do not think that it is wise or just reasoning to say that a thing which is right in itself, beneficent in its objects, may be in the future perverted into a wrong, nor do I anticipate it.

I have watched the progress of this scheme from the time
that it was first introduced into the other house many years
ago down to the present time, when it has taken its present
shape as presented by the senator from New Hampshire. I
have watched it with deep interest and intense solicitude.
In my opinion, it is the first step, and the most important
step, that this government has ever taken in the direction
of the solution of what is called the race problem; and I
believe that it will tell more powerfully and decisively upon
the future destinies of the colored race in America than any
measure or ordinance that has yet been adopted in reference
to it—more decisively than either the thirteenth, fourteenth,
or fifteenth amendments—unless it is to be considered, as I
do consider it, the logical sequence and the practical continuance of those amendments.

I think that this measure is fraught with almost unspeakable benefits to the entire population of the South—white
and black. Apart altogether from the material aid—and
that cannot be overvalued—apart from the contribution of
this bounteous donation of money, it will give an impulse
to the cause of common-school education in that section
which will tell on the interest of the people through the
long coming future. It will excite a new interest among
our people; it will stimulate both state and local communities to more energetic exertions and to greater sacrifices,
because it will encourage them in their hopes in grappling
and struggling with a task before whose vast proportions
they have stood appalled in the consciousness of the inadequacy of their own resources to meet it.

It is true, as some gentlemen have stated, that before
the war the common-school system did not flourish in the
South. We had an education there, and an educated
people whose culture was as high as that of any people on
earth. They were a people—one-fourth of them at least,
perhaps—who had all the function and discipline and intellectual development that the finest education could give,
not only from their own colleges at home, but from the best
universities in America and Europe. It is true that, owing
to the sparseness of our population and to other causes, the
common school did not thrive; and there were prejudices
against the common school as an efficient means of diffusing

education—prejudices they may be called, but such as are now entertained and expressed by some of the ablest writers in the North. Be that as it may, though the common-school education did not prevail in that section to as great an extent as in other parts of the country, they were a better educated people than one would imagine from the statistics of illiteracy. They were educated in the school of American citizenship, and they reached a discipline and a maturity of thought and an acquaintance with public and social duties that showed itself in a war in which grand armies stretching nearly across the continent found themselves baffled with alternate victory and defeat, and the fate of this Union held in the balance for four years. No ignorant and debased population could have stood before such a power with such heroic resistance for such a time.

But the result of the war overthrew the conditions of society; and colleges, schools and academies shared in the general crash and desolation. In that section the educated classes suffered more than all others. They were more impoverished than any other class, and their children more imperiled by falling back into ignorance than any other class; and now the common-school system has become the indispensable factor in diffusing education generally throughout the South.

The people of the South have attempted to meet the emergency. They have rebuilt, in a large degree, their colleges, academies and schools in the towns, villages and cities, and they have made great sacrifices. Although the remark has been made more than once that it is impossible for any except those who live in their midst to know the extent of the efforts and sacrifices that they have made, I must yet call attention to it here.

Guizot, in one of his great speeches, once said that the overthrow, prostration and demolition of the political institutions of a country were equal in the political world to the swallowing up of a city by an earthquake, and that it would be as difficult to reconstruct the one as it would be to resurrect and rebuild the other. Extravagant as the illustration is, we have learned by a costly experience that there is much truth in it. Yet we have made the effort; and our people have taxed themselves, and are still taxing themselves, at a rate that is equal in some of our states to that of any other section of the Union.

But the progress has been slow, the difficulties have been great, the burden has been grievous, and we stand, I say, almost appalled by the immense obstacles in the way. The generous, wise and beneficent action of the government proposed by this measure, as I said before, will reanimate and infuse new hope in our people; it will be a manifestation of respect and confidence and affection which will draw them into closer relations, if possible, to the government, and dispel whatever impressions past events have produced that it stands in an attitude of sternness and hostility toward them. . . .

We have, as I said before, schoolhouses; we have teachers, and the material for making teachers. All that we need is the money to apply to these ends. We can carry on in the rural districts this instruction for four months in some of the states, as in my own, and in the cities and towns for eight months; but we have not the means for prolonging the tuition. If we had, the blessings of education would be multiplied beyond the mere proportion of the extension of the time; for such is the character of the occupations of our people that they are not able to send their children to school in large numbers at any one time and for any very protracted period. The culture of the cotton crop, especially in the lower portions of the Gulf States, requires nearly all the months in the year. They begin in the early part of the year, sometimes in December of the preceding year, to bed up the land; the field work goes on until in July; then we have a short vacation through August into September, and then the children go in larger numbers to the schools until about the middle of September, when cotton-picking commences, and continues until Christmas, and often later. But if our terms were prolonged, as they would be if we had the means of employing the teachers, there would be all through the year children sent to those schools for short periods where they are now excluded by the shortness of our present period. . . .

I would regret very much if the amendment offered by one senator should, by its adoption here, mar and impair the effect of this bill—I mean the amendment which pro-

poses that the fund shall go into the hands of federal agencies and be distributed by them to the exclusion of the state
officers.   The effect of such an amendment would be a dis-
crimination.   It would give to the measure, instead of its
present generous and beneficent aspect, a harsh and ungra-
cious look and effect.

Senators have expressed the opinion that this fund will
not be fairly administered; that such is the prejudice of
race, that such is the darkening influence of slavery, that,
with the best intention, our people and officials are incapable of administering this fund equally and equitably to all.

I say that I should regret the adoption of such an amendment for the reason that it would change the entire aspect
and character of this bill and show that this government
intended to keep up discriminations; that, while it is animated with a desire to benefit and improve and elevate and
edify one race, it looks upon the other as an object of distrust
and suspicion.   It would be the enactment of the color line.

Mr. President, the surest way to make a people worthy
of trust is to trust them; and the surest mode of producing
alienation and of making them stand aloof in sullen opposition—or, perhaps, active obstruction and antagonism—upon
such a subject as this is to treat them as objects of distrust
and disapprobation, and to manifest toward them a want of
confidence which they feel that they do not deserve.   I say
with entire confidence that this distrust is not deserved;
that senators are mistaken as to the state of feeling in the
South with reference to the education of the negro.   The
people of the South find that the most precious interests of
their society and civilization are bound up in the question
of his education, of his elevation out of his present state of
barbarism.   .   .   .

I should regret the proposed amendment for more reasons than those which I have given.   It would impair the
working of the common-school system of the South, or of
any other section of the country, to introduce two sets of
agencies in its administration.   Instead of being a harmonious coöperation of state organization and national aid,
there would be, perhaps, an antagonism—certainly discon-
nected effort and discordant forces.   There would be both
time and money spent, which, if you used a single agency

under the present system already occupying the ground, would be concentrated in one harmonious effort. Besides, as it is now, the agencies which this bill selects are the agencies which are amenable to the public opinion and the restraining moral sentiment of the people among whom they will operate, whereas the other would be in the hands of comparative strangers, who would have no relation to the constituency in which they are working and would be uninfluenced by the supervision of the people at home. They would be responsible to no one there, to no restraining public sentiment, but simply to the appointing power at a great distance, too often governed by political considerations instead of the interests intrusted to them.

I said at the beginning of these remarks—and I have protracted them much further than I intended—that, in my opinion, this bill is a decided step toward the solution of the problem of race. The problem of race, in a large part, is the problem of illiteracy. Most of the evils, most of the difficulties which have grown up out of that problem, have arisen from a condition of ignorance, prejudice and superstition. Remove these, and the simpler elements of the question will come into play with a more enlightened understanding and a more tolerant disposition. I will go with those who will go farthest in this matter.

Liberty cannot be manufactured by statutes or constitutions or laws. It is a moral and intellectual growth. It is the outgrowth of men's natures and feelings, and passions and instincts and habits of thought. A people who remain ignorant and superstitious and debased cannot be made free by all the constitutional guarantees and statutes with which you surround them. You may force power upon them, and subject others to their rule, but the great attribute of self-government, and that real liberty which comes from it, you cannot confer on them while they remain ignorant and in bondage to their own passions and to their own prejudices and superstitions.

Sir, in my opinion, institutions and laws and governments, and all the fixed facts of society, are but the material embodiment of the thought of a people and the substantial expression of their inner life; and liberty, which is the culmination of them all, is a boon that cannot be conferred upon men, but, to be permanently possessed and enjoyed, must be earned, as the reward of the development of our moral and intellectual faculties.

> No state stands sure, but on the ground of right,
> Of virtue, knowledge, judgment to preserve,
> And all the powers of learning requisite.

Mr. President: No one has the right to predict that this or any class of people will not rise to that plane of intelligence and moral elevation necessary to the enjoyment of this great blessing, and therefore refuse to vote for a measure like this, which proposes to aid them in their effort to emerge from that condition which centuries of barbarism have entailed upon them. For my part, I say that I would leave no legitimate effort unused and no constitutional means unemployed which would give to every human being in this country that highest title to American citizenship—virtue, knowledge and judgment.

I am not an optimist as to the rapid progress of the black people in education. However earnest they may be, there will be great difficulty, even with the aid of the Federal Government, in establishing effective schools for all. We are yet but in the incipiency of this great work—hardly gone further than establishing the educational machinery on the ground. A task of colossal magnitude is before us, and a dense mass of ignorance has to be penetrated; but, sir, whatever of disappointment may attend it, whatever of failure, whatever of error and mistake—and even abuses of trust—may cripple and embarrass this movement, the great idea of popular education which has animated the North, and is animating the South, and in which this bill has originated, will inspire both to guard and guide the vast host in its slow, hesitating but onward advance to knowledge and true freedom.

SIR WILFRID LAURIER

CANADA, ENGLAND, AND THE UNITED STATES

[Sir Wilfrid Laurier, P.C., G.C.M.G., LL.D., Canadian premier and statesman, was born in the Province of Quebec in 1841. He graduated at the College of the Assumption, and entered upon the practice of law, subsequently taking to journalism. His interest in public affairs, his French-Canadian origin and sympathies, and more especially his aptitude in the delivery of speeches in the English and French languages, gave him great influence. When thirty years of age he was elected to the Quebec Assembly. In 1874 he was chosen to the Dominion Parliament. Two years afterwards he gained a seat in the Dominion Cabinet as Minister of Inland Revenue, being by this time the leader of the Liberal party in the Province of Quebec. In the general elections of 1896 Sir Wilfrid Laurier received an overwhelming majority of French-Canadian votes, carried the elections, and became premier of the Dominion. In 1897 he was knighted. His settlement of the Manitoba School Question, in which he incurred the opposition of the Roman Catholic hierarchy, was at length pronounced a wise one, and his administrative measures have strengthened the Canadian sense of unity. The following speech was made in response to a toast to Canada, at a banquet in Chicago, October 9, 1899, the anniversary of the great fire of 1871 in that city.]

I VERY fully and very cordially appreciate the very kind feelings which have just now been uttered by the toast-master in terms so eloquent, and which you, gentlemen, have accepted and received in so sympathetic a manner. Let me say at once, in the name of my fellow-Canadians who are here with me, and also, I may say, in the name of the Canadian people, that these feelings we will at all times reciprocate—reciprocate not only in words evanescent, but in actual living deeds.

I take it to be an evidence of the good relation which, in your estimation, gentlemen, ought to prevail between two such countries as the United States and Canada, that you have notified us, your next-door neighbors, in this day of rejoicing, to take our share with you of your joy. We shall take back to our own country the most pleasant remembrance of the day.

We have seen many things here to-day very much to be admired—the imposing ceremonies of the morning, the fine pageant, the grand procession, the orderly and good-natured crowds—all these are things to be admired and, to some extent, to be wondered at. But the one thing of all most to be admired, most to be remembered, is the very inspiration of this festival.

It is quite characteristic of the city of Chicago. As a rule, nations and cities celebrate the day of their foundation or some great victory or some national triumph; in all cases, some event which, when it occurred, was a cause of universal joy and rejoicing. Not so, however, of the city of Chicago. In this, as in everything else, she does not tread in beaten paths. The day which she celebrates is not the day of her foundation, when hunters and fur-traders unconsciously laid down the beginnings of what were to develop into a gigantic city; neither does she celebrate some great action in which American history abounds; neither does she commemorate a deed selected from the life of some of the great men whom the state has given to the nation, though Illinois can claim the proud privilege of having given to the nation one as great as Washington himself.

The day which she celebrates is the day of her direst calamity, the day in which she was swept out of existence by fire. This, I say, is very characteristic of Chicago, because, if history recalls her destruction, it also recalls her resurrection. It recalls the energy, the courage, the faith, and the enthusiasm with which her citizens met and faced and conquered an appalling calamity.

For my part, well do I remember the awful day, for, as you well know, its horrors were reverberated far beyond the limits of your country; but of all the things which—I was then a young man—I most remember, of all the acts of courage and heroism which were brought forward by the occasion, the one thing which at the same time struck me most was the appeal issued by the business men of Chicago on the smoking ruins of their city. They appealed to their fellow citizens, especially to those who had business connections in Chicago and whose enterprise and energy had conferred honor on the American name, to sustain them in that hour of their trial.

Mark the language. The only thing they asked was to be sustained in their business, and if sustained in their business they were ready to face and meet the awful calamity which had befallen their city. Well, sir, in my estimation, in my judgment, at least, that was courage of the very highest order. Whenever you meet courage you are sure to meet justice and generosity. Courage, justice, and generosity always go together, and therefore it is with some degree of satisfaction that I approach the toast to which I have been called to respond.

Because I must say that I feel that though the relations between Canada and the United States are good, though they are brotherly, though they are satisfactory, in my judgment they are not as good, as brotherly, as satisfactory as they ought to be. We are of the same stock. We spring from the same races on one side of the line as on the other. We speak the same language. We have the same literature, and for more than a thousand years we have had a common history.

Let me recall to you the lines which, in the darkest days of the Civil War, the Puritan poet of America issued to England:—

"O Englishmen! O Englishmen!
In hope and creed,
In blood and tongue, are brothers,
We all are heirs of Runnymede."

Brothers we are, in the language of your own poet. May I not say that, while our relations are not always as brotherly as they ought to have been? May I not ask, Mr. President, on the part of Canada and on the part of the United States, if we are sometimes too prone to stand by the full conceptions of our rights, and exact all our rights to the last pound of flesh? May I not ask if there have not been too often between us petty quarrels, which happily do not wound the heart of the nation?

Sir, I am proud to say, in the presence of the Chief Ex-

ecutive of the United States, that it is the belief of the
Canadian government that we should make the government of President McKinley and the present government of
Canada, with the assent of Great Britain, so to work together
to remove all causes of dissension between us. And whether
the commission which sat first in the old city of Quebec and
sat next in the city of Washington—but whether sitting in
Quebec or sitting in Washington, I am sorry to say the result
has not been commensurate with our expectations.

Shall I speak my mind? (Cries of "Yes!") We met a
stumbling block in the question of the Alaskan frontier.
Well, let me say here and now the commission would not
settle that question, and referred it to their particular governments, and they are now dealing with it. May I be permitted to say here and now that we do not desire one inch
of your land?

But if I state, however, that we want to hold our own
land, will not that be an American sentiment, I want to know?
However, though that would be a British sentiment or Canadian, I am here to say, above all, my fellow countrymen,
that we do not want to stand upon the extreme limits of our
rights. We are ready to give and to take. We can afford
to be just; we can afford to be generous, because we are
strong. We have a population of seventy-seven millions—
I beg pardon, I am mistaken, it is the reverse of that. But
pardon my mistake, although it is the reverse, I am sure the
sentiment is the same.

But though we may have many little bickerings of that
kind, I speak my whole mind, and I believe I speak the mind
of all you gentlemen when I say that, after all, when we go
down to the bottom of our hearts we will find that there is
between us a true, genuine affection. There are no two
nations to-day on the face of the globe so united as Great
Britain and the United States of America.

The secretary of state told us some few months ago that
there was no treaty of alliance between Great Britain and the
United States of America. It is very true there is between
the United States of America and Great Britain to-day no
treaty of alliance which the pen can write and which the pen
can unmake, but there is between Great Britain and the

SIR WILFRID LAURIER

Photogravure after a photograph from life

United States of America a unity of blood which is thicker than water, and I appeal to recent history when I say that whenever one nation has to face an emergency—a greater emergency than usual—forthwith the sympathies of the other nation go to her sister.

When last year you were suddenly engaged in a war with Spain, though Spain was the weaker party, and though it is natural that men should side with the weaker party, our sympathies went to you for no other reason than that of blood. And I am sure you will agree with me, that though our relations have not reached the degree of perfection to which I would aspire, from that day a new page has been turned in the history of our country. It was no unusual occurrence before the month of May, 1898, to read in the British press of American arrogance; neither was it an unusual occurrence to read in the American press of British brutality.

Since the month of May, 1898, these expressions have disappeared from the vocabulary. You do not hear to-day of American arrogance; neither do you hear of British brutality; but the only expressions which you find in the press of either country now are words of mutual respect and mutual affection.

Sir, an incident took place in the month of June last which showed to me at all events conclusively that there is between us a very deep and sincere affection. I may be pardoned if I recall that instance, because I have to speak of myself.

In the month of June last I spoke on the floor of the House of Commons of Canada on the question of Alaska, and I enunciated the very obvious truism that international problems can be settled in one of two ways only: either by arbitration or war. And although I proceeded to say immediately that war between Great Britain and the United States would be criminal and would not be thought of for a moment, still the very word "war" created quite an excitement in this country. With that causeless excitement, though I was indirectly the cause of it, I do not at this moment find any fault, because it convinced me, to an absolute certainty, that between your country and my country the relations have reached a degree of dignity and respect and affection that even the word "war" is never to be mentioned in a British Assembly or in an American assembly. The word is not to be pronounced, not even to be predicated. It is not to be pronounced at all. The very idea is abhorrent to us.

I repeat what I then stated, that war between Great Britain and the United States would be criminal in my estimation and judgment, just as criminal as the Civil War which desolated your country some thirty years ago. Whatever may have been the mistaken views of the civilized world at the time, the civilized world has come to the unanimous conclusion that the War of the Rebellion was a crime. The civilized world has come to the conclusion that it was a benefit to mankind that this rebellion did not succeed and that the government of the people, by the people, and for the people did not perish from the earth.

Your country was desolated for long years by the awful scourge of the Civil War. If there is anything of the many things which are to be admired in this great country of yours, the one thing, for my part, which I most admire is the absolute success with which you have reestablished the Union and erased all traces of the Civil War. You have done it. What is the reason? I may say, as has been uttered by the President of the United States—I took down his words: "No responsibility which has ever resulted from the war is tainted with dishonor. We have succeeded in establishing the cause of the Union, because no blood was shed to reestablish the Union except the blood which was shed by the sword; not one drop of blood was ever shed except by the power of the law, and what were the consequences?"

You had the consequences, in the war with Spain, when the men of the Blue and the men of the Gray, the men who had fought for the Confederacy and the men who had fought for the Union, at the call of their country, came back to fight the battles of their own country under a united flag. That was the reason.

My friend Mr. Cullom said a moment ago that he might believe me almost an American. I am a British subject, but to this extent, I may say, that as every American is a lover of liberty, a believer in democratic institutions, I rejoiced as any of you did at the spectacle which was represented at Santiago, El Caney, and elsewhere during that war.

Sir, there was another civil war. There was a civil war in the last century. There was a civil war between England and her American colonies, and their relations were severed. If they were severed, American citizens, as you know they were, through no fault of your fathers, the fault was altogether the fault of the British government of that day. If the British government of that day had treated the American colonies as the British government for the last twenty or fifty years has treated its colonies; if Great Britain had given you then the same degree of liberty which it gives to Canada, my country; if it had given you, as it has given us, legislative independence absolute, the result would have been different —the course of victory, the course of history, would have been different.

But what has been done cannot be undone. You cannot expect that the union which has been severed shall ever be restored; but can we not escape—can we not hope that if the union cannot be restored under the law, at least there can be a union of hearts? Can we not hope that the banners of England and the banners of the United States shall never, never again meet in conflict, except in those conflicts provided by the arts of peace, such as we see to-day in the harbor of New York, in the contest between the "Shamrock" and the "Columbia" for the supremacy of naval architecture and naval prowess? Can we not hope that if ever the banners of England and the banners of the United States are again to meet on the battlefield, they shall meet entwined together in the defense of the oppressed, for the enfranchisement of the downtrodden, and for the advancement of liberty, progress, and civilization?

HENRY LEE

EULOGY ON WASHINGTON

[Henry Lee, general in the Continental army, was born of a distinguished Virginia family, in 1756. At thirteen he entered Princeton College, and graduated in 1773. When but nineteen he entered the service of his country, and became a captain of cavalry in the army of Virginia. He was one of the most dashing, vigorous, and successful officers in the Continental army. He took part in the battle of Germantown, and after being advanced to the rank of major he successfully attacked the British post at Paulus Hook, opposite New York. In 1780 he was promoted to the rank of lieutenant-colonel. After the war he became a member of the Virginia legislature, and in 1786 went as delegate to the Continental Congress. He supported the Federal Constitution in the convention held for its ratification. In 1792 he became governor of Virginia, and continued in office three years. He returned to Congress again in 1799, and was chosen by that body to pronounce the oration in memory of Washington. In 1814 he suffered injuries in a political riot, which terminated fatally March 25, 1818. He was noted for his graceful and effective oratory, and was chosen to deliver the following eulogy shortly after Washington's death. The address was made in Philadelphia, December 26, 1799.]

IN obedience to your will, I rise, your humble organ, with the hope of executing a part of the system of public mourning which you have been pleased to adopt, commemorative of the death of the most illustrious and most beloved personage this country has ever produced ; and which, while it transmits to posterity your sense of the awful event, faintly represents your knowledge of the consummate excellence you so cordially honor.

Desperate, indeed, is any attempt on earth to meet correspondently this dispensation of Heaven ; for while with pious resignation we submit to the will of an all-gracious Providence, we can never cease lamenting, in our finite view of Omnipotent wisdom, the heartrending privation for which our nation weeps. When the civilized world shakes to its center; when every moment gives birth to strange and momentous changes; when our peaceful quarter of the globe, exempt as it happily has been from any share in the slaughter of the human race, may yet be compelled to abandon her pacific policy and to risk the doleful casualties of war, what limit is there to the extent of our loss? None within the reach of my words to express; none which your feeling will not disavow.

The founder of our federate Republic—our bulwark in war, our guide in peace, is no more! O that this were but questionable! Hope, the comforter of the wretched, would pour into our agonizing hearts its balmy dew. But alas! there is no hope for us; Washington is removed forever! Possessing the stoutest frame and purest mind, he had passed nearly to his sixty-eighth year in the enjoyment of high health, when, habituated by his care of us to neglect himself, a slight cold, disregarded, became inconvenient on Friday, oppressive on Saturday, and, defying every medical interposition, before the morning of Sunday put an end to the best of men. An end, did I say?—his fame survives, bounded only by the limits of the earth and by the extent of the human mind. He survives in our hearts, in the growing knowledge of our children, in the affection of the good throughout the world: and when our monuments shall be done away; when nations now existing shall be no more; when even our young and far-spreading empire shall have perished, still will our Washington's glory unfaded shine, and die not until love of virtue cease on earth, or earth itself sinks into chaos.

How, my fellow citizens, shall I signal to your grateful hearts his preeminent worth? Where shall I begin in opening to your view a character throughout sublime? Shall I speak of his warlike achievements, all springing from obedience to his country's will—all directed to his country's good?

Will you go with me to the banks of the Monongahela, to see your youthful Washington supporting, in the dismal hour of Indian victory, the ill-fated Braddock, and saving, by his judgment and by his valor, the remains of a defeated army, pressed by the conquering savage foe; or, when op-

pressed America nobly resolved to risk her all in defense of
her violated rights, he was elevated by the unanimous voice
of Congress to the command of her armies? Will you follow him to the high grounds of Boston, where to an undis-
ciplined, courageous, and virtuous yeomanry his presence
gave the stability of system and infused the invincibility of
love of country; or shall I carry you to the painful scenes
of Long Island, York Island, and New Jersey, when com-
bating superior and gallant armies, aided by powerful fleets
and led by chiefs high in the roll of fame, he stood the bulwark of our safety, undismayed by disaster, unchanged by
change of fortune? Or will you view him in the precarious
fields of Trenton, where deep gloom, unnerving every arm,
reigned triumphant through our thinned, worn-down, unaided ranks, himself unmoved? Dreadful was the night.
It was about this time of winter; the storm raged, the Delaware, rolling furiously with floating ice, forbade the approach
of man. Washington, self-collected, viewed the tremendous
scene; his country called; unappalled by surrounding dangers, he passed to the hostile shore; he fought; he conquered. The morning sun cheered the American world.
Our country rose on the event; and her dauntless chief, pursuing his blow, completed in the lawns of Princeton what his
vast soul had conceived on the shores of the Delaware.

Thence to the strong grounds of Morristown he led his
small but gallant band, and through an eventful winter, by
the high efforts of his genius, whose matchless force was
measurable only by the growth of difficulties, he held in
check formidable hostile legions, conducted by a chief experienced in the art of war and famed for his valor on the
ever memorable heights of Abraham, where fell Wolfe,
Montcalm, and, since, our much lamented Montgomery, all
covered with glory. In this fortunate interval, produced by
his masterly conduct, our fathers, ourselves, animated by
his resistless example, rallied around our country's standard
and continued to follow her beloved chief through the
various and trying scenes to which the destinies of our Union
led.

Who is there that has forgotten the vales of Brandywine,
the fields of Germantown, or the plains of Monmouth? Every-

where present, wants of every kind obstructing, numerous and valiant armies encountering, himself a host, he assuaged our sufferings, limited our privations, and upheld our tottering Republic. Shall I display to you the spread of the fire of his soul by rehearsing the praises of the hero of Saratoga and his much-loved compeer of the Carolinas? No; our Washington wears not borrowed glory. To Gates, to Greene, he gave without reserve the applause due to their eminent merit; and long may the chiefs of Saratoga and of Eutaw receive the grateful respect of a grateful people.

Moving in his own orbit, he imparted heat and light to his most distant satellites; and, combining the physical and moral force of all within his sphere, with irresistible weight he took his course, commiserating folly, disdaining vice, dismaying treason, and invigorating despondency, until the auspicious hour arrived when, united with the intrepid forces of a potent and magnanimous ally, he brought to submission the since conqueror of India; thus finishing his long career of military glory with a luster corresponding to his great name, and in this, his last act of war, affixing the seal of fate to our nation's birth.

To the horrid din of battle, sweet peace succeeded; and our virtuous chief, mindful only of the common good in a moment tempting personal aggrandizement, hushed the discontents of growing sedition; and surrendering his power into the hands from which he had received it, converted his sword into a ploughshare, teaching an admiring world that to be truly great you must be truly good.

Were I to stop here, the picture would be incomplete and the task imposed unfinished. Great as was our Washington in war, and much as did that greatness contribute to produce the American Republic, it is not in war alone his preeminence stands conspicuous. His various talents, combining all the capacities of a statesman with those of a soldier, fitted him alike to guide the councils and the armies of martial toils, while his invaluable parental advice was still sounding in our ears, when he, who had been our shield and our sword, was called forth to act a less splendid but more important part.

Possessing a clear and penetrating mind, a strong and sound judgment, calmness and temper for deliberation, with invincible firmness and perseverance in resolutions maturely formed; drawing information from all; acting from himself, with incorruptible integrity and unvarying patriotism; his own superiority and the public confidence alike marked him as the man designed by Heaven to lead in the great political as well as military events which have distinguished the era of his life.

The finger of an overruling Providence, pointing at Washington, was neither mistaken nor unobserved when, to realize the vast hopes to which our revolution had given birth, a change of political system became indispensable.

How novel, how grand the spectacle! Independent states, stretched over an immense territory, and known only by common difficulty, clinging to their union as the rock of their safety, deciding by frank comparison of their relative condition to rear on that rock, under the guidance of reason, a common government through whose commanding protection liberty and order, with their long train of blessings, should be safe to themselves and the sure inheritance of their posterity.

This arduous task devolved on citizens selected by the people from knowledge of their wisdom and confidence in their virtue. In this august assembly of sages and of patriots Washington of course was found; and, as if acknowledged to be most wise where all were wise, with one voice he was declared their chief. How well he merited this rare distinction, how faithful were the labors of himself and his compatriots, the work of their hands and our union, strength, and prosperity, the fruits of that work, best attest.

But to have essentially aided in presenting to this country this consummation of her hopes neither satisfied the claims of his fellow citizens on his talents nor those duties which the possession of those talents imposed. Heaven had not infused into his mind such an uncommon share of its ethereal spirit to remain unemployed, nor bestowed on him his genius unaccompanied with the corresponding duty of devoting it to the common good. To have framed a constitution was showing only, without realizing, the general happiness. This great work remained to be done; and America, steadfast in her preference, with one voice summoned her beloved Wash-

ington, unpracticed as he was in the duties of civil administration, to execute this last act in the completion of the
national felicity. Obedient to her call, he assumed the high
office with that self-distrust peculiar to his innate modesty,
the constant attendant of preeminent virtue. What was the
burst of joy through our anxious land on this exhilarating
event is known to us all. The aged, the young, the brave,
the fair, rivaled each other in demonstrations of their gratitude; and this high-wrought, delightful scene was heightened
in its effect by the singular contest between the zeal of the
bestower and the avoidance of the receiver of the honors
bestowed. Commencing his administration, what heart is
not charmed with the recollection of the pure and wise principles announced by himself as the basis of his political life!
He best understood the indissoluble union between virtue
and happiness, between duty and advantage, between the
genuine maxims of an honest and magnanimous policy and
the solid rewards of public prosperity and individual felicity;
watching, with an equal and comprehensive eye, over this
great assemblage of communities and interests, he laid the
foundations of our national policy in the unerring, immut-
able principles of morality, based on religion, exemplifying
the preeminence of a free government, by all the attributes
which won the affections of its citizens, or commanded the
respect of the world.

"O fortunatos nimium, sua si bona norint!"

Leading through the complicated difficulties produced
by previous obligations and conflicting interests, seconded
by succeeding houses of congress, enlightened and patriotic,
he surmounted all original obstruction and brightened the
path of our national felicity.

The presidential term expiring, his solicitude to exchange
exaltation for humility returned with a force increased with
increase of age; and he had prepared his farewell address
to his countrymen, proclaiming his intention, when the
united interposition of all around him, enforced by the eventful prospects of the epoch, produced a further sacrifice of
inclination to duty. The election of president followed; and

Washington, by the unanimous vote of the nation, was called to resume the chief magistracy. What a wonderful fixture of confidence! Which attracts most our admiration, a people so correct, or a citizen combining an assemblage of talents forbidding rivalry and stifling even envy itself? Such a nation ought to be happy, such a chief must be forever revered.

War, long menaced by the Indian tribes, now broke out; and the terrible conflict deluging Europe with blood began to shed its baneful influence over our happy land. To the first, outstretching his invincible arm, under the orders of the gallant Wayne, the American Eagle soared triumphant through distant forests. Peace followed victory; and the melioration of the condition of the enemy followed peace. Godlike virtue, which uplifts even the subdued savage!

To the second he opposed himself. New and delicate was the conjecture, and great was the stake. Soon did his penetrating mind discern and seize the only course continuing to us all the felicity enjoyed. He issued his proclamation of neutrality. This index to his whole subsequent conduct was sanctioned by the approbation of both Houses of Congress and by the approving voice of the people.

To this sublime policy he inviolably adhered, unmoved by foreign intrusion, unshaken by domestic turbulence.

> "Justum et tenacem propositi virum,
> Non civium ardor prava jubentium,
> Non vultus instantis tyranni,
> Mente quatit solida."

Maintaining his pacific system at the expense of no duty, America, faithful to herself and unstained in her honor, continued to enjoy the delights of peace, while afflicted Europe mourns in every quarter under the accumulated miseries of an unexampled war—miseries in which our happy country must have shared, had not our preeminent Washington been as firm in council as he was brave in the field.

Pursuing steadfastly his course, he held safe the public happiness, preventing foreign war and quelling internal discord, till the revolving period of a third election approached, when he executed his interrupted but inextinguishable desire of returning to the humble walks of private life.

The promulgation of his fixed resolution stopped the anxious wishes of an affectionate people from adding a third unanimous testimonial of their unabated confidence in the man so long enthroned in their hearts. When before was affection like this exhibited on earth? Turn over the records of ancient Greece; review the annals of mighty Rome; examine the volumes of modern Europe: you search in vain. America and her Washington only afford the dignified exemplification.

The illustrious personage called by the national voice in succession to the arduous office of guiding a free people had new difficulties to encounter. The amicable effort of settling our difficulties with France, begun by Washington and pursued by his successor in virtue as in station, proving abortive, America took measures of self-defense. No sooner was the public mind roused by a prospect of danger than every eye was turned to the friend of all, though secluded from public view and gray in public service. The virtuous veteran, following his plough, received the unexpected summons with mingled emotions of indignation at the unmerited ill-treatment of his country and of a determination once more to risk his all in her defense.

The enunciation of these feelings, in his affecting letter to the President accepting the command of the army, concludes his official conduct.

First in war, first in peace, and first in the hearts of his countrymen, he was second to none in the humble and endearing scenes of private life. Pious, just, humane, temperate, and sincere; uniform, dignified, and commanding, his example was as edifying to all around him as were the effects of that example lasting.

To his equals he was kind; to his inferiors condescending; and to the dear object of his affections, exemplarily tender. Correct throughout, vice shuddered in his presence and virtue always felt his fostering hand; the purity of his private character gave effulgence to his public virtues.

His last scene comported with the whole tenor of his life; although in extreme pain, not a sigh, not a groan escaped him ; and with undisturbed serenity he closed his well-spent life. Such was the man America has lost! Such was the man for whom our nation mourns!

Methinks I see his august image, and hear, falling from his venerable lips, these deep-sinking words:

"Cease, sons of America, lamenting our separation; go on, and confirm by your wisdom the fruits of our joint counsels, joint efforts, and common dangers. Reverence religion; diffuse knowledge throughout your land; patronize the arts and sciences; let liberty and order be inseparable companions; control party spirit, the bane of free government; observe good faith to, and cultivate peace with, all nations; shut up every avenue of foreign influence; contract rather than extend national connection; rely on yourselves only; be American in thought and deed. Thus will you give immortality to that Union which was the constant object of my terrestrial labors. Thus will you preserve, undisturbed to the latest posterity, the felicity of a people to me most dear; and thus will you supply (if my happiness is now aught to you) the only vacancy in the round of pure bliss Heaven bestows."